DRAGON
GOD OF THE
HINDU KUSH

THE RETURN

WAYNE T HAALAND

DRAGON
GOD OF THE
HINDU KUSH
THE RETURN

WAYNE T HAALAND

Jack Flashhardt and his half-brother, Billy Howling Dog, break free from Fort Leavenworth and escape to Singapore. But are they really free or are they being manipulated by Marine General Harmbruster of the super-secret Eagle's Aerie spy agency into finding a missing US biological bomb, so terrible, the US is afraid to look for it in the Hindu Kush Mountains of Southwest Asia—Afghanistan! But now the terrorists have come to America, and the brothers must scramble back to the USA to stop Mara Bhutto, the al Qaida operative, and her gang of crazed, blond and blue-eyed Bosnian Mujahideen.

ISBN (Hardback):   979-8-89381-046-2
ISBN (Paperback):   979-8-89381-047-9
ISBN (eBook):   979-8-89381-048-6

508 West 26th Street KEARNEY, NE 68848
402-819-3224
info@medialiteraryexcellence.com

Contents

Dedication I
Epigraph II
Prologue III
Chapter 1 1
Chapter 2 11
Chapter 3 13
Chapter 4 22
Chapter 5 25
Chapter 6 33
Chapter 7 35
Chapter 8 41
Chapter 9 43
Chapter 10 44
Chapter 11 46
Chapter 12 53
Chapter 13 58
Chapter 14 61
Chapter 15 68
Chapter 16 72
Chapter 17 76
Chapter 18 85
Chapter 19 94
Chapter 20 98
Chapter 21 103
Chapter 22 107
Chapter 23 115
Chapter 24 124
Chapter 25 130
Chapter 26 132
Chapter 27 138
Chapter 28 144
Chapter 29 156

Chapter 30 159
Chapter 31 162
Chapter 32 166
Chapter 33 168
Chapter 34 171
Chapter 35 177
Chapter 36 180
Chapter 37 183
Chapter 38 184
Chapter 39 188
Chapter 40 194
Chapter 41 198
Chapter 42 209
Chapter 43 211
Chapter 44 213
Chapter 45 216
Chapter 46 219
Chapter 47 221
Chapter 48 227
Chapter 49 228
Chapter 50 230
Chapter 51 237
Chapter 52 243
Chapter 53 249
Chapter 54 252
Chapter 55 256
Chapter 56 261
Chapter 57 269
Chapter 58 274
Chapter 59 275
Chapter 60 276
Chapter 61 278
Chapter 62 289
Chapter 63 295
Chapter 64 302

Chapter 65 303
Chapter 66 310
Chapter 67 315
Chapter 68 324
Chapter 69 329
Chapter 70 333
Chapter 71 336
Chapter 72 338
Chapter 73 340
Chapter 74 350
Chapter 75 351
Chapter 76 359
Chapter 77 362
Chapter 78 367
Chapter 79 370
Chapter 80 373
Chapter 81 378
Chapter 82 385
Chapter 83 387
Chapter 84 398
Chapter 85 417
Chapter 86 424
Chapter 87 425
Chapter 88 429
Postscript 436

Dedication

Among the Texas patriots who died at the Alamo, 6 Mar 1836, were THE IMMORTAL THIRTY-TWO. These men were distinguished by the fact that they were the only Texans to respond to Col. Travis's appeal for help while surrounded by General Santa Anna's Mexican Army forces. The 32 men actually penetrated Mexican lines to join the doomed fighters in the Alamo. This book is dedicated to my ancestor, Squire Damon, one of those 32 fallen heroes.

"The bravest are surely those who have the clearest vision of what is before them, glory and danger alike, and notwithstanding go out to meet it."
— Thucydides

The wise general will use the highest intelligence of his army for the purposes of spying, and thereby he will achieve great results.
— Sun Tzu

Si vis pacem, para bellum —
If you want peace, prepare for war

Prologue

A cavern in the Hindu Kush Mountains of Afghanistan

Mara Bhutto glared at the Russian FSB agent sprawled on the ground in front of her. Mo Poo, the giant Chinaman, pushed him down again and shouted in broken English with his distinctive, rumbling voice, "FSB acting alone? How you find our training camp?"

Bruno Baeder Utecht, the blond, once handsome Russian soldier, briefly struggled against the two other giant Chinamen pinning him to the floor. "I told you. I can't say—it's *Of Special Importance*—meaning top secret." Bruno looked up at his former friend, Mara Bhutto. Despite her beauty, she terrified him. Two of the massive Chinamen were easily holding him on the cold rocky ground in front of the sheer Shangrilan cliffs. The odors they emitted were horrific—a mixture of unwashed body odors, garlic, and some kind of horrible sauce that made their breath unbearable— so bad he could almost taste their smells.

Exasperated, Mara shouted, "Not an answer, Bruno!"

Before he could respond, Mara—a former Chinese Second Department field agent—asked, "Bruno, why're you here? Looking for the American bio-warhead?"

The Russian shook his head, said nothing. She nodded to the eight feet tall leader of the cavern's inhabitants; Mo Poo lowered his glaring eyes, smiled at Bruno. He pulled a long knife from a scabbard on his belt, then sliced open and pulled down Bruno's ragged, dirty pants, exposed his slim hips; the Chinaman held the knife in front of Bruno's eyes, waited for the Russian to quit writhing. He grabbed a testicle as if he was grabbing a goldfish in a tank, slashed it off with the knife.

Bruno screamed until he ran out of breath, then sobs alternated with more screams until he yelled, "Yes! Yes, yes, any—thing!" He stared up at Mo Poo's hideous face, torn open and permanently scarred the year before when Jack Flashhardt's pet Caspian tiger had attacked him.

Mo Poo held the red mass on his huge hand, squeezed until the bloody plum popped out of its jagged skin sheath, then tossed it into his huge maw and chewed with gusto. Blood and fluid spurted out of the healed open wounds on his huge face, splashed onto Bruno. He rumbled in his basso voice, "How is that, you stupid little Fan Gway? You tastes good, tiny foreign devil."

Starved in his captivity, Bruno still managed to wretch green bile over his body, onto the floor.

Mara felt her own stomach heave, nauseated at the horrific sight. Vomit rose to her throat, she quickly swallowed, tried to control innards. She was as terrified of her Chinese comrade as was the captive writhing on the ground.

Bruno shut his eyes momentarily, and then with halting words, looked fearfully at Mo Poo while he gasped his answer to Mara. "It… it began when Mo Poo's former servant, Cyvual… he… he delivered Jack's Khyber knife—the Dragon God's knife—to the American Embassy in Beijing.

Chapter 1

Fort Leavenworth, Kansas

Jack Flashhardt, ex-Marine, finished his early morning sit-ups, rolled over on the concrete floor to restart his push-up routine. He paused to wipe sweat off his face with a drenched towel; he thought about quitting, instead he thrust his hand under the pillow on his bunk and pulled out a scrap of paper. He read the verse out loud:

A BOLD MAN'S MANTRA
I WAS MOUNTED ON A SNOW-WHITE STEED,
YES, A FLASHHARD LAD INDEED
MY COCKED PISTOL WAS LOADED AND READY,
STAND AND DELIVER, SAID MY VOICE SO STEADY.

The mantra inspired him and after putting the verse away, he mustered inner energy and pushed himself to continue exercising.

Finally finished, he carefully spread the threadbare white towel on the metal frame bunk to dry, then focused on a picture taped to the concrete wall. His former girlfriend: Ashley's lovely, laughing face, blonde hair tumbling down over her shoulders, wide-set hazel eyes penetrating the cell's gloomy, gray atmosphere.

Looking beyond the picture, he stared at a strip of white caulking that filled every joint in the concrete walls. The caulking was there to thwart any attempts to hide anything in a crevice: he stared at the ribbon of whiteness until it slowly faded into the mental image of a glacier, where he found himself lying on his back, watching the sunrise splatter gold over the white snows. He relaxed, took a deep breath of thin, fresh, high altitude air; he enjoyed the solitude, the sun warming his cheek.

Pounding steps: someone in the passageway snatched him back to reality. The first thing he had noticed inside was increased auditory sensation: sometimes there were measured strides in the hall, often-times there were shuffling, aimless padding, but there were never hurried steps like those he heard skidding to a stop outside his door. He quickly stood and waited for anything.

Lock clicked, slammed open. The solid steel door swung wide, revealed his brother in the doorway: Billy Howling Dog, his childhood playmate, his teenage antagonist, his grown, red-faced half-brother, and Marine Corps comrade-in-arms. A big smile on his face. They had not seen each other during Jack's six months in Solitary.

"Billy—how you doin'?" he asked. A sneering guard had told him Billy had become addicted to Oxycontin, an opiate-based drug. "Dumb shit's popping *Hillbilly H*," the guard had proclaimed.

"Hey, Jack. Whoa—what happened to you?" Billy's wide-setgrey eyes widened as he surveyed Jack's new, heavily muscled body, then he strode forward and the two embraced.

Jack Flashhardt glanced down at his new body. "I powered up 'cause there's nothing else to do in Solitary." He thought of the long pounding hours, running in place. Push-ups going on and on. Using the cot as rudimentary weights. Handstands, leg lifts. All to relieve the boredom; all to achieve exhausted dreamless sleep in soul-killing Solitary. All in case *they* returned. "And 'cause a guard and two prisoners, including the Dock Warden, tried to do me last fall, two weeks into my stay in this luxury pad."

"Do you!" Billy's grin vanished. "What happened?"

"Managed to dis-invite them. Dock Warden left with his balls halfway to his liver and his nose looking like a broken egg. He said he'd be back."

"Whoa!" Billy sat on the bunk to listen.

"Then I got a big bowl of very spicy clam chowder one night. An' a pitcher of water." Jack made a gesture with his hands. "This time six of them came in the middle of the night. They got me down, poured another quart of water down my throat."

"Huh?"

"Threw me in The Hole."

"What's that?" Billy leaned forward.

Jack took a deep breath. "A lidded concrete drainage sump in the back of the laundry. Too narrow to sit, too low to stand. They shut the lid… total darkness. Musta fed me a laxative or a poison because I crapped and crapped. All that chowder, all that water."

Astounded, Billy winced. "Holy shit!"

"Yeah, holy is right. That was probably the only thing that saved me— God. We talked a lot—who knows how long." Jack raised his arms, stretched up on his tiptoes. "When I finally managed to push the lid off—it was covered with a fifty five gallon barrel of fuel oil—I couldn't walk or even stand. A Trusty found me, washed the shit off with a fire hose."

Billy, an astonished look on his face, asked, "How long?"

Jack sat down next to his brother. "Seventeen hours."

Billy put his arm around him his brother. A big grin spread across his dark-skinned, striking face, shattered his brother's account. "Jack, I think we gotta shot at getting' out of here!"

"Yeah, right!" Jack replied with a scornful tone. "My only choices of getting out are in nineteen years, six months, and a wake up." He wiped a drop of sweat off his nose. "Or out on a one way to an underground condo in Peckerwood Hill Cemetery." A rueful smile at his brother. "But what're you doing here, Billy? Who gave you a card opener to my cell?"

Glancing out the door, Billy Howling Dog stroked his short but growing black braids, looked back at his older half-brother. "They sent me over here to *USDB* from the Warden's office. You got a visitor and I was 'sposed to tell the Day Watch to bring you. But they're all out on coffee break. Only, like, the video monitor guard there. He couldn't leave his station. Keyed a transmitter, sent me over."

Jack was woefully reminded that he was, unlike his brother, in the highest security part of Fort Leavenworth—*USDB*, which housed murderers and other felons with sentences of seven or more years. He exclaimed, "A visitor! Dad? He has news about the appeal?" *Hope surged.*

Billy shook his head, his black braids danced on his broad shoulders; his white man's grey eyes sparkled, his teeth flashed as he smiled.

Jack gestured around his stark cell. "Nobody else knows about this 'cept Ashley." *Would his gorgeous blonde ex-girlfriend blast back into his life?* He glanced at the only decoration in the cell: the picture of Ashley. Pouty lips that could kiss forever—lips that would never kiss him again, according to her. He felt a flush of painful loss.

"Nope," Billy interrupted his mental whining. "Check this out—it's General Harmbruster's aide. He pulls me into the Warden's office, asks me about your Dragon God knife. I said you lost it in the caverns—last year. Now he wants to see you ASAP."

Suddenly suspicious, Jack looked into Billy's eyes. "You using?" "Yeah, but I'm cool. Cept for my dreams—the Hindu Kush dragon's hauntin' me big-time. Wish we'd never stole the emeralds…"

Jack glanced at his brother. *Billy's conveniently forgotten that he pried the gems off the statue, not me. But the old monk had said, 'Take the emerald shield, guard it for the rightful owners.'*

Jack sat on his military-perfect, made-up bunk. Wiped sweat off his face, his stubby short blond hair, interrupted his brother. "General Harmbruster. He's doin' a *Vocati Ad Servitium?* A call to service?" He punched the air. "I'm not goin' down that road again. Anyway, I can't leave the cell without an armed escort. Too dangerous. Guards say everybody in here wants a piece of me. Unless… we're ready to make my breakout."

Billy grimaced. "I'm goin' with, Bro. I'm goin' if we got a chance of gettin' outta here!"

Jack swung a fist in the air. "Don't be stupid. You've got a much less sentence."

"Bro, Chief Talking Dog made me swear a blood oath to cover your rear. So—"

Jack snorted, "Don't give me tribal mumbo jum—"

"Hey!" Billy exclaimed. "Don't be dissin' the Chief. He an' grandma practically raised you after your ma bailed." He walked to the door, looked into the hallway. His strong body odor infused the sterile cell's atmosphere. "I figure the general wants you for another impossible mission like last year. And if you get out, I'll get out, too. I was freakin' wrong back in Afghanland when I said this dump'd be better than the bush. I'm ready to return to my starrin' role as a blood-suckin' war machine."

Jack laughed. "Ohh, you baddie! But I'm not lookin' for another working vacation in Southwest Asia," Jack felt his imaginary hopes of a pardon crushed.

"Bro, I get dreams—bad ones. Your Dragon God's after me," Billy said with a frown. "We gotta go back, get rid of the emeralds. An' anyway, face it—you're the best hill-humpin' raghead killer around. That's why the general wants you."

Taking a deep breath, Jack stared at his fingers. "Let's do it. Hump on outta here." He glanced at Ashley's picture on the concrete wall. Pulled it down, carefully folded it, stuck it in his pocket. He looked at the unopened letter—he guessed, believed, somehow knew it was from his long-gone mother. Decided to leave it on the shelf above the sink. No point in opening that bitter childhood chapter.

The brothers peered into the hallway, saw no one about, cautiously set out for the admin center.

"Wait a minute," Jack said. He returned to the cell, grabbed the letter, stuffed it in the pocket with Ashley's photo. Maybe freedom would bring him the courage to open the letter.

The military prison's high security concrete bulkheads quietly echoed their tentative footsteps; they rounded a corner, an unseen inmate from the level above shouted an alert: "Traitor's out!"

Yells repeated the alarm, echoed down the halls, through the two-tier cellblocks. Individual calls became a clamoring, cup pounding, bar-rattling chorus: "Traitor! Mother-fuckin' traitor! Get the America-hatin' bastard. Scum-suckin' asshole!"

Jack felt tendrils of fear. Thought of retreating to the quiet safety of his cell. But a flush of shame, surge of anger—a swell of resolve overcame his doubts: *a thought of blue skies unscreened by prison bars, a herd of wild horses galloping through green and brown Montana prairie grass, an American flag rippling in a fresh Bighorn Mountain breeze, frosty white clouds billowing and passing above the snowy peaks.* The black hole of a drainage sump.

Clenched his fists at unseen enemies and their chants of hatred in the dead, gray, hellish prison. *Smash things, bash prisoners,* he thought. Looked up at the security cameras: red *active* lights not showing. *Someone turned the all-seeing cameras off. The guards know what's going down: good or bad? They after me too?*

A minute later, the screams, chants, shouts all suddenly stopped.

In the ensuing eerie silence, from around a corner, the brothers heard a weird, wavering, high-pitched voice singing a creepy song:

We're comin' to get you two.
We're gonna make you an asshole new,
Ain't gonna be no cruise on the Med,
We're gonna make you… DEAD!

"Slimy, silly Shakespeare in the halls?" Jack whispered as the last word, shouted louder, echoed through the concrete caverns.

"Some guy's a joke," Billy nervously agreed. "Thinks he can rhyme—I'll rhyme his ass."

The two rounded another corner of the wide, gray, cellblock hall, encountered five prisoners led by a huge multi-tattooed, spider-like white prisoner with a long torso, giant arms, short legs.

Billy recognized the former Army sergeant: he was in for murder and for selling stolen weapons—from a National Guard armory in Madison, Wisconsin—to *God's Purpose,* a white supremacist force in Tillamook, Oregon.

Muscles piled on muscles—his neck looked the same size as Jack's waist. Jaw square like Jack's but a huge under bite, like a maniacal bulldog. Blue eyes like Jack's, but beady and close-set. Blond hair like Jack's, but shaved—a bulldozer of a figure, as though a creator had taken Jack's form, added lumps of flesh and bone, then squeezed haphazardly, and pounded the figure from all sides.

Guy was so ugly, a dirty look would send any but the bravest, most foolhardy, suicidal man scrambling to a telephone to make a 911 call for help. In the background, a fat, white-haired, flat-faced guard watched. Licked his thick lips with eager anticipation.

"Hey, guys, we got a date with the warden," Jack addressed the group with a neutral voice. "You can only get sloppy seconds." He noticed horrid tattoos all over the muscle man's exposed skin. As the man's physique flexed, the devil faces grimaced, scowled, appeared to snap their fiendish, gaping mouths.

"You ain't goin' nowhere, traitor!" the leader growled. His eyes glared with hate under drooping eyelids. "Been waitin' for you to come out, Flushhard. Fix you up right now. Don't need no warden. Resistance is fee-u-tile!"

Jack Flashhardt saw that he was two inches taller, at six feet, then the monstrous man, whose wide body blocked the passage. "I'm innocent, pal. Can't we all just… ?"

His Brule Sioux half-brother raised his fists, yelled, "Get outta the way, fucker, or we'll go through you." At six feet one, taller than Jack and twenty pounds heavier, he showed no fear on his dark face.

Two more white prisoners: one tall and skinny, the other average size. Both had shaved heads, wore orange prison garb. Last two were black men, who didn't normally hang with the whites— they wore pale blue doo rags on their heads.

"Ax em if'n they wans' give up, take a beatin', bro," one of the blacks said.

"Yeah, I's gonna mess up his pretty boy face," the second black guy exclaimed. "Maybe get some white meat, close ta the bone."

First one added, "Ohh, those pretty blues, long eyelashes! Sweet!"

The white leader shook his head. "Na, this deserter scum's goin' way beyond a beatin' or a screwin'."

"Come on, Mister Bobby," the other sunken-cheeked black whined. "He's too pretty ta waste. Looka those carved cheeks—that handsome chinny-chin-chin. I wanna rub those cheekbones tween my legs. He looks like one a those Hollywood stars."

Tattoo snarled, "I want this traitorous, arrogant filth dead."

Starting to feel totally trapped, Jack said, "Guys, I'm no traitor. I'm an all-American sunshine boy. I sent in an absentee ballot last election. "I'll even vote whiney, guilt-ridden liberal. I'd volunteer for jury duty… well, skip that last… "

First black guy exclaimed, "Oh, I like talk-back bitches! Yummy."

His heart pounding like a berserk jackhammer, Jack responded, "You guys think maybe you could sign up for anger management or sexual harassment classes?"

No more taunts from either side as the aggressors advanced on the brothers. Suppressing fear, Jack glanced at Billy. The rape thing changed their long-debated escape plan, made during their trip to Leavenworth in chains, the year before. They hadn't counted on forced sex. They couldn't fake a whipping in order to get admitted to the hospital if it ended in rape. He stared at the complex tattoos of devil faces on the leader's arms and neck. The faces snarled: the five prisoners attacked. Three piled on Billy, he went down. One man flew off the pile, another screamed, rolled away.

Jack punched Tattoo in the midsection—like hitting a concrete block— pain flared up his arm. Guy grabbed his wrist, flung him against a bulkhead like a skinny rag doll: stunned, he bounced off, back to Tattoo like a kid's ball on a stretchy rubber string. The man wrapped his hands around Jack's slender middle, squeezed. Garlicky rotten-meat breath was horrendous. A second man punched him in the back of the head, once, twice. Twisted away: guy missed, hit Tattoo.

Jack swung at Tattoo: midsection, then an uppercut to the monster's lantern jaw—no effect. Sunk teeth into a fiend's image on Tattoo's collarbone: felt it crack. Saw the letters—KGC—in the mouth of a demon illustrated on Tattoo's neck. Jack fought harder.

Desperate, he stuck a thumb in the muscle man's left eye, gouged it out.

Tattoo squealed, squeezed. Jack felt his ribs popping, smacked the dangling eye as he struggled to breathe.

Agonizing howl, Tattoo fell to his knees, clutched his face.

"Dude, see my point of view?" Jack taunted. Kicked Tattoo in the head as he would a resting soccer ball: head thunked, twisted away. Sharp pain in the foot.

Second black attacked: Jack punched him twice, guy fell.

Grabbed from behind, he head-butted backwards, heard a smashing crunch, screech of pain. Arms released, he swung around, kneed the guy, then took two steps, field goal-kicked the other man on top of Billy.

Freed, Billy jumped up, yelled a taunting, "Get some!" punched his attacker twice, a third time. Grabbed him by the ears, lifted him, threw his head into the bulkhead. Man grunted, collapsed.

Jack hit the last guy, knocked him senseless. "Piece of cake!" he shouted, then winced as pain shot through his ribcage.

Billy Howling Dog screamed a Marine Corps war whoop: *"Ooraw!"* Jack recoiled from the noise.

Four more white convicts rounded the corner, waded into the brothers. Knife slashed at Jack: he threw up his left forearm, the knife sunk home.

A biting, searing pain. He ignored it, desperately pushed against the wielder so he couldn't free the knife for another stab. The two crashed into each other; Jack got his free hand under the other's jaw, pushed his head back. Fingers slipped into the man's mouth; he yanked them out just as the man clamped down with his teeth. Grabbed the man's lower lip, dug his strong climber's fingers in, stripped it away from the guy's face, flesh ripped to the jawline, the bloody flap dangled, danced. Prisoner howled, fell to the floor screeching.

Knife had penetrated his arm, protruded on the other side, a halo of fiery pain expanded. Swung his wounded arm backhand at a second man, the knifepoint slashed the guy's face: an ear-shattering, wailing cry!

He felt intense pain, a sucking, freeing sensation when he pulled the knife out. Saw blood splatter the floor, realized it was his, felt a sickening sensation sweep through his body. He slashed a man who was on his knees, gripping Billy's leg.

Man squalled, held on: Jack hacked again, got him in the shoulder blade; guy arched his back, the knife wrenched out of Jack's hand.

Billy rolled free, picked up the wounded convict, threw him into two advancing men, charged the pileup, punching wildly. Jack punched the last leaning man in the face, guy careened off the floor, collapsed.

Dizzy, Jack swung around, steadied himself against the bulkhead, saw the guard lift his baton. Jack looked around, no convicts standing. Forced himself to appear stunned, held still. Hit in the forehead, saw stars, consciousness faded to a dim reality. Fell to his hands and knees, landed on unconscious Tattoo, still cuddling his dangling eye. Waited again. Looked at the demon visages—they scowled, snapped at him. The images were terrifying. Thought, *Wait a minute—he's out cold. How can he flex the tattoos? I must be hallucinating.* The guard's kicks began lifting him off the floor. He struggled to his feet, leaned against the concrete bulkhead, snarled at the guard: fearful, the old man drew back. Jack reached in his pocket, felt the letter and the picture: safe. And the escape was on.

Chapter 2

Lying side by side on hospital ward gurneys, two prisoners, badly beaten, were unconscious. A male nurse hovered over each, wiping blood away from lacerations. Another nurse finished switching IV bags on the former officer and turned to the Indian. A female doctor—a lieutenant—hovered nearby.

Marine Major Zack Broyer, short, trim, black, wearing a neatly pressed khaki uniform, looked at the two prisoners again, sniffed at foul odors in the room, tried to breath in shallow gasps.

Broyer pointed at Jack. "How bad's Flashhardt?" He felt inward glee, guiltily suppressed it for a moment, then reveled in it: the naked white man looked beaten to a pulp, his face swollen, smelled like antiseptic. *Serves the traitorous prick right.*

The doctor, a slightly overweight brunette, with a bulging forehead, pale white skin and hooded brown eyes, pointed at the twitching patient and said, "I'm going internal—take a quick look at his abdominal section, check for bleeding. Plus, he hasn't regained consciousness—MRI showed brain swelling. Doesn't look good. Broken wrist, a stab wound—closed that up— no big deal. Several cracked ribs."

"Strange," Major Broyer said. "I always heard this guy's so unbeatable. Somebody kicked his ass big time."

The brunette doctor brushed her bangs back, looked at the Marine with an amazed expression. "Guard said there were nine attackers."

"That's all? Guy's some kind of Oriental fight artist. An animal—he shoulda been able to handle them. Not so tough after all."

The Assistant Warden entered the ward, responded with a wondering tone, "The nine were all down. Guard cowering in a corner. Flashhardt and the Indian were still standing."

The doctor pointed at Billy. "He's in better condition. But he shows signs of drug influence. A baggy in his pocket—*Hillbilly Heroin.* Oxycontin. Opiate-based."

Broyer shrugged, didn't look at the second body. "I don't care about a drug addict. Can Flashhardt travel? I need to get him to Washington."

"Not a chance," the doctor spoke with a firm voice. "I'm sending them to the hospital in town. These guys need a full-on trauma center."

The major grasped the doctor's white sleeve. "Unless you need to operate to save his life, you stabilize him, I'll take him to Bethesda where I can monitor his recovery, if he does." *Which looks unlikely.*

The doctor's mouth dropped open, she closed it, looked grim. "He can't travel. It might take a month before he can."

Broyer shook his head. "Nope—send him today. By noon. I'll have an air ambulance standing by at the airport." He pointed a finger at the doctor. "My orders are to get him to D.C., an' I don't—" *Give a shit whether the traitor puke is dead or alive.*

"What about the enlisted prisoner—the Indian?" the doctor pointed at Billy's unconscious form.

"I don't need him," the major retorted.

Leaning against the wall, the Assistant Warden stepped forward, announced, "Take them both. Warden doesn't want this to go on report. They came together, they leave together, if they die— they die together. Somewhere else."

"Alright," the major turned away. "Just get them ready to go to Maryland, ASAP." *The general's plan,* he thought. *It's working... slightly.*

Chapter 3

Naval Medical Center, Bethesda, Maryland

Jack Flashhardt saw Death on the glacier for the third time that day. Tall, impossibly thin—looking as skinny as Jack had after his escape from the Taliban prison the year before—Death was dressed in a skintight, black snowsuit.

It snowboarded across the glacier's white expanse. First time it had just appeared, hovering in the starlit sky. The second time it had paraglided to Jack's location from the deep blue, pre-dawn sky. Now, dawn's first rays turned the snow golden, the sky a lighter blue, but the black spirit absorbed all light, reflected nothing.

Death skidded his snowboard to a stop, splashed cool, moist snow on Jack's face, sat down, flashed a ghastly, gray-faced grin that highlighted blood red teeth glistening in the sun. *"I've been waiting for you. I'm glad the fight got you out of Leavenworth. Now you can climb Chomolungma— Mount Everest. I'll be waiting on top—it'll be grand! You've always wanted that peak. Now you get—"*

Jack turned away, woke up. He was in a hospital room. IV ending in his arm, oxygen tube jabbing under his nose. No pain—a dreamy, drugged feel to his body. A beautiful blonde vision dampening his face with a cold cloth. Fell asleep.

Woke: saw two men—they resolved into Marine General Harmbruster and his twin sitting in chairs next to the bed. Wearing khaki uniforms, the stars on their collars glinting.

Tried to speak. Throat was dry, croaked, "General, didn't know you had a twin."

The shaved-head general flashed a wide, Eisenhower grin from his tanned, handsome Prussian visage. "Seeing double? No, Jack, my boy, just me. You're back among the living. Prognosis, excellent." Jack peered closer and noticed heavier wrinkles on the general's face then he had seen the year before.

"You gave us a scare—had some apparently serious injuries from your incident two days ago, but the doc says you're managing an amazing recovery. You'll be up and about in a few days. Doesn't seem possible, but there it is." The general glanced at Jack's new musculature. "Maybe because you've grown a buncha muscles since I last saw you."

Thought of beautiful Penel's words, spoken in the Hindu Kush Mountains the year before as she scooped mineral water from the spring with her hands and poured it into his mouth: "Drink and be restored. These waters have wondrous healing powers. For now and forever." *Maybe she had something going with the water thing. I do feel better than I should.*

"Incident?" Jack sat up, winced. "General, I had the crap beaten out of me by some maniacs at Leavenworth. Where am I? Where's Billy?"

"Bethesda Naval Hospital. Your brother's fine. I wanted you close by so we can take good care of you." The senior officer poured water in a glass, regarded Jack with intense, wide-set blue eyes as he sipped.

"I appreciate your concern, General," Jack said. He fingered the bandage over his stab wound. The injury had made the fingertips on his left hand numb. *He thought, Where the hell was your concern when I got courtmartialed last year? All in your cause. And I'm not a captain anymore, asshole—I'm a convict!*

"You deserve it, lad. You've paid a heavy price for your patriotism."

"Why, General?" Jack unconsciously pulled the bandage off his stab wound, tried to rein in his anger.

"Look, Jack. You know I was unavailable—deep-cover in Africa, Agent David Holland was in Syria, Major Nakamura was in flight school," the general said. "G WOT—the Global War on Terror—keeps us hopping. We didn't know about General Farley's sneaky initiation of your Article Thirty Two hearing and court-martial 'til it was too late. And you know the records of your Hindu Kush LIIT bomb recovery operation are sealed, couldn't be used at the court-martial."

Suddenly feeling dizzy, Jack swallowed, then summoned failing energy and responded, "So, what's the deal, General? Why'd you send your aide to Leavenworth? I figure I got a right to know, since it almost killed…"

General Harmbruster smiled, put down his glass. He eagerly stood, walked around the room. "That you do, Jack. The fact is we need you to explain a mystery."

"Who's gonna win the Series this year? Sorry, General, no TV in Solitary."

The general leaned forward, whispered, "A package, containing an old knife—a short sword, really. It was delivered to the front gate of our Embassy in Beijing. Had this written on it." He took a worn piece of cardboard from his pocket and held it in front of Jack's eyes:

To Flas-hard
From Cyvual

Who the hell is Cyvual? And why a sword?" The general held up a two-foot-long, thin package wrapped in a dirty linen cloth.

Jack slumped back, mused, "Cyvual. Named after a character in an ancient Greek play: Silenus." Jack tried to focus on the general's face. "Get it, sir? Cyvual—Silenus? Different spelling, same meaning. Sigh-view-all."

"A play?"

"Yes, sir. Odysseus and the Cyclops. By Euripides. The Greek hero landed and went ashore looking for food and water. This character, Silenus, warned Odysseus that the inhabitants of the island the Greeks had landed on —Sicily—were cannibals. Called the Greek hero, *'Luckless Stranger.'* Added *'Strangers, the Cyclops say, supply the daintiest meat.'*" Jack fell silent.

The general prompted. "So? What's all that got to do with the Khyber knife in this package?" The general unwound the linen wrap, handed the knife to Jack.

"It's a message. A warning," Jack said. He regarded the knife.

Losing patience, the general growled, "Explain!"

Jack took a deep breath, put the knife down after poking a finger in the empty gem settings. He glanced at the general, wondered if the whole conversation was to set him up for last year's stealing of the rare purple diamonds out of the knife's hilt. "It's like this, General. I was given this knife by a sect of Buddhists or Hindu priests—I don't know which—but, I lost the knife during the battle with the Chinese and al Qaida in Herotmere. In the cavern. By sending me the knife, Cyvual is telling me that when we bombed the cavern to bury your lost LIIT bomb, we failed. Cause if he could get out and away from the bad guys who had enslaved him, so could they."

The general thought a moment and whispered, "And that means they might have the bio warhead. The GBU-200." His eyes widened. As Jack regarded him, he saw the general's face go white, as though the blood had been instantly sucked out of his head.

"Exactly!" Jack added. "We thought the B-52 strike Agent Holland and I called in would bury it all. There musta been another way out of the cavern."

"Jack," the general whispered. "This could make Iran-Contra, or the Army's poisoning those Blacks in San Francisco years ago, even Abu Ghraib look like kindergarten games. If the existence of the LIIT warhead gets out... if it is traced back to the US of A, there's gonna be hell to pay. Generals, bureaucrats, politician are gonna be running for cover like cockroaches in a lit-up kitchen."

Jack said with a cynical tone, "Not to mention maybe twenty million deaths, if someone uses the bio bomb."

"Maybe more," the general added with a whisper. "They don't call it the LIIT bomb for nothin'."

"Long Island Iced Tea." Jack smiled. "Yes, sir, somebody had a sense of humor when they named it. An evil mix of deadly strains. Instead of Vodka, rum, tequila and gin, it's got what-? Anthrax, Smallpox, Spanish Flu?"

The general stood, nodded as he paced around the small room, stumbling once over a leg of Jack's IV stand, almost ripping the IV out of Jack's arm. He stopped, pointed a finger at Jack. "You gotta go back, Captain. No one else available has a combination of your climbing and intelligence expertise, your leadership skills, your mountain combat experience." The general leaned forward, smiled.

"I can't point to one young man in the Marines that can climb into those high mountains and carry out intelligence gathering and or combat like you can." The general paused and surveyed Jack's battered face. "I must say, you don't look bad considering how many prisoners attacked you and your brother. I checked your records—you don't have any special hand to hand training. Looks like another one of your grand efforts."

Jack rubbed his forearm where the IV needle was inserted. "I grew up on a ranch in Montana, General. My grandfather and my father were both Marines. And I was a wrestler in high school." *How many solitary hours shooting arrows, stalking prairie dogs, throwing knives and hatchets under long Montana summer days, alone as an only child on the ranch, except for Indian cowhands who pumped him full of the Indian Way?*

"Well, you garnered an excellent background, Jack, however you did it. Now I want you to put all your skills to work for America, once more into the fray."

"To do what, General?" *Look for the lost Air Force bio bomb payload in some godforsaken canyon or high pass in Afghanistan? Stop crazy Muslim terrorists, end up in Leavenworth again? So you can pick up that third star? Forget it, pal.* He picked up the weapon from his lap, put the heavy knife on his bedside table.

"One of NSA's Echelon Spy Sats assigned to *Eagle's Aerie* intercepted electronic communications originating in Baluchistan—southern Iran. Words popped up after a massive search and comparison of computer files: *Bruno Utecht, Saladin's Fist, Shangri-La.* The computers found two of the terms in an action-rep you gave me in Islamabad last year, when you returned from Afghanistan. Remember? Just before the stabbing attack from—what was her name?"

Glancing at the knife, Jack suppressed a shudder. "Mara Bhutto—the Black Orchid. Pakistani, also a Chinese assassin-type secret agent. Tried to shish-ka-bob me. Did: sixty-some stitches. Stayed away from foreign babes ever since."

The general chuckled. Jack thought, *Guy loves the mention of blood— even when his own men are bleeding.*

"Anyway," the general continued, "this *Saladin's Fist* is—we think—a terrorist cell that's planning on hittin' American domestic targets." The general looked at Jack with widened eyes. "Maybe with the bio bomb payload. And the name, Bruno Utecht—I remember meeting him at your welcome home party in Islamabad last year. Young Russian officer with a German name and an attitude."

"That'd be my pal, Bruno. He's Russian FSB—the spy guys. Tried to grab the *Long Island Iced Tea* bug bomb for Russia. Coincidently, he's pals with Mara Bhutto."

Jack thought of the handsome Russian. "His grandfather was a German V-2 rocket scientist. Captured by the Soviet Army. Grandpa served as an American spy in Star City. Adopted a Lebensborn baby during the war, born of a Norwegian woman."

"Lebensborn? Sorta rings a bell," the general leaned forward, stared incredulously at the stab wound on Jack's forearm. It was almost fully healed.

Jack self-consciously put his arm under the blanket. "Hitler's program to create the Master Race. Lebensborn kid was Bruno's dad, and was raised in Russia after the war by the scientist stepfather. Bruno, the grandson, is a loyal Russian, despite his German heritage. He's rich, as well. The U.S. paid beaucoup spy bucks into a Swiss account for the grandfather, who ended up in a Gulag when he was caught spying for our side, never touched the money. Bruno's dad was a committed Communist, never touched it either. So it just sat there. Bruno says he's not spent any of the dough. He's a committed patriot."

"Well, Captain, to more recent events," the general said. "Last month, I tried to send a rifle company in a squadron of V-22 troop carriers. Into their training camp in KGCV 409, the valley on the Chinese border—you called it Shangri-La—but it was impossible to land. The pilots reported the winds were too intense. They went back a second time—same problem."

No, General, Jack mused, *that's a minor problem. I was convicted for desertion and treason—that's the real problem. So why don't you take a long hike with a short-fused bomb up your hinder?*

A nurse walked in: blonde, piles of curls, peaches and cream complexion—a wonderful smile over big breasts. A familiar whiff of apples and roses perfume. "Time for your pain medication, Captain." She looked at the visitor, was unintimidated by his rank. "Five minutes, General, then I'm givin' this hunk a bath."

Jack looked again, saw two nurses. "Hey, girls, wanna go out for a drink after work?"

The long-legged, slender blonde giggled. "It's just me, honey. Usually I'm enough. Nurse Reynolds—Commander to you. Hold that *'drinks thought'* until you're better. You're goin' nowhere for now, honey." She glanced at the long knife, added, "My! Is that toy an indication of the length of *your* weapon?" She giggled again, left the room, saying, "And remember, I outrank you. When we go for that drink, you'll have to follow my orders to a *T*."

The general, not used to levity from underlings, stared, shocked.

Jack laughed, responded to the general's comment about the inaccessibility of the valley. "High winds, narrow openings in the cliffs, General." He looked, saw two pills in two hands and two glasses of water, wondered whether he was overdosing or seeing double again. He palmed the pills, drank the closer water. "Never get cruise missiles in there, either." *Pictured the huge, snow-covered Hindu Kush peaks looming over the remote valley the natives called Shangri-La. I wonder why it's called 409? he mused.*

"Right," the general agreed. "We sent mountaineering recon teams— they tried to go over the mountains twice, but our climbers couldn't hack it. They turned back. Bad weather, avalanches, crevasse fields, altitude sickness. Your Shangri-La doesn't sound like paradise to me."

Jack suppressed a yawn. "What's it all got to do with me, General? I'm just a poor, innocent, all-American boy serving twenty years in Leavenworth because I worked for you." *Guy's crazy if he thinks I'm going back to the Hindu Kush for him.* "General, you offered me a chance to go back to law school last year, remember? You said I could become a JAG—a Judge Advocate General officer—for the rest of my Reserve tour. I put that aside to help you out with the LIIT bio bomb."

Sitting back, the general smiled. "That was commendable, Captain. Outstanding, really. You and your team did a great job, stopping that operation, even if you didn't recover the payload. Delivered to America, it coulda killed millions." His eyes narrowed into a calculating look.

"And where'd my volunteerin' get me, General? I shoulda listened to my dad: like, never volunteer."

The general frowned, shook his head. "Bullshit! Your father was a wonderful Marine. Deadly, cool—absolutely fearless. You're just like him. But you used some unfortunate tactics in Pakistan. *Nemo est supra leges*— no one is above the law."

"Got you there, General. *Silent leges inter arma*—during war, the laws are silent. I did what I had to do."

"Exactly! You got it done each time, without whining or asking mom for permission." The general stood, walked around the room in a restless manner, turned back to Jack. "You're right—you did what you had to do— even when it got you in trouble. That's why I want you to take a recon team over the heights, into 409— find out what's going on. I'm confident that you'll succeed where others have failed."

"So you can get my convictions dismissed after this? And Billy's?"

"No guarantees, but I'll put forth max effort in your cause. I promise, I'll deliver after your mission." The general sounded sincere.

Yeah, right! Too sincere, Jack thought. "Everything I did last year was to solve your problems, General. Look where it got me."

Shaking his head, the general looked sad. "I know, Jack. But you stole that Pakistani Caribou aircraft, paid for those Pakistani stolen weapons with illegal drug money. Nobody asked you to do that. And then your brother busted General Farley's jaw in the courtroom. That was ill-advised—to say the least."

"Billy did that when General Farley lied on the witness stand." Jack smiled at the memory of Billy going through the MPs, vaulting into the witness stand, laying out the short general. "We needed everything we took to complete *your* mission, General. And when I couldn't get weapons from our military, a British SAS man gave me the drug money to buy black market weapons. To use against the Taliban. We didn't have time to put in requisition forms—you know all that."

Harmbruster leaned forward. "And a great job, you did. But that's the past, son. Now, I need you to climb into that valley, KGCV 409, and let me know what's going on. We think the payload is still there. We… we may have to destroy the whole valley to stop…"

Jack stared at the general. Shangri-La—it's a populated, I have friends there…"

"Can't be helped," the general said with a firm voice. "Those germs, properly spread, could kill tens of millions."

"What about my brother, Billy? I'd need him."

"I'm afraid the Indian has to go back to Leavenworth. Serve out his sentence. General Farley insisted on that—he's still pissed about his jaw." Jack tried to restrain a smile as an image of the pompous, chubby general with a big white bandage holding his jaw in place, popped into his mind. "You don't understand, General. Billy Howling Dog serves under a blood oath from his maternal grandfather, Talking Dog. He has to protect me." He yawned, felt serious drowsiness sweep over his body.

"We'll talk about it as soon as you're up, Jack. Rest now."

Intending to ask if KGCV 409 had anything to do—he fell into an instant dream: his drill instructor at OCS, Bulldog Mahoney, was screaming a date—April 9, 1865. "Lee surrendered to Grant on that day, you dummy!" Bulldog yelled. "And remember, shit for brains, the Knights of the Golden Circle."

Jack instantly woke, heard the general say to himself as he rose and left the room. "Son, I'm glad to see your positive attitude. Duty, loyalty— that's the ticket. Semper Fidelis, Captain Flashhardt."

Chapter 4

A jangling telephone awoke Jack. Morning by the light from the window. Head felt better already, ribs still very stiff, forearm stab wound good. It was his dad, Bill Flashhardt.

"Jack, how the hell did you and Billy end up in Bethesda? Are you okay?"

"I'm fine. You at the ranch, Dad?" *He sounds sober.*

"Just drove home from golf with the senator. Over at Red Lodge Mountain Golf. Bought a season pass for three hundred fifty bucks. Mrs. Hansen told me about you and Billy's accident. How are you?"

"I'm—" Jack looked around. Was momentarily distracted at the realization that his dad, a real tightwad, was well on the way to health and happiness, evidenced by his splurging for a season golf pass. "Not good, Dad. Could you come? It's time. I hate to make you travel so far, but I'm weak and… gaunt from the beating. It's time to let it be." They had codenamed their planned breakout, Gauntlet. He hoped his dad got the message.

"Are you sure, son? I'm pretty busy right now. You sure comin' back there is the right thing to do?"

Jack realized his father was trying to talk him out of the planned escape. "Absolutely, Dad. I might need an *operation.* I just have to see you. I miss you so much." He sat up and tightened his grasp on the telephone. "You can *deliver* a little cheer. I know I'll be in a better place if you visit. And you can say hello to Billy. That'll mean a lot to him. And I need redemption."

Remembering and understanding his son's secret communications, Bill reluctantly agreed, "Okay, son, I'll catch a flight back east right away. See you soon."

Jack said goodbye, slumped back on the bed. He was gratified that he and Billy had solved their father's problems by resurrecting the ranch, but now it was their turn. They had planned an escape if the brothers could fake a mishap, make it to an outside hospital: Bill had purchased forged passports at the Southern California border town of San Ysidro, and had assembled other necessary items.

After a moment's thought, he called Billy's ward and asked for his brother. Billy was in rehab, so he left a message.

His half-brother came at 1800 hours. Unlike Jack, who was pale from his imprisonment, the half-Brule Sioux offspring of Bill Flashhardt and an Indian maid at the ranch had a dark complexion that made his flashing smile and grey eyes bright.

"How's it goin', bro. You getting good?" Billy stroked his braids. His grey eyes had the Oxycontin look. Jack wondered how Billy had so obviously obtained *Hillbilly Heroin* in the hospital.

"No," Jack responded with a wink. "I'm feelin' real bad. And you were right. The general wants me to go on another mission. Soon as I'm better."

"Great! But whaddya mean, *you*? Don't I get to go?"

"I asked. The general said no."

"That's bullshit, Flashy! You need me to cover your six."

Jack winked again. "Dad's coming to visit. And as soon as I'm better, I'll be outta here. Take care of yourself in Leavenworth."

Winking back, Billy growled, "Thanks a lot, asshole! I'm gonna go break somethin'!" He stormed out of the room.

Jack grinned when Nurse Candy Reynolds entered. With a big smile, she locked the door, stripped away the bed sheets, carefully removed his bandages, began to give him a him a hand bath. He smelled a hint of aromatic perfume. Relaxed, shut his eyes and enjoyed the moment.

"Ever been washed by a commander?" she giggled. She brushed her big breasts against his bare chest as she washed his neck. Her breath was sweet. One sniff and he wanted to kiss her wonderful lips.

"First time I've been this helpless," Jack responded. "And been molested by a peaches and cream blonde."

Nurse Reynolds said, "Call me, Candy. All my favorite patients do." She carefully washed his battered and bruised ribcage, then drifted the washcloth lower, to his hip, to his groin. "And helpless?" she exclaimed. "It appears to me that a heat-seeking missile has just readied for launch. Oh, my!"

Shutting his eyes, Jack shivered, then said with a quavering voice, "I've been in a cage for six months."

Candy grasped him, gently squeezed, began to wash him with a fresh warm cloth. "You should've called 911. I would've made emergency house calls."

Wonderful sensations flushed Jack's body from head to toes. Moments later, he felt bare breasts brush his chest. He opened his eyes, saw peachesand-cream complexioned, curly-haired Candy carefully lower her slender, naked body onto him. She took his erection inside, leaned over, barely brushed his chest again with her wonderful breasts. A hint of strawberries filled the air, exploded in his brain.

Chapter 5

The brothers awaited their father's arrival: Jack with eager, loving anticipation, Billy with typically ambivalent feelings. Jack glanced at the wall clock— ten AM. Dad was overdue. He rubbed his ribs, thankful that they were only cracked; touched the stab wound on his forearm: it was totally healed over but the skin still felt rough.

The plan to endure a beating had worked— they were outside Leavenworth's walls. Next would be escape, then an attempt for Jack's redemption.

Handsome, tan, and fit, sixty-year-old Bill Flashhardt had done an amazing turnaround in the six months since he had purchased back the Flying Eagle Ranch from the Crow Nation, who had won it away from the family after a bitter lawsuit over the legality of the original 1883 sale when Jack's great-great granddad purchased the land.

Bill had quit drinking to excess, his blue eyes were bright, clear, and his facial skin had lost a blotchy complexion. He was upright, healthy, and brisk in manner. He had plunged into an exercise regimen and rehabilitation of himself and the Montana ranch, which had been neglected for three years under the Indian tribe's stewardship.

Walking into his son's room, Bill shouted, "Hey, Billy, Jack. Great to see you guys." He put a bag down, which contained civilian clothes, fake passports, cash and credit cards, kicked it under the bed.

The father and sons exchanged emotional greetings, hugs, backslaps. Bill covertly checked Billy's eyes— they were clear. He turned up the bedside radio and gave a detailed report on the state of the ranch; they more quietly discussed the loan— secured by the Afghan treasure— Jack and Billy had set up in Singapore to finance the repurchase of the ranch.

Bill finally asked, "So the General wants you to climb back in the saddle?"

Jack exchanged glances with Billy, responded, "Yeah, he call you?"

"That he did," Bill affirmed. "Said he thought he could get everything turned around if you'd go back to the Hindu Kush."

Jack restrained rage, collected his thoughts. "Dad, even after you and Senator Jensen got me transferred to the United Nations, the general interfered and I ended up responsible for the deaths of hundreds of men in Afgone-land and Pakman-land. Not to mention the Chinese dudes in the caverns. I don't want to be that kind of the person. I can still see the scenes in my nightmares— luckily most of the faces are gone." He thought of the giant Chinese guy— *Mo Poo: hideous, slash-opened, bloody face, teeth showing through the wounds from the white tiger's claws.*

Bill pounded a fist on the bedside table, sending a glass flying, startling both his sons. "Son, I know exactly what you mean. But you chose to be an officer of the Corps, just as I did. You're not a librarian or a school teacher. Deal with it or you'll sink in a morass of whining self-pity. And remember, those who died at your hands made their choices, too— put themselves at risk." Bill paused, picked up the fallen glass, continued, "I'll never forget what you wrote me. What that temple monk told you in Afghanistan: *You're a Kshatriya— a unique and powerful member of the warrior caste. It's your dharma— your duty to fight. You'll make the earth a lake of blood."* Bill smiled at his bedridden son. "Powerful words."

Jack sat up, gestured for his father and Billy to come closer. "The general's got his own agenda, Dad. He doesn't care about us. I don't trust him."

"Me nuther," Billy added. He rearranged his short braids.

Bill protested but acquiesced after Jack whispered over and over, "Twenty years, Dad. Twenty years. Once we make Pakistan, and I gather evidence— I can prove I'm innocent. Or else I'll be in my forties when I get out of here." He glanced at Billy, added, "Well, me innocent, but then there's Billy's boxing exhibition and tap dance on General Farley's jaw." He delivered the final argument. "We gotta get Billy out of the prison system, get him off *Hillbilly H."*

Bill looked at the two sons he adored, slowly nodded his head in agreement. "I love you two— I'm proud of you— no matter what happens, we know the truth."

After a lunch of great tasting, sweet red pepper tuna sandwiches and iced tea, served at Jack's bedside by an enlisted orderly, Bill hugged his sons, whispered he would bring a rented ambulance to the ER entrance the next day at 0600 hours.

The next morning: Jack in a wheelchair, Billy pushing, Commander Candy Reynolds attending, trailing an IV pole on four wheels. Down corridors past a nurse and security station: the security guard asked, "Where to, Ma'am?"

Candy punched an elevator control, answered, "MRI unit, Sergeant." The Marine sergeant said, "I have no record of movement." "Movement, sir." Billy ordered the Marine.

The Marine punched a keyboard, stared at his computer monitor. "I'll need written authorization to move the patient, Ma'am."

Jack sat quietly, his head slumped to one side, his eyes closed.

"What? You think he's going to fly away, Sarge?" Billy asked. "Look, I can't—"

The elevator door beeped its arrival, slid open. Candy pushed the chair in, hit the down button, looked back at the guard. "We have a schedule around here, Sergeant. Patient first, your paperwork later."

To the first floor, past kitchens and supply wards, and outside from the Medical Center. Candy stopped Billy under an overhang. She looked up. "There's a video camera once you move onto the sidewalk." She knelt and kissed Jack with ardor, smiled. He inhaled her strawberry perfume. He felt her breasts against his chest, sensed a flush of passion sweep through his body, squeezed her hand. She whispered, "You've made an amazing recovery. Come visit me when you're back. I'll show you what *a whole lotta lovin'* really means."

"You won't get in trouble over this?"

Commander Candy flashed a brilliant smile. "Don't worry, I'll tell them you and your brother broke away on your own when I was talking to the MRI unit. I'll give you five minutes head start."

Three hours later, at Dulles Airport outside Washington, D.C., the brothers stood in line, waiting to present their tickets to Singapore. Jack had died his blond hair black to match the photo in the fake passport his dad had purchased in San Ysidro. He looked around, scratched his healed forearm.

Billy, his beloved braids cut off, disguised as a Catholic priest, also glanced around, shifted feet constantly.

"Quit fidgeting. Try to look more like a dickhead tourist, less like a criminal."

"I *am* a dickhead criminal— and an escapee," Billy retorted.

"You didn't have to go. Especially to Pakistan. Me, I gotta go to clear my name. Make up for my stupidity."

Billy sighed, "So you say. But Chief Talking Dog told me to cover your lame ass— no excuses." He rubbed his head, searching for his lost braids.

"You're not carryin' are you?" Jack asked.

"Not much," Billy reassured him.

Reaching the head of the line, the two presented their tickets and fake passports. Both held their breath as the bored American Airlines ticket agent looked at their IDs and tickets, then stamped the paperwork and returned each packet. Jack stuck the paperwork— his name was now Samuel Flashman, named after his part Indian ancestor— in an envelope containing five thousand dollars his dad had given them.

While they waited for the flight, Jack took the worn photo of Ashley out of his pocket, spread it on his thigh, smoothed it out. Billy glanced at it. "You miss her— call," he suggested.

Jack looked around, walked to a bank of payphones. He punched in Ashley's cell phone number from memory. It rang: she picked up halfway through the first ring, asked, "Frank?"

Quelling a sense of dismay, Jack responded, "It's me."

Her voice lost its excited tone. She said, "Oh. Jack. Where are you? I thought you couldn't take or make calls from... Solitary." Her voice evinced no sympathy.

"I'm out." He stopped himself from announcing where he was, glanced around the gate area.

"Transferred to minimum security? Or you got a pardon?" Ashley sounded incredulous.

"No. I gotta go. I just wanted to hear your voice."

"Don't tell me—," Ashley's voice evoked rising anger. "In fact, don't tell me anything, convict. Goodbye!" She disconnected.

The gate attendant called a second time for first class passengers. Jack looked at the payphone, slammed it and walked to the gate.

They found their first class seats, sat down. The 747 was crowded in the rear sections.

"Hey!" Billy exclaimed. "First Class! Musta caused Dad a bundle! But we got a baby in front of us— it's sure to wail."

"Have a little sympathy. This's all new to a baby. And the cabin air pressure'll make it cry."

"There you go," Billy grumbled.

"You'll see things differently when you have kids." *Ashley. Our lost baby.* "Things woulda been so different," he mumbled.

"Maybe so, if I live that long." The Indian responded to the first statement, glanced at his brother, recognized Jack's sorrowful expression. He pounded his brother on the thigh. "Chasing you around, covering your ass ain't the healthiest lifestyle in the world." He accepted a glass of champagne offered by a smiling Asian hostess in a tight-fitting blue dress. He checked out the girl's figure. "But it does have rewards. Government transport so sucks compared to this." He popped three 40mg Oxys he had stashed in his hip pocket of his priest's suit, settled back to druggie dreams. Jack pulled out the unopened letter, stared at it. Fought the urge to open it. What could his mother say after being MIA for twenty years? *I hunted all winter when I was twelve,* he thought. *Shot, skinned, cured coyote furs. Made a coat. Figured that'd lure you back. Hah!*

The flight was uneventful, although the two tensed in Los Angeles during a well-timed airline switch to Northwest Airlines. They worried again, many hours later, prior to landing at Changi International Airport in Singapore. Through Customs, where a smiling, moon-faced Chinese man in a blue suit and red tie stamped their passports and welcomed them to Singapore. Armed guards carrying submachine pistols that looked like P90s, ignored the two Americans, stared at Arab-type men as they passed.

The two crossed the hot sidewalk through a humid, tropical-smelling atmosphere; spotted a uniformed Asian chauffer holding up a sign saying, *F E R,* their agreed upon symbol for the Flying Eagle Ranch. The two accompanied him to a waiting Mercedes limo with sighs of relief. Without instructions, the smiling driver pulled into traffic on East Coast Parkway, an impossibly crowded expressway, drove around a traffic circle with a freshly painted giant anchor being erected in the center of a huge flowerbed, and headed on to the financial district. An incredible amount of skyscrapers jutted into the almost invisible sky.

"We made it, Billy," Jack said. "Seemed too easy." He peered through the darkened rear window, looked for signs of attention from potential followers, saw nothing obvious.

"Yeah? I liked the first class seats, the limo, but what exactly have we made?" Billy asked for the tenth time. "Go home, we'll be back in prison—"

"Where we'd be jumped again by patriotic prisoners," Jack interrupted. "I told you— I asked the general to give us pardons as a condition of helping him. He stalled again."

Billy shut his eyes "So, we're not going that route."

Jack's voice rose with passion, he exclaimed, "Exactly! I figure if we're free, we got a better chance at getting me a reversal or a pardon. Screw him! We'll get sworn depositions from General Hammar, from Robert Arses— the SAS guy, maybe the Hunza tribal leader— Sergeant Major, and we can start an appeal process. Prove my innocence. Prove I was railroaded."

The limo stopped and a liveried door attendant opened their door, unloaded their bags. Billy looked up at the twenty-story, pure white Singapore Hotel, exclaimed, "Wow! Dad's payin' for all this?"

"He's footing everything on this escape-vacation. And tomorrow we're meeting the bank that helped with the loan to buy back the ranch." He glanced at the hotel situated in the midst of about fifteen acres of lush gardens. "I couldn't resist when Dad told me the name of the place— *the Shangri-La Hotel*."

"Yowzer!" Billy exclaimed as they entered the front doors. Massive palm trees, a hundred feet high, were growing in the marble-floored lobby. Ponds, streams, island restaurants abounded. An artificial rainfall with intermittent fake lightning flashing over a lake.

"Quite a pad. Beats the hell out of a foxhole in Afghanistan, huh?" Jack stopped at the check-in parlor.

Billy laughed. "Or a dumpy Pakistani hotel."

Fifteen minutes later, they reached their nine hundred dollar per night suite. While Billy enjoyed the view, smelled fragrant jasmine flowers floating in a bowl on the table, Jack mussed the bed sheets, walked into the bathroom, wetted glasses, placed them about. "Don't get used to the view— we're not staying," he said. "Take a quick shower, then we're outta here."

"That so sucks— how come, Flashy?"

"In case American agents are trackin' us." He grabbed a "Do not disturb" sign and hung it on the doorknob. "Let's hurry. We're done establishing our new lifestyle."

An hour later, a dilapidated trishaw— a three-wheeled bicycle pulling a carriage— delivered them to a quay on the Singapore River. An old wooden, two-masted bugis prabu boat, with a little, pitched-roof house on the main deck, was waiting next to the dock. Jack called out, "Hello? Yu… Fuk Up?"

A fat old Baba— a Malay Straits-born Chinese on the stern deck answered, "Welcome, Mr. Flesh-hurt, honored guest."

Jack and Billy stepped aboard the battered but clean boat; a young, bare-footed Chinese boy cast off, pushed the traditional Malay boat— about fifty feet long— away from the dock and jumped on the craft. The waterfront smell was strong, soon was not noticeable.

Billy inspected the boat, then the craft-filled waters as they drifted into the channel. "I liked the hotel better, but this view is great."

"After we rented a limo, a suite, traveled first class, who's gonna look for us on this ancient tub of a sailboat?" Jack asked.

"Hey, you got something there." Billy checked out the water— it looked murky. "At least I hope whoever's chasin' us ain't smart as you. I'd hate to go back in chains, like last year."

Jack looked up and down the quay. He saw no one lurking or staring in their direction. Watching Billy move to the rear of the boat, huddle with the boy, he guessed his brother was trying to score drugs, wished he could do something to stop Billy. He looked around the dock area again, the nearby waters, saw no one loitering or watching. No police, no secret agent types, no muggers.

Yu Fuk Up started the diesel engine and moved farther into the channel, headed south out of Singapore towards a group of islands to the south.

An hour later the deck boy dropped anchor between two jungle islands that Fuk Up identified as St. John's, and Lazarus Island. After digging through a dirty canvas sport bag, Jack and Billy donned fins, masks, and snorkels, dove into the warm waters and swam among spectacular coral reefs. Jack felt the usual tension and tightness in his chest— stemming from childhood near-drownings— increase as he looked across the water for police and secret agent types. He thought of the arid lands he was headed toward and smiled. *Can't drown there,* he mused. Marine Major Zack Broyer pounded on the general's office door.

"Enter," General Harmbruster growled.

"General, Captain Flashhardt and his brother arrived safely in Singapore."

Harmbruster leaned back in his chair, smiled. "Everything's going to plan," said. "That boy is goddamned predictable as the tides."

"He's an escaped prisoner, General," the major protested.

Harmbruster grinned. "Yeah, but he's our escaped prisoner."

Chapter 6

Zhang Poon t'ang, a clandestine special agent in the Second Department's Analysis Bureau—the People's Republic of China's equivalent agency to America's CIA, and known by its acronym, SD, sat in the bar of the Singapore Hotel, hoping to encounter Jack Flashhardt, the American spy. Flashhardt had been face ID'd as a suspected American agent by the new digital photo recognition system the Malaysian government had installed at its International Airport. An informer had tipped Second Department to the American's arrival, and Zhang, in Singapore as part of a Shanghai dance troupe, had been jerked out of her dancer's cover by her superiors when a computer had declared Jack to be on a Chinese *SD Wanted* list.

She had rushed to the hotel, had been too late to observe the American and his assistant check in, but was reasonably hopeful the Americans would go to the bar, have a drink to unwind from their flight. A boring hour later, she decided to give up on that idea.

Zhang fidgeted—an observer would have wondered whom the strikingly beautiful, athletic young woman was waiting for as she stroked her long hair out of her very dark Asian face.

Minutes later, she approached the American's room, bearing a bouquet of flowers purportedly from Hotel Management. She was startled when she recognized a dark purple orchid amongst the fragrant blooms: it reminded her of Mara Bhutto—the Black Orchid: her bunkmate and friend at a Chinese subversive warfare training camp on Hainan Island two years ago. Mara had saved her last year in Kabul after Zhang had turn coated and sold critical information on the location of a missing USAF biological bomb to the CIA.

Arriving at the American's suite, she noticed the door was ajar. She knocked and waited. No response.

Her heart hammering in her chest and throat, she pushed open the door. "Management," she called in English.

Inside, a solid-looking white devil: about thirty-five, light brown wavy hair, brown eyes wide set. A handsome, tanned face, tall, dressed in a dark blue suit. The man whirled and stared. He was not the room's occupant: too old, too heavy.

"What d'you want?" he demanded.

"Fl-flowers for guests," Zhang stammered. She visually checked out the room: beds unmade, dirty clothes on the floor, a half-empty whiskey bottle tipped over on a table, the convenience bar door hanging open. The sloppy Americans had gone out. She returned her attention to the intruder.

"Who you?" she asked with a firmer voice. "Identify, please, or I call Security."

"Relax, lady. I work for the American Embassy. I'm lookin' for the guys staying here." He pulled a leather folder out, flashed a badge and put it away.

"Please check in with Hotel Security," Zhang said. She brushed the small .25 semi auto in a pocket with her free hand, considered shooting the American intruder, rejected the impulse—he was too handsome. She chided herself for being distracted by shallow thoughts, but he was…

"Get lost, girl, I'm busy."

Zhang put the flowers down on the table, retreated, a faint blush tinting her dark skin and African-Asian features. Where were the Americans? Why was this agent chasing them? She had been told the two had been involved in the American ordnance rescue mission in Afghanistan. That they had destroyed the sought-after, high tech weapon she had sold to the CIA: another reason she had been ordered to meet them and find out their intentions. After she left the room, she extracted a cell phone from her pocket, ordered a covert search for the Americans, and an agent to tail the American agent in the hotel room.

Chapter 7

Finding it hard to relax, Jack Flashhardt glanced around, looking for observers on the second afternoon as they climbed aboard Yu Fuk's boat. "What a day!" He watched a line of pelicans fly over the harbor waters off the port bow. The old man started the rattling diesel engine and headed into deeper waters.

Billy glanced across the harbor at the Singapore skyline a half mile away. He mused, "You dragged my ass all over Singapore, looking for that Chinese gem guy." He looked at the boat again. "Then back to this dump!" Jack grimaced, stared into the harbor waters.

Billy continued, "We gotta find that guy. Last year when you gave him the one rock, he said it and the last purple diamonds were worth a mil each. So we know that last purple thingy from the sword scabbard's worth a bundle."

A young woman, looked about twenty to twenty five, slim and attractive, dressed in a halter and cheongsam, a Chinese skirt with a slit almost to the waist, revealing a beautiful, well-muscled leg, came from below deck carrying cold beers on a wood tray.

Billy held up the frosty bottle. "Twenty four bottles in a case, twenty four hours in a day. Some say coincidence—I say—great planning, God."

"What happened to the boy?" Jack yelled to the boat owner, after clicking bottles with Billy.

Yu Fuk Up, looking nervous, left the helm, waddled up to the bow where they were sitting. "The boy run off, damned Singapore trash. This girl name China Mist, she better. She a Nonya—a Straits born girl. Little English speaking, but more reliable." His voice sounded tentative.

Billy cursed under his breath, said, "Boy owes me for some H…"

The brothers both inspected the attractive girl standing before them with hungry eyes that had been deprived of beautiful feminine sights for six months. She was short but very pretty, had muscular

35

arms. She smiled, had a cinnamon odor, large eyes that could be maybe traced to her Malay forebears.

"Yes," Fuk Up confirmed to Jack. "Smart. Ver' reliable. Not like trash Peranakan boy." *Old guy's selling her too much,* Jack thought.

"Peranakan?" Jack asked.

"Means not pure Chinese. Got Malay blood," Fuk Up waved a dismissing gesture as he answered. He returned to the helm.

Jack snorted. "Prejudice rears its ugly head. Thanks, anyway."

The girl smiled, said nothing as she walked away. *No English?* He turned to Billy. "Anyway, you're right. We made out great on the diamonds for the ranch loan deal."

Billy grinned. "Good thing the Crow Nation needed dough to start a casino."

"Indian casinos—redskin's ultimate revenge on white men," Jack observed.

Billy responded, "The Crow got their payback when they won the lawsuit. Anyway, if you're done with social comment bullshit, let's get going. I'm getting seasick again on this tub—whaddya call it? Bogus prayer boat?"

"Bugis prabu. You don't look seasick—you look drunk." The prepaid cell phone he had purchased earlier, rang.

Billy watched his brother speak and listen.

Jack yelled at the boat owner, "Let's head back." He turned to his brother. "Bingo! That was Loo On Sat. He wants to meet."

Billy leaned over and threw up into the water. He wiped his mouth with the back of his hand. "The diamond guy from last year?" His voice was shaky.

Jack smiled at his brother's discomfort, lounged back on the deck. "Exactly," he added.

Twenty minutes later, the boat slowed, bumped against a wood pier. Jack checked out his brother. "Still seasick? Or just lovesick over China Mist?"

Billy belched, finished a beer, crushed the can on the gunwale. "Great legs! Ain't gettin' nowhere, though. She says, 'Go 'way. My father kill me if I date white.' I said, 'I'm an Indian.' She sez, 'You no look Hindi man— you got Amelican eyes.'"

The two stepped off after Yu Fuk tied up alongside the quay. Still laughing over his brother's frustration, Jack hailed a cab and directed the driver to take them to the Overseas Chinese Banking Corporation on Orchard Road.

"The road," their driver said, "it was just a dirt trail in the Nineteenth Century…"

The street cut through the biggest shopping district in Singapore. Each shopping center was more amazing than the last— the architecture ranged from traditional Chinese to the most modern structures.

In front of the bank, Jack paid and tipped the taxi guy five Singapore dollars. Inside, after submitting Jack to a retinal scan, a short, fat, assistant manager led the two to a conference room. He escorted Jack to the deposit room, removed a box from the rows of many boxes, then accompanied Jack to the conference room.

After the man departed, Billy opened the box. "There's only two rocks in here! Somebody bagged our stolen jewels!" He held up the twenty-five carat, dark green emerald, tossed it on a piece of white linen on the table.

Jack assured him, "I've got the rest in another bank. For security. This one's just our sample." He put the other gem—a ten-carat flawless purple diamond, cut in an oval, on the linen in the center of the table.

The door opened and the same manager escorted in an elderly, goateed man dressed in a dark brown Chinese Mao suit. Jack recognized and greeted the man, then introduced him to Billy as Loo On Sat. Jack explained, "Mr. Sat arranged the loan against the two purple diamonds last year."

Mr. Sat smiled, the wrinkles around eyes crinkled like crumpled old paper. He nodded his head several times and sat down. Avaricious eyes darted to the two gems, widened. He stood, leaned closer, his breath puffing out in short gasps. Jack wondered if the guy was having a heart attack.

"Mr. Flashhalt, where did you find this emerald?" he asked. "It appears perfect—it must be fake!"

"The same ruins we recovered the diamonds," Jack responded. He and Billy exchanged nervous glances.

"May I?" Mr. Sat's hand trembled, then picked up the gem as soon as Jack nodded an assent. "Is it real?" he whispered. "A very ancient, unique style of cut. Never imitated. I've only seen renditions in scrolls, descriptions in books." He studied the gem through a jeweler's loup, whistled. "I did not believe flawless emeralds could exist, except in legend. Can it be? This is one of the gems of the first Ch'in Dynasty? There were two hundred perfect stones. The only ones in the world. Identical, all from a single emerald mine in Tibet. On the eastern slopes of Chomolungma. Very famous. Distinctive teardrop shape. Unique color. Very famous. The Emperor Shih Huang Ti had them cut and incorporated into a fabulous dress for his Number One concubine, Fagem Fuk b'est. That was in your Sixth Century B.C."

"Interesting," Jack faked a yawn. "Musta been quite the babe." Despite his apparent disinterest, he kept his eyes on the gems.

The old man's slanted eyes slowly scanned the room. "Much more than interesting, Master Flashhalt. They are national treasures of legendary proportion. Eight of them are locked away in the *People's Struggle Museum* in Beijing. One hundred ninety two are missing. Have been missing for over twenty five hundred years."

Billy said, "Well, we co-inc-i-dently got one hundred ninety two emeralds." Jack kicked Billy under the table.

The old man sat back in his chair, astonishment on his face. "Legend has it," he said with a quavering voice that gave the words an eerie air, "that an invading dragon from Tibet—I remember, Mao mentioned the legend as a way to foment enthusiasm for the invasion of Tibet back in the Fifties'— kidnapped the Royal Concubine. Only her necklace, made of the eight emeralds—and dropped by her—was recovered."

"Well, your legend's close to the mark," Billy interjected. "We took them from a dragon statue in—"

Jack kicked Billy's shin again, quieting him. "If we had them, what d'you think they'd be worth?"

Sat said without thinking, "I could not get involved in this. The stones are worthless for they are priceless! The political overtones—a Chinese national treasure! Legend has it that all the two hundred stones will reunite only when China's ready to resume the role of *Center of the World*." "So what would we do... if we had them?" Jack asked.

"Donate them to the Chinese government—that would be the safest course."

"Bull-*shit*!" Billy cursed. "I risked my life for those jewels. They woulda been lost in the avalanche, anyway, if I hadn't taken them, humped them outta those mountains. Tell him, Jack."

"True," Jack added, giving up on denial. "They would've been lost— maybe forever. An avalanche wiped out the temple the emeralds and diamonds were in—"

"So we ain't gonna just give 'em away," Billy concluded.

Sat picked up the emerald, put the loup to his eye, inspected it. "The legends are true—perfect—no occlusions, cracks or chips." He removed the loup. "Maybe you could hire an attorney, negotiate a donation for a certain reward. Not I, but one could ask for fifty million dollars American." Sat looked at Jack, added, "Of course, they must not be separated. There are countless poems about the two hundred. Very significant number."

He picked up the purple diamond. "This stone is perfect, like the other two of last year, but smaller. It would retail in the States or Europe—in a setting—for more than a million five hundred dollars. I will give you a quarter million Singapore dollars."

"Make that three hundred fifty thousand American dollars and you've a deal," Jack counter-offered.

"Done," Sat responded with a too eager smile that he quickly suppressed.

Jack studied the old man's face, wishing he had asked for more. "Make a cashier's check to Bill Flashhardt. Mail it to Red Lodge, Montana, USA. I'll arrange for this bank to release the diamond when it gets confirmation from my dad, just like last year."

The three men turned their attention back to the emerald. As he wrapped the gemstone in the cloth, put it back in the box, Jack wondered if they would ever derive any more benefits from the treasure. "Maybe we should just give the emeralds back," Jack offered to his brother. "I gotta feelin' we're headed for a lot of trouble, big trouble if we don't. And at least we got the ranch back for Dad."

The Chinaman bowed, quickly left the room. He glanced back at the two from the doorway, then disappeared.

Jack turned to Billy. "Let's go get the emeralds." *I hope the rest of the emeralds are still there. If some bank employee knows fifty million dollars is sitting in his bank, how safe are they?*

Chapter 8

David Holland, the man who Zhang Poon t'ang had encountered in Jack Flashhardt's hotel, and a mid-level CIA field agent in South Asia, glanced at his watch: 1800 hours. His Hong Kong and Shanghai Bank contact was late. She had promised, in return for an American passport for her father, who had stayed in Hong Kong after the British gave up the colony to Communist China, to steal and deliver the American's safety deposit box at 1730 hours. With the treasure in hand, he was sure he could complete his mission: to convince the Flashhardt kid to co-operate with General Harmbruster and go on the general's mission to Afghanistan.

When the prisoners had escaped Bethesda, *Eagle's Aerie* analysts had studied Flashhardt's traffic patterns from the year before and determined the two escapees were probably headed for Singapore, where an operative, Army Captain Michel Nakamura, had reported that they had secreted a jewel treasure looted from an ancient temple in Afghanistan.

Eagle's Aerie had contacted the Embassy and Holland had volunteered to follow up when he recognized Jack's name from their past work in Pakistan. It had not been hard to find the bank Flashhardt had used. Holland thought of cold mountain passes, hordes of dead Taliban and al Qaida the Marine escapee had killed, and shuddered.

He watched a mob of loud tourists and dancing locals hurrying down the street. Some kind of festival, he figured. Singaporeans knew how to party. He sipped his gin and tonic, inhaled the scent of mint from a crushed leaf on the top of the glass. Thought of his wife and two boys back home. He could be at a little league game, eating fresh popcorn, watching his sons play ball. His wife sitting next to him in makeshift stands, squeezing his thigh and clapping her hands whenever one of their boys excelled.

A cab skidded to a stop in front of the tiny sidewalk café. His contact, Ann Siang, a tall, attractive Chinese woman in a tan Western dress suit, got out of the white London cab carrying a brown leather satchel. She stumbled, righted herself and walked stiffly to his table. Her face was chalky white, despite her Chinese ethnicity. He wondered if she was wearing stage makeup.

Holland glanced at the heavy bag she struggled to lift to the table. "Success?" he asked. "That's wonderful."

Ann Siang, her lips squeezed tight, sat, nodded an affirmative.

"Awesome, Ann," Holland grasped her hands. She pulled away, he tightened his grip, asked, "What's wrong?"

Slipping off her chair, Ann gripped his hands tightly, fell to the pavement. Her silk jacket slid open, he saw her blood-soaked right side. "What happened?" he asked.

"They're coming. *SD*. I got away. They're right..." Holland reached for his cell phone.

Chapter 9

The day after they sold the purple diamond to Mr. Sat, Jack and Billy sat in another conference room at ten AM, in the Hong Kong and Shanghai Bank on Orchard Road. The sterile-smelling room was as featureless as the last bank they had visited, but this room was on the tenth floor and had a view of the river. The Eurasian bank manager directed the two security guards to put the safe deposit box on the table, then left the room, shooing the guards before him.

Jack regarded the green metal box. When he had filled it with the emeralds, he and Billy had been on a high: they had destroyed the USAF LIIT bomb, they had rescued Jack's fiancé, Ashley. He briefly wondered where Ashley was, who Frank was.

"What're you waitin' for?" Billy exclaimed. He opened the box: it was empty!

Stunned, Jack slumped back. Billy stood, looked inside the box, cursed, "What the fuck?"

Chapter 10

Reading the decoded *SD* email again did not change the words: *The American is in Singapore.* Mara Bhutto, the former secret Chinese *SD* operative, sat back, stared at the words she had intercepted. Jack was in Asia! Emotions poured through her mind: love, hate, failure.

She jumped to her feet, walked as calmly as possible through the cave system to Bruno's cell. Outside the door, she aimed a flashlight through the small opening hacked in the makeshift plank door: the Russian spy was curled in a fetal position. Once aware of the light, he stretched out, carefully sat up.

Mara removed the wood bar across the door, entered. "Bruno?" His foul odor hit her nose.

"Yes, bitch," Bruno's whispered reply sounded strained.

"Tell me about Jack," Mara demanded. "Does he know the bomb still exists? Is that why he is here?"

"Jack? The amazing… jihadist slayer? I haven't seen him since we parted in Abad, last year. He returned to America, under arrest—that's all I know."

Mara stared at Bruno. "I don't have time for games or subterfuge, Bruno. D'you want me to call the giant cannibal, Mo Poo? He's completely de-manned—he'd love to streamline you in the same way."

Bruno's hands jerked towards his violated groin. His voice increased with fright, "Mara, we're pals! So is Jack. Why did you do this to me? I'm a soldier. You had no reason or right—"

"Shut up, Bruno. You're a filthy European! A white man. We're not pals. I hate you with every particle of my being. And Jack! I want to crush him!"

Staring up at copper-skinned Mara, Bruno exclaimed, "You're halfwhite! Which half is it, Mara? Which half do you hate? You're a Catholic, not a Muslim. Your God is white." Bruno paused, looked up at Mara. "Is that why you tried to kill Jack last year?"

Fuming, Mara ignored his question asked, "Jack's in Singapore. Are you two working together? Is he on his way here?"

"I certainly hope so, Mara," Bruno stiffly stood up. "Before I move from the appetizer list to the main course for that filthy Chinese bastard. And I need something to sterilize my wound, Mara. Please!"

Mara looked at the formally handsome Bruno. When she had first met him, he was young, well-muscled, blond, blue-eyed—the European ideal. Now he was filthy, bearded, smelly, gaunt, sick. "I'll get you some alcohol," she relented. "But you'll have to treat yourself—I'll not fondle your filthy jewels."

"Jewels? just one now!" Bruno jested with a bitter tone.

Slamming the door shut, Mara barred it and strode down the dimly lit hall. She wondered if Jack was coming. Hoped Jack was coming. Thought about making love to Jack, wondered if she ever would. Dreaded his coming.

Chapter 11

Shaken by the loss of the gems, Billy and Jack caught a cab to the Singapore Hotel.

Despite the "Do not disturb" sign, the linens had been changed, the room had been picked up. Billy spotted a card on the bathroom counter, read it out loud. *"David Holland. American Embassy.* What the hell's he doing here? How'd he get on to us?" He turned it over — handwritten words stated: *Jack, you're a jewel of a guy. Call me.*

"I'm guessing, hopin' he's the guy who has our emeralds," Jack responded. He sprawled on a couch in the sitting room.

Billy crossed the polished-bamboo wood floor, handed the card to Jack. "Call him," Billy ordered. "I was gettin' used to bein' real rich—but the feeling's disappearin' fast." Billy pounded a fist into the other hand, ground his teeth, slammed a pillow against the TV. He looked up at Jack, asked, "What's Dad gonna do with the money Sat's sendin' him?" He pulled a plastic sandwich baggy out of his pocket, popped two Oxycontins.

Jack frowned, said nothing about the Oxy. "The senator's going to spread it around. Political contributions. Dad and the senator figure they can buy political pressure to get us a Presidential pardon." Restless, he rose, began pacing. "Dad has a picture of General Harmbruster givin' me the Silver Star last year. And the one taken when the President of Pakistan decorated me. Wish we'd had them during the trial." He slammed a fist into his palm. "They'll go a long ways towards annulling our felony convictions, make us whole again."

Billy picked up the pillow, pounded it again.

Jack regarded his brother, took a deep breath. "Billy, how'd you get started on Oxy? What's that all about?"

Billy stared at his brother with hate-filled eyes. "What d'you know about pain, asshole! Star-blessed life. Always got everything you ever wanted. Lived a rich kid life on the ranch. I grew up in a rundown singlewide on the Rez, an' I was too embarrassed to ever let white kids visit."

Jack felt anger rise, stepped it down before he spoke. "Doesn't look like you ever missed a meal, pal."

"You had a dad!" Billy accused.

"You had a mom!" Jack shot back. "So what—"

"Yeah," Billy grimaced. "What say we quit bitchin' and—"

"Get on with our real problems," Jack finished.

"You got it, bro." Billy flashed a smile. The two bumped fists.

Jack heaved a sigh of relief, called the American Embassy, asked for David Holland. After several minutes, Holland came on the line.

"Hey, Jack, long time. How's it goin'?"

"Yeah, hi. You didn't thank me for last year."

"Sorry about that—I been busy in Iraq. Duty calls, another crisis, you know?"

"Yeah, right. You guys are like busy little beavers—running around, damming the shit outta the world's problems. So you visited. What's up, dude?"

Holland laughed. "Your hotel—great pad—you guys're livin' the high life. Beats Bharakan Prison, huh?"

"Damn! You knew I was imprisoned there?" Jack snarled. He swallowed a string of swear words. "Why didn't you get me out?"

"Hey, we weren't worried about you. A Pakistani prison? Come on! Buncha A-rab and Pak ragheads. And we wanted you to take Hammar out with you. We figured you'd need him to help you. And he was agreeable."

That admission stunned Jack. He wondered if he had ever had a moment of free will in Asia during his first forward deployment. He took a deep breath. "So what's up, now?"

"The general was a little irritated when you checked outta Bethesda without saying goodbye, but he got over it when he saw you headin' for Asia. I knew you'd wanna meet me in Singapore. Talk over old times— after all, I'm a gem of a guy, like you," Holland laughed. "I'm on Napier Street, but let's meet at Molly Malone's Pub for a late lunch. It's on Circular Road in Chinatown, it's a lorang—that's a lane—right behind Boat Quay on the river. Just tell a cab. Half hour."

"You wouldn't have any pals along, bent on sending us back to the States?"

"Don't sweat it, Jack. I'm down with your escapade. C'mon over." Jack hung up, said to Billy, "He's got the emeralds." "I'd like to kill the prick!" Billy exclaimed.

"Actually, he's a pretty good guy," Jack observed. "I met him in Billings when he was a fibbie—FBI—working with the District Attorney on the ranch lawsuit. Then, in Islamabad, he gave me the cell phone we used. To trigger the blow-up of the bomb."

"A peach of a guy. Guesh I'll just pit him."

Jack ignored Billy's drug-induced slur. Smelled an armpit—it was horrendous. "I'm taking a quick shower."

After cleaning up, dressing in shorts, polo shirts and hiking shoes, the two took a cab to Molly Malone's. It was a pub that could've been in Lower Manhattan or Dublin: outside second floor painted red, first floor Irish green; with the words, *Molly Malone's* over the door, a "No gum chewing" sign tacked to it.

Inside, they saw Holland, dressed in a light blue suit, his brown hair neatly combed, sitting on a stool at the dark mahogany bar. A female clothes manikin's legs were comically sticking through the ceiling above the bar. Four uniformed US sailors were sitting at a table, drinking and bellowing out songs.

"Hey," Holland called. "Jack. Old buddy. Good to see you." He held out a hand, Jack ignored it.

"Hey, Billy," Holland said. "How's it feel to be free?" He noticed Billy's eyes, looked closer, said nothing, but his wide-setbrown eyes had a questioning look.

"Great, ashhole," Billy said.

"Let's sit in a booth. I ordered corned beef sandwiches— they're a specialty of the house." Holland signaled the bartender, a slight Asian, ordered three beers. He grabbed the tray of sandwiches, carried them to a booth. "Hope Leavenworth's crap chow didn't make you two vegetarians."

At the booth, Jack ate half of the very juicy, flavorful beef sandwich, then demanded, "How'd you get our gems? Why'd you steal them?" "Slow, down, Jack," Holland smiled. He watched the server, held out ten Singapore dollars, the guy put down three bottles of brown ale.

"No slow down!" Billy demanded. He picked up a sandwich, added mustard, finished it in three bites.

"I rescued your gems—they were being stolen."

"Thanks," Jack said in an unfriendly tone. "Where are they?"

"In a safe place. Singapore was too hot. Some Chinese guys were after your treasure. Bribed or threatened a bank employee. I intercepted the deal, sent the gems by diplomatic pouch to the Embassy in Islamabad. Boxed up and labeled as evidence in a 'drugs for bullets' investigation. Says "Do not disturb. Singapore—"

The sailors overrode his words with an even louder Jailhouse Rock parody:

"Taliban One said to Mullah Four,
Get the boys ready for a holy war.
Throw rocks,
Everybody throw rocks.
Raghead Three said to al Qaeda new,
I'll pay you to kill an American, too."

"—nobody'll look at the package for probably six months. Luckily, the local DEA guy is in Baluchistan for a couple of weeks, setting something up," Holland resumed. "The gems will be safe there. And that'll give you time to help out the general. He wants you to go back to Afghanistan, check out the camp in that Hindu Kush valley, KGC 409."

With a disgusted expression, Jack stood, threw his sandwich crust down, finished his ale. It was bitter. "Let's get outta here, Billy."

"Hold your horses, Jack," Holland exclaimed. "We got a doable deal here. Win-win. Your country really needs your help—it's urgent. And you owe me—I saved your gems."

"You don't get it, Dave," Jack said. He glared at Holland, continued, "I don't give a rat's ass about those emeralds. I almost got whacked big time in Pakistan last year. I lost a close friend fighting for you guys. I gave up a lot to fight for my country."

"Poor you," Holland smiled. "Grow up, Leatherneck. Your country needs you. We're at war."

Jack glared down at the CIA agent. "Yeah, it needed me last year and I gave at the office. And the thanks I got was my country threw my ass in Fort Leavenworth to rot for twenty years, so I don't owe anybody squat. I'm not going back for you, the general, or the Dragon God's emeralds." He glanced at Holland—the agent stared, open-mouthed.

He and Billy left the pub, waved down a Mercedes cab, directed the driver to the hotel. In the taxi, Jack noted his brother's tight lips, said nothing, noted his own hands shaking, sat on them.

At the Shangri-La Hotel, Jack opened the door to their suite: an Asian man pointed a pistol at him! He gestured for them to come forward with a beckoning hand. Jack tried to block Billy from entering, but another man, younger, ran forward and pointed a pistol at Billy's forehead.

Hearts pounding, the brothers raised their hands. The intruders were young, looked like teenagers, wore tight-fitting black suits, white shirts and thin blue ties, had shoulder-length black hair.

The room had been searched. Clothes were thrown around, the sofa and chairs were torn apart. The first Asian demanded, "Where the emeralds?"

"What're you talkin' about?" Jack snapped.

The man gave an order in Chinese, the other man hesitated, then cocked his pistol, leveled it at Jack, a frightened expression on his face.

"Hold on," Jack cried. "Don't hurt me! Please, I'll do anything. Please don't hurt me. I'll give them to you."

He walked toward the small refrigerator, opened it, removed a bottle of champagne. The second man shouted another order. Jack threw the bottle, hit the gunman in the shoulder, charged into him. Grabbed the gun hand, crashed over the sofa. Landed on the guy, heard a grunt of pain. Pistol slid away. Guy's smell was rank. Billy attacked the other man, a gunshot rang out, a window shattered.

Terrified for his brother, Jack head-butted the guy, slammed a fist into ribs. His superior weight gave him an advantage but he was sprawled half over the sofa and the boy twisted loose. Both scrambled in the direction of the fallen pistol. The boy reached it first, Jack dove on him, knocked him into a table and chairs, grabbed the hand holding the gun. It fired twice, the loud bangs next to Jack's ear sent shooting pains through his head. Heard a crash behind him, Billy stepped on the boy's wrist with one foot, stomped the guy's fingers with the other. Bones crunched, shattered under his foot. The boy screeched.

"Need a hand?" Billy asked. He was panting from exertion and excitement. He picked up the champagne bottle slammed it over the boy's head. The bottle didn't break but the cork shot out with a bang that made the combatants flinch. Fizzing wine poured over the boy's face.

"That's good champagne! Don't waste it!" Jack cracked, relieved that Billy wasn't hurt. The first guy was crumpled, unconscious, on the floor next to the bulkhead where Billy had thrown him.

"Didn't have a milk bottle," Billy grinned, helped his brother to his feet. He took a swig of the spilling champagne. "And you were lettin' the kid shoot up the place. We might hafta pay fer the damage."

Jack searched the body, found no new weapons. Billy dragged the boy across the room, threw him on top of the other body.

"Let's get outta here," Jack said. "Too much riff and raff lying around." Grabbed the sports bag he had left in the room, threw personal items and clothes in it, added the two handguns. They were Chinese Tokarevs. He put on his flexible ceramic shirt, threw the other to his brother. "Things are heatin' up. Wear this."

"What's so special, Flashy?" Billy looked at the shirt, which appeared to be made of soft leather with a gray tint.

"*Vestis virum reddit*—the clothes make the man, dude. Dad picked them up on the Internet. The malleable ceramic-infused titanium molecules realign, and harden when a force like a bullet hits the shirt. He tested them. Can take a .50 caliber round or even the double punch of a Russian AN 94."

"Way cool!" Billy fingered the fabric.

"Yeah, when hit, the flexible vest hardens, spreads the shock wave throughout the entire shirt. Unlike Kevlar armor, you don't get a massive bruise where the bullet strikes."

"Sounds very science fictiony," Billy exclaimed. "But if everybody wears these, how do you pop a guy?"

Jack picked up the telephone, said over his shoulder. "Sock 'em in the nose." He chuckled, and added, "The shirts're experimental. Dad got 'em from this guy who's developing them in California."

When the operator answered, he reported a break-in to the operator, hung up. "Let's blow this over-priced dump for the time being."

The two hurried to the elevators, relived the fight as the elevator swiftly sank to the lobby. Outside, they looked around for other pursuers, saw no one acting suspicious. Climbed into a Mercedes taxi, ordered the driver to the Boat Quay, silently watched to see if anybody was following.

Chapter 12

Free of the cab driver's presence, and walking on the quay to Fuk Up's boat, Billy began, "So what—"

Jack nudged him in the ribs, pointed at a stranger on the two-masted bugis prabu. He glanced at his watch: 1730 hours.

"You know," Billy whispered, "all in all, I like the CIA guy's approach a tad bit better than those crazy gooks at the hotel."

"Yeah, me too," Jack agreed in a low voice. "But how'd those guys know about the emeralds? Mister Sat told someone. I figured him for a straight-shootin' guy."

Billy snorted. "You say straight shootin', I say he straight stabbed us in the back."

They crossed to Yu Fuk Up's boat, Billy added in low tones, "Your indignant speech to Holland was great, but we gotta get outta Dodge, and his offer of a ride to Pakmanland would be as good as anyplace else, bro. We're goin' there, anyway."

Jack wiped his brow. It was hot, humid. He admitted, "Pakistan? Yeah, I know."

Billy added, "Holland could get us through any problems like leaving used bodies lying around the hotel suite. Get us a ride to Islamabad. So why don't you get off your high horse?"

Jack responded, "It's just, like, I hate being manipulated by these assholes. Why should we jump just because they say so? They threw me out of the Marines. Nobody's invited me to re-up. It's not like I'm duty-bound. Screw 'em."

"Yeah," Billy agreed. "I know what you mean. But I guess I'm more used to it. You've been part of the white man power structure all your life. I've been, like, on the redskin side of the equation."

Jack snorted. "Okay, but we were on the track to fill our own dance card and they jerk us back in line like a coupla puppets. It just pisses me off."

"You gonna whine a lot more, I'll really need some Oxy."

"Okay, I won't. I wonder who the babe is?"

Drawing closer, they saw China Mist, Yu Fuk's new employee, swimming in the water, scrubbing the side of the boat with a hand brush. The old man was hovering at the stern.

The other person, a tall, attractive Asian female, dressed in white shorts and a red shirt, tied under ample breasts. Long legs splayed out—a very muscular body—she was sitting on the deck of the boat, her long black hair tied in a ponytail. She wore a red *LA Angels* baseball cap. When she stood, Jack noticed her slim hips jutted out at a wonderful, saucy angle. He felt a surge of passion sweep through his body.

Stepping aboard, Jack noted the woman's large green eyes had an Asian slant but no epicanthic fold. Realized she was a striking, gorgeous mixture of Asian and African. "Waiting for us?" he asked hopefully.

The young woman smiled. "Hi, guys. You're Jack Flashhardt. You're Billy Howling Dog? I'm Zhang Poon t'ang. I work for ChiRep Institute for International StratStudies." The black girl had an American accent, a strong animal odor that was disturbing.

Billy smiled, moved closer.

Jack observed, "Sounds spyish. And your name sounds—"

"No jokes on name, please, I got enough of that last year in Newport Beach." Zhang smiled, directed her next response to Billy, who had invaded her body space, now towered over her slender frame. "I'm visiting Singapore, working for the cultural attaché to Chinese Embassy. Second Department's Analysis Bureau asked me to check you guys out. You've something belongs to People's Republic. Something I'm an expert in." She took Billy's offered hand, looked into his eyes. Her gaze flicked over his muscular body, his chiseled, dark-skinned face.

Jack said, "And that would be?" He could see Billy was pre-empting his own imagined assault on the beautiful girl. He sighed, forced down powerful desire.

Zhang grinned, her face looked American when she smiled. "Don't be coy. You possess national treasure. My country wants back."

"Babe, I'd say you're a national treasure," Billy offered. "What's a cultural whatever do? Can I do you?"

Zhang's smile broadened. "Thank you. I'm Wayang singer—that's Chinese opera—and waist drum dancer. My troupe is here from Shanghai. I was asked to help out, 'cause I studied history of the *Concubine Emeralds* at Beijing University."

How'd you find us?" Jack asked. He looked up and down the quay, saw no apparent backups loitering. He heard China Mist still splashing as she scrubbed the side of the boat. Yu Fuk Up was at the stern, avoiding the new visitor and his passengers. The hot, humid atmosphere was oppressive.

"Hey, Fuk Up," he called. "Can we please get cold drinks?"

The old Baba turned, a fearful expression on his face, uttered a harsh string of words in Singlish—Singaporean English. China Mist immediately climbed onto the boat, went below, dripping water. She appeared minutes later, carrying a tray with three glasses of iced tea, and an attitude. After the three took their drinks, she stalked away.

"Just following directions," Zhang said. "No one told me how we found you. But you're white men in Singapore. How hard could it be?"

Jack watched China Mist retreat, sipped his cold tea. Said, "Anyway, we don't have the emeralds anymore. They were stolen."

Zhang, staring at China Mist's back, looked startled at Jack's words.

"Like, we was hoping for a reward," Billy said. "A big one. Equal to what they're worth."

"The gems are priceless!" Zhang protested. "Where are they?"

"Oh, we kin find a price, all right," Billy answered. "Fifty million bucks."

"Doesn't matter," Jack said. "We don't have them."

Zhang looked into their eyes. "The Second Department won't believe. You're in grave danger. You must return gems. This come all way from my uncle. He's—"

"What makes you so sure they belong to you guys?" Jack asked. "We claim right of salvage."

"Yeah, I humped 'em out of the Hindu Kush, not outta China," Billy exclaimed.

Zhang, with a frightened expression on her face, said, "You cannot defy the Second Department! The entire Chinese government!"

"Yeah, like, I doubt the entire Chinese people give a damn about Billy and me. All my life I heard: 'Eat your vegetables. People are starving in China.' Well, if you guys were so hungry, you should have looked up the emeralds a long time ago, sold 'em and bought chow. As in chow mien."

Zhang looked nervous, laughed without mirth. "Guys, this ver' serious. No time for joke. You could die."

"How come you have an American accent? And you're black." Jack asked.

Zhang frowned, "Complicated family history. And I talk funny because I got in a little trouble last year. In Afghanistan. My superiors were very mad. I went to Los Angeles for six month— stayed with American relatives in Orange County until I got things straightened out back home. The time give me a chance to work on my accent, my English."

"Sorta like us goin' to prison," Billy said, glanced at his brother. "For trouble in Pakistan and Af-went-land."

Zhang smiled and her eyes grew distant, "If you call Orange County a prison. I grew fond of fish tacos, Corona Beer, the Crab Catcher in Newport Beach. Sitting on the jetty, sailboats and yachts cruising by. Watching people catching fish on the pier, Sunsets over Catalina Island. How it go?

Sittin' on the dock of the bay, watching the tide roll away?"

"Yeah, Rubio's fish tacos," Jack sighed. "Civilization in a tortilla."

"Minnow-munchers!" Billy snorted. "I'll take a ballpark hotdog any day."

"So, can you get emeralds back?" Zhang asked. "I get you a reward." She cast a glance up and down Billy's body. "It's important to me. This is my first mission after my rehabilitation."

Jack said, "First, we'd have to make a little side trip to that wonderful Disneyland of Asia—Pakmanland. Where mutton is rancid, rice is starchy, and sunsets are smoggy."

"Sounds awesome! Can I come? Where is it?" Zhang asked.

"I'll do everything'n my power to make you come." Billy slowly smiled.

"Let's break up the love fest," Jack said. "I don't think hauling a Chinese agent around Asia is the best idea I've heard today. Billy, I'll tell our pals—the guys who're always lookin' out for our best interests—that we'll go. Maybe they can arrange a lift." He went below, grabbed a local prepaid cell phone he had purchased at the hotel.

Jack pulled Holland's card out of his wallet, called the CIA agent. When he answered, Jack said, "Dave, I've reconsidered the value of your offer—can you arrange transport to Pakistan?"

"Great! The general'll be stoked. I'll get you a ride," Holland sounded excited.

"Where to?" Jack asked.

"Islamabad. I'll meet you at your hotel. You're on your way to Pakistan, pal."

"Lucky me," Jack said. "But the hotel might be a little hectic—we had some problems with a couple of Chinese dudes in suits in our suite."

Holland paused. "You're just down the street from my office. Your hotel's got a big padang—about a five acre field—and in the middle of it's a huge jungle park and a lake—I'll meet you at the boat statue on the east side of the water in an hour."

Jack hung up, looked at Billy and Zhang: the two were facing each other and holding hands, oblivious to their surroundings. They had made a strong personal connection and were now busy exploring it. He felt a pang of regret, mixed with happiness for his brother. He called, "I'm meeting Holland. I'll be back in a couple of hours." "Watch out for Chinese goblins," Billy advised.

Jack thought, *Let's hope you're not embracing one.*

Chapter 13

The sunset, through rose-tinted, clouded fingers, barely glowed on the waters of the lake. The *Shangri-La* Singapore Hotel's miniature jungle was lush, filled with birds and monkeys that quieted as darkness grew and the inhabitants worried about imagined and real threats. The fragrant odors of night-blooming flowers filled the air.

Jack found Holland sitting on a bench on the shore. A bronze statue of a Malay fisherman standing in a small boat was barely visible a few feet from the shoreline. Giant lily pads—two feet across—surrounded the boat, were faint glistening pink orbs.

The CIA man's face was barely visible in the growing darkness, he smiled, flashing his teeth when Jack said, "Hey."

"How's it goin? I'm glad you changed your mind."

"Not many options, Dave." He thought about mentioning the Second Department people, rejected the idea, then did. "I'm gettin' too popular with some *SD* guys."

"We know all about the Chinese spooks," Holland said. "But bottom line's what counts with the general. So you're in."

Jack tried to read Holland's face—it was getting too dark. "So, I'm back in the Corps? Or is it the CIA?"

Holland chuckled. "I don't think you're pullin' any time in grade on this one, Jack, but what the hey, you're already rich. And I hear your family got your ranch back."

Jack checked the darkening western sky, saw a faint movement on the other side of the five-acre pond.

A thud, a splintering tree branch: both men ducked into long grass, Holland pulled a silenced gun—rapid-fired at shadowy, running figures coming out of the jungle behind them.

Two men fell, one stumbled, three continued. Shouts from the other group, now running around the lake.

"C'mon!" Holland yelled.

He and Jack rose and sprinted along the darkening shore: Holland reloaded, Jack yanked up a short metal sign stake in his path. Holland spotted several lights ahead, grabbed Jack's arm, pointed at a stream in their path. The two splashed into the warm water, grabbed and broke reeds, submerged under the bank and breathed through the makeshift snorkels. Jack felt his fear of water, from two childhood near-drownings, tighten his chest muscles. He squeezed the quarter-inch metal stake, forced himself to suck air through the reed.

Seconds later he felt thudding footfalls from approaching hunters, heard splashes from others wading upstream. A small creature skittered up his bare leg. He shuddered, drifted his free hand over, brushed a crab or some other critter away.

The pursuers thrashed about in the water, finally moved away. After endless minutes crawled by, Holland rose, nudged Jack. The two peered about, trying to see in the darkness. Shouts: a man jumped off the bank from behind. A shot rang out, Holland grunted, shot his attacker once, then slumped face first.

Jack rose out of the water, threw himself at the attacker, knocked the gun aside. Stabbed him below the ribs with the metal rod, felt a pant of air. The man held a kris—a wavy-bladed dagger— above his head. It glinted in the moonlight. Jack jumped on top of the guy, grabbed the knife-wielding wrist, knocked him into the stream, held him underwater. The man struggled, weakened, finally stopped moving.

Jack turned, pulled the gasping, groaning Holland out of the water. Dragged him up the bank. Holland was clutching his upper abdomen with one hand, his pistol with the other.

"How you doin'?" Jack asked.

"Hurts bad," Holland said. He panted, "Any others?"

Jack looked around, listened. "Think they left just the one guy."

Holland whispered, "Jack—we need you to go to 409—" his head fell back, he struggled, raised it: "Seletar Airport. Go to the FBO. I arranged a ride… a guy you know—"

"Don't worry about that stuff. We need to get you help."

The wounded agent looked up at Jack, "Get me to hotel… parking lot. Someone waiting… Embassy."

Jack took Holland's weapon, stuck it under his belt, hoisted Holland up, held him with a fireman's carry, felt hot blood soak through his shirt, trickle down his back, as he hurried through the fake jungle, across a meadow towards the hotel. Every few seconds, he jerked around, checked for hostiles. Holland was breathing with raspy gasps. Startled birds squawked whenever the two men drew near.

At the edge of the parking lot, Jack lowered Holland to the ground behind a clump of bushes, looked again for pursuers. The agent was breathing but unconscious. Just then, a black car arced across the lot, headed directly to their position, as though the driver could see in the dark.

Jack pulled the pistol. The car skidded to a stop. A slender young woman jumped out, ran to their position.

"Over here," Jack called unnecessarily.

"I got Agent Holland on GPS," the woman responded. Jack lifted the now unconscious agent by the arms, looked around, dragged him to the car. The girl opened the passenger door.

"Hurry—he's hurt bad," Jack instructed.

The Asian woman, about twenty-five, slender, attractive, with short dark hair and a small stature, asked with a British accent, "What happened?"

"No time!" Jack exclaimed while he pulled the body onto the seat. "Get him to a doctor. I'll call in a sitrep. Hurry!" He spun around, checked out the surroundings, then headed for the main hotel buildings after the woman drove away.

He entered a poolside door to the lobby, panting more from stress than exertion, looked at the expanse behind, saw no one who appeared interested in him. Pulled his shirt over the weapon, walked quickly, water still dripping in his wake. He was angry at himself: Holland was injured, maybe dying, because Jack hadn't accepted the original assignment. Another headstrong mistake had hurt a good man. *Grow up!* he swore to himself.

Chapter 14

In the air-conditioned hotel suite, Jack threw the door lock, his mind tormented by a jumble of thoughts. He jumped in the shower, washed the blood, the grime, smell of rotting muck, and dirty water off his body. Changed into fresh clothes; he snatched his and Billy's remaining belongings, threw them in their sports bags. Checked the deodorant where he had secreted the diamond: it was safe. Completed quick research on the Internet and checked out of the hotel on the suite computer.

Outside, he grabbed a loitering taxi and directed the driver to the Boat Quay.

When the cab dropped him off, Jack told the driver to wait, then hurried to Yu's sailboat. Lights from the opposite bank sparkled on the river, outlining Zhang, who was sitting on the stern, her feet hanging over the gunwale. He stepped aboard, approached her. "Where's Billy?"

Her teeth and eyes flashed white in the darkness. "He's taking an opium nap. Sit down."

Jack sat next to the Chinese girl, suppressed his attraction to her. He caught her strong body odor—it was entrancing.

"Am I coming with?" she asked.

"I guess I'd rather have you with us than following us—especially since Billy has the hots for you."

Zhang giggled. "He's insatiable, but I put him down. Then the opium kept him down. Does he use a lot?"

"Hey, he's been in prison, like, for six months."

Zhang put her hand on Jack's upper thigh. "He say so have you, Jack. You're a very attractive man. Singapore's full of beautiful women."

His thigh burned where she was touching him. She casually slid her hand to his inner leg, tensing and untensing her fingers.

"I haven't had time for romance, what with half the population trying to rob me and the other half tryin' to kill me." He looked at her face, but it was too dark to see her expression. "Some of your friends attacked me at the hotel. Again. Can you call them off?"

Zhang ignored his request. Her hand lightly stroked his leg, she slid it up and down his inner thigh.

"Billy's asleep," she said.

Jack looked at the beautiful girl, longed to envelop her. Forced himself to his feet, called below, woke Billy. "Big trouble, dude. We gotta hit the road. And you got your wish."

"What up? Pakishtan?" Billy muttered as he climbed to the deck.

"They're sendin' us to Shangri-La. Where's Yu and China Mist?"

"The babe's around. Fuk up—whatever—had to go somewhere. I paid him off, so we're good to go." Billy crossed the teak deck, hugged the Chinese girl. She smiled innocently at Jack, looked more like a Newport Beach bartender than a Chinese spy. "Zhang's comin'," he added.

"Dude," Jack protested for form, "This might be the *Love Boat* but—"

"Jack," Zhang said. "Like you said, either I go with you or I follow. I work for the Second Department but… you guys need a friend," she grinned, kissed Billy on the lips.

"See?" Billy chuckled. "We shave—er—save the Chinese spy community money if we travel together. And we gots an inside track on the bad guys."

"Hey!" Zhang protested. "Since when does wanting national treasure back make my country the bad guys?"

"Holy shit! I'm running a circus," Jack complained. "Let's just get outta here before someone else decides they want a free ride an' shoots us for the price of a ticket."

The three climbed in the big Mercedes cab; the driver drove through the Central District, raced across Singapore, then along winding, narrow jungle roads toward Seletar Airport. On the way, Jack related the lake incident until Billy yawned and fell asleep.

Jack stared out the window at the overhanging trees, illuminated by the cab's headlights, imagined thousands of Japanese soldiers riding bicycles through the jungles to their successful attack on the British in 1939, at the start of the Second World War.

Wondered if Zhang Poon t'ang was another Asian warrior creeping up on the white man's fort. Wondered whether he could count on his drugged out brother.

Agent Holland had passed out before he could say who the pilot that they knew was, that would carry them to Pakistan. But it had to be someone he had met the year before. He reviewed the pilots he had encountered: Jimmy Jinks, the Air Force pilot who had carried him from the Afghan mountains to Quetta, Pakistan, after his escape from the Taliban prison— unlikely; General Hammar, the Pakistani who had escaped Bharakan Prison with him the year before—possibility; Charlie Davis, the young Texan deserter who had helped steal the Air Force Caribou that had landed Jack in Leavenworth—strong likelihood.

Remembered for a second the young pilots who had died when their helicopter blew up just after Jack and Chopstick Mick had parachuted into the Hindu Kush. Young, handsome, full of life—dead. His mind zinging, thoughts returned to Holland. He'd said he had a wife, two kids in Wyoming. Another American, hurt chasing bad guys away from America's gates. Hopefully not going home in a casket covered by the Stars and Stripes.

Charlie Davis proved to be their pilot and was easy to find— his white, T-tailed twin engine Citation jet was first in a line of parked private aircraft in front of Seletar Airport terminal. Under lights that illuminated the parking area, Charlie was polishing the windshield while a maintenance crew, despite the pre-dawn hour, washed the sleek airplane. A smell of jet fuel permeated the area.

"Charlie!" Jack shouted. "Long time no see."

Looking down from a stepladder, the blond pilot said, "Hey, Captain Jack," clambered to the tarmac. The tall, skinny youth held out a hand, smiled. "I heard you got thrown in Leavenworth, then checked out of the government housing on your own. Great to see you!" He glanced at the beautiful girl with Billy, greeted the Indian with sparkling blue eyes, a lopsided grin under a bushy mustache.

"Whose jet, Charlie?" Billy asked. "Last time we saw you, you were flying a single-engine putt-putt Bonanza for General Hammar."

Charlie grinned, patted the Citation. "I'm working for—" he looked around, whispered, "General Hammar and his new partner, Rama Razi Muhammad. Giant fat guy lives in Iran. He's the biggest dope smuggler from Afghanistan to the Golden Triangle. I just delivered a load of H. Big consumer item in Singapore. Agent Holland got DEA to put my deserter status aside, got me transferred outta the military." He leaned forward, "I'm undercover."

"Congrats. Being a dope smuggler for the U.S. is a perfect cover, Charlie," Billy observed in an equally low voice. "Got any free samples? Trade you a t-shirt that says: UNDERCOVER."

"The general's here in Singapore?" Jack asked over Charlie's laughter.

"Yeah, he always wanted to retire to Singapore," the pilot responded. "You gotta visit him. He's got, like, a pad on this, like, huge river. Stocked with Malay babes. A small army of Pakistani guards. Totally awesome, dude!"

"Dave Holland got shot last night," Jack added.

"You're shittin' me!" Charlie was astounded.

Jack thought, *I see a pattern here: Charlie, a deserter. Now he works for DEA. I'm a deserter. The whole thing was a set-up so I'd be useful to General Harmbruster. But I figured that. Then they put me through a mock —totally bogus trial—then Leavenworth, just so I'd be a perfect operative? Is General Harmbruster that cynical?*

"True story. I was with Holland," he said. "He sent me to you. Said you'd give us a hop to Abad."

"No sweat," Charlie looked around. "I'm running a small load of heroin to Chen nai, an east coast port city in India. Then Karachi for a refuel, then Abad." He shook his head. "Holland shot. Hard to believe. Hurt bad?"

"I don't know," Jack said. "Not good, but it was dark, and they almost got me, too."

Charlie looked at the approaching sunrise. "Well, if somebody's after you, we'd better get outta Dodge. You guys ready?"

"Do we need to go through Customs?"

"I'm already cleared—one of the benies of working for fat guy Rama—think Jabba the Hut."

Fifteen minutes later, the Citation CJ2 cleared the runway, banked to the northwest. Jack sat in the second seat, listened to Charlie announce over-flight to Malaysian air traffic controllers, while he looked down at the jungles of Singapore, the mile-wide waters of what Charlie called Serangoon Harbour. Checked the cabin, Billy and Zhang were smooching. Wondered how dangerous the Chinese operative was—at least she seemed open, honest. Maybe that was her ticket. He looked at the green jungle, brilliantly highlighted by the morning sun. Checked out the digital instrumentation displayed before him, found the altimeter, watched the digital numbers spiral up as the Citation continued a steep climb.

"I'm beat," he said, "takin' a nap."

Charlie grinned. "Go for it."

Three hours later, the steward—an old black African with a British accent and a stooped back—served cucumber and feta cheese sandwiches, and iced tea, to the three Americans and Zhang. Charlie wolfed his sandwich as he started a descent to Chen nai, the city formerly called Madras, on the east coast of India. Jack looked at the brown earth below: countless farms broke up the vast stretches of land—the countryside looked tired. Jack wondered what fertile America would look like after going through the thousands of years of farming India had endured.

He asked if he could land the jet and Charlie assented. It went smoothly, after Jack adjusted to the speed of the jet. He had never landed at a speed over one hundred miles per hour.

Following a quick refuel, the old steward exchange packages and heavy cardboard boxes with a dark-skinned Indian. Jack and Billy lent a hand to speed up the process, and the jet continued towards Karachi.

An hour after take-off, Jack went to the galley for coffee. Billy was asleep. Zhang was reading a magazine, the steward was also asleep. In the galley, Jack poured two cups of coffee, put them in the microwave.

"Need any help?" Zhang approached, stood next to him—close.

"You want a cup?" he asked.

"No, I want you." Zhang's gaze was intense, her eyes were staring into his. She brushed a hand against his crotch, rubbed it. The microwave beeped. He felt his skin flush. He inhaled her animal odor.

"Sounds good to me," Jack responded. "You're a very desirable babe. I could really… but first, go check with Billy, then let's get it on."

Zhang giggled, her big eyes squinted. "I don't want to wake him. I'm not sure he'd share. But I own me."

"Look, Billy's my brother, so forget about it." He took the two coffees, pushed past Zhang, headed for the cockpit. Thought righteous but frustrated thoughts. Switched to visions of a comely Asian body, long legs wrapped around his head, large breasts filling his hands. That wonderful animal smell…

Four hours later, the Citation swept around the north end of the smog and dust-decorated city of Islamabad; to the north, Jack recognized the brown Margalla Hills. Just to the south of the hills, he watched as the huge Faisal Mosque, with its four tall minarets, passed under the right wing. Each of its four towers was twenty-five stories high. The giant mosque, tallest in the world, looked so unlike anything in America, it could have been an alien artifact, transferred whole from another planet.

Looking down at the crowded streets, he wondered whether bronzeskinned, long-legged Mara Bhutto was alive and strolling on one of the wide Islamabad avenues.

Jack took out Holland's silenced Smith & Wesson, flipped the cylinder open: it still held two bullets. He wondered why Holland had carried it— using this revolver was like throwing pebbles at a crowd, even with its sixinch barrel. Jack determined to acquire two M-9 semi auto Beretta pistols before he left Islamabad.

The Citation flew west of Islamabad airport by ten miles, landed south of the city at an airstrip Jack remembered as Kilgar Khan Airport. Someone —probably Charlie's new crime boss—had built a steel hanger next to the collapsing WWII hanger that was half way down the taxiway. When the jet taxied to a stop, a small tractor approached, two men in tan coveralls worked for a moment; the tractor pulled the quieted Citation into the hanger.

"Okay, lovebirds, we're in sunny Southwest Asia. Let's rock and roll," Jack called as he passed his brother and Zhang Poon t'ang, and climbed down the rear hatchway.

Billy stood, stretched and called, "How we gonna git to Gilgit?"

"That's the question of the day," Jack stuck his head back in the cabin. "I talked to Charlie about renting a private charter—he's gonna try set it up for tomorrow morning. At least we don't have to worry about Customs." He heard a vehicle approaching, glanced up, saw a military truck bearing soldiers approach the hanger. The sight kicked his heart into overdrive.

Chapter 15

The black Sudanese steward proved able to deflect the soldier's curiosities when they arrived at Kilgar Khan Airport: he served them cold drinks in the hanger while the Americans and Zhang remained in the jet, with curtains closed over ports, and supplemental, ground-based airconditioning going full blast.

Watching through a slightly parted curtain, Zhang saw the steward pull the beret-covered officer aside and slip him an envelope. Minutes later, the army unit left the hanger, drove away.

"I need a bath, need to buy some clothes," she announced after the four travelers climbed in a new Range Rover and headed up a gravel road to Islamabad, twenty miles to the north. She glanced at Billy—she was sore from his constant attention. She felt gooey, her thighs were almost sticking together.

"We'll stop and pick up some clothes, get a hotel, try and get the flight in the morning," Jack said. "If we can't do that, we'll have to go overland, disguised as, like, natives. Or maybe climbers."

Zhang glanced at the Americans and laughed. "Billy and I'll so pass for locals," she pointed out. "But a blue-eyed white guy?"

"Raghead cap, sunglasses, spray-on tan," Jack said.

Charlie drove into the Blue Zone—one of the neighborhoods of the city—stopped at a one-story storefront that had merchandise on tables in front of the run-down store.

Zhang mumbled at the poor quality and cleanliness of the apparel, but managed to find what she needed while Billy, Charlie, and Jack, sat at a table and drank black tea, served by the proprietor. When she was finished, and had stuffed the clothing in a plastic bag, the brothers purchased nondescript loose trousers, long shirts, vests, jackets, and Afghani karakul caps. When they completed their selections and paid for everything, they took the Range Rover to the Holiday Inn and rented a two-bedroom suite.

Over a dinner of spicy curried chicken, rice pilaf, and chapatti bread, washed down by a local beer—Red Pilsner—Charlie and the three travelers discussed the trio's plans upon reaching the mountain town of Gilgit.

Zhang didn't reveal that she had been there the year before, as an agent for the Second Department, China's version of the CIA.

Zhang had traded a dozen Stinger missiles to the Taliban who found the lost American bomb that had been automatically jettisoned from a burning B-52. After she had found out the capabilities of the biological weapon, she had turned around and given its location to the American CIA in exchange for a US passport and ten thousand dollars.

Pursued by agents of China's Second Department, who had orders to capture her and strict orders to not harm her, she had fled, been captured by a SD agent, Yassar Ahmoud, then released after revealing the bomb's location under the threat of torture. Only her relationship as a grandniece of Hu Jintao, the general secretary of China, had saved her. But after the second escape, she had been sent by worried relatives to America.

She recalled Yassar Ahmoud, her captor, and what he had said: "I'm in a hurry. You're a beautiful woman—I'll blind you. You're a famous waist drum dancer—I'll cut your feet off. You come from a rich and powerful family but you'll not write them after Hakim chops off your hands. You'll not call your family for help—for I'll rip out your tongue. Then I'll release you to live as a beggar in the streets of Kabul. Think about it for one minute."

Words spilling out of her like machinegun fire, Zhang had told everything she knew about the bomb's hidden location in the Hindu Kush.

"You look uncomfortable, babe," Billy Howling Dog, the American Indian patted her arm, stroked it.

Zhang shuddered, "Just a bad memory."

"What was it?" the suspicious, unapproachable one asked.

"I was captured last year in Kabul by a Pakistani agent—Yassar Ahmoud."

The two Americans exchanged shocked looks. Jack said, "Mara?"

"Who're you talking about?" Zhang asked.

"Yassar Ahmoud was a Pakistani woman, Mara Bhutto, in disguise," Jack responded.

"Mara Bhutto? My friend, Mara? That's impossible!"

"He—she crossed paths with us—got whacked in the Hindu Kush," Billy added.

"You knew her?" Jack asked.

"I don't believe it!" Zhang shuddered again. Cold terror crept up her back. "Mara was Yassar Ahmoud? In Kabul, Ahmoud threatened to blind me, cut out my tongue, my hands, and feet. I told him everything. I've never been so frightened in my life. Mara would never—"

"Oh, yeah," Jack affirmed. "But she's dead: a giant Chinese dude wrung her neck and the USAF dropped a mountain on her head."

Visibly upset at the revelation that her friend Mara Bhutto had donned a disguise, had captured her and threatened to torture her, Zhang rose. "I have to report in to *SD*—I'm going to the room."

After she left, Billy said, "She's shook, Flashy. But she's great, you know?"

"Yeah, too bad she works for guys committed to robbing us of the treasure, killing us dead, if they so decide."

"Well, there's that," Billy grinned. "But hey, every broad I ever met had a few hang-ups. And she's gorgeous—more than anyone I ever met. And she's great in the rack."

"Well, there's that," Jack agreed.

"I seen her focusing in on you—you know I'm gettin' in pretty deep." Billy nervously patted his pockets.

Jack smiled at his brother, wished he could get through to him about the drug addiction. "I can see that, I'm glad one of us is keeping his head out of a sexual fogbank."

Billy relaxed, laughed. "I dunno, Jack. Your buns been in the oven ever since we went to Leavenworth. You gotta be done by now."

"Yeah, I'm cooked, ready to blow up, ready to scrape my burned crust," Jack agreed. "Is that enough about my pathetic sex life? 'Cause I gotta set up a meet with General Farley. Get a few things straight."

"Like, are we gonna get our jewels back after we check out Shangri-La for the spy guys?"

Jack smiled. "You got it, bro." he glanced at his brother, took a deep breath. "One more thing. You're hitting the *Hillbilly* shit pretty hard."

"Pain, bro."

"Bullshit! You're not injured."

"Hey, Dad hits the sauce every night. What's the diff?"

Jack responded, "He doesn't hit it for breakfast, lunch and din-din. I love you, but lay off or stay behind."

Billy looked down for long seconds. "Okay, bro, I'll give it a shot."

Jack gazed at his brother, hoped he was sincere. "No pun intended?"

Billy laughed. "There it is."

Sometime in the night, Jack groggily woke when the door opened. The faint illumination from the window revealed a naked woman walking across the room. His heart raced from fear—China Bitch! He had barely survived her midnight attack in Haartgard the year before. But this dream girl was too slender—it must be Penel! His beautiful mountain girl of the Hindu Kush.

She smiled, climbed in bed. He thought about asking her how she had traveled to Islamabad, why she had dyed her blonde hair black. She kissed him and he forgot about questions and dreams. Her smooth skin, hard muscles electrified him along the complete length of his body. Her knee forced his legs apart, rubbed against his groin. She ran her fingers through his short hair, kissed him passionately. He got an immediate erection, entered her hot, wet center, had an instantaneous orgasm. She kissed him again, rose and left the room.

"Hey, Penel, wait," he called as the door shut. He opened his eyes, stared at the dream-torn bedding.

Chapter 16

Dawn: Jack sat in the Range Rover, reflected on his sexual fantasy dream of the night before, wished it had been real. Wondered for a second whether it had been. Watched the half-moon set over Rawal Lake, in the western reaches of Islamabad. Eastern sky to his left was brightening. Two scrawny ragtops riding pathetic-looking donkeys along the lakeshore. He had suggested that General Farley meet him in the park, hoping that the open expanses of mown grass would prevent the general from ensnaring him in some way. He saw a Humvee leave what he remembered from the year before as Peshawar Highway, then bounce on a dirt road that circumnavigated the dark waters. He patted Holland's revolver for reassurance, thought, *the general's an American, for God's sake: relax!* The Humvee slammed to a halt, a man climbed out, stepped into range of the headlights.

General Farley, dressed in desert BDUs, and another American, moved forward from the vehicle. "I'm here," Farley announced.

"Agent Holland was shot in Singapore," Jack said.

Farley stared up at Jack, downward curving mouth in a cherub face, pop-eyed pale blue eyes glinting in the dawn's light. "I heard. You sayin' you did it?"

"Not me—we were pals. We were meeting, discussing me comin' here. I don't know who—it was dark—Chinese *SD*, I think. I had asked for a ride to Islamabad. Dave and I were meetin' in a grove of trees at my hotel, we were jumped by a gang."

"He should've had more security," Farley observed.

"Either that or more trees."

"What d'you mean?" Farley's voice was harsh.

"To hide behind. I had to run for my life."

"You abandoned him!" Farley accused. His mouth curved downward even more.

"No, he called the Embassy, I carried him to the hotel parking lot. A woman showed up, took him to the hospital. How's he doing?"

"Why would they be after him?"

"Just bad luck," Jack responded. "He stuck his nose in my business and got popped."

Farley snarled, "So your screwed-up approach to life got a valuable agent hurt. I hope you're satisfied. Anyway, General Harmbruster wants you to go into the hidden valley, 409."

Curious, Jack asked, "What do you think about that, General?" He knew the Army officer had always hated him.

"Now that you're outta the Corps, I don't care what you do. Join the CIA, *Eagle's Aerie*—whatever. In my opinion, you were the worst kind of military officer, but your climbing skills make you the best possible asset for this mission. And we can't employ US troops in Pakistan right now. So the various letter agencies have hired ex-Special Service types like you to do their dirty work."

"Dirty work? The general called me a captain."

"He's a sentimentalist. You're a convicted felon, stripped of all rank." General Farley slightly smiled, happy at the thought. Then his smile broadened, and his teeth gleamed as the sun rose, lit up his cherub face.

Jack felt a sinking feeling, pressed on, "General, what exactly do you want me to do?"

"Go to Gilgit. I'll send Major Nakamura there with your final instructions. Anyway, all we want you to do is check out a suspected terrorist cavern in the mountains. Maybe call in cruise missiles when you get on site, if warranted. I'll send a Fire Scout in to laser designate any targets you find. Fully autonomous UAV made by Northrup Grumman."

"Nothing can fly into the valley," Jack pointed out. "We've tried in the past."

Farley grimaced. "Yeah, well, then I'll give Nakamura illumination gear and we'll send you a fourpak out of Camp Rhino from a Ground Launch Cruise Missile launcher." Farley scowled again. "If the illumination system fails, put a thermal spot on the target. That'll work just as well."

Jack observed, "Pretty hard to 'reach out and touch somebody' in those mountains. Wind patterns will knock the Tomahawks offline."

Farley snarled, his mouth moved into its familiar downward curving bow. "At 550 mph, they'll blow through any wind gusts and take the camp out, smartass."

"I want a pardon. If you promise one when I complete the mission, I'll do it," Jack bluffed. "I want those railroad tracks back."

"No way! No captain's bars for you. After the mission, your ass is goin' back to prison."

"Then forget it. I'm gonna try and reopen the case. With new evidence."

"Give it your best shot, convict. You're nothing but a dumbass kid with no experience except climbing high and havin' an unlikely adeptness at killing bad guys." Farley's voice dripped with scorn. "But if you want a free rein in Pakistan and Afghanistan to gather evidence for a new trial, you'll complete this mission first, or I'll tell Pak authorities to have your ass before lunch." He glared at Jack. "And you'll carry a microchip implant, so I can keep track of you."

Alarmed, Jack stepped back. "What d'you mean?"

"An advanced BTID—a battlefield target identification device." Farley gestured, and the short, thin soldier who had hung back, moved forward, placed a pack on the short grass, and pulled a horse needle-sized punch out of it. He grabbed Jack's arm, shoved the sleeve up and jabbed the punch in the forearm. Farley, a small smile on his face, watched closely as Jack restrained a wince.

The medic, using tweezers, shoved a rice kernel-sized chip in Jack's arm, then squirted super glue from a tube on the wound.

Pushing his sleeve down, and feeling totally violated, Jack asked, "Did you bring weapons and ammo?"

The general pointed a thumb at the Humvee. "Four M-9 Berettas, two hundred rounds. Satellite photos, four encrypted ISRs—intersquad radios. An encrypted sat cell phone. Two M-4s with video scopes. Plenty of ammo, and two ATN night visions."

"I'll want more M-4s, or 16s, and an OICW."

Farley shook his head. "The Army doesn't have an one available since they shitcanned it, but I'll check with the Marines, see what I can do. I'll send it up separately, if I can find one."

"Money for climbing gear, chow?" Jack asked. "We'll need ropes."

Farley pulled a large envelope out of the Humvee, handed it to Jack.

"That's five hundred grand in rupees. You'll have to scout around Gilgit, see what you can buy. After our teams failed to reach the terrorist camp, they were sent to the Syrian border last week. Took their gear with."

"One more thing, General. About a year ago, the armorer at Camp Hansen showed me a XM-199, the laser gun. I want one."

"Goddam, you don't want much," the general snarled. "What do I look like—a REMF? But I'll see what I can do."

Jack thought, *Rear Echelon Mother Fucker. Yeah, you do look like one.* But he couldn't stop feeling enthusiastic. He grinned. "Thanks, General, wish me luck." He walked to the Humvee, a corporal unloaded two cargo bags, put them in Charlie's Range Rover. A tall, skinny, dark-skinned Pakistani man, dressed in a green uniform, climbed out, smiled nervously, asked for Jack's passport. He handed his and Billy's real passports to the man. The guy pounded entry prints onto blank pages, signed them.

"Now you're legally in Pakistan," the short general said as he approached. "Though I must say, you took an unorthodox path to get here. Typical of you. But I hope you complete the mission," the general added with a tight voice, as though he were forcing good wishes through a mouth full of broken glass.

Jack started the Rover, drove back to the Grand Trunk Road, turned east toward the hotel. Wondered, *What lies ahead in Gilgit? The next stop on this crazy, hell-for-leather expedition for redemption.*

Chapter 17

Major Lialot Soongoon, a short, thin man with a trim British mustache, longish black hair for a military man, a lean, dark-skinned face with an eagle beak of a nose under piercing eyes, watched Jack Flashhardt enter the bar-dining room of Gilgit Lodge, formerly Serena Lodge, the most popular gathering spot for foreigners in the small mountain town. As he watched the confident, handsome American cross the room, he wondered why the young man was so favored by certain elements of the American military and yet was so scorned by others.

Wearing a dark green Pakistani undress uniform, the major stood, held out a hand to Jack, smiled. "Captain Flashhardt, welcome back to my country." He sat down, gestured at a chair next to the blazing fire in the open field stone fireplace. "I was so happy when you called from Abad. I'd be honored to buy a drink for a holder of one of my country's highest awards—the Hilal-I-Juraat—awarded, I'm told, by President Zardari, himself. 'For conspicuous bravery against Taliban invaders of my country.'" He leaned forward. "What was it like to meet my president?"

Jack flushed, stammered, "Th-thank you, Major. It was cool. But now, *Nunc est bibendum*—It's time for a beer. My brother and I had a long trip from Abad." *Does he know I was arrested and imprisoned for an alleged assassination attempt on* President Zardari? *That I escaped? Is he going to arrest me?*

"Unfortunately, it'll have to be tea or coffee," the major said. He glanced at the many mullahs sipping coffee and tea in various parts of the dimly lit room. "They don't serve any alcoholic beverages anymore in the entire region."

"Why not?"

"Since the Taliban mullahs have been pushed out of Afghanistan, they've come here, and enforced blue laws in the Territories, because of their stupidly strict religious convictions. They pretty much run the civilian sector." The major smiled with an apologetic air. "So, the bus ride from Islamabad was hard? I could have sent a chopper."

"Long," Jack responded. "My brother and his companion are resting." He glanced around, noticed many hateful glances from darkly clad, longbearded men in the room; but he felt semi-secure dressed as a civilian. "You know, your mullahs should spend their extra energy and mis-directed anger on your roads, not on blue laws. Most countries have roads with potholes. Your highways have semi-connected bomb craters masquerading as potholes."

"You're not one to talk, my dear Captain Flashhardt," the major laughed, broke off and signed for a coffee and a refill of his tea. "Your topographical rearrangements on the eastern flank of the Hindu Kush Mountains last year were colossal. Luckily, your bombs landed on the other side of the contested border, so not my concern."

Jack thought of the USAF B-52 attack he had called in to bury the lost Air Force biological bomb in a mountain cave.

"So what brings America's *Master of Mayhem* to my Control Area of Responsibility?" Major Soongoon asked.

"I'd like your permission to pass through and check out a suspected training camp in the contested zone," Jack responded.

"Satellite intelligence shows new al Qaeda camps?" the little major asked.

Jack looked at the dapper major. "Right. I guess they're set up in a cavern in the Hindu Kush. We've some satellite evidence of ingress and egress from China, but other than that, no HUMINT. That's why I'm here."

"Well, in any case, General Harmbruster—your old commander—has already paved your way. He sent a company grade officer to ask permission for the pass-through. Here he comes now—I believe you know him."

Jack swung around and was both heartened and dismayed to see Army Major Mick Nakamura approaching their table. Mick, nicknamed Chopstick by his fellow OCS students when they discovered he hated Oriental food, had been Jack's close friend at Stanford University.

He knew Chopstick Mick, a short, wide, heavily muscled Japanese American, would walk across swamps full of gators to pick a fight with any perceived enemies. Mick had helped Jack in his previous actions in Southwest Asia, but had also acted as a secret operative for General Harmbruster and had entangled Jack in the general's schemes. They had fought side by side, even after Jack discovered Mick's treachery, and had finally parted as friends. Now, the two shook hands, hugged each other.

Mick and the major exchanged greetings. Jack wondered if Mick was here to help the Pakistani major take him down. *No, he's an American, dammit! He's on my side.*

"Welcome back to the Disneyland of Southwest Asia, buddy," Mick enthused. He was wearing rough climber's garb like Jack's. "I'm glad you're out of the mess you got into last year." He grinned, his black eyes disappeared in folds of flesh, and his canine teeth— longer than normal— showed. When he smiled, his teeth were prominent, making him look ready to chomp a raw fish or tear out an enemy's throat. He had thick arms that could rip anything off a bad guy.

"I guess we're both workin' for the general again," Jack said. "At least we got the cards on the table this time, right? And I need you to help me out with a written statement for a new trial back in the States."

"Anything, buddy," Mick said. "I was deep in Syria when it all came down. I didn't know about it until you were convicted."

"So, you're along to help." When Jack heard the word *convicted*, he tried to forestall a glance at the major—but failed. He noticed that the major was intently listening.

"Right, buddy." Mick crinkled his Asian eyes in a smile. "I flew over from Camp Rhino in Ka-bullshit. I have updated satellite imagery on the valley, but it doesn't show anything new. I brought you and Billy climbing boots per your request: Kayland Ice Climbers—no crampons, though. Two ropes—9.8 mike mikes."

"Kinda light ropes, Chopstick," Jack commented. "New?"

"No," Mick responded, "but all I could find. An' I swiped a half dozen of the test model P2 body-powered safety suits—"

"I've heard of them," Jack interrupted. "Do they really work?"

"Better than long johns," Mick responded. "The piezoelectric and peltier threads in the suit convert body movement and thermal differences into electrical power that heats or cools your body, depending on the outside temp."

"So you create energy as you walk? But you'll look like an overmuscled Spiderman," Jack said.

"Don't worry—I brought white BDUs with no insignia, regular cammos, a couple of SAS E an' E survival tins." He took two hand-sized metal pacs out of a leg pocket and tossed them on the table. "Also, a package that was overnighted from Camp Hansen. I peeked. A weapon, but no ammo?"

"Laser gun," Jack smiled. "I'll show you how it works when we get to the valley."

Mick continued, "Sweet! I arranged for a supply drop in KGC 409, so we don't have to haul everything over the mountains. And I had the armorer put SAWs and new Sapis armor systems in redundant drops."

Mick smiled, added, "Guess what? I went to Flight School. I'm a pilot. I flew up here in a Cobra." He glanced at the major. "Thanks, sir, for letting me park at your base."

"Dude, congrats! I just wish we could take your helicopter into Shang —uh, 409," Jack said.

"Wanna go for it?" Mick asked.

"Ain't no way, Chopstick. Robert Arses tried it last year, General Harmbruster tried it twice this year. Winds are too violent. The Hindu Kush peaks catch the jet stream, funnel winds over the valley in a weird way. That's why the valley's so isolated. Can't fly in there—it's like a blindfolded ride at Magic Mountain. And you gotta be nuts to go for it. High avalanche danger, hidden crevasses that come out in… probably Alaska." He glanced at Mick. "Nuts—that'd be us, of course."

The major stood, leaned forward. "If the baddies are there, will you share some of the glory with your Pak allies?"

"Are you kidding?" Jack asked. "It's all yours, if you want. I'm not lookin' for a dustup. But you guys don't cross west of the Durand Line, do you?"

The major sat back, deflated. "No," he admitted.

"I'm weak on local history," Mick said. "What's that, again?"

Major Soongoon responded, "A British officer, Lord Durand, surveyed the Afghan-Pakistani border in the 1890's and an 1893 treaty set the line between the two countries. Anyway, it expired in 1993 and now the border's in dispute. Where you're going is in the disputed territories." "Speakin' of glory," Mick interjected. "I got a Silver Star for the Hindu Kush battle last year, Jack. Thanks for putting me up. 'Course the citation was classified." He leaned over and poked Jack in the chest to emphasize his words. "You deserved one, as well."

Jack thought of the cell in Leavenworth, grimaced with anger. "I got a Silver Star, as well, and I was up for a Navy Cross for my escape from the Taliban. But they cancelled the nomination after I was charged." "You heard about Omar Johnson?" Mick asked.

Jack thought of his college roommate for a second. "No, not a word since the trial. I figure he wrote me off. Green Beret and all that shit. Probly couldn't handle havin' a so-called traitor for a friend."

"No, not true. He told me you got a raw deal. Anyway, he got shot when he went with Task Force 121. Those Special Forces dudes who're hunting and killin' old-line Baathist insurgents in Iraq."

"Shot!"

"Lost his leg—right at the knee," Mick said. "He's out of the Army— partial disability. Back in his hometown. Portland."

"Damn, Long-legged Omar, could run like the wind—what a shame! Giving up a leg for a buncha ungrateful Iraqis."

"Hey, remember his Hunza irregulars? They were shit hot!" Mick protested.

"Yeah," Jack admitted. "You're absolutely right! Those little guys were great last year. How'd Omar—"

The major leaned forward, interrupted, eyes glinting with eagerness. "I wish I could lead troops into your 409. I smell a victory. But the local tribes forbid action against the Tali—Mr. Seighder!" Soongoon stood and smiled a greeting.

A white man, tall, slender—about forty years old—handsome, with white-blond hair to his shoulders, striking green eyes, a deeply-tanned face and a wide, thin-lipped mouth, extended a hand and shook with Soongoon. He smiled, revealing a missing tooth in front. The two small Asian teenage girls behind him were wearing rough, ill-fitting mountaineer clothing, wore their black hair tied back in buns. Jack quickly realized that the girls were identical twins and were probably Nepalese or Tibetans.

Major Soongoon glanced at his watch, said, "Mr. Seighder, you're right on time. Meet these Americans. They, too, are venturing into remote highlands."

"Where you headed?" Jack looked up at Seighder, held out his hand. The lofty, thin man had a crazy glint in his eyes, wild hair that stuck in all directions.

"Call me Gran Crew. I'm going to China," the man responded with German-accented English as he moved forward and shook Jack's hand, then Mick's. The girls, appearing to be about fourteen or fifteen, followed and stood behind Seighder after he entered and sat down. Both had their hands folded together, both looked downward, but couldn't repress mischievous glints in their eyes as they checked out the group with quick glances.

"Really!" Jack exclaimed. "Was it easy to get a visa to travel the KKH into China?"

"We'll travel the highway as far as Hunza, but then—" Crew leaned closer, "we'll sneak around Godwin-Austen and into China. I'm searching for Shangri-La. The valley of the long-lived."

"Where's Godwin-whatever?" Mick asked. He and Jack exchanged glances, each wondering why the guy was looking for the secret valley in the wrong country and the wrong mountain range.

"K-2. It was surveyed by Godwin-Austen in the 1850's," Jack said. "Called Chogori by the locals."

Mick leaned forward. "K-2! Second highest mountain in the world."

"First guys up—an Italian team reached the summit in 1954. It's a death dealer to the inexperienced or unlucky." Jack said, stalling to collect his thoughts. He looked at Seighder again, wondered if the guy was CIA or one of Farley's flunkey's, bent on some HUMINT work in China.

"Well, we don't plan on climbing—we're goin' around it," Seighder added.

Major Soongoon rose, and gestured for the others to follow him while he walked through a heavily engraved wood door, into a private room off the bar. A black potbelly stove in the corner heated the room, but a tiny flow of smoke cast a pall under the wood beam ceiling.

A waiter followed into the poorly-lit room with a fresh pot of tea in an over-sized brass kettle with a long curving spout. He put the pot down, removed from a bead-covered canvas bag, a bottle made to resemble a rocket. The label proclaimed, *Red Army Vodka*. He placed it in the center of the rough wood table next to a cluster of glasses. The major picked up a scratched-up glass and poured. He placed the full glass in front of Jack, who sat across from him, then proceeded to fill glasses for Mick and Seighder. With a mock-sinister accent, he said, "We have our ways to get around the cursed mullahs."

Jack made a pretext of sipping the spicy vodka, then put the glass down on the scarred surface of the rustic table. He glanced over his shoulder at the two girls hovering behind Seighder. "Sharwa?" he asked.

The girls smiled when he recognized and named their tribe, but did not speak.

Startled at Jack's correct guess, Seighder said, "Yes, they're Sherpas. I bought them in Karachi."

"Bought them!" Chopstick Mick exclaimed with an angry tone.

Seighder waved a hand in a placating manner. "Not what you think."

"What's to think, asshole!" Mick rose, his voice incensed. "You can't own two kids just because they're Asian!"

"Calm yourself," Major Soongoon interrupted. "Mr. Seighder purchased the Sharwas out of enslaved prostitution. He is returning them to their tribal lands in Nepal."

"They agreed to guide me in return for their freedom," Seighder added. "So I don't have to go through an established guide service. Easier, that way, to slip through Nepal, into China."

"Seems like a lotta work to chase a myth," Mick, looking chagrined, observed with a shake of the head.

"Last chance, really," Seighder said with a grimace. "You see, I've got AIDs." He frowned, hit a fist into his other palm. "A moment of weakness in Mandalay. Prettiest damned Burma girl you ever saw. Little Muslim bitch!" He glanced at Jack, then chanted in a rolling, deep voice:

On the road to Mandalay,
The dawn comes up like thunda,
Outta China 'crost the Bay!
By the old Burma Pagoda,
A Burmese girl thinks o' me;
Come back, British soldier;
Come you back to Mandalay!

"Rudyard Kipling, of course," Jack observed. Seighder nodded his head, added:

The mist is on the rice-fields,
The sun is droppin' slow,
She'd git 'er little banjo
An' she'd sing 'Ku-la-lo!'

He stared at unknown vistas for seconds.

"So how do you feel about Muslim girls now?" Mick asked with a slight smile.

Seighder stared at the two Americans, glanced at the major, who Jack remembered was a Catholic. "I kill 'em at every opportunity. Men, as well. We're in a thousand-year-war an' I'm gonna make sure I do everything I can to lower their population while I'm still around."

Jack and Mick stared at Crew Seighder, chilled by his words.

Realizing he had cooled the conversation, Seighder rose and asked, "Say, how'd you recognize the girls? You a climber?"

Jack glanced at Mick. "The clothes looked familiar. Like pictures my dad took of Sherpas when he climbed Everest."

Seighder sat back. "Thought you mighta been to Nepal."

"I've heard stories Shangri-La is in the Hindu Kush," the major observed.

Seighder shook his head. "Outposts here and there, claimants, really. They've popped up wherever glacial water contains a certain mixture of minerals that are incredibly healthful. But the real—the main one—is in the remotest part o' China. Headwaters o' the Nu River in Yunnan Province."

Still shocked by what had happened to Omar, his college roommate, Jack half-listened to the major and crazed Crew Seighder, wondered if the guy was just probing, wanting to trail along on their expedition to ShangriLa.

Chapter 18

Jack and Mick excused themselves, returned to the bar. Mullahs stared at them and muttered obviously hostile and unintelligible remarks.

The Americans watched a white girl enter the room, accompanied by two local men. She wore baggy, blue snowboarding trousers, a heavy red coat over a thick, woolen sweater. Her light brown hair was cut short, almost a buzz cut. No shrinking violet, she confidently walked past admiring Pakistani men.

Despite her burly figure, her face was beautiful, with high cheekbones, a firm jaw, a perfect nose, beautiful eyes that sparkled even from across the poorly lit, Gilgit Lodge's dining hall. She was about five-foot-nine in her heavy hiking boots.

Zhang and Billy, looking like they had just romped a mile across their bed at high altitude, entered, and Jack introduced Zhang to Mick. The Chinese agent noticed Jack looking over her shoulder, turned, checked out the young woman on the other side of the bar. Billy, sipping a cup of tea, did as well.

"An American," Zhang observed.

"How can you tell?" Jack asked.

"No women in the world look or dress like Americans," Zhang added. "Nor look straight at the world like confident, world-ruling Americans."

"That's 'cause American women are the most beautiful in the world," Billy said.

Zhang hit him on the arm, "What'm I? Dog meat? Anyway, she's fat!"

"Hey, you're from OC. You're an American babe, and you're gorgeous. Best lookin' babe between the Hindu Kush and the Himalayas," Billy responded with a quick smile.

Zhang hit him in the arm again. "They're right next to each other, you big yak ox!"

"Just kiddin', babe." He glanced around the room again and added, "What happened to this joint? Used to be a bar, now it's a raghead boutique."

Jack watched Billy smile, transforming his hard-planed Indian face to something resembling mere mayhem on two legs. He felt a surge of love for his brother.

Billy glanced at Jack, asked, "What's an American doing way up here?"

"Dunno. Must be part of an aide mission. Maybe a doc like—" he thought of Amy Anderson, who had hung herself in their shared Taliban prison the year before, after her captors had repeatedly raped her.

Just then, another white man entered the room, sat down at the white woman's table. Jack stared, amazed when he recognized Dickey Arses.

"Billy, Mick—check it out—it's Dickey, the SAS guy from Shangri-La. The guy we saved at Haartgard last year."

Mick and Billy swung around again, agreed.

Billy said, "What the hell's he doin' here?"

Jack stood and approached the Brit he and his friends had rescued from the isolated valley of Shangri-La. Dickey had been trapped for over two decades after the Soviet Army had destroyed the only known access tunnel to the valley, and had escaped when Jack had found the secret tunnel into Shangri-La. "Hey, Dickey," he called.

The Englishman glanced up, stood, bellowed, "What the 'ell you doin' in these heathen lands, Jack, me boy?" Dickey didn't look like a teenage Leonardo DiCaprio anymore. Still had blond curly hair, blue eyes under shaggy eyebrows, still had the big nose only mothers and plastic surgeons could love. His face and body had thickened in the last year, but he still wore his infamous black silk top hat.

Jack looked at the young woman. Short blonde hair—almost a man's crew cut. "Hi, I'm Jack Flashhardt, from Billings, Montana."

She responded, "We're neighbors—I'm Caylynn Jones. From Boise, Idaho." The two smiled, shook hands. Caylynn had very strong fingers, a firm grip, a mountaineer's dark tan that made her pale blue eyes stand out, and a brilliant smile on a strong Nordic face. She had taken off her jacket, but still looked very hefty in a grey, yak wool sweater.

Jack said to Dickey, "Come to my table for a few minutes. I need to talk to you."

The tall Englishman followed Jack and asked, "What's with the dyed hair?"

Jack rubbed his head. "Disguise. I escaped from prison."

"You're joking! Heard about the prison thing. A bit nasty, what? After all you did for God and Queen—er—Country?"

"A lot nasty. Sit down," Jack said. He introduced Zhang Poon t'ang.

Dickey tipped his black top hat to Zhang with a sweeping flourish, grinned and nodded at Billy. The two touched fists.

Billy said, "I thought you were long gone after we saved your ass last year. Back to the white cliffs of Rover."

"Dover," Dickey and Mick corrected at the same time.

"Dude, what're you doin' here?" Jack asked.

Arses grinned sheepishly, his blue eyes twinkled. "I'm tryin' to get back to Shangri-La, actually. Miss it, what?"

"Unbelievable! You're stuck there for ages, and now you wanna go back?"

"What's up, Jack? How'd you shake your sentence?" Dickey glanced at Zhang, who was sitting up, listening intently.

"We're on a mission," Jack said in a low voice.

"A mission to Shangri-La," Mick added.

"Whatever for?"

"A terrorist cell. Been training there, evidently," Jack said.

"But the caverns are collapsed! No way in." Dickey protested. "And anyway, your government backhanded you for your efforts last year."

Zhang interrupted, "There's another underground route into your Shangri-La, but it's heavily patrolled by Muslim terrorists, Tajik members of Jaish-e-Muhammad. Through Kashgar. From China."

Jack looked at the Chinese agent. "Well, that would be easier, but I'm not looking for a cave fight with a bunch of crazy Tajik mullahs. We'll sneak over the peaks."

"You climbin' to bloody Shangri-La! You could take me!" Dickey exclaimed.

Jack looked at the Englishman. "Dude, you're no climber—you've said so yourself. Why're you so hot to get back to the valley, anyway?" Dickey smiled, admitted, "Bloody mission. MI6 is worried about the same Shangri-La training camp, as well. I volunteered to check it out. The firm tuned me up at Fort Monckton in Hampshire, sent me out braying for support and muttering *Semper Occultus*." "What's Semp Occult-whatever?" Mick asked.

"Always secret," Jack responded.

"It's the MI6 motto," Dickey explained.

Jack stared at Dickey. "Why would they send a non-climber to the toughest range in the world?"

"Misrepresented meself to get the operation when I heard about it," Dickey grinned. "Truth is, I miss the place. Spent too long there. Can't fit in back in Merry Old England anymore. Been here in Gilgit fer two weeks, tryin' to figger a way into Shangri-La. But the cavern entrance you blokes found last year is collapsed."

"We destroyed it with a B-52 strike after we set off the avalanche and blew up the bio bomb," Jack explained. "Anyway, Dickey, how've you been since you left the valley? Any illness?"

Staring at Jack, the Englishman toyed with a saltshaker. "None," he answered. "Didna expect any, didna get any."

Jack glanced at the others, asked, "Any physical injuries?" "Nothing that didn't heal up in a few days," Dickey responded.

"What's with the medical analysis?" Mick asked.

"Oh, I was just wondering," Jack explained. "The inhabitants of Shangri-La have this kooky theory that they never get sick. An' live longer than most. Way longer. What's with the fat chick?"

"Caylynn? I was trying to talk her into climbing over the bloody peaks. And takin' me," Dickey said. "She's had a bit of bad luck with her team. And they lost their permit to climb."

"The fat babe's a climber?" Jack asked. "Bring her over. Let's get to know her."

Dickey returned to Caylynn's table, leaned over, whispered in her ear. She spoke to the Pakistani men sitting with her, then joined Dickey, walked over. Her baggy pants rustled as she approached. Jack watched the big woman draw near, wondered how she could climb, heavy as she was.

Dickey introduced Caylynn to Mick, Billy, and Zhang, the two sat down.

"I hear your team had some bad luck," Jack said.

With a wan smile that didn't prevent her facial beauty from shining through, Caylynn said, "Did we ever! We have… we had a permit to climb Rakaposhi. My first major peak."

"Rakaposhi—25,000 plus feet high. That'd be a wonderful summit to pick up."

"You're a mountaineer!" Caylynn sat straighter.

"We've climbed in the Hindu Kush," Jack swept his hand at Mick and Billy. "What happened to your team?"

Caylynn looked down, frowned. A crease appeared in her flawless face, between her eyebrows. "Two of the team had a mishap on the KKH— the Karakoram Highway—the old Silk Road from Islamabad to China." She pointed towards the door. "About twenty miles north of here. They were transporting gear to Base Camp. Bandits held them up." Anybody hurt?" Jack asked.

"One of the team was shot in the knee, one was stabbed by a bandit."

"You're kidding!" Mick exclaimed.

She shook her head. "Luckily, they escaped with their lives, but their climb was over. Then the other two came down with hepatitis. They went home last week."

"Expedition born under a bad star?" Billy asked.

Caylynn nodded. "I stayed behind to ship our expedition gear home. I got everything back from Base Camp today. What a mess!"

Jack half-listened to the conversation, thought about the failed expedition's gear. With luck, they could acquire all they needed to climb over the Hindu Kush range, into Shangri-La. "Sell some of your gear?" he asked.

Caylynn looked at him, asked, "Why? Are you climbing? Do you have a permit? What're you doing on this side of the world without gear?"

He shook his head. "No permit, but I know the local Pakistani Army base commander, Major Lialot Soongoon. He's helpin' me out."

Billy exclaimed, "I'm the only redskin in the world who has to drag his red ass up crazy fuckin' snow-covered rock piles every time I turn around."

"What're you attempting?" Caylynn glanced at Billy, leaned closer to Jack. She looked more friendly and very interested.

Jack smiled, checked out her beautiful face, her possibly impressive breasts hidden under bulky clothes. "Nothing exciting. We're just trekking into… an isolated local valley."

Caylynn sat back, looked disappointed. "Then you don't need much in the way of gear. I don't have ropes, anyway. They were stolen during the robbery."

"Well, there's no pass to Shangri-La—we'll clear over twenty-two thousand feet—that's more'n sixty-seven hundred meters—where we're goin'. We definitely need gear—tools, belts, for starts. I was hoping to find some here in Gilgit." He glanced at Mick. "I'd like better ropes, as well." He wished he hadn't named the destination.

"Shangri-La. Dickey called it that also," Caylynn asked. "That's a place in the novel *Lost Horizon!*"

"True," Jack agreed. "But it's just a Chamber of Commerce nametag. It's what the locals call the valley where we're headed. Sorta like Aspen, Colorado, locals call that region Paradise."

"Yeah," Billy added, "Montanans call our state, Big Sky country. Like you call Idaho, famous spud-land."

Dickey rose from his chair, an angry expression starting to form across his brow. "That's not—"

"So how's your brother?" Jack cut off Dickey's protest at the characterization of Shangri-La.

"Not bloody good," Dickey said, settling back. "Had a spot of trouble six months ago. Got in a tangle with some Uighur terrorists. Then the People's Army caught him trying to cross the border out of China on the Karakoram Highway."

"You're kidding!" Jack exclaimed.

Dickey nodded. "He's serving a one-year sentence. He's okay—he'll be out in six months."

"Sorry to hear that," Jack said. "He's a great guy. Saved my life in Afgone-istan last year."

Caylynn persisted, "So you can get a permit but you're not climbing a peak. At almost seven thousand meters, you'd have to be very close to one of the Hindu Kush summits. I'd sell… give you all the gear you need—" "That's great!" Jack exclaimed.

"I'd give it to you if you let me go along, help me capture a peak on the way," Caylynn finished. Her eyes sparkled, she leaned forward, her lush red lips parted with excitement.

"Forget it," Jack shook his head. "We're too busy to bag a summit." Caylynn slumped back, disappointed.

Billy and Zhang, who had been subdued by the big woman's presence, said goodnight and repaired to their room, holding hands as they walked. Several heavily-bearded Pakistani men frowned and mumbled at the display of affection. Jack noticed one fellow angrily rise. He was quickly restrained by another man at his table.

Settling back after the perceived threat, Jack and Dickey relived their year-ago battle to save China Bitch from being raped. Mick enthused about the battle at Haartgard, when Islamic fundamentalists had tried to overrun and destroy the ancient Shangrilan fortress.

Finally growing bored at the war stories, Caylynn excused herself and left the room.

A half hour later, with a slight altitude headache as an excuse, Jack left the dining room, went outside. The full moon was so bright it was hard to look at it. Snow-covered mountains on all sides gleamed brilliant white. He looked up at the hugely steep mountains, wondered if their climb would be accident-free. Thought, *Confident in my abilities, Billy's, Mick's. But what about the others?*

He walked through the cold air to the lodging section of what had been the Serena Lodge the year before: a Swiss-type, timber-structured hotel with a sharply pitched roof, its balconies and windows trimmed with intricate woodwork. Out of the corner of his eye, he caught movement behind him, suddenly wished he had Holland's pistol as he hurried inside. His room, the same one as last year, had a bed, a small antique table, two chairs, a television that still didn't work, a wood floor covered by a large Afghan rug. He locked the door, looked around, thought of Melinda O'Reilly, the flamboyant Time Magazine correspondent who had seduced him in this same room—she had been a sensational, if fleeting and selfserving, disruption in his life.

Unpacking his bag, he took out the long knife and the scabbard the old English monk from Quetta had given him the year before. Recalled Hilton's words: "This scabbard's made out of a sacred white Komodo dragon's hide. The silver and gold trim is from Tibet." *Varanus Komodoensis, the scientific name of the Komodo Dragon.*

And then, later—just before Hilton was shot, "Listen: go to my Dragon God. He holds the sword for this scabbard. Save you in the end, it will."

Okay, Yoda. He tossed the empty scabbard in the air, caught it, thought of the desperate battle the year before, when he had lost the knife he had taken from Dragon God's temple: *climbing up the caldera rim on the escape rope. A huge hand grabbed his ankle. Mo Poo, the giant Chinaman, looked up: his bloody face ripped open from the tiger's attack. Desperate, Jack pulled the Dragon God knife. Slashed the giant across his upturned face, the knife slipped out of his hand as the screeching giant grabbed his face.*

A knock at the door interrupted his thoughts. He cracked it open and a smiling Zhang brushed by him, sat on the bed. He looked in the hallway for Billy, asked, "Where's my brother?" He thrust the knife into the scabbard and put it into his pack.

Zhang answered with a smug air, "He's exhausted and asleep. He took four Oxys. Anyway, I told you, I'm my own woman. I have plenty to share."

"What's really up, Cher? I mean Zhang?"

"You're going into Afghanistan. I want to go."

"Hey, I said you could come along to Pakistan, not go on a grand tour of Asia. Anyway, you're not a mountaineer. Those heights are brutal beyond your imagination. You could get cerebral edema, pulmonary edema. And we can't waste time carrying an amateur out of altitude. You screw up and you'd be toast!"

Zhang thought for a moment. "I'm in excellent condition—probably better than you. I'm a professional dancer. I'll chance it." She rose, moved close to Jack, pressed her body against him, rubbed her groin against his, put her arms around his neck. "Billy can attest to my body's condition. D'you want to make an independent survey?"

Jack laughed, grabbed her wrists. "Babe, you may be in excellent condition, but you're puttin' me in the red zone." He tried to push her away, she tightened her grip. "The other problem is the KKH. It's a road loaded with bandits. We'll have to hire a truck to take us north on it."

Zhang freed him, waved her hands in dismissal. "Your friend flew here in a helicopter. Even if we have to go by truck—you're a warrior—you'll get us through."

A knock at the door interrupted them.

Chapter 19

Jack crossed and opened the door—Caylynn Jones, the American climber, stood in the hallway. He stepped back. "Join the party."

The big woman entered, stopped when she saw Zhang move to the bed, sit down with an air of ownership. "I'd like to talk to you about the climb."

"Welcome to the club," Jack said. "I'm startin' to feel like an adventure travel agent. Why don't you two work out my schedule while I go back to the dining room for a midnight snack."

Zhang burst into laughter, rose. "Awesome, I talk to you guys tomorrow. I think Billy's rest is over. See you later." She strutted out of the room as though she had conquered all in it.

Watching her leave, Caylynn said with a hint of irony, "I didn't realize she was with *both* of you. I'm sorry I interrupted."

Jack barked a nervous laugh. "Zhang's a Chinese Communist agent. She's along to keep an eye on us for her government, and 'cause Billy is smitten with her. Nothing to do with me. We were just talking about the climb into the Hindu Kush."

"Chinese! Why would they want to watch a couple of American trekkers in Pakistan? Are you still in the military—or something more?"

Jack went to his bag, pulled out a bottle of Russian vodka and a cloth bundle that he unwrapped to reveal two small stemmed crystal glasses. "Cheap Russian spicy vodka, expensive Russian antique glasses. Glasses are a gift from our assistant guide after my dad and I climbed Mount Elbrus."

"You're carrying glasses into the heights?"

"Hah!" Jack exclaimed. "I always bring them to Base Camp for luck. Reminds me what my dad always drilled into me: If you don't think you can make it to the top, remember, you can always make one more step. And then one more. Never quit, ever."

"He must be quite a man."

Jack frowned. "He took a bad mental hit after we lost the ranch to the Crow Nation, but—"

"That was your ranch?" Caylynn interrupted. "I remember my parents talking about the lawsuit. It was famous."

"Yeah, but we bought the ranch back last year. The Crow had run it down pretty bad. Most of the cattle were sold off."

"Probably the drought didn't help," Caylynn offered.

Jack nodded agreement and held up the bottle. "Anyway, Dad's off the booze and forging ahead. I'm proud of him."

He filled the two small glasses; they twinkled in the light from the lamp. "The Russians balance these glasses on their elbows, then drink without spilling." He picked up a glass, balanced it on his bent arm, steered it toward his mouth until it fell off, bounced and spilled on the thick woolen rug. He glanced sheepishly at Caylynn, refilled his, offered the other glass to Caylynn. She accepted it, looked skeptically at the contents. She added, "Hope you climb better than you balance Russian glasses."

The two laughed, exchanged warmer glances. "Elbrus? You're doing the Seven Summits?"

"Correctomundo. I've also done Mount Aconcagua—at 23,000 plus feet—the highest mountain in South America; Kilimanjaro, highest in Africa."

"So you have McKinley, Everest, and Vinson in Antarctica left to do. And Australia. I'm impressed. I've never summited anything important." Caylynn sipped the vodka, grimaced. "Not by your choice of drinks, though. This's horrible!"

Jack, enjoying her open personality, her frankness, pointed his glass at a chair and sat down in its companion.

Sitting, Caylynn put her glass down, said with a firm voice, "You need gear. I want a summit. I've traveled halfway around the world." "Rock and ice walls are all you've ever done?" "Yes," she answered defensively.

With a dismissive tone, Jack concluded, "You're what my circles would call just a chalk bag-toting rock rat. You in good enough shape to make almost seven thousand meters?"

"Yes," she answered eagerly. "I'm acclimated. I've hiked the slopes of Rakaposhi for three weeks."

Jack gazed at the beautiful woman, wondered how fat she really was under her bulky clothes. He felt a flush sweep through his body. Thought, *I've been celibate for too long. And she's got a gorgeous face, more curves gotta be good.* "I need your gear. I'll get you a first ascent. You'd be the first ever on that peak."

"The first?" she asked.

"You get to name it in the Mountaineering records. I already have one in the Hindu Kush. I called it MistMount."

He added, "But no free rides, no short roping, and no bolting. That is, drilling holes for safety ropes. I climb clean. Leave no traces."

"That'd be awesome!" Caylynn leaned forward, her lush lips parted with excitement.

"No stage climbing, not expedition-style. We just go for it, balls to the walls."

He sank to his knees in front of her, touched her lips, traced her jaw with his fingers, moved his hand to her long slender neck. His unexpected actions froze her. "A first ascent. You'd go down in the record books, Caylynn Jones."

Mesmerized by his words, startled into stillness by his touches, she stared into his eyes. He spread her vest, started on the buttoned-up sweater under it.

"You, standing on a summit. You can see forever, massive Himalayas to the east, snow-covered Hindu Kush all around, emerald valleys below." He pushed the sweater and vest off her upper body, unbuttoned a silk shirt. She still made no move or protest.

Surprised at how slender her upper body was under the bulky clothes, he pulled her shirt off, gazed at her large breasts. Put his head between them, breathed in her aroma—slightly cinnamon. He heard her gasp, then sigh.

He pulled her to her feet, ran his hands down her sides, undid her pants. "The top of the world. When you know you're going to make it to the summit—when you know the mountain grants permission, adrenalin shoots through every cell: raw energy pours out of the earth, out of the mountain, into your body, out your fingers, every hair on your head alive with the electricity shooting out. If there's lightning, you're a lightning rod. Because you know the summit is yours. You're gonna make it. Jet Stream wind blowing on your face, lenticular clouds flying overhead like swooping swallows, powerful sunlight, almost lethal in intensity, air so thin, so pure you could bottle it—sell it to flatlanders who'll never know that it's as good as sex."

He pushed her bulky pants down, was astounded at her long, slender form. "Well, almost."

Caylynn broke out of her trance, giggled, kissed him passionately, pushed him to the bed, shoved him down. Pulled the long Afghan shirt off his body, stripped away his pants. Grasped his erection and exclaimed, "Sweet!"

Chapter 20

Pausing at an approximate altitude of fifteen thousand feet as the sun brightened the eastern sky over the Himalayas with a golden hue, Jack shifted his eighty-pound pack, regarded a snow-topped serac that looked about ready to shed its mantle of white. A stiff breeze had begun blowing at first light. Snow was curling off the upper lip of the icy serac cliff that towered to their front. Higher and to the left, he saw a black spec in the middle of a white expanse. The spec either wavered from a refraction of sunlight, or moved across the expanse. A flash of light, glinting off a patch of ice, or maybe a lens, blinded him; when his vision cleared the spec was gone.

Downslope on his rope, Billy and Caylynn were about thirty feet apart. She had been climbing with no difficulty. Mick, pulling a sled of camp gear like Jack's and Billy's—no problem. Zhang and Dickey were also on the second rope. All the backpack-laden climbers were in a straight line, following Jack's steps across the wind-packed snow, their foot crampons keeping them from slipping.

Dickey, carrying the lightest pack, was struggling. Jack had started a rest step procedure so the weaker climbers could maintain: after each step, the climber would lean back on a stiff rear leg, forcing the skeletal bones to take the body's weight, thereby giving the climber's muscles a chance to rest. They had started with a one breath pause on each rest step, but now had progressed to three breath pauses between steps. He worried that the inexperienced team members would not be able to make it over the ridge, even with the rest step regimen, as they climbed to highest altitudes. The fact that they were not climbing in stages increased the risks, but he wanted to rush over the heights before any of them had a chance to get altitude sickness.

The six had begun climbing the eastern slopes of the Hindu Kush at midnight of the second day in the region thirty-five clicks north of Gilgit, utilizing a brilliant moon that stood over their shoulders as they toiled up the mountainside.

Jack waited until all five halted below him. As he watched the trudging climbers, strung along the two ropes, he wondered what

Penelope Kong, the beautiful tribal queen of Shangri-La, whom he had met on a tumultuous day the year before, was going to say when he showed up with Caylynn. He checked the snow consistency for the hundredth time—it was still dry. Suddenly, a lenticular cloud mass paused over the northern ridges, indicating high winds aloft. More clouds quickly spread across the sky, blocking out the sunrise.

"A storm's coming," he stated with gasping breaths when the others stopped just below him. He looked upslope. "We'll move a hundred meters. To that rock ridge, pitch tents. Make snow walls on the north side of the tents for wind barriers."

The climbers trudged downwind until Jack, in the lead, stopped on a small flat area, about five meters across, just below a snow-crusted rock ridge about three meters high. He threw his pack on the snow, untied the rope attached to his sled, unwrapped his tent. He arched his aching back, and then began erecting the shelter.

The wind was strengthening; he had a hard time controlling the flapping tent, so he shoved it under his pack and began cutting snow blocks from a wind-packed drift. Caylynn and the others dropped their packs and helped; soon the three teams had constructed walls for each tent—a meter high and two meters long, jutting away from the rock ridge.

After the tents were pitched, Jack set up a tiny gas stove to melt snow for hot tea, while the others crawled in tents: Billy and Zhang quickly disappeared into one tent; Mick and Dickey squirmed into the third tent. Caylynn put teabags in the team's oversized cups and waited as the snow slowly melted at a high altitude speed of almost zero.

As pans full of snow finally changed to water, Caylynn prepared tea and fought her way through the steadily increasing wind and drifting snow to serve the other team members. When she finished, she pushed into the low-to-the-ground two person tent and settled next to Jack.

"Hey," he greeted her. He idly wondered, *Can you get laid at 5,000 meters? And what was that speck I saw moving above us in the high ridges?* Pushing worries out of his mind, he concentrated on his beautiful tent-mate. She handed Jack a large plastic mug of hot tea, he sniffed the acrid odor, sipped the scalding black tea—a relaxing sensation swept through his body.

"How long will the storm last?" she asked.

"Chopstick Mick is checking on his laptop," he responded. "He'll let us know."

"Chopstick is a pretty rude nickname," Caylynn commented.

"He can take it—he's Army."

Just then, they heard Mick shout above the howling wind. Jack reversed directions in the cramped tent, stuck his head into the maelstrom of swirling snow.

"Outlook is thirty six hours," Mick yelled. "Big blow comin' out of China."

"May as well rest," Jack said. "You tell Billy. And pass out Diamox." He handed a small bottle to his friend.

Mick waved an acknowledgement and turned away.

"Hey," Jack yelled. When Mick turned back, he added, "I might have seen someone way upslope. Maybe we should stand watches."

"No one can move or find us in this storm," Mick yelled over the howling wind.

Nodding agreement, Jack retreated into the tent, clumsily reversed directions again, wondered if they would have to retreat after the storm.

The two finished their tea, then exchanged an affectionate kiss and fell asleep, after Caylynn turned over, snuggled her back against Jack.

A pounding on the tent, different from the sounds made by the windflapped walls, woke him. When Jack peered into the blowing storm, Billy was hunched over, back to the wind, melting snow over the stove; Mick was pulling food out of the packs and divvying it up. Jack glanced at Caylynn—she was still asleep. He picked up their cups, crawled outside, ate two bags of dry snacks while he waited for tea. It was almost dark. He heard a hacking cough coming from Dickey's tent.

When water was finally hot, he filled two cups, re-entered the tent. "Hey," he called. "Hot tea."

Caylynn was awake, her lovely smiling face peeking out from her bag, and accepted a cup. "How long will we be stuck here?"

Jack frowned. "Probably until tomorrow." He broke open a granola bar. 'Why don't you tell me about yourself?"

Caylynn sipped her tea, smiled shyly. "Maybe you wouldn't want to know."

"Why not?" Jack laughed. "You an ax murderer?" Caylynn frowned, did not answer.

"Come on," he urged. "You grew up in Idaho—are you a Mormon?" Her mouth turned down slightly. "Of sorts," she said. "I… I was… married. I belonged to a… conservative branch of the church."

"Hey, I grew up in Montana," Jack exclaimed. "Polygamists?"

Caylynn looked down. "My sister and my cousin. We all were… we all married this bishop's son, Jacob." She looked into Jack's eyes with a sad expression. "We were sorta forced into it by our mother."

"Nice lady, I'll bet. Those dudes always have those biblical names. Why is that?"

With an angry tone, Caylynn said, "Because they're sinless!"

"I get the feeling you don't include your husband."

"He killed my cousin and my sister."

Jack reached out, touched Caylynn's arm. His fingertips were still numb from the stab injury, but he could tell her muscles were clinched tight. "Killed! Why ever for?"

"They got pregnant."

"He—"

Caylynn's words rushed out. "He didn't want children. When she got pregnant, he killed my cousin first—poisoned her—claimed she suicided. Everybody believed him. Then my sister died, fell from a ridge while rockclimbing with Jacob—he was always looking for buried KGC treasure. Nobody's that unlucky. The county did an autopsy—it showed she was… pregnant, as well. He was arrested, but the community leaders rallied and he was let out on bail. Then…"

Horrified, Jack automatically sipped his tea—it had grown cold. "You got pregnant?"

Caylynn snorted. "I thought I was. But I wouldn't let him near me. I moved out, I was going to go back home, but he came to the house unexpectedly when I was there picking up some clothes…" she stopped.

"You don't have to— "

"I killed him." Caylynn's voice was defiant. "Hit him with a lamp. Then a poker. I ran. I wouldn't have had a chance in that tightknit community. I had a passport from a choir trip to England the year before, I left the country—fled to Europe. I met some climbers from Colorado. I wanted to get high. Get clean."

"High mountains are purifying," Jack responded. He wanted to say more but he was at a loss for words. What she had done made sense. Running hadn't, but it was too late to lament that act. He put his arm around Caylynn's broad shoulders, hugged her. Her body odor was pungent and she was trembling as fast as the tent was flapping from the storm's winds. He wondered what the KGC she had mentioned really meant. And was it the same as KGC 409, where they were heading? And was Caylynn telling the truth about her objective? Was her true intention a visit to KGC 409?

Chapter 21

The next morning, the team dug out of the snowdrifts that had totally encased their tents, looked at clear deep blue skies. Perfect lens-shaped clouds, called lenticulars, hovered over the high summits, indicating high winds aloft.

Mick pointed at the white clouds. "Problem?" he asked.

Jack glanced up. "Hard to say. The summits are in the jet stream most of the time. It's always windy up there. We should be alright."

A half hour later, after drinking hot tea and wolfing down packaged oatmeal, the group packed, roped up and continued upwards, post-holing in Jack's stomped out footprints through thigh-deep fresh snow.

Strung out ten meters apart, they took a break after an hour, still separated in case one of the climbers fell in a crevasse.

Mick, who was inspecting the upper slope, called, "That serac—the ice wall—about ready to shed its slab snowcap."

"Cause an avalanche. In that upper snowfield," Billy added.

"Exactly!" Jack agreed. He stamped a foot to test the snow consistency. "We're in its fall line. Too risky. All that dry snow from the storm. I don't think it's bonded to the snowpack. We could climb that ice wall to the side. Or retreat down the mountain. But Zhang and Dickey... could never scale the ice wall—it's a two hundred meter cliff. We need to go down, try another approach."

"Yeah, I'd even have trouble on that ice," Mick exclaimed. "Anyway, I don't have toe crampons."

"Lose a couple of days if we start over," Caylynn complained.

The group fell silent, stared at the potential avalanche field beside the ice wall.

"Other option... is for Billy and me to climb the serac," Jack said. "Set off the avalanche. Then you others can safely proceed up the snowfield... join us on that upper ridge."

"I want to climb the serac, too!" Caylynn protested. Un-intimidated by the vertical serac, she added, "That's my baby."

Jack regarded the Idahoan, remembered she was a rock rat. She'd probably have no trouble with the serac, and she was handling the altitude. He thought back to their first sexual escapade in his hotel room, repeated last night in the tent, smiled at the memories.

After more discussion, all agreed to the plan of dis-arming the serac and the potential avalanche field. Before they split up, all checked their avalanche transmitter-transceivers to ensure the small pocket radios were working.

Jack, Billy, and Caylynn dropped their packs on a rockpile, the brothers undid their sleds, and moved single file to the base of the ice wall. Jack carefully inspected the rope—no frays, but it looked weather-beaten and old. He wished he had new ropes. *General Farley, who knows squat about climbing, nonchalantly dismissed our lack of gear,* he thought. *Like to see the fat little turd dangling on the end of this rope, wondering how sound it is.*

The three proceeded to climb, one at a time, the vertical cliff. Jack was in the lead.

He swung one of his two ice axes, buried it in the ice wall, kicked a toe crampon into the ice and lifted himself two feet. He repeated the moves until he reached the end of the thirty-foot expanse of rope that separated him from Billy. He drove a piton into the bluish-white ice, clipped a Fader carabineer to it, attached the rope. He waited while Billy attached a handheld, steel Petzl ascender to the rope, watched him slide it up as far as he could reach. When it locked, Billy pulled himself up to a new foothold. He repeated the process of using the ascender and an ax to ease the climb up the rope.

When Billy stopped, Jack began the next pitch while Caylynn, who was using her ice axes rather than an ascender, moved up.

Disaster struck an hour later when Jack heard a scrape far above, saw a flash of blue, shouted "Ice!"

The slab skinned over his left shoulder, glanced off Billy, knocking him away from the wall, ricocheted and squarely hit Caylynn's head and upper back, also knocking her away from the wall! The restraining safety pitons ripped loose from the lowest to highest! Popped one by one, until the two lower climbers, attached to Jack's rope, which was hooked to his waist harness, were suddenly supported by Jack's desperate grip of his two axes and his crampons, which were jammed in a crack in the vertical wall.

He did not look down. Billy's grunt, his rasping slide, Caylynn's abbreviated cry, and the huge jerk on his waist harness where the rope to Billy was attached, was all he needed to know.

The ice broke loose, Jack slid ten feet down the wall, caught a tiny ridge in the ice, popped off when the two below jerked his rope, slid again. One axe fell away.

Terrified, yelling, he caught a toe on a crack, swung his remaining axe into the ice, desperately hung on to it with both hands.

He concentrated, gasping for air as he stared at the blue ice inches from his face, shouted, "Billy, you guys okay?"

"Dropped my axes. They're just below me, on a ledge. Chick's… unconscious… or dead."

Jack immediately realized the dreadful truth: his grip was slipping. He tried to dig his fingers in, lock them on the axe handle. His brother and Caylynn. He had to hang on until they could regain their balance. Numb fingers on his left hand slipping. "I can't hold. You gotta get back to the wall."

"Can't!" Billy yelled. "She's too heavy—pullin' me away."

Caylynn, regaining consciousness, weakly called, "Help!"

Jack stared at the ice ax, just inches away. "Caylynn, grab something —I can't hold on any longer." He glanced down, Billy and Caylynn were both hanging free. She looked dazed, was pawing the air, kicking.

"Swing! You've got to get back on the ice."

He was slipping, he dug his fingers in tighter, tried to find a foothold— his crampons scraped rock, found nothing. His numb fingers began to cramp.

"I can't hold!"

Caylynn swung her body. The pressure increased as the seconds crawled. Jack tried to look, couldn't see. He felt a jolt as her rope hit the cliff, heard a twanging snap.

Caylynn wailed "No-oo!"

Pressure on Jack halved and the girl screamed for two hundred feet, until she dashed against wind-swept rocks at the base of the serac.

Chapter 22

Jack tried to loosen one hand, grab a crack, but his desperate grip failed. He fell, swung his axe and dug it into the ice wall. It scraped, caught— jerked him to a stop—ripped out, he slid again.

He swung, jerked to a halt, kicked his toe crampons into the wall. Hung onto the axe.

Lower now, Billy had landed on the ledge where his axes rested. The downward pressure disappeared.

After five minutes of just holding on, salvaging physical and mental recuperation, the two watched those below pulling the body off the rocks. They silently continued towards the top of the serac, each enduring ghastly thoughts.

Jack regretted he had used the old ropes. Questioned why he had taken the girl to the mountain. *Was it for sex? Her gear? I should've told her to get lost. Stupid ass!*

His dismal reverie stopped when another chunk of ice sailed past, missing him by inches. He glanced up, saw a man duck back.

"Watch it, asshole!" Billy yelled.

"Not me—someone up there. Throwing shit at us!" Jack pounded a toe crampon into the serac, pawed into a pocket and pulled his M-9, fired twice. He saw a flash of movement, fired again. A half hour later, on the almost-level top, Billy fell to his knees and cursed, "Son of a bitch! Hardest thing ever happened. Who'd you shoot at?"

Jack looked around, saw no one. Checked the snow—there were tracks leading to the edge and then away. Put a hand on Billy's shoulder.
"Someone dropped that ice chunk on us. Look at the tracks!"

Billy glanced down. "I'll kill the sonofabitch." He put his hands on his head.

Jack put an arm on his brother's shoulders. "*Nemo sine vitio est*—No one is without fault. We shouldn't have used these old ropes."

"Still—it was a bitch of a thing. And stick the goddam pig Latin!"

"I know, Billy. I'll never forget the—" *the sounds, the screams— racing through my head.*

"Who did it?"

Jack looked around, looked at the disturbed snow, indistinct tracks leading upwards. "I dunno. Someone doesn't want us up here."

Jack and Billy turned, carefully moved fifty feet to the snowcap, which was about twenty feet long and six feet thick.

They kicked and stomped it loose, watched it plummet to the snowfield far below, where it smashed into the steep slope, bounced once, then rolled.

As they had suspected, an avalanche built from a tiny stream to a gushing, smashing cascade. The roiling snowmass roared past the lower climbers, who were hiding on the lee side of the ice serac. Jack glanced at his watch: 0900 hours. Caylynn had only touched his life for a little more than forty eight hours: beautiful, intelligent, forceful, a daring mountaineer, a wonderful, caring, intimate lover: dead. He ground his teeth, hoped he had shot the culprit.

Jack and Billy transitioned to the main snowfield by crossing a ledge, then trekked down to the rest of the team.

Mick had melted snow, prepared tea. He poured the hot liquid into the arrival's cups. "What happened?" he asked in a low, tired voice.

"A chunk of ice, knocked her out, knocked both of them off the serac wall. Someone did it. Threw it down at us. The rope severed on a rock or an ice ledge."

The others stared, shocked by his words.

"We almost all three went," Billy muttered, stared at a new mound of packed-down snow. "Jack was slippin', she was flailing, I couldn't do anything with her pullin' me away from the wall."

Mick pointed at the mound of snow. "We buried her so ravens wouldn't get her. We can retrieve the body…"

"Later," Jack finished. "After all that," he pointed at the peaks above, "we'll come get her. Take her home." He thought, *What a mess! But we can't turn back.*

He trudged to the mound, knocked the snow away until he found

Caylynn's head. He gently brushed snow from her face, stopped when he encountered a bloody mass. She had hit a rock. *At least, if they cremate her, I'll take some ashes to a summit. Somewhere, Caylynn, you'll get your first summit.* He dashed tears out of his eyes, swallowed guilt.

They finished their food, forced down hot tea, silently started up the steep slopes. Jack kept watch but saw no movement above.

When the sun began to set over the wildly rugged Hindu Kush, casting a golden glow over the cliffs of ice and rock, the five climbers slowly trudged over the highest stone ridge, buffeted by cold, strong winds that whipped across frozen drifts.

Ten minutes later, they spotted a series of one-story buildings made of quarried granite, spread across a flat area the size of half a football field.

The biggest, a one-story temple, was also situated at the highest spot. It had a thick rock slab roof, and hovered over the already darkened, far below valley of Shangri-La. Snowdrifts sprawled halfway up the walls of the shrine complex.

Billy looked around, pointed. "Hold on a minute! Wasn't this where we set off the avalanche that took out the temple? The dang thing's back!"

"Yeah, you're right," Jack responded. He stared at the buildings, tried to remember what the site had looked like a year ago. Remembered setting and exploding the nitroglycerin, remembered the avalanche sweeping the temple ruins away. It had not been a dream.

Someone had restored the temple complex, and built the temple on a site safe from avalanche. He looked around the area, saw one running figure, then a second dart across an expanse of snow on the heights far to the north. He didn't raise an alarm, wondered who could run at the almost seven thousand meter altitude.

The group entered the temple, their panting breath hanging in the air, flashlights probing the corners of the structure. The wide vestibule's walls were decorated with painted art. Three complex themes were depicted: monsters fighting humans, humans and monsters fighting gods, and gods and humans attacking monsters.

Ignoring the art, Billy entered the main temple, called out, "Goddam!
The bigass gold worm is back!"

The others followed, stared at the golden dragon that dominated the temple. It was ten feet long—had two big front paws. Two horns on the ugly head were carved ivory, decorated with filigree gold. The angry eyes were red gems and the bared teeth were also large rubies cut to resemble bloody teeth.

"*Dracoserpens Lung orientalis*—Oriental dragon." Jack said in a hushed voice.

Zhang, who had been mesmerized by the Dragon God, asked, "This is where you stole the emeralds?"

"Yeah," Jack answered, "this's the dragon dude that supposedly stole 'em from your Emperor's Chinese concubine. If you believe in legends." *Who the hell put the big-ass dragon statue back on top of the ridge? Gotta weigh tons. And who was running across that snowfield?*

The five collapsed on the stone floor, broke out food. Jack set up a battery-powered lantern, sat by the door, kept guard. Mick set up an antenna and text messaged a sitrep to General Farley's headquarters in Islamabad.

They all shared bread, sausage, cheese. Mick heated tea, Dickey took out a leather bag of red wine: they all talked about the Dragon statue; all knew the story of the explosions that had caused an avalanche, destroyed the temple complex and saved Haartgard. They tried to imagine who had lugged it back up the mountain. Talked to help ignore Caylynn's death.

Jack's thoughts turned to the valley below: wondered again whether Penelope was still single: shut his eyes, pictured her—she was so like his former girlfriend Ashley in looks, he always confused them in his mind: tall, slender, long-legged, spectacular wide-set eyes, pouty lips—beautiful, with thick, long tangled blonde hair.

Remembering her sharp wit and sharper personality, he wondered whether she would welcome him.

"So what's all this about Shangri-La?" Zhang changed the subject. "Is it the Magic Kingdom of Asia? You know—like Disneyland?" Billy laughed, Dickey snorted an accompanying guffaw.

"I've been here twice," Jack began. "I met Dickey after I made a training parachute jump and a freak updraft blew me into the valley."

The Englishman observed with a dry tone, "Dropped outta the sky like a wraith, tried to steal my gels, the bugger."

Jack laughed. "Not exactly true, I was just contemplating it." He glanced at the Englishman. "Who wouldn't think about stealin' them? Anyway, deal is, these people claim they're descended from deserters of Alexander the Great's army during his travels through Asia in the Fourth Century B.C."

"Might be true," Mick said. "You'd think you're in Norway or Sweden or Minnesota—they're all blonde or redheaded, blue or green-eyed."

"Except for the Muslims up at the north end of the valley," Dickey said. "But the True Hunza—that's what the Shangrilans call themselves— do have a museum of sorts—no bloody Elgin stolen Greek exhibits, but there is a bronze shield, or apis, and a cuirasse— an intricately decorated breastplate on exhibit—looks like a Greek hoplite's armor to me. But they're stuck in a pre-industrialized society—just like everybody else in the region. Only thing semi-modern is their guns."

"They're Animists, as well," Jack added, "for they worship the Dragon."

Dickey shifted, continued, "I was serving in the SAS. Was stuck here in 1979. During the Soviet invasion. Bloody Russians discovered, then blew up the only tunnel into the valley—they did that in all parts of Afghanistan to cut off sanctuaries—so I tried to escape over these mountains. But deadly crevasses, frightful avalanches always pushed me back. I'm not like Jack here—he's an expert on such, knows the ways to avoid sudden death."

Jack thought of Caylynn for a second, added, "And then the peoples of the valley were plagued by these Chinese dudes—Grendel-like monstrous guys. Cannibals." He moved to the entrance, nervously searched the perimeter of vision in the faint light cast by the lantern, saw nothing but snow, ice and rock. He turned back and added, "Can you imagine? People trapped in a beautiful valley: no tunnels out, no airport 'cause of the high winds, almost impossible to get over the heights. An isolated paradise."

The rest of the group looked around the temple, avoided each other's eyes, shifted uncomfortably, looked at dark recesses.

Dickey added, "Well, and then there's the KEGYA—"

"—know a little about the giant man program," Zhang interrupted as Jack rejoined the others. "But rumors only. Chairman Mao started it in the Fifties." She glanced around. "None of you know much of China, but in the bad old days, when the European Colonial Powers had their way, they always sent their biggest soldiers and diplomats to China. So Chinese people thought all white men were giants."

Zhang sipped water from a plastic bottle, continued, "So when the Communists took over, Mao ordered the *Second Department*—it was called the *People's Collective Shield* before it began spying internationally—to gather big people from all over China. Forced them into a breeding program called… *Giant Leap Up*." She noticed ironic smiles on the listener's faces. "It's true! They hired former Nazi doctors and scientists from South America and Western Europe, brought them to China to work on the program. But it failed during its second generation—I don't know why."

"Mo Poo," Jack added, "the rebel's leader—dude was almost eight feet tall—told me some of these giants fled here to the Hindu Kush, some— including his son—went into the wild Himalayas."

"Others reportedly migrated to the extremely wild region of the headwaters of the Nu River in Yunnan Province," Zhang said.

"Anyway, Mo Poo hated China and especially white men, 'cause of the ex-Nazi doctors," Jack finished. He tried to remember where he had heard of the Nu River.

"They may've been big dudes," Mick objected. "But we kicked their giant asses in the cavern caldera under this very mountain."

"Well, sort of," Jack agreed. "But if I remember right, we had to fight our way outta the caverns. Run like hell for our lives. It was touch and go for a while."

"So, Dickey," Billy asked, "how come you're goin' back to Shangri-La after we busted our asses getting' you outta there last year?"

Dickey grinned. "Simple. I miss Wantonal. We'd fooled around a bit— a lot, actually. Didn't realize I rather loved her until I left. And tops o' that, I didn't fit in too well in fast-paced UK after twenty-five years in Shangri-
La. Too, too fast for me: musical groups called Rancid, Primal Scream, Outkast—I was the outcast. No Sound of Music. So when SAS offered me a chance to return, investigate the training camp, I jumped."

"Wait a minute," Zhang said. "Twenty-five years? You said you were in the SAS when you came here. Something doesn't add up. You're too young." She sat up, appeared to listen intently.

"Righto, well, it's a secret. You age less in the valley below. Just like it says in the book, *Lost Horizon.* If you drink the tarn waters. That's why I look so bloody young. Actually, I was born in '55."

"That would make you… over fifty-five!" Zhang exclaimed.

"Righto," Dickey grinned. "Cuz the Shangrilans believe one thing— they claim that if you tipple the waters more than once, you live almost bloody forever."

"Where do we get these waters?" Zhang asked. She leaned forward.

Dickey smiled. "You'll get all you want in the valley. You'll find the locals quite friendly. You see, there's a problem in Paradise. Folk're quite infertile, inbreeding or some such rot. Have to be to keep the population down if you live a long time. I guess." He looked at Mick. "That makes the True Hunza wild for outsiders." He glanced at Zhang, added, "Except maybe for wogs. You're a new breed to them."

Zhang's green eyes blazed. She sat back, nibbled on a crust of bread, grew quiet.

Jack exclaimed, "Hey, Zhang's one of the team, now. Don't be calling her a—you know, wog."

"Er—sorry, Miss Zhang," Dickey smiled. "Old habits die hard. No harm intended."

"We need rest, Jack," Mick broke into the awkward silence. "Dickey and Zhang are draggin' ass."

"So'm I," Jack said. "It's hard to work on aerobic stamina in the slam. We'll spend the night here but we'll need to stand guard. Whoever tossed those ice chunks at us might still be around. I saw two guys about a half hour ago. To the north. Didn't look friendly. I'll take first watch." He regarded the exhausted team, sprawled along the walls. "No need to travel in the night. We're on the western slope, so we should be out of the avalanche zone by the time the sun comes over the ridge—as long as we avoid danger zones."

Chapter 23

Jack fought sleepiness during his second watch, from 0300 to 0600. At 0510, he thought he saw movement as he gazed at the most distant temple structure, a small stone hut. It was barely visible in the dark, as clouds had blocked the starlight.

His heart went into overdrive and he stood still, holding his breath. A slight wind pushed whispering snow over the drifts, but there were no other sounds, just his breathing and the pounding in his ears.

A footfall behind him, he whirled: it was Mick.

"Hey," the short Army officer quietly called. "Didn't mean to startle you. Get some rest."

"Not you," Jack responded. "I thought I saw something. You wait here, I'm gonna check it out."

Mick illuminated his watch. "It'll be light in a few minutes. Wait."

"My night vision's good." Jack turned, pulled the pistol out of his parka pocket. He walked into the fading darkness, paused to sharpen his night vision, listened to the whistling wind. After a moment, he moved across wind-packed snow until he reached a small ridge that led to a steep western slope. Above it, the eastern sky was turning to a pale whitish-blue, signaling the approaching sunrise. He looked down at the valley to the west: all darkness.

Seeing nothing unusual, he turned, headed back towards the temple complex. Out of the corner of his eye, he saw movement, started to spin around.

One of the boulders rose, turned into a giant figure, knocked the gun out of his hand with a numbing blow, grabbed him; Jack tried to pull away, the big man was overpowering, lifted him easily and marched toward the western slopes. Jack struggled mightily, but was unable to break the giant's grip. Heart hammering in his ears drowned out the wind. He yelled, the giant stopped and threw him down the sixty degree slope.

With a last grab, Jack desperately clutched the man's coat, hung on with his climber-strengthened fingers.

There was a distinct traveling crack that Jack recognized instantly: avalanche!

He and his attacker began to slide, then were sucked under and tumbled by the accelerating mass of snow. Trying to swim to the top of the massive wave, Jack felt his assailant grab him, twist him down, use him like a surfboard. He felt the man's knees pressing on his midsection. He tried to twist away but the giant held him by his arms, kept him under, used him like a sled. He tried to breath, his mouth filled with snow—he couldn't get air.

The leading edge of the roaring avalanche crested and broke like a giant wave, the two tumbled end over end, still locked in an intimate embrace as each clutched, desperate with terror, to the other.

Jack could not tell what was up and what was down, but suddenly he felt like he was dropping through the air instead of being tumbled by the onrushing snow.

A slamming, crashing jolt—movement slammed to a halt: the roar of the avalanche continued but he and the other, now under him, had crashed into a nook that was out of the assaulting avalanche.

His senses slowly reorganized and he realized that he was surrounded in complete silence: the avalanche had moved on to lower parts of the range. He was alive. The giant was under him, unmoving.

He prepared to fight for his life, but as he twisted out of the other's grasp, he felt no resistance. The man was still unconscious or hopefully dying if not dead.

He had expected to be locked in the concrete-like grip of packed avalanche snow, but when he was able to move, he felt around and realized the two had

He pushed himself to his feet, looked around his refuge. A glimmer of light towards the interior of the cavern.

He felt for his pistol, realized it had been lost in the tumbling descent. Dug freezing snow out of his collar area and his wrists. Pulled out his combat knife, stumbled towards the light.

A giant hand banged into his knee, seized his ankle, jerked.

Jack fell on his back: was dragged, kicking, yelling. The giant seized his hair, pulled him around. Jack swung, kicked again with his free foot. Knife dropped, gone!

The giant wrapped his massive arms around Jack's middle, lifted him, began pounding him against the floor like a bag of stuck-together ice. He tried to pry an arm away—useless. Slamming blows. Hard, impossible to breath; he thrust his hand around every time he hit the rock floor, found the knife! Slashed, the blade skidded off something that turned the blade.

In the complete blackness, his gasps for air mingling with the giant's explosive wheezes, he felt the other's body with his other hand. Ignored the pain, the inability to breath, the gathering blackness, he stabbed past his stomach, felt the knife penetrate a parka, sink all the way to the hilt.

The giant screamed, an agonizing cry that deafened Jack. He pulled the knife back, thrust upward. A hot gush seeped between his glove and parka sleeve, flowed up his forearm. The giant started to lift him, weakened, failed. Jack slumped into the giant's now soft embrace, relaxed, faded into semi-unconsciousness. He awoke, was lying stretched out, feet together, hands at his sides. He felt no cold—the P2 safety suit was still working its warmth magic. A flickering light. Throat dry—he fumbled in a thigh pocket for a water bottle, found nothing: it had fallen out in the nightmare trip down the mountain. He glanced around, saw a near-naked man seated on a white limestone platform —familiar: guy looked like the same monk he had encountered a year ago in the Dragon temple. Still apparently frozen in place. Shaved head—but with a new, dangling pony tail on the back of his head; muscular body, shiny yellowish skin in the light of a flickering oil lantern. Impossible to determine his age: looked adult but no wrinkles. Could be forty, could be seventy years old. Black eyes, unnoticing, unreadable.

The monk looked up, said in a high, monotone voice. "*Kshatriya*—you have returned as expected. You are now a full member of the warrior caste. You have achieved your dharma—fulfilled your duty to fight your opponents. You make the earth a lake of blood, an icy grave for many. You used the *Dragon Athane*—the sword you carry—well."

Still in shock, Jack responded, "Yeah, that's me, K-shit—er, past tense, I guess. How's it goin'? I see you're still chillin'." Jack patted, then looked at the bare rock floor he was lying on. "You're still a little light on the interior decorations. Say, I know someone who could do a makeover. Maybe a sofa, a recliner, Tiffany lamp or two?"

The monk ignored or did not understand his weak attempt at humor.

"You can now overcome your mental pain. We will teach you more of *The Way* very soon." Jack glanced around. He was in a cave of some kind, rock walls illuminated by the oil lamp at the monk's feet. Shadows made the guy's face spooky, like a flashlight under the jaw at summer camp. "Got any Kentucky Fried Chicken around here? I'd like to jump in the hot fryer.
A drink of water, at least?"

The monk did not smile, did not respond. His black eyes were unreadable. He pointed at a pitcher on a low table against the cave wall, then said, "Now you must go to Chomolungma to be examined."

"What the hell're you prattling about?" Jack demanded. "You guys have been on me like flies on—well what do you want? And ain't you guys a little mixed up? You act like Buddhists but preach like Hindus."

The monk looked up. "Buddha was the ninth *avatar* in the Hindu religion. You may be the tenth—or you may foreshadow the coming of the avatar, Kalki."

Jack looked over his shoulder—the walls of the cavern were rock and ice. No decorations, nothing resembling a temple. "Java like tar?" "No, avatar," the monk corrected.

"Oh yeah, I saw the movie. An' I'd love to go to Mount Everest, but I'm on a mission. How do I get out of here? Where's the big dude?"

"You killed him. He was removed, returned to a place where his kind could care for the remains. Thank you. You did well a cycle ago. You destroyed the demon egg in Dragon God's lower realms and removed most of the pestilent giant Chinese invaders." The monk made a dismissive gesture with one hand, continued, "Unfortunately, as you just discovered, there are still a few in the caverns below. And KEGYA remains an irritant."

"KEGYA," Jack said, "Sounds familiar."

"Our bitter enemies. You'll know more of them as events progress."

Jack suppressed an urge to urinate, asked, "So what's the deal on Kalki?"

The monk responded, his voice lilting in a quasi-chant. "*Lord Kalki*, the Lord of the Universe, will mount His swift horse *Devadatta* and, Dragon God sword in hand, travel over the earth. He will kill those Age of Kali thieves who have dared dress as kings."

"Why not just call 911? I'd rather go for a swift horse ride in New York's Central Park," Jack said. "Killing thieves doesn't sound much like fun. Do that and new thieves pop up. What's the point?"

"*Kalki* will free us from the shackles of the evil *Age of Kali*. After all the imposter kings have been killed, the residents of the world will become transcendentally pure and human society will bring forth progeny in the mode of goodness."

Jack smiled hopefully. "Goodness is… er, good, but more importantly, how do I get out of here?"

The monk pulled out of his quasi-trance, pounded his thigh with a clenched fist. It was the first time Jack had seen him move in their two meetings. "Our entry's totally blocked by your avalanche."

Jack felt for his radio transmitter, it was in his parka pocket. "I have an avalanche beacon. My friends'll find me."

The monk stared into his eyes with a flat gaze. His black eyes revealed no emotion, reflected no light. "You have capped our entry and path with a hundred foot lid of avalanche-packed snow. On a fifty degree slope. Your friends tried, gave up and moved down the slopes."

"Doesn't sound good," Jack responded. "Don't suppose you have a bulldozer or backhoe? An elevator? No, I guess you wouldn't—as I remember, you guys aren't into *things*. So how do I get outta here? I need to reach Haartgard."

"Yes, you must go down to the valley. But it won't be easy. To go through the interior is to deal with the Big Ones—fire and ice, as well."

Jack felt a sinking feeling. "You mean like my old buddy, Mo Poo. Just as soon not."

The monk faintly smiled. "I can understand your reluctance. Our order avoids him and his whenever possible."

"I guess so, they prob'ly look on you guys as tiny little appetizers. So how do I get past them?"

The monk stared, did not look encouraging. "Can you endure pain?" "Hell, no!" Jack exclaimed.

The monk rose. He wore only a loincloth and flimsy leather sandals. "Can you swim?"

"Hey. I took YMCA swim classes. Swam across the west thumb of Yellowstone Lake from Pumice Point back home in Montana. When I was a kid."

"Then come with me. And pray to Vishnu and your Christian god for deliverance from the Big Ones." He picked up the lamp, turned and walked into the three-meter-high by about a meter-wide chamber entrance. Jack pulled a small flashlight out of a cargo pocket, aimed it at the cave floor. The air grew warmer on his face as they descended at a slight angle, Jack pushed off his hood, unzipped his parka. The aches and pains from his tumble down the mountain started to attack his upper body. It felt like he had wrenched his back, the pain increased as minutes passed.

An hour's hurried walk on downward leading steps, lit by guttering oil lamps that hung from the walls of the cavern chamber. About every hundred meters they passed an alcove in which sat a meditating monk.

His guide passed a branching opening and paused at an iron-bound door about six feet high and four feet wide, made of thick wood planks. A heavy iron crossbar secured it. The monk turned and appraised the American. "Beyond this lies the *Big Ones* realm, are you sure you want to take this path? Remember the bridge you crossed last year? Over the river you called Styx? The big ones have blocked off our trail, and guard it, ever since your battle last year. We will have to enter the water, float under the bridge, climb to the road on the other side. The glacier-melt water will be cold at first."

Jack looked over his shoulder, back at the near-naked monk. "Or stay down in this icebox and work on my cave tan like you're doin'? I guess I'll forge ahead. I need to get to Haartgard."

"There's more. They have caught on to our drifting past their barriers. They fling oil in our paths, then light it."

Jack stopped. "Tunnel of burnin' love, huh? So, I get to chill and fry at the same time? I can't wait. Still no elevator? Guess not."

The monk said nothing, lifted the weighty-looking iron crossbar out of its cradle, grunting with the effort, pushed it aside, pulled the massive door open.

Beyond, the cave remained unchanged, the door looked like it had been added as an afterthought. But the sound of rushing water came out of the darkness.

"The river you call Styx, the River of Death." the monk said. "We call it *Kalki's Wash.*"

"Not me," Jack said. "It was Robert Arses who named it last year, when we were trying to get to Shangri-La, to rescue his brother, Dickey." The two rounded a curving corner, a dim light from somewhere far above cast a faint glow that illuminated a river about twenty meters wide. Small chunks of ice twinkled brightly in the light.

"The source of the underground river is melting glacial ice that comes in contact with a hot area created by rising volcanic magma. The same geological condition that causes the *Dragon's Lung* lake to be permanently heated."

"So, you guys were the ones that created the mountaintop vent that forced the faked hot air and sulfur fumes out of the dragon statue's mouth and nose," Jack suggested. "In the temple."

The monk looked over his shoulder, his teeth flashed as he smiled for the first time. He was missing a tooth in front. "Not our order, people far more ancient. Our order is only twenty-five generations from our founder."

"Whatever, dude. Why didn't you fix it when it broke?"

"Cheap theatrics created by those ancients when they were establishing their religion," the monk replied. "After the overland access trail was destroyed by earthquakes, no one visited anyway." The monk stopped. "Take off your boots, hang them around your neck. We float from here."

"Why? I like this trail. Cozy for a bat-filled cave: warm, dry. Water looks chilly."

"The Big Ones watch from the bridge. You would be killed. This way, you have a chance." The monk waded into the rushing water, stood, knee deep, waited, no expression on his face.

Reluctantly, Jack sat on the rock floor, stripped off his boots, tied the straps and hung the boots around his neck. He stepped into the water: it was frigid. His feet, not heated by the piezoelectric and Peltier threads in the suit began aching immediately.

"Hurry, we have little time before hypothermia overcomes you." The monk splashed into the water, grabbed a chunk of floating ice, and Jack followed. He paddled hard to keep his head above the water, felt that he would pass out if he submerged it.

"Don't splash," the monk cautioned.

The two swept around a bend and in the gloomy distance, Jack saw the bridge he had crossed twice the year before. It was an arching span built of cut stone with a small stone hut at the highest point. He grimaced, remembered the horrid smell of rotting human remains that he had discovered in the hut the year before. He paddled, hit a chunk of ice. The blow snapped him back to reality: his feet were numb, fingers ached like they had been smashed with a hammer. He looked up, the bridge was overhead—no one was visible; the monk was angling towards the opposite shore. Jack dog-paddled frantically, and caught up to the monk just as he lifted himself onto a ledge a half meter above the water.

The monk leaned over, grabbed Jack under the armpits, helped him scramble onto the rock surface, where he sprawled on his side.

"Hurry, we need to run," the monk said as he pushed Jack's boots onto his feet, laced them up.

"Can't feel my feet," Jack complained. "Got a blanket? Arggh— preferably electric?"

"You won't feel anything if you don't rise. Let us go to Shangri-La. We are past the lookout. Hurry!" The monk pulled Jack to his feet and partially supported him as they moved up a narrow trail cut out of the rock cliff that hung over the water. Moving up the trail, each step felt like it was a stop-action shot in a movie scene, overridden by his panting breaths. Minutes later, Jack's feet began to respond and he was able to quicken his pace from a shuffle to a stumbling jog along the path to Shangri-La.

Chapter 24

During the entire day's descent, after the avalanche and a failed search for their leader, Chopstick Mick watched upslope, over his shoulder: he saw a tall figure, obviously not Jack, as the man wore dark clothes, dogging their trail at noon. He spotted two more figures at mid-afternoon. Whoever it was did not come close, did not threaten the shrunken team.

They had started a rescue descent to the avalanche scene but had given up after they realized there was no possible way to explore or penetrate the avalanche area without more skilled climbers. Zhang and Dickey were not up to the task, and after a short-lived attempt, they all had reluctantly given up. Nevertheless, they had to drag Billy away from the scene.

Numb with shock at the loss of their leader, Mick carefully, timidly, led the team through two major crevasse fields, on a long traverse through soft snow up to their knees, around obvious avalanche threats, down a narrow, icy, scree-filled ravine. He had never been a team leader on a mountain, and his fears were constantly aroused by distant booming avalanches as the day progressed.

Finally, at eighteen hundred hours, they dropped completely below the snowline, hit a road two miles south of the ancient fortress Haartgard. After an exhausting hour's hike over the pounded-hard cobblestone road, just after dark they reached the outlines of a village of shattered buildings.

Disappointed that they could not see and appreciate the impressive thirty-foot-high battlements of the gloomy old stone structure from a distance—it was almost a hundred meters long from end to end as it nestled against perpendicular granite cliffs—Dickey forged ahead of the others. Shocked by the devastation, he inspected the destroyed village as they passed through it. The avalanche Jack and his brother Billy had set off the year before on the mountaintops high above must have crushed the entire hamlet: only a few walls remained standing, but signs of new construction stood out.

"What in the world happened here?" Zhang asked. "It looks like a war zone."

"Don't look at me!" Billy exclaimed. "It was Jack's idea. When we came outta the cavern that led to this joint, a buncha ragheads were about to overrun the fort. Jack figgered an avalanche would stop the attack."

Dickey adjusted his top hat, added, "We all pulled back, inside the mountain caverns, then Jack sent half the mountain done on us. He intended to smash the village, crush the roof of Haartgard. Amazing, really, but it looks like it worked. Killed all the bloody attacking ragheads. Musta been an extraordinary lot of raggedy, dick-headed popsicles in the Spring."

Laughter at Dickey's gallows humor died away as the feeling of ghostly presences seeped through the group; the four drew near the gates, an unseen guard on top of the parapets challenged them.

"It's me, Dickey Arses. Open the bloody gates!" the Englishman yelled.

After shouted commands, the double gates swung open and the Officer of the Watch, a muscular young blond man hallowed, then embraced Dickey.

Not bothering to introduce the others, Dickey eagerly swept across the fifty-foot wide, flagstone-covered courtyard, arm in arm with his friend. The others followed him through twelve-foot-high double wood doors into a reception hall and eating area with a high ceiling. Ancient, faded tapestries hung against the walls, high up near the ceilings.

Two young blonde girls were directing three cloaked maids in the clearing and clean-up of a long wooden plank dining table. Mick recognized the twins, no more than sixteen, who had seduced him on his first visit.

"Mick!" they squealed and ran to hug him. "Come see who's here."

Remembering what Dickey had said about the valley inhabitants enthusiasm for outsiders, Mick introduced the twins to Zhang. The bubbly, braided girls led the team to the kitchen, where they all spotted a man seated, back to them, eating.

"Jack!" Billy shouted.

Astonished, the others clustered around their leader, shouting questions in a relieved burst of happiness and enthusiasm. He stood and the entire team hugged and slapped him.

Wincing, he exclaimed, "Easy, guys, I'm pretty beat up from my shortcut down the mountain."

Dickey asked the cook, a Muslim woman, to dish up a meal while they listened to Jack tell how he had survived the avalanche by a whisker, and had just arrived after coming through the caverns they had used the year before, that ended in the castle, Haartgard.

The Muslim woman, wearing a black, ankle-length dress and a white hijab or scarf on her head, returned several times with large bowls containing mounds of chicken, boiled potatoes, lamb chowder, and a large loaf of crusty black bread.

"Too bad the Middle Eastern Jews and Muslims can't take a page from these folks," Mick observed.

"After last year's battle, the women of the two tribes parleyed, agreed to end hostilities," a young woman's strong, British-accented voice came from the doorway to the kitchen. "The fact that most of the muj men were dead, helped." All turned. The Americans and Billy recognized the Princess, Penelope Kong.

She was dressed in tight black silk pants half-covered by knee-length, polished black leather boots, she wore a tight grey woolen sweater that barely concealed the curve of her breasts, a finely embroidered red and white vest. Long blonde, wavy hair cascaded over her wide shoulders, and Penel's spectacular face was accented and softened by a spray of freckles across her nose and under her smoky eyelashes.

Dickey smiled, hugged his Shangrilan friend.

Jack also stood, embraced the beautiful girl, then laughed and kissed her. "Babe, I've been thinkin' about you ever since I crossed under the peaks." *Rosy-skinned, velvety, sweet.*

Penel pulled away, frowning, "Not before that?"

"All the time, babe," he assured her, then kissed her again; she drew away again. He was staggered by her beauty.

"Thou hath taken thy time returning," Penel's voice had a testy inflection. Jack and Billy exchanged a glance. Billy, a sympathetic smile on his face, hugged Zhang, who also looked cross.

"I had a little problem after I left here," Jack picked up a drumstick, brandished it. "I'll tell you about it."

Penel fixed a cold stare on Jack. "Wantonal died in the avalanche. My sister is dead."

Shocked by her words, Jack exclaimed, "I'm so sorry."

"What'n bloody hell happened?" Dickey demanded, an astonished look on his face.

Penel frowned, rubbed her brow, looked at Jack. "We all retreated into the caverns as thou instructed. After Dickey and your Hunza warriors left, Wantonal realized our dear aunt Ing, a very old lady, was missing. She went back to the fortress to assist her—thy avalanche caused the roof to collapse the front section of Haartgard. They were both buried."

Jack felt a flush of horror, shame, and dismay course through his battered body.

Mouth agape, Dickey Arses yelled, "Wantonal's dead?"

"Yes. Dead, mourned, buried." Penel gazed at Dickey for a long moment. "She was already dead when thou left us and departed for thy outside world."

Penel looked at the others, then commanded, "Jack, come with me." She led him upstairs to her apartment. The two-room suite was spacious, clean, with bright colors and elaborately-carved furniture.

The living room fireplace was constructed of handcrafted brown bricks, and faced with sparkling white quartz. A plush, red Afghan rug covered the floor in front of the fireplace. A large window, with handcarved mullions, revealed a scene over the outside fortress walls: showed a wonderful view of early stars over the western mountains across the valley. Far below, terraced fields crept up the valley floor to the base of the darkening mountains.

Still rocked by Penel's revelation about her sister's death, he leaned against the fireplace, watched the queen of the True Hunza, but his thoughts were of Wantonal. The first time he had seen the now-dead girl, she was standing next to the tarn pool below the waterfall, wearing only her leather pants: *she had murmured a husky hello, dried him with a large wool shawl when he waded out of the bubbling hot springs. She accidentally— playfully?—brushed her full, bare breasts against his chest when she raised her hands and toweled his hair. He had inhaled a hint of saffron, fought an urge to embrace her. Still nervous, he had restrained himself until she looked into his eyes with an inviting smile. Her beautiful look, her hand, slowly stroking his hip with the shawl.*

Crossing the room, Penel put her arms around Jack, kissed him ardently, drew back. "The coldness thou shewest in our last meet, thank God, is missing. Thou're as changeable as the seasons. In our first encounter, you were passionate beyond belief. In the second, you were as cold as the snowmelt waters of Falls Everlasting. You said thou wert in love with another."

"Yeah, well, 'the another' is history. Anyway, I've got presents for you," Jack responded. He noticed her speech patterns were evolving: the year before she had exclusively used thees and thous. "I picked them up in Singapore." He reached in his huge backpack that Billy had carried down the mountain, pulled out two gift-wrapped packages.

Delighted, Penel sat on an intricately handcarved, straight-back chair, and pulled the first wrapping away. Inside was a delicate gold crown.

Jack placed it on her abundant blonde mane. "You're a queen. After your dad died in the attack. I figured you could use a crown."

The second box contained a delicate gold chain with a one-carat diamond hanging from it.

"Beautiful!" Penel exclaimed. Jack crossed the room, his boots echoing off the wood floor, and fastened the necklace around her throat. He leaned and kissed the back of her neck.

"You're favored with a royal welcome," Penel exclaimed. She kissed Jack. After a breathless moment, she led him into the bedroom. A blue silk bedspread covered a down comforter on the double bed. She stood straight, next to the bed. Pulled the covers aside.

Jack hurriedly undressed her. Her rose-petal skin, like no other woman in the world. Smooth, velvet. Smelling like honey. Lips like in the song— sweeter than wine.

"Leave the crown on, I've always wanted to—" "Seduce a queen?" she whispered.

Chapter 25

"The American is coming!" Drug dealer Rama Razi's words shocked Mara Bhutto. She lowered the satellite phone for a second, looked around the lit-up cavern entrance in the Shangrilan mountains southwest of Kashgar. The lights were powered by a solar PV system packed in from the Chinese city by camel. She put the cell back to her ear. The American could only mean Jack Flashhardt, the Marine she had fallen in love with, tried repeatedly to kill, had finally defended in the white man's battle with Mo Poo, the giant Chinaman. The cell's reception was broken, she moved outside.

The cell regained its signal and she heard, "My pilot, Charlie Davis, delivered him, his brother, and a Chinese *SD* agent. To Islamabad. Four days ago!" the fat Palestinian screamed with fright.

"Nice of you to be so accommodating," Mara said with a sarcastic tone.

"I knew nothing! The pilot knew them as friends last year," Rama squealed.

"Calm down. Why didn't you tell me sooner?" Mara asked the drug smuggler, her financial backer.

"I've been trying to reach you. If only you'd finished him off last year," Rama wailed. "He knows Davis. He's too close. I have to act now.
I'll have the pilot eliminated at once."

Mara considered whether Rama was vulnerable to Jack Flashhardt, rejected the idea. "Don't worry, Jack's not concerned with drugs."

Rama Razi's home base was Chanbahar in Baluchistan, a province of southeastern Iran. "He won't go to Baluchistan. No doubt, he's coming to me. In the Hindu Kush. Somehow, he's learned of my plans." Mara felt a tremor of fear. She had failed in every attempt to kill Jack Flashhardt in the previous year, despite her prowess as China's most able assassin.

"But I'm helpless!" Rama wailed.

Bronze-skinned Mara, tall and slim, squeezed her green eyes shut, thought of her seven-hundred-pound partner. Rama Razi was right—the hugely fat man, dubbed Jabba the Hut in American drug enforcement circles, would be helpless in any attack on his home base. He couldn't even get out of bed. His guards would probably run away. She ran her fingers through her chopped short hair, wished she could apply lipstick to her lush lips. "Don't kill the pilot. He's a good source of information on Flashhardt." *Jack and his country, America,* she thought. *Both will pay for daddy's magical floating act on the hangman's scaffold. Hugely. Jack Flashhardt—I hate you!*

Chapter 26

Just before 0200 hours, Chopstick Mick Nakamura and Jack Flashhardt crawled over a rocky crest, a hundred meters above the Muslim village at the north end of the valley.

"One dumbass guard is prone, catching rack time!" Mick stared at the image on his laptop. Moments earlier, he had launched a *Wasp*, an unmanned miniature aircraft. With a twelve-inch wingspan, the silent aircraft carried a day camera and an infrared camera for night vision capabilities. He glanced at Jack, who was yawning. "Hey," he complained.
"Wake up! You shouldna been bangin' your babe all night and all day."

"It's late, I'm tired, it's the altitude. I'm cold—my love life's not the problem." Jack grasped Mick's elbow, pointed at the image of a sitting guard, barely visible behind a granite boulder. Beside him, the second guard was curled in a fetal position, not moving. "Anyway, let's go inside. *Audaces fortuna juvat:* Fortune favors the bold."

Mick, ever eager for battle and mayhem, hummed in delightful agreement, then added, "Do the guard."

Jack pulled Penel's bow off his back, notched an arrow. "I'm glad I brought this."

"The second guy will wake up," Mick protested. "And if you miss…"

"I practiced yesterday," Jack responded with a confident air. "This is where Chief Talking Dog's lessons'll pay off. From when I was a kid back on the ranch."

Mick reflected on his partner's words as Jack pulled the bowstring back. He had been astounded when after a few close misses, Jack had repeatedly hit quarter-sized coins at a range of thirty meters.

The string twanged, the arrow flew across the expanse, shot into the guard's mouth as he completed a yawn—his last.

The arrow sunk into the man's spine, just below his skull, paralyzing and silencing him immediately and forever. The other guard did not stir.

"Holy shit!" Mick whispered.

The pals rose and crawled around a mass of boulders, dropped down a shoulder-width, snow-filled ravine, crept past the dead guard.

"Kill him?" Mick whispered as he nodded at the sleeping man.

"Yeah, better," Jack whispered back.

Mick pulled his leg back, kicked the man on the side of the head with a soccer-style kick. He hauled the unconscious man behind a boulder, pulled a combat knife and slit the guy's throat. Jack turned away at the sight of spurting blood that splattered off the rocky ground. *Welcome back to mayhem, Jack*, he thought. *Will I ever get used to this crap?*

Inside, their M-9s drawn, they moved along a twisting, dimly-lit corridor, obviously designed to prevent a missile penetration. A faint hint of sulphur in the air. They moved past two roughly-clad soldiers sleeping under a makeshift electric light hanging by a cord on the cavern wall; one was lying against each side of the ten-foot-wide corridor.

"Kill them?" Mick whispered hopefully.

"No, someone might find them," Jack whispered. He flushed an image of spurting blood.

Mick drew his knife, looked at the sleeping men, whispered, "Who cares?"

"Guys're sleeping. Not gonna wage destruction on us."

"Their loss," Mick whispered. He knocked the one man's head towel off, grabbed his long hair, slashed his throat. The man glared, horrified: tried to scream, gurgles came out. He bounced, died.

Mick turned to the second guard. His sleeping companion's kicking thumps had roused him. He sat up, stared at Mick's Asian face with sleepconfused eyes. Mick clamped a hand over the man's mouth, slammed the knife into his heart. The guy's eyes flew open, bulged. His body trembled for long seconds, stilled. Mick pulled the first body behind a row of barrels while Jack nervously kept watch. Mick dumped it, returned to the second, threw the body on the first, took a business card out of his hip pocket and sailed it onto the dead man's chest.

Jack removed the head scarves from the bodies, threw one to Mick, wrapped the other on his head. It smelled rank, felt greasy to his touch, gave him the creeps. He could imagine Ashley, his old girlfriend, saying "Ee-yu, kudies!" He picked up rags from a pile and tossed them on the blood patches in front of the boxes.

Continuing silently forward, the two emerged in a huge cavern with high rock ceilings. The two removed their goggles in the faint light cast by far-off standing arc lamps. A growling generator powered the lights. They crept around the edge of the huge room on a well-beaten path. Floodlights on long, drooping extension cords highlighted obstacle courses and firing ranges in the middle of the cavern. They heard the hum of another generator in the murky distance.

A hacked-out hallway, about six feet by six feet, branched to the right. The two turned into its dim interior, passed several wood plank doors, each with a wood bar holding it closed. A moment later they encountered carvedout steps leading downward. Descending a few steps, they heard voices. Peering around the corner, Jack saw an unbelievable sight: Mo Poo, the giant Chinaman, and Mara Bhutto, the bronze-skinned female terrorist, sitting on boxes on the cavern floor. The almost eight-foot-tall Mo Poo towered over Mara, the Pakistani-Chinese double agent.

Jack pulled back, his heart pounding: he thought of the numerous confrontations with Mo Poo and Mara in the Hindu Kush last year—the imprisonment, the escape… for a second he was thrown into the still vivid memories of the year-ago battles: *he swung around, saw the giant man standing in the middle of the mountain pass, barely visible in the mist. Jack's heart, already pounding in his ears from the hike into the mountain pass, accelerated when he recognized the ugly giant with the distinctive peaked cap. "You killed my dot-ter," Mo Poo rumbled. A voice deep enough to cause avalanches.*

"—Americans already in the valley," Jack refocused on the present, heard Mo Poo's voice snarl in real-time.

Mara answered, "How d'you know?"

They're pals again! Talkin' about me.

The giant: "As Sun Pin, the great-grandson of the philosopher, Sun Tzu, said: *'One who does not use spies will not be victorious.'* One of mine own saw a group come over the high ridges from Pakistani borders.

"How many?"

"My man tried to stop them, failed. He fetched me, I saw them travel on the heights, towards Shangri-La. Down the slopes came HIS native mongrel brother and the fat Jappo; a female of China, and the British spy, formerly of Shangri-La."

"No troops? And why did Jack come out of the caverns separately, as my woman reported." Mara asked. "He expects to take the bio pile from you with a handful of men?"

Jack stifled a gasp when he heard Mara casually reveal the LIIT payload was in Mo Poo's hands. He thought back to last year when he had seen the bomb in the cavern far below the Dragon God's temple: *he glanced at the slender GBU-200 biobomb. The bomb's rear access panel was dismantled. The bio payload had been removed!*

Mo Poo's rumbling voice disrupted his thoughts. "I sent one of mine to discourage him and his invaders—no, not invaders—probably just a reconnaissance team. My man killed one of their team—a female. Later, he crept close to their encampment at the Dragon God's temple, to discover their intent. There was an avalanche: he and Flashhardt disappeared. Dead, I thought."

"Dead!" Mara exclaimed. "You said—"

"But his friends reached the valley floor separately in cur-sed Haartgard."

Listening to Mo Poo describe his near-death gave Jack the creeps. Mick nudged him and restrained a giggle.

Jack spotted a ladder to a ledge. He touched Mick's arm, pointed. He and Mick climbed the short ladder to a carved-out shelf, where boxed supplies were stored.

While Jack settled down behind the boxes to listen again, he envisioned the ugly underground volcanic caldera where he had destroyed the bomb—minus its payload—with Dickey Arses' nitroglycerin.

Mara's voice interrupted his thoughts: "If the Americans just now came into the valley, it will be days before they attack. We'll have time to get away."

"Get away?" Mo Poo's voice rumbled. "Never! We must smash, crush the white vermin!" Jack recalled the giant man had sworn he hated all white men for what the German Nazi scientists had done to him and his kind during the Chinese government's attempts to breed giant soldiers.

Mara responded with a sorrowful tone, "I fought Jack more than twice. I was defeated every time. Easily. He's a clever, evil devil."

"Your force outnumbered him by five to one in Herotmere," Mo Poo snarled. "Yet he smashed you."

"You giants outnumbered him by the same factor," Mara responded. "Still, he and his friends easily fought through your force, escaped the caverns."

"He is *too* smart a devil," Mo Poo agreed. "But now we must set up a defense. You will need time to prepare for the America attacks. I—"

Jack heard approaching footsteps, whispered, "Let's get outta here before all their praise causes my head to swell an' stick in the tunnel."

"No, let's see what they're planning, where the biobomb is," Mick whispered. A clattering sound interrupted them.

The giant Chinaman and Mara Bhutto paused, looked up towards the Americans' hiding place.

"Careful!" Jack cautioned in a whisper.

"Not me," Mick whispered back. "Must be a rat."

They saw Mara Bhutto come up the steps towards the ladder; they drew back, into the darker shadows.

Mick raised his pistol. Alarmed, Jack put a hand over the weapon. "Wait, someone's coming."

A muj wearing a long black shirt hanging over ragged brown pants walked past, Mara turned, retreated down the steps as the muj uttered a greeting.

"Let's get outta here," Jack whispered again.

Mick responded, "Should we finish these two? This is a great chance."

Jack thought about shooting Mara, fighting their way out of the cavern. Couldn't do it. "We need backup," he murmured back. "We'll stop 'em later. We'll blow them and their mujahideen pricks home to their 72 virgins.

After we find out where the bio stuff is."

The two crawled down, ran up the steps, along the corridor. They emerged into the large cavern, a man across the way shouted something, Jack yelled back, "Allah Akbar!" The man screamed the same chant, turned away.

The two continued across the main cavern, entered the hall to the outside, approached the lit-up area where Mick had hidden the two bodies. No one was about, so they hurried on to the entrance, peered outside. The dead entry guards had not been discovered. Jack illuminated his watch—it was 0500 hours. Grinning he slapped Mick on the shoulder.

The two ran, bouncing from boulder to boulder in the dawning light, laughing at their success. Jack sobered when he remembered the LIIT payload was still out there. Again, he realized, everything he had done the year before had been for nothing. *I went to prison, sat in the sump, lost my girlfriend, lost my commission in the Marines, almost got killed—for what?*

Chapter 27

Sitting at and standing around the pine wood breakfast table in Fortress Haartgard's huge kitchen, Jack's team made way for a newcomer. It was Xander Kong, Penel's brother, a young man of about nineteen years, tall, very skinny, with red hair, a massive amount of freckles and a huge Adam's apple under a receding chin. He looked like the picture of his father hanging in the Reception Hall.

The smell of cooking bread mingled in the air with other fragrant breakfast odors. The room was lit by fat guttering candles mounted in brass holders screwed into the wall. Copper and iron pots hung on the walls, light brown wicker baskets were piled in a corner.

Jack said, "After checking out the enemy's terrain, I've got a pretty good idea what I want to do."

"And that is?" Dickey asked.

Jack looked around the table, exchanged glances with Billy, Zhang, Mick, and Dickey. "We can't call in an airstrike, and the way the tunnels are set up—"

"Cruise missiles wouldn't penetrate," Mick interjected.

"Right. Cave is way too big," Jack agreed.

"So it's up to us," Billy said. "Great!" he added with a moan.

Regarding his brother with a grin, Jack offered, "Hey, this's what we're here for: ragheads up to no good. When Chopstick and I were in the cave, we heard Mara and the big dude—yeah, our old pals, Mara and Mo Poo are here—mention an attack on America. Check this out: the LIIT bio stuff—it's still kicking around. The Chinese dude's got it." The others stared at him in disbelief.

"I went through all that crap last year for nothin'?" Billy exclaimed.

"When I put the explosives on the bomb, I noticed the warhead compartment had been opened. Because I was scared of anthrax, I didn't hang around to check it out." He looked around. The others had various expressions on their faces of dismay, surprise, boredom. "So we're gonna take out the mujahideen force guarding the training camp. Then we'll destroy the giant Chinamen's base camp inside the cavern."

"Not just the long drink of water, it looked like at least fifty men in the encampment," Mick said.

"No shit!" Billy exclaimed. He tried to hide a half-smile.

"Yeah, I'd call it a target-rich environment," Jack responded. "We're gonna get some!"

He spread a large satellite photo Mick had brought, across the table. Weighted down each corner with a salt shaker, a dish of butter and a mug of black tea. First, he pointed out the northern end of the valley, then the buildings in a village just to the south of the cavern entrance.

"They'll be ready for us—throw up a defense. I figure they'll have a security perimeter," Jack stabbed the photo map, "right here on the outskirts of the vil."

"House to house fighting—I love it!" Mick exclaimed.

"We don't have a big enough force," Jack speculated. "Penel will only give us men, led by Xander here, if they volunteer. She won't force anyone to fight for us." He looked at Mick. "I've got about five hundred thousand Pak rupees."

"We have no use for thy outside world monies," Xander waved an arm in dismissal, rejecting the offer.

"We'll give you our extra weapons and ammo after the battle," Mick offered.

Red-headed Xander grinned, pumped an arm. "Now thou talkest. Done!" he eagerly exclaimed. "But what is that strange weapon? What does it?" he pointed at the boxy rifle Jack had placed on the table.

"The OCIW," Jack answered. "It's a 20 millimeter weapon. Each shell has a mini-computer in it—like a brain. The sighting video camera's laser determines the range to… say, a boulder. The computer in the shell explodes it just above and past the boulder."

"Thy words are beyond my ken," Xander responded.

Mick added, "It's still experimental, we can't give it up, anyway. But we can give you a dozen M-21 rifles, some pistols. We'll school you on the SAW."

"I have ten friends I can convince to go," Xander exclaimed with an eager tone.

"Not enough, Flashy," Billy opined.

Jack nodded his head. "Right… but General Farley promised cruise missiles. They might penetrate the wind currents—make it easy for us— aww, I doubt it. Xander, just tell your guys what Gunny Dan Daly told his troops at Belleau Wood."

"What was that?" Chopstick Mick interrupted.

Jack smiled, sat back. "World War I. Belleau Wood, France. The Marines were pinned down in their first battle with the German Army. Gunny Daly yelled to his troops, 'Come on, you sons a bitches! D'you wanna live forever?' He jumped up and led the Fourth Brigade in a bayonet charge that overwhelmed the Krauts, took the vil of Lucy le Bocage."

"You Marines," Mick marveled. "Bragging even about stuff a hundred years ago."

"OohRah!" Billy exclaimed.

Jack added, "Well, we're short of Marines and soldiers, so prob'ly we're gonna have to snooker 'em." "How so?" Xander asked.

Jack peered at the photo map, scratched his head. "We'll set up a trap, timeless—true—but it should work on these dumbshit ragheads. We'll put an ambush team in place about here." He pointed to a line of boulders along the road to the village. "Then we'll send a small-time fake attack on their perimeter. When the defenders respond, our skirmishers will retreat like spanked scaredy cats. Probably, the mujs won't be able to resist giving chase, and when they follow into the open, we'll ambush 'em, pound 'em with the OICW. Dickey, that's you. Don't worry, it's easy to use. I'll school you. Then we'll hit 'em with the XM-199. Mick, that's you." "What's that?" Dickey asked.

Jack pulled a short, very strange-looking weapon out of a stiff polyurethane bag. "Developed by the Joint Non-Lethal Weapons Directorate in Quantico. It's a laser gun. It shoots an energy beam. When it hits the victim, it makes the water molecules in his cells boil. It produces heat far beyond the human tolerance for pain. It's impossible to stand up to it." He turned it on, aimed a light beam at the stonewall. A curl of steam from moisture in the rock—nothing else happened.

"Laser—ain't it supposed to shoot a death ray or sumpin'?" Billy asked.

"Don't think it's much, huh? Check this out—don't worry—I won't hurt you." Jack aimed the weapon at Billy's forearm, activated it. Two seconds later, Billy howled and dove for the floor. Horrified, he stared at his wrist, expecting to see a hole or burning flesh. He saw only a slight red spot on his skin.

Jack laughed, "It was developed by the Non-lethal people in Quantico. It scares the living shit out of the victim. Absolutely impossible to endure, and terrifying to encounter. Those mujs'll go running home like lightninglicked mustangs in a High Plains storm. Mick, that's your job. I figure they'll give up at that point."

"What if they don't give chase?" Dickey asked.

Grinning, Jack hacked the map with his pen. "Then it's run 'hell for leather' and back to the drawing board. If we're still breathing." "What about you, Jack?" Mick asked.

"While you guys have everybody distracted, Billy and I will take out anybody left inside. Billy and I are goin' caving. Rat-hunting."

"Ohh, man," Billy groaned, rubbing his slight wound, "I hate spelunkin'! Rats and bats and shit. Ugh!"

"Some might think you're not lookin' forward to this," Jack observed.

"I know that's bullshit!"

Billy glanced at Zhang, then the others. "Alright—you busted my chops. I'm just used to whinin'. I can't wait to kick their asses. Let's get some! OohRah!"

Mick checked his watch. "The material airdrop is scheduled in a half hour, Jack."

"Okay, let's adjourn for now," Jack responded. "Come on, Mick, let's go get our gear. Then, we'll practice our attack, tune in the locals on the modern rifles."

Outside, they crossed the flagstone-covered courtyard, mounted onto the double seat of a waiting wagon pulled by a big black Morgan horse that crapped on the courtyard to signify its start.

The driver, a boy of about twelve years, exited the wooden gates after a guard opened for them. Just outside the avalanche-destroyed village, they heard the drone of a four-engine C-130 high above the valley.

Jack gazed at the dramatic, snow-covered Hindu Kush peaks, the cloudless skies, prayed that the new parachuted Copterbox system would work. It was a specially designed paper box with a honeycomb cushion that had an altimeter release system for the chute.

"There," Mick pointed at a black speck that drifted down from ten thousand feet over the peaks. It grew larger, proved to be a large, tumbling box. A white mushroom parachute opened, arrested the supply canister, but swirling winds caught the chute and pulled it into a high canyon where it impacted on a cliff, shattered into tiny pieces, cascaded down the crags.

"Not good," Jack muttered. "That's why the cruise missiles won't work."

"Don't worry, they got a back-up drop, just in case," Mick responded. "They'll come around again. I'll call them an' tell' em to set the altimeter for a terminal phase parachute opening, like they use with the Quick-MEDS packages."

Jack looked at the dust cloud, agreed, "That'll work—shoulda done it the first time."

Fifteen minutes later, a speck appeared, materialized as a four engine C-130. The monstrous four-engine airplane dropped between the peaks surrounding the valley, dramatically bobbed and weaved in the turbulent air over the valley. The engines roared as the pilots tried to maintain altitude and bearing.

A box drifted out of the sky, grew larger as it plummeted to the surface. The cargo plane rose and veered out of sight.

This box tumbled longer, deployed its chute close to the valley floor, far towards the south end of the valley.

"Not good," the boy said.

"Let's go get it," Mick ordered.

"We can't go to that end of the valley," the boy responded. "The KEGYA—"

"Get your ass in gear, kid," Mick demanded. The boy still hesitated, so Mick grabbed the reins and urged the horse forward; an hour later, they reached the large container, sitting in a small, terraced alfalfa field, a parachute flapped in a breeze.

Mick handed the reins to the boy, who kept staring, wide-eyed, at a rocky ridge that bisected the valley floor, just a half mile to the south. He kept muttering, "The KEGYA, The KEGYA…"

Mick cut away cinched black metal bands and they loaded ammo boxes, a SAW, cases of MREs, a large first aid pac, rifles, various other supplies.

On the way back to Asgard, Jack questioned the boy about his fear of the drop point but the boy refused to answer. Jack figured the boy was worried about some religious taboo.

An hour later, they watched several young men unpack the wagon. After the unloading and storage in a room off the tan-colored flagstone courtyard, surrounded by cut stone gray walls, they repaired to the kitchen, which had become their unofficial office.

Chapter 28

A loud knocking at her door awoke Mara Bhutto. Already dressed, she rolled out of the low bunk in her spartan cell, answered the door. A young guard, his eyes wide with fright, exclaimed, "You should come at once."

Five minutes later, Mara stared at the two dead mujs, piled one on the other behind a stack of boxed supplies. Black-appearing blood lay in pools around the bodies. She saw a white card on the chest of one of the men; she bent to pick it up. In English, it stated: *Quality control effort by USARAAC.* Confused and wondering what the letters meant, Mara looked at the bottom of the card. Words across the bottom stated: For questions, call U.S. Army Raghead Attitude Adjuster Center. 1-800-URF-ucked. Suddenly understanding, Mara crumpled the card, ground her teeth, looked up at the muj, who beckoned her to follow.

At the entrance, the muj pointed to the dead sentries, piled behind a rock. One had a cut throat, the other an arrow through his mouth. She inwardly shuddered at the gruesome, blood-soaked scene. Beyond them, Mara saw the first glimmer of a cloudless dawn.

Enraged, she pulled her Chinese Tokarev 54 pistol, shot into the dead bodies, continued firing.

Her pistol empty, Mara was confused when unceasing gunshots still sounded. Suddenly, she realized the gunfire was coming from the outskirts of the village. *The Americans!* she thought. *So soon!*

She ran out of the rocks, raced towards the perimeter lines, where the local mujs were standing guard. She caught a flash from the sky, looked up and saw four cruise missiles impact and explode on far cliffs, one after another, a kilometer away. She involuntarily ducked, was elated that the missiles had gone astray.

Dashing to the perimeter, she saw that the perimeter guards were excitedly firing at retreating attackers. One, two, and then three different teams of aggressors turned and fled, screaming in fright. A muj jumped into the road. "Follow—let's kill the cowardly

144

whoresons." He turned and ran forward. All the mujs rose and followed their leader.

"No! Hold the lines," Mara yelled, but she couldn't shout her commands loud enough over the men's triumphant war cries. All pounded into the growing light, firing with no discipline, yelling and screaming as they ran. As many shot into the air with triumphant gestures as did those who shot at the fleeing attackers. *Totally forgot their training*, Mara thought.

In less than a minute, the attackers and pursuers disappeared from her sight; Mara heard continued gunfire and shouts as the dawn's light increased.

Mo Poo and two other giant Chinamen emerged from the cavern, strode stiffly, towering over Mara when they reached her. Mo Poo turned his hideously scarred face, a souvenir of Tigger's attack last year, glared down at her, his huge black eyes widely open.

An eerie silence grew, was suddenly punctured by the bloop and shattering crashes of heavier weapons. Wild gunfire broke out. Mara struggled to see what was going on—it sounded bad.

Long moments later, terrified mujs appeared, running in the open, weapons abandoned.

Machinegun fire arced through the running men from an east flank ambush in the rock piles along the road, men fell and tumbled as the red tracers cut through the air and the runners. Airbursts from a small cannon impacted above the men, knocking more to the ground. Suddenly all halted, wailed in terror, raised their arms, threw themselves to their knees in supplication.

The machine gun stopped, then crashed out again, bullets buzzed by Mara, two Chinamen grunted, slowly sank to their knees. Mo Poo cursed, knocked Mara to the ground, threw himself beside her. The two crawled and scrambled across the dusty rocks, rushed to the safety of the cavern. Mo Poo dragged one of the wounded giants.

Jack and Billy, standing on a narrow ledge thirty meters above the cave entrance, watched the battle unfold.

"Looks like fun," Jack exclaimed. "What say we drop in, give them a couple of warning shots between the eyes?" "Funny!" Billy responded.

Each had a gas-operated, delayed recoil-action AN 94 slung over his shoulder, loaded with thirty-round magazines with second magazines reverse-taped to them. They carried two additional sixty round doubled magazines in thigh pockets of their cargo pants. Each wore the ceramicinfused, malla-titanium armored vest shirts their dad had given them. Strapped to their heads were VS-7 night vision goggles, which made them look like bug-eyed space aliens.

The two jumped off the ledge, repelled down the cliff on ropes they had attached to cracks in rocks.

At the base of the cliff, they unslung their rifles, peered into the cavern opening. Seeing nothing, Jack threw a smoke grenade, Billy heaved a M-67 HE grenade. After the explosions, the brothers plunged into the cave, side by side.

A muj loomed out of the smoke, Billy yelled, "OohRah!" Fired a tworound burst, the man slumped to the side.

Jack shouted, "Let's go!" He ran forward. They each fired at surprised men, Jack shooting left, Billy right. More men behind barrels, the two fired on full auto: shredded wood fluttered through the air, water gushed, bodies fell away as the 5.45 millimeter assault rifles fired at the overwhelming rate of 1800 rounds per minute.

Jack threw another grenade, yelled, "Reloadin'." He reversed his magazine, pounded it home, charged the weapon.

Billy fired the last of his double magazine, shouted, "Reloadin'!" Jack raised his rifle to cover his brother.

The two ran ahead, rounded a corner. Now in the large cavern lit by a bank of floodlights on a pole above a generator. Jack fired double-punches into the generator until the lights faded out.

Charging across the cavern, a squad of men held up when the lights went out. Rounds wildly ricocheted around the two Americans. Jack felt a punch to his still tender ribs, staggered but did not fall. An RPG round sizzled overhead, impacted behind. Both were stung by fragments of slashing metal, slicing rock fragments.

The mujs were clearly visible through their goggles: the brothers shredded them with auto fire, switched to double punches, knocked down fleeing survivors.

Jack and Billy ran to the right, cleared each room fronting on the central cavern. The first two rooms were offices, torn to shambles, papers lying everywhere. The third was an armory, Jack threw a grenade; they ran on to the next hewn-out room.

The floor shuddered from multiple explosions, Billy cursed, "Goddammit! You're gonna bury us!"

Opening the next door, Jack saw a man tied, hand and foot, suspended from steel hooks in the rock ceiling, unconscious or dead. He moved on to the next room, threw it open, saw movement, fired a burst of auto fire. Screams, groans, silence.

"It's the Russian!" Billy shouted from his rear. "Utecht."

Jack paused in astonishment, then continued around a corner. A huge Chinaman rose in front of him. He switched out of auto, shot a double round that didn't slow the Chinaman. The giant cursed, stepped forward, struck Jack with a backhanded swing. He flew against a wall, slumped— stunned—to the cavern floor. Chinaman advanced, loomed over him, raised a fist. Double round to the head from Billy, the giant fell to his knees, sprawled face first on top of Jack. He tried to move the huge corpse, couldn't. Guy stunk horribly. Finally, he squirmed out from underneath the lifeless body with Billy's help.

Other side of the huge cavern, beyond the obstacle course, a flare shot up. Bounced off the cavern topmost, fell to the floor, burned brightly.

"Reloading!" Jack yelled. Heard the SAW's distinctive blasting far to the rear. 20 mm rounds exploded. Figured Mick and Dickey must be coming. AK chatter, shots ricocheted off the bulkhead next to Jack. Billy yelled in pain. Jack dropped to one knee. Switched to auto, fired an entire magazine of suppressing fire at the flashes across the cavern, yelled, "Tell me!"

"Just scratches," Billy's voice was strained. "Pricks don't like me."

"Right—no Welcome Wagon here!" Jack hollered. Entered what looked like an exit tunnel, forced himself to move down a long straight stretch, step after step, nerves jangling: two men loomed out of a nook in the tunnel, flashes from gun barrels, Jack felt punches to his protected midsection, dropped both attackers with a long automatic burst that sent slashing pain through his ears.

Glanced at the fallen bodies—they were blond! Penel's people? *Oh, shit,* he thought. *I shot the wrong guys. But what're they doin' here?* Heart pounding, breath in short gasps—*Don't hyperventilate, stupid!*--looked ahead, saw no movement, threw a grenade, another punch to the midsection. Flew against the wall. Sprawled to the rock floor.

Figure loomed over him: backlit, face hidden.

"Alive! Well, Jack, you proud of yourself for destroying our training camp?" Mara aimed a pistol at him. Pulled the trigger. A fiery blast. Another shock to the midsection. He groaned.

"Mara," he gasped, showing more pain than he felt. "Resistance is futile."

"Stop your stupid jokes. I can't believe you've succeeded again. What are you doing here? I thought the American authorities threw you in prison. Mo Poo said you were killed on the heights!"

"The reports of my imprisonment and demise are pre-ma-ture." Jack raised on one elbow. "What're you up to, Mara? Killed any innocent women and kids lately?"

With a smile in her voice, Mara whispered, "I'm coming to visit America."

"Do you have the bio warhead, Mara? Is that what this is all about?"

"I wish! No, your friend, Mo Poo has that secreted away. I'm trying to talk him… never mind, Jack. Your troubles are over." Mara's face turned, a dim light revealed her beautiful face. She snarled. "I've wanted to do this for a long time. You've frustrated me for the last time. This will end it!"

"Mara, we were pals, almost lovers…"

Mara aimed at his head, he squeezed his eyes shut, kicked his foot at her legs. Knocked off-balance, Mara's shot missed! Rock shards sprayed the side of his head when the bullet hit the rock floor. Then, a click. Gun was empty or had mis-fired. Desperately felt for, found his dropped M-4. Raised it, Mara turned and ran. He jammed the rifle between her feet, sprawled her on the rock floor. Aimed at her back, hesitated. She rose and ran away. He couldn't pull the trigger. She faded into the darkness, disappeared.

In the distance, the SAW stopped firing, a grenade exploded, silence fell over the massive grotto.

Billy emerged from the darkness, looked around, sank to his knees next to Jack. "You okay? Jesus, your head is bleeding like a stuck pig!"

"I'm a stupid asshole! Let Mara escape."

"You shoulda whacked her," Billy agreed. "Done whinin' 'bout your loser soft streak? Let's get outta here."

Jack responded, "Gotta collect Bruno—he's probably tired of just hangin' around."

"Ohh, that's cold," Billy giggled.

Standing, Jack kicked something. He leaned down, saw a small notebook. Picked it up, jammed it in his pocket.

"What's that?" Billy asked.

"Dunno, let's boogie." He lightly rubbed his head, pulled a rock chip out of his scalp.

They retraced their steps, re-entered the cell where Bruno Utecht was bound, hanging from the ceiling. His head and slumped back were inches from the cavern floor.

Jack looked at his former UN associate, cut his wrist bindings with the Dragon God knife, asked with sarcasm in his voice, as he lowered the Russian to the floor, "Bruno, old buddy, you just drop in as part of your outfit—what was it? The 106th Parachute guys? Or you still hanging out as a secret James Bond-type agent for Mother Russia?" "Jack, thank God!" Bruno said. "My arms!

"Yeah," Jack answered as Billy helped the Russian to the floor. He pulled a water bottle out of his cargo pocket, held it to Bruno's mouth, poured. "Billy, check around. Bruno looks like he just crossed Death Valley on foot."

"My arms—my arms are dislocated."

"That'll teach you to hang around with nothin' to do," Jack forced a chuckle. "We can fix them. Billy, grab his other arm. On three shove it back in place." He and Billy each grabbed a wrist and an elbow, put a foot in Bruno's armpit. On the Jack's count of "Three." they shoved Bruno's arms into place. He groaned horribly. Jack poured more water into the Russian's mouth, splashed it over his face.

"What's Mara up to?" Jack asked.

"If you... didn't find her," Bruno shivered from pain. "The bitch probably... left the way I came in—China entrance."

"Oh, I found her," Jack said. He tried to block an image of Mara's gun barrel, aiming at his head. The click. "She tried to dust me. Luckily... anyway, she ran."

"Filthy bitch!" Bruno exclaimed. He pressed his elbows against his ribs, grimaced. "I wish I had her and that cannibal bastard, Mo Poo, in my sights." Billy took off his coat, spread it over Bruno's upper body.

Five minutes later, Dickey, Mick, Jack, Billy, and Bruno, met at the point where the entry tunnel spilled into the camp's training cavern. Xander's men brushed by them, cautiously went inside. The brothers were assisting the staggering, weak Russian out of the cavern. Astonished to see him, Mick stared at Bruno, who sank to his knees on the ground. He hadn't shaved in days, his greasy blond hair stuck in all directions, making him look like a Hollywood star on a drunken rampage.

"We found him hangin' out in a cell," Jack explained. "The Hunza?" he asked.

Mick glanced at the shivering, pain-stricken Russian, then responded, "No serious casualties. They're guardin' the twenty-two healthy prisoners, treatin' the three wounded. Nine local Muslims and two of the big ones died. I don't know what went on inside."

"The captured survivors—all locals," Dickey added. "No Chinamen."

Mick pounded Jack on the back. The two high-fived. "I'm still amazed how you do it. I mean, attacks that always win." Jack embraced Mick, yelled:

We few, we band of brothers;
He that sheds his blood with me
Shall be my brother;
And men now-a-bed
Shall think themselves accurs'd they ain't here.

"Bloody Shakespeare!" Dickey enthused. "Slightly amended, you crazy American!" He laughed, clapped Jack on the back, slammed fists with Billy. "And we suffered almost zero friendly casualties. And you were right
—the bloody ray gun scared the crappers outta them. Every bloke that Mick hit, dropped his weapon, screamed, ran like a bloody bat outta hell. And the OICW… he broke off and regarded the weapon. "Amazing!" he concluded.

"Hey, Veni, Vidi, Vici," Jack said with a smile.

Mick snorted a laugh, his eyes disappearing as he grinned. "I came, I saw, I conquered. What Caesar said when he kicked the Arab's asses in Syria. Perfect!"

"Didn't mean to brag—anyway, it's not all good." Jack waved at the cavern. "There's two blond guys way back at the other side of the cavern," Jack added. "I shot them. Your guys, I'm afraid."

"No," Dickey shook his head. "None of the True Hunza went into the bloody cavern."

"They were members of *Saladin's Fist*," Bruno interjected.

"Lebensborn terrorists."

"How's that, dude?" Jack asked, relief and elation surging.

"Like Hitler's Lebensborn. These're all blond, blue-eyed. But they're Europeans—Muslim Bosnians."

Jack fingered the bullet holes in his jacket, mentally thanked his dad for supplying the civilian armored vest that had saved him. "So we didn't get them all. And the survivors escaped." He glanced at Billy, added with a defensive tone, "But it wasn't our job anyway. We were only supposed to check this place out, not shut it down. What should we do with the prisoners?"

"I dunno," Dickey scratched his head. "We don't want to PUC them— that is, make 'em prisoners under control. Too bloody much trouble and expense."

151

"Let's execute—" Mick started.

"I say let the locals free," Jack interrupted. "Interrogate 'em, then warn 'em. They've taken some heavy hits in the last year. Must be tired of fighting other people's battles."

"We'd better check with Penel," Dickey decided. "She's the queen bee around here."

"Send a messenger," Jack concluded. "I wish we could get an interrogation team in here, but I guess it's up to us." He could feel adrenalin draining away.

"So what're you doin' here, Pilgrim?" Mick asked Bruno with his fake John Wayne accent.

"FSB sent a small recon team to check out *Saladin's Fist*," Bruno answered. "I led it because I had operated in this region last year with you Americans. We walked into a Tajik ambush, only I… survived." "You found anything out?" Jack asked.

"Our supposed friend, Mara Bhutto, and our enemy, Mo Poo, are the leadership of the training camp."

"What'd you tell them?" Jack asked.

"Everything…" Bruno shifted. "She said talk or be de-manned. At first, I remained silent." Bruno grimaced and shifted his weight from one side to the other, again.

"She didn't!"

"Not her. The big one. His amigos held me down, he cut a… my testicle off and ate the bloody mass right in front of me." Bruno shut his eyes. "For a second, I was afraid he'd make me eat it!"

"Ugh!" Dickey turned away, swallowed several times.

"That'd do it for me," Billy sympathized. "I'd sing the *'Winnie the Pooh and Tigger Too'* fight song on one leg, if need be." "You alright?" Jack asked.

"At least I'm here," Bruno glowered. "But I'd like to get those two in my sights. I'm definitely calling my superiors at Lubyanka Square, tell 'em to put the hit on those Bosnian pricks that're running away."

The group's hostility towards their injured Russian friend evaporated in an instant.

152

"Okay, let's gather the paperwork, anything else we can find, conduct questioning of the captives, then head back to Haartgard," Jack suggested. He glanced at the bedraggled Russian, remembered how clean-cut the leanfaced guy had been when he first meet him: polished black boots, a neat undress uniform, a smart Russian green beret. He dug a bottle of aspirin out of a pocket, gave Bruno four tablets. "What's our pal Mara up to, Bruno?"

"She has trained fanatical Muslim Bosnians to be terrorists," Bruno said. He shifted his weight, adjusted Billy's coat over his shoulders, trying to find comfort. "They're all Europeans. Like the ones you shot. Blonds. No one would give them a second glance on the streets an' parks of Moscow or St. Petersburg."

"Or London," Dickey added.

Or Kansas City, Jack thought. He glanced at the red splotches where Billy had been hit by shrapnel on the head and neck, fingered his own minor wounds. Felt a small lump, worked a rock chip out. Remembered the notebook Mara had dropped, retrieved it, handed it to Mick. "Farley's spooks might be able to glean somethin' from this. Mara dropped it when she ran. Lotta paperwork inside."

"I'll put guards at the exit," Mick suggested. "Make sure those tall crazy dudes don't try and crawl back to whack us."

"Good idea," Jack enthused. He helped Bruno settle to the ground, rest against a boulder.

Splitting up, the team searched every room, taking cell phone photos of documents to later email to General Farley's headquarters in Islamabad; they collected paperwork, two undamaged laptop computers, a cell phone, a passport-sized photograph of a young European man. By noon they had everything piled up at the entrance. Mick also text-messaged an immediate situation report to the general that included a description of the action: twenty-three enemy dead, fourteen seriously wounded, seven with minor wounds, and a report of the escaping terrorists from the training camp.

Penel's brother, redheaded Xander Kong, spoke to the Muslim prisoners in a language incomprehensible to all save Dickey, who nodded and smiled at various intervals during Xander's speech.

When Xander finished, the Muslim leader gave a lengthy, guttural reply, bowed to Xander, then to the entire team.

"Says they're gonna be bloody good little ragheads," Dickey interpreted. "Says the leader—the one you've said is Mara Bhutto, forced them to provide security an' support to the training camp. There were thirty or so candidates, all blond and blue-eyed Bosnians, but only ten still in the course of training. *Fingers of the Fist*, he called 'em. Whatever that means."

Blond, blue-eyed men, Jack thought. *All gone. Where? What the hell's this all about?*

After downing a MRE—military rations in a package—lunch of spaghetti and chunked chicken, Jack, with the help of Xander Kong, set up two interrogation teams comprised of one of Xander's men paired with Mick, and one with himself. They spent the afternoon questioning the Muslim prisoners, learned nothing of value, even after they were supplied text-messaged questions by General Farley's Intel staff in Islamabad.

Billy went to Haartgard with a messenger and returned with a wagon and horse to carry Bruno Utecht back to the fortress. Riding with him on horseback was platinum blonde Penelope, who sat and surveyed the battleground with a satisfied smile on her face. After a glance at Bruno, she dismounted, pulled a liter bottle out of a saddlebag, and encouraged Bruno to drink the healing tarn water.

Nearby, raven-haired Zhang, who had arrived with Penel, was sifting through the pile of paperwork they had collected and weighted down with rocks.

When the princess learned they intended to let the prisoners free, she stormed over to where Jack and Xander were interviewing the last prisoner, to protest the decision.

The Muslim blanched when he realized she wanted to execute him and all his men. A short, slender, middle-aged man, he fell to his knees, pulled his graying hair in anguish, wailed in terror.

Jack regarded the warrior princess. She wore tight, natural suede pants, a blue silk shirt under a black wool vest. On her head was a knitted red beret. She stomped her knee-length black boots in anger and her long blonde hair bounced on her shoulders.

When she wound down from a tirade about how her people had been continually plagued by the Muslim valley inhabitants, Jack pulled his pistol.

"Here, go ahead. Kill 'em all. May as well do the women and children, too. Can't have 'em raisin' new terrorists."

Penel looked at the black Beretta, down at the cowering man and finally at Jack. She took the pistol, aimed it at the now-squalling man. Said, "You're right, they'll raise new terrorists. They crazy as well. You save them, they just come back screaming, 'Allah orders, blow you up.' You give them medical help, 'Allah says blow you up.' Build them a school, they'll scream, 'Allah says, blow you up'." She stared at the cringing man, scowled with frustration, re-aimed the pistol.

Chapter 29

Aiming a glass at Jack, Penel threw it. The glass hit her bedroom fireplace, shattered. Another followed, hit Jack's shielding forearm. Red wine splashed over his shirt.

"Babe, easy. I'm not leaving this minute."

With a furious look, Penel ran at Jack, her fist pulled back. He stood, not defending himself. When she drew near, she slugged him on the cheek, began to cry, then hugged him, buried her face in his neck.

He rubbed her back. "You're not so tough. You proved that when you couldn't waste the prisoners, so lighten up. You have to understand—I need to clear my name. I have to get back to Pakistan to do that. And I've left an American climber's body in the heights—I need to take it down to Gilgit, ship it out."

"It'll keep. Buried in the snow," Penel said, her voice devoid of sympathy. "Anyway, you just want to recover the Dragon shield emeralds."

"That's Billy's gig. I want to give them back to China. Zhang says if we don't return the gems, *SD* will come huntin' for us."

Penel pulled back, punched him in the ribs, accused, "You sonofabitch!
You have a thing for her!"

"You were a lot sweeter when you used, like, more thees and thous, and less SOBs."

Penel hugged him again. "I'm sorry. I just don't want to lose you again. I can keep you safe in Shangri-La."

"Are you kidding!" Jack exclaimed. "Last year I was in gunfights, was chased by giant cannibal Chinamen, was in more gun battles, blew up a mountainside in a huge struggle for this fortress. This morning another vicious battle. Shangri-La—what a joke! This's one of the most dangerous places in the world."

"Outsiders bring their troubles to our peaceful valley!" Penel exclaimed.

"Any more peaceful, an' I'll expire. Anyway, I gotta go outside the valley to fix my problems," Jack replied. "I can't just sit here. I'm wanted. I escaped from prison. I have to use this opportunity to clear my name. I can't run all my life."

"Last year, it was my time," Penel murmured into his neck. She pulled away. Regarded him with her beautiful, intense eyes. "But I didn't become pregnant. Last night was different. Yesterday, I felt the tug of fertility. Last night was a good time to make a baby. You cannot leave a child like rust scraped off a Khyber knife."

At first confused by her change of subject, he responded, "We'll cross that bridge later. I promise I'll come back." *Jeez,* he thought. *A baby. What a wonderful thought. But in Shangri-La? I can't raise a kid here! Be like livin' in a mausoleum.*

"Toast that promise with the waters from the Tarn of Long Life." She took a cork-sealed ceramic pitcher off the mantel, poured two glasses of water, held up a glass, commanded, "Remember, these waters promise health and long life."

Jack drank the entire glass of sulphurous, slightly mineraly-tasting water. "If this stuff doesn't kill me first." He looked at the beautiful girl. *Is she really pregnant? Am I going to be a dad? I can't leave my kid in this disaster of a place.*

He had a sudden thought, "How long since you've been back to the glacial melt tarn waters?"

"Wantonal and I went often, but I have not been since she died."

"You drank any of that water?"

"No reason." Penel raised her glass. "I toast you. I toast me. I toast our child."

Jack leaped across the room, knocked the glass out of her hand.

Shocked, Penel said, "I'm sorry I threw the glass at you."

"No, not that. You told me last year your women hardly ever get pregnant. Have a lot of miscarriages."

"True, that is Dragon God's way of keeping our population in check."

"No, what if it's something else? You say the waters attack foreign stuff like germs, viruses, inflammations, stuff like that. What if it attacks a fetus as a foreign invader. That'd explain the many unsuccessful pregnancies. Maybe, when women drink the waters at the wrong time, they miscarry."

Penel pondered his suggestion. "You knocked the water away. You want this baby!"

Yeah, I do, he thought. *But how the hell do I get her out of here?* "If you're pregnant, of course I want the baby. That would be the most wonderful thing to happen. But I'd want you to come out. I'd want my son or daughter born in a modern hospital in America—not this…"

Penel stared at Jack with an expression that moved from love to anger. She concluded, "I'll not let you leave Shangri-La."

Chapter 30

Mara Bhutto hated camels. She hated one-humped and two-humped camels equally. This one was a one-humped, former Arabian racing dromedary, and it felt the same about Mara. It spit in her direction. She dodged the gooey missile, climbed aboard the squatting animal and hung on as it groaned horribly. It heaved up after several well-aimed kicks and headed north, across a brush and sand-covered plain, followed its companions away from the mountains that sprawled across the southern horizon and wrapped around to the west. The thumping and swishing sounds from the pads of the camels' feet were a unique and exotic medley of sound as the beasts of burden moved along a sandy trail.

She sighed, thought of the forthcoming odyssey: fifty kilometers on this miserable camel to the town of Shaymak on the Oqsu River, then a bus or auto ride for another one hundred seventy kilometers to Dushanbe, the capital of Tajikistan, where her partner, Rama Razi could send a jet to pick them up.

After a meeting in Rama's headquarters on the Sea of Oman, they could continue to Tehran, then America. There, she would repay Jack Flashhardt, settle with those who had killed her father, reimburse them all with justice and vengeance. Mara smiled at the anticipation of her future. But to accomplish it all, to destroy Jack, she would need Rama's financial support, and the Bosnians' unconditional loyalty.

Twenty camels trotted before her. The surviving giant Chinamen were fleeing to a refuge in Tajikistan and were escorting Mara's reduced team of *Saladin's Fist* warriors to Shaymak, which was probably a miserable collection of mud brick hovels just like everywhere else in this part of the world. For a moment, the thought of sitting in the *Tavern on the Green* amidst the lush summer greenery of Central Park in New York dazzled her. She wondered how long she would have to wander the most degraded parts of the world.

The seven remaining Bosnian *Fingers of the Fist* were strung out in front of her. Mo Poo, the giant Chinaman, was riding a quarter mile to the right flank. Mara was surprised at how the terrain changed north of the Chinese border: almost flat tablelands. She had expected high passes choked with snow, cliffs to avoid, avalanches to dodge.

Seven *Fingers* remaining: a disaster wrought by the vicious Americans. Hopefully, she had enough warriors to cause chaos in America. A firestorm of chaos. Like the explosive fire from the Americans that had so foiled all her plans last year—almost as though the Dragon God had forcibly stopped her planned attack. Its presence had ruined all her plans to destroy San Francisco's population with the captured American biobomb.

Now she had blond, blue-eyed men that no one would profile at America's borders. She prayed to God that the Swedish passports and the Canadian tourist visas were waiting with Rama Razi. With the proper paperwork, the invasion of the U.S. by *Saladin's Fist* would be easy. She swore in a low voice, "Dragon God be damned to hell! Jack Flashhardt be damned to eternal hell!"

Mara glanced at the stars that filled the sky above. Draco, the dragon, was high in the sky. Also, she suspected that soaring dragon eyes— American satellites—would pick up the caravan but would never suspect that it was anything other than a nomadic tribe wandering through the wild lands, perhaps heading to market in Shaymak. Unless they were caught in the open, in daylight.

Positive musings shattered when she realized Jack Flashhardt—if he was still alive after her shot to his chest—could communicate by a satellite cell-phone and warn the American authorities of the Fist's escape. She knew that they had to reach Shaymak before dawn: if they didn't, the Americans could send UAV aircraft to verify who they were, then hunt them down and coldly kill them without a shred of regret that only a pilotless machine could have. She glanced at the stars—they had about three hours before first light.

Under her legs, the camel pissed without pausing, after being stimulated by a stream of urine from the camel to its front. Mara sighed when the pungent scent assaulted her nose, wished she were in Abad, Karachi, Hong Kong, even Kabul. Anywhere but under the

Draco constellation, under a colossal sea of stars on the highlands of Tajikistan. She shut her eyes to the natural beauty and concentrated on the death and destruction she would cause in America. But she was unable to stop looking up at the constellation Draco devouring Ursa Minor. She wondered whether the Dragon God could or would somehow stop her again. She reached in a pocket, trying to touch the al Qaeda code book. It was missing!

Chapter 31

Contemplating the boiled eggs that squatted on his plate like a couple of malformed dud cannonballs, Jack counted his mixed blessings: alive, healthy, still desired by some, still wanted by many, still hated by General Farley. He mashed the eggs.

Zhang slid into the booth in Haartgard's kitchen, sat across from him, smiled a good morning. Her shiny black hair was tied in a ponytail: wearing her Angel's baseball cap, she looked beautiful, like the actress Lucy Liu, American more than Chinese.

"Where's Billy?" he asked.

"Opium pipe dreams," Zhang responded. "Tell me what you know about the local waters. Do they really extend the people's lives? Is this really the Shangri-La of folk tales?" She put her foot in his lap, rubbed it back and forth.

Jack gasped, forced himself to ignore her actions. He noticed her slanted green eyes had the wide open look that was so striking against her flawless dark brown skin. He tried to cross his legs, she pushed harder—he felt a flush of desire course through his body. "I don't know, the water seems to have effects, but I'm no scientist. Talk to a biologist. I think it's a lot of crap."

Mick joined them—he sat next to Jack, then Dickey Arses arrived and crowded Zhang over until she had to remove her foot from Jack's lap.

A veiled woman with smiling eyes served a platter of thickly sliced, fresh wheat bread that smelled wonderful. She put down a dish of yak butter next to it, then poured black tea for all.

"Hey, Dickey," Jack asked, "now that your babe, Wantonal, is no longer around, you gonna stay in Shangri-La?" He grabbed a chunk of bread, pushed the strange-smelling butter away.

"Is that what goes as sympathy for a passing in America?" Dickey asked with a grumpy tone. He pushed the yak butter farther away, selected a piece of bread, bit into it.

"Hey, Penel's sister was great, but she's been dead for almost a year. She ain't even still warm, dude."

"Rather." Dickey held up a cup in a toast. "Here's to Wantonal. May she rest in peace." He looked in Jack's eyes. "You came off much luckier."

"Dude, Penel's great, but I gotta get outta here. I have too many problems to be taking an extended vacation in Shangri-La. For starts, I need to look up your brother and get a statement from him. For my new trial." He glanced at Zhang, who smiled, then ran her foot up his leg, under his pants.

"Yes, well, you'll find him in a Kashgar prison, as you know," Dickey said. "Did I tell you he had a spot of trouble?"

"Yeah, but you said he's okay. How's Milady?" Jack thought of the Kafir warrioress who had worn full-facial striped war paint. Long wavy black hair over her naked black skin. Thought of their sex after his escape from the Taliban prison camp: her sweet breath, red lips swallowing him with passionate kisses, wonderful breasts. Incredible passion. Coming together: rolling, falling, laughing, giggling, panting.

Zhang rubbed his leg again, jolted him back to reality—she smiled, thinking his visible memories of Milady and physical stirrings were caused by her.

"Dying or dead, I heard," Dickey observed with relish.

"No!"

"Taliban got her just like they got her husband the year before, 'cording to my brother, Robert. Buried her, stoned her to a bloody pulp."

Jack avoided that awful mental picture, thought of Milady's son, Kim:

eight or nine, sweet kid, wanted a dad in the worst way, now—no mom either. War sucks!

"Let's knock off the reminiscing bullshit, Pilgrim," Mick said. He pushed the butter to Zhang, speared one of the wonderful-smelling, sizzling lamb chops on a platter the cook had put on the table. "When are we getting' outta here?"

"Yes," Zhang said as she rubbed Jack's upper thigh under the table and pushed the unwanted butter across the table to Jack. "My superiors don't believe you're still co-operating. I was just text-messaged that you've seventy-two hours from midnight tonight to hand the gems over to *SD*. After that, they'll apply force again. I tried to respond, but couldn't get through to stall them off."

Jack removed her foot from his leg. "We'll go over the hump tonight. Start around 2000 hours. That way we'll avoid avalanche danger. We'll climb all night."

"Still plenty bright, if it's clear," Mick grinned. As always, his eyes disappeared in his face. "Two days over the hump, assuming good weather and no illness, then a day to Abad, assuming no road problems. Pretty tight. "Can I stick with you guys? I smell blood and thunder."

"I don't trust General Farley to let us take our gems outta the Embassy," Jack said. "So we're gonna tell him we're resting up here for a few days—I did get shot in my body armor an' I'm sore." He rubbed his breastbone. "Then we head back, slip into the Embassy there in Pakistan before he expects us."

Billy arrived, pulled up a chair. "So, we're gonna steal the gems outta the Embassy? I love it." He glanced at Jack's severely angled face, added, "You got a fever or sump'n? You're all, like, red-faced."

Zhang quickly removed her foot from Jack's crotch.

"Leave me outta that, Pilgrim," Mick objected. "I'll just claim no comm 'cause of dead cell batteries."

"What about that chip thingy Farley stuck in you?" Billy asked.

Jack glanced at Zhang, relieved that Billy had arrived. He looked at his brother's grey eyes—they appeared clear. He fingered a small bandage. "Funny thing, the chip popped out yesterday. Just a jab with a knife and a little squeeze did it." He said to Dickey, "Can you blow up the Shangri-La tunnel to China without us?"

Dickey swallowed tea. "I told the prisoners that was a condition of their parole. They reluctantly agreed. I'll use nitroglycerin from Haartgard's armory."

"That'll do it," Jack said. He thought of the avalanche he and Billy had set off with the nitro Dickey had supplied last year. It had saved Haartgard from the Muslim attack that was about to overwhelm it. "I've been thinking, Mick. After you return the weapons, we'll need your help to retrieve the emeralds." He glanced at Zhang, who was sitting, quietly, demurely. He pulled out a piece of paper and a pencil and began to outline a plan.

"Oh, oh, here it comes," Mick sighed. "Now, I gotta pay for the fun I've had wastin' those Taliban fuckers. I just hope you pull off a sneak and snatch as slick as you smacked that camp."

Chapter 32

The seventeen-year-old Bosnian boy, the youngest of *Saladin's Fist*, was writhing on the ground. Puffs of dust flew up when his elbows and feet pounded the ground with rapid thuds. The rest of the group had dismounted and were gathered around the boy in the ghostly-lit predawn scrublands southeast of Shaymak, Tajikistan. They were murmuring to each other.

"What's wrong with him?" Mara Bhutto asked. She shifted the pack on her back.

The leader of the Bosnians, Mikhail al Slovenly, twenty-five and the oldest of the *Fist*, his face to the spreading light, leveled intense blue eyes on Mara. She noted again his handsome features: he looked a lot like Jack Flashhardt, but without Jack's new muscled form. The similarities in facial appearance were dis-orienting: high cheekbones, a sculptured face, a broad forehead, heavier eyebrows, but the same piercing eyes as Jack's. She shook her head, tried to listen.

"—very painful," she heard him say.

"What?" she asked. "What's so painful he should hold us up? We have to get to Shaymak before daylight or we're dead." She glanced at the others. All were standing or kneeling in a circle, regarding the writhing boy. "Don't you understand? If the satellites see us, realize we're not nomads, we're dead."

"Boils," al Slovenly repeated. "He has a severe case of boils. He can't ride because of the pain."

"We mustn't stop," Mo Poo rumbled. "Delay will give the white rats in the sky a chance to catch us."

Mara looked at al Slovenly. "You're sure he can't ride? Can't you strap him to the camel? A little pain…"

Slovenly spoke to the boy, the boy mumbled words, Slovenly turned to
Mara. "He has boils on his belly as well."

"Are you sure he cannot travel?" she demanded. She felt rage rising in her body: rage at Jack's American satellite and UAV eyes,

166

ready to peer down at them and send down devastation; rage at the stupid camel, rage at the weak squirming boy on the ground.

"Yes," al Slovenly responded with a shaking of his head.

Mara pulled out her Tokarev 54 pistol, aimed at the suddenly screaming, scooting boy's head and shot him. His head hit the ground, bounced once. Mara's pistol now casually pointed in al Slovenly's direction. She said, "No time for a burial. We'll leave money at the local mosque, send mullahs for the body. Let's mount, move along."

Fright showing in his staring eyes, al Slovenly quickly agreed. Mara fantasized for a moment that the blond Bosnian was Jack. Her finger tightened on the trigger, but she restrained herself. "*Saladin's Fist* cannot be stopped by mere pain. You men are the best of the best. Don't you want to avenge your families back in Bosnia? Aren't you tired of shaking your fists at invisible enemies in the sky? This boy was weak. Only men can carry out what must be done. Are you warriors for the Army of Islam or little boys wailing in the dust?"

With frightened, sullen expressions, the men jumped on their camels and the tiny caravan hurried northwest, towards Shaymak, on the dirt road that passed through scrub brush and sparse grass. In minutes they encountered the shallow, ten-meter-wide Oqsu River, turned north on a riverside dirt road towards Shaymak. To their right flank, the eastern sky over the snowy northern remnants of the Karakoram Mountains showed the first orange-tipped hints of dawn.

Chapter 33

After dropping Zhang off at the Marriott Hotel on Aga Khan Road, Jack and Billy, disguised as two bearded American trekkers, arrived at the American Embassy on Ramna 5 Road in a Pakistani Army pickup supplied by Major Soongoon and driven by a soldier from Soongoon's Pak Army base in Gilgit. It was 1000 hours and growing hot. They both were exhausted, but wanted to finish their goal of dropping off Caylynn's body.

The ride down the KKH, four hundred kilometers—about two hundred fifty miles—on the old Silk Road to Islamabad, had been boring, bouncy, and dusty. Caylynn Jones' long body, still frozen, wrapped in a ground sheet and canvas, and packed in snow by two of Major Soongoon's soldiers, had ridden in the back.

The Marine guards at the control gate of the compound, looked at their fake American passports. The Sergeant of the Guard asked a couple of questions about the dead American they had supposedly stumbled across during a trek, waved them through, after giving directions to sign-in at the main entrance before taking the body around to the Embassy morgue.

Fifteen minutes later, after registering their assumed names and supplying their passport numbers to a Pakistani clerk at a desk in the entrance, they went around to the morgue, hauled the frozen body, wrapped in a gray woolen blanket, out of the truck. Jack told the Pak soldier to wait.

The brothers carried Caylynn's body to the morgue, a nondescript room with bare walls—with Billy holding the legs, and Jack the shoulders. She suddenly sagged at the waist and they had to struggle to keep her body from dragging on the floor. A Pakistani technician, asleep with his head on his desk, woke when they entered and directed them to put her on a low table.

After they put her down, Jack paused for a moment, put his hand on the covered head, felt the cold through the wrapping. He turned away, suppressing thoughts of her screaming fall, her death.

From there, the Pakistani civilian orderly sent them to an office on the second floor where they turned over Caylynn's personal effects and passport, then filled out a report describing the Idaho girl's place of death, as well as the details of the supposed discovery.

The relieved brothers donned their sunglasses, left the office, which was manned by another Pakistani—a middle-aged man. In the passageway, they saw cherub-faced General Farley, dressed in civilian clothes, hurriedly enter the hall from an office, about twenty paces away. He glanced at them, then crossed to another office.

"Oh, shit!" Billy exclaimed. He touched the karakul cap that was pulled low over his wide-set grey eyes.

"Shut up," Jack whispered. He bent to tie a shoelace while Billy looked down at his boot. Farley glanced over his shoulder one more time at the two lean young men, paused, then disappeared through a door.

They headed for an elevator, entered: Mick was waiting in the elevator. On the lowest level, the brothers followed Mick, who had arrived separately and had obtained a key to the evidence locker from the Marine OD in the security office.

Mick walked to the locker, entered and left seconds later, after sticking a piece of duct tape over the locking mechanism. He disappeared around a corner, a half minute later the loitering brothers entered.

In a matter of moments, they found the taped-up wood box containing the emeralds. Billy stripped away a piece of tape, pried opened the heavy box with his Kay bar knife, grunted with satisfaction when he saw the gems, individually wrapped in tissue paper.

After removing Mick's duct tape and exiting thorough a side fire exit, they walked to the truck, threw the box in the truck bed and heaped a mass of melting snow over it. Ordered the black-bereted, bearded soldier to drive to the main gate.

A young Marine guard, trying to look stern in his BDUs and helmet, stopped them at the entry. He carried an M-16 at port arms. "Sir, you must return to the Embassy offices."

His heart pounding, Jack eyed the closed gate, wondered whether he could talk the driver into crashing through it. "What's the prob, Marine?" he asked in a level voice. "I need a drink after offloading that body."

"Sir, I was informed you forgot to sign out," the Marine stated in a humorless voice with a southern accent. "Please turn the truck around." With a sinking heart, Jack signaled the driver to go back.

Outside the Embassy main building, Jack and Billy climbed out, exchanged glances and headed for the front door.

"Think they're on to us?" Billy asked.

"Probly. Or maybe General Farley's missin' us and inviting us to stay for lunch."

"Don't want MREs. Maybe we won the Pakman Lotto."

"Damn! You're an optimist," Jack complained. "Just keep walking." They climbed the marble steps, entered the main hall, reluctantly walked to the sign-in desk. The clerk turned the log around, pointed to where she wanted them to sign out.

Billy and Jack did so, then turned. Billy stumbled, Jack grabbed his elbow, steadied him as they walked away. At the gate the guard stopped the truck again. Jack glanced back at the vehicle bed. The snow had partially melted—the top of the jewel box was showing.

"Have a nice day, sir," the Marine said. He glanced at the pile of melting snow and the top of the box.

"Thanks, General," Jack responded. He urged the driver to move away with frantic pointing of his fingers, below the level of the truck's window.

The truck moved slowly, the guard watched the truck bed as it slid past, said nothing. Sighing with relief, Jack directed the soldier to take them to the Marriott Hotel.

Chapter 34

Pouring the tissue-wrapped emeralds all over the hotel suite's table, Billy broke into a broad grin, showing his flashing white teeth against his dark face, howled with pleasure. "We done it, Red Ryder!" He tossed the wooden crate on the wool-carpeted floor, ran his fingers through the gems, unwrapped a dozen. "Hey," he added, "remember the movie?" He picked one up, his grey eyes flashing, whispered, "My precious, my precious." he ended with a wicked cackling laugh.

Jack looked at the dark green mass. Sparkles from the dozen gems flickered, sent shifting rays of light all over the suite. An eerie, foreboding sense swept through his body.

Zhang Poon t'ang emerged from Billy's bedroom. She wore tan military-type pants, boots, a white silk shirt with rolled up sleeves. Her hair was up rather than in her usual ponytail.

Jack watched Zhang run her fingers through the gems. He wasn't astonished when she palmed one, casually slipped it into her pants pocket.

"What now, bro?" Billy asked. He had not noticed Zhang's actions.

"We gotta work a deal with the Chinese government. After all, that's why Zhang's here. We'd better survey the gems, make sure we have 'em all.
Count 'em, Billy, I'm gonna order us some
chow." "Also, order a beef chowder,"
Zhang asked.

"Champagne, too," Billy commanded. I wanna celebrate."

Jack arranged a room service meal of steaks and fries, the chowder, a bottle of cheap Australian champagne. After ordering, he took a leisurely shower. For a moment, he wondered what his Australian pal, Gil Acton, whom he had worked with in the UN in the Islamabad offices, was up to a year later. He finished shaving, put on clean clothes, rejoined Billy and Zhang.

Billy said, "One ninety. We're missin' two."

"No," Jack glanced at Zhang. "Remember, one's in the bank box in Singapore. So—"

Sensing his intent, Zhang said, "I'm sorry. I took one to prove to my superiors that…" She pulled out the gem she had taken, put it on the table.

Jack relaxed, took a small bottle of *42 Below Vodka* out of the refrigerator, poured it in a glass, added ice. Remembered it referred to the 42nd parallel in New Zealand, not a temperature. He turned back to the couple sitting over the gems. "So, what're we gonna do?"

"You must return the emeralds to my government," Zhang exclaimed.

"If you don't—"

"First," Jack added, "we gotta go to Singapore, get hold of General Hammar for that statement about the stolen Caribou airplane. It was one of the biggest things against me at the court-martial. I need the General to explain why we needed that plane." He thought of his other witness, Dickey's brother, wondered how he would get the Brit's statement while he was in a Chinese prison.

"What're we gonna do with these?" Billy ran his fingers through the unwrapped emeralds.

"You must take to Singapore," Zhang said with a shrill commanding tone.

Jack pointed out, "That means we hafta risk smugglin' the gems through Customs here and in Singapore."

"Too risky," Billy interrupted. "Some snoopy Customs guy could find 'em. We'd be screwed."

"Why don't I report in to General Farley, tell him we just arrived. See what he has to say. Maybe he'll get us a military hop to Singapore," Jack concluded. He called General Farley, got a voicemail, left a callback number.

"You're dreamin' if you think Farley'll help us," Billy said. "Call your buddy, Charlie Davis. He can get us around the border bullshit."

Jack selected Charlie's stored number, called him. Another voicemail. He left a message, asking about a ride to Singapore.

"Get to Singapore," Zhang directed. "Get last gem, return to my government. You cannot stop to talk to some general. You can talk after you resolve the turnover." She shook her head. "Delay could mean the Second Department loses patience, turn you both into tasteless Kung Pow Chickens. That would be deadly." She stared at the gems.

"Never did like that Chinese chop chop," Billy exclaimed with a scornful laugh. "What the hell's some rumdum Chinese outfit gonna do ta us?" he scoffed. "I'd love to go up against a buncha stupid gooks."

Zhang regarded Jack with humorless eyes. "Who gave you that scar on your back? The one that wraps around to your ribs?" "Mara," Jack responded with a sinking feeling.

"Yes. A Chinese agent. Second Department agent. A special agent just like me, Jack."

An hour later, someone pounded on the door. Jack felt the suite's walls closing in on him. He motioned for Billy to cover up the gems with a towel, answered: it was General Farley.

The short Army general with the downward-curving mouth stalked into the room. "You're back. Why didn't you report in? GPS tracking shows you're still in the 409 valley."

An aide paused in the passageway, looked around the room. He was tall, skinny, had red hair and was dressed in BDUs.

Jack swallowed a snide reply, decided to act friendly, then couldn't. Said in a poor imitation of Farley's singsong voice, "Thanks, Jack. You did a helluva job, your country's grateful for your timely, heroic action. And you managed to kill three of the ten members of *Saladin's Fist*. Great work! You boys want to put in for Purple Hearts for your wounds? And thanks for returning all the special weapons I gave you."

Farley sneered. "Yeah, right—message and all that. What happened to the chip in your arm? Why didn't you report in to the Embassy?"

Jack sat down and added, "By the way, check your voicemail—I left a message a few minutes ago."

Farley eyed Billy, smiled. It wasn't a pretty sight. "Wait a minute," he exclaimed. "I saw you two in the Embassy. What were you up to?"

"We were delivering a dead American we found," Jack responded.

"What about the chip?"

"Musta fell out. And why would we report to you at the Embassy?" Jack asked. "So you could arrest us, send us back to Leavenworth?"

"Exactly." The general laughed with a mean expression on his face. "It's not like it was hard to find you. My staff has been keeping their eyes on hotel registrations at the major hotels."

Jack shut his eyes, mentally kicked himself, took a deep breath.

"General," he asked, "did you hit the bad guys when they escaped into China?"

"China? You wanted us to fire cruise missiles into China? That'd go over big in Beijing, you numb nut."

Jack winced again, asked, "General, can you get us a ride out of here?"

The brigadier general rocked on his heels. He was dressed in desert tan BDUs, the lone star on each collar flashed when caught by the overhead light. He glanced at the table, at Zhang. "Only ride you shitbirds get is one back to Fort Leavenworth, Kansas."

"C'mon, General," Billy said. "I'm sorry I busted you in the chops." The short man glared, said nothing, stared at Zhang.

"Sir, can we contact General Harmbruster?"

"He's busy in Okinawa. At Camp Hansen."

Zhang broke the silence. "These men are in my custody, General. My country, The People's Republic of China, requests that these men be turned over to PRC security forces. In Singapore."

"Who're you?" Farley demanded. "Why d'you want these men?"

Zhang pulled an ID card out of her purse, handed it to him. "People's Liberation Army Institute for International Strategic

Studies. These two are under arrest for stealing rare artifacts from People's Republic. You're interrupting an arrest and interrogation."

The general regarded the ID, looked at Zhang. "You're a field agent for China's Second Department? Then why Singapore?"

"That's where the crime occurred," Zhang responded. "These men have already confessed. They will identify and turn over the stolen goods in Singapore, then will be taken to Beijing for trial. But we request that you deliver them to Singapore, where Second Department arrest warrants are waiting."

"General," Jack protested with an alarmed air, "don't turn us over to *SD!*"

The man smiled, returned the ID. "You really did it this time, Flashhardt. Once a common thief, always a common thief. So much for your prattling about the necessities of the moment." He turned back to Zhang. "I'll call your offices in China. If this checks out, my government will be happy to co-operate."

General Farley smiled again, pulled out a wallet. "If what you say is true, I'll have a jet transport waiting at Abad International in the morning." He handed Zhang a card. "Call my office for details." He looked at Jack, did not attempt to contain a wide grin, walked out.

Jack spun around. "That was a brilliant idea!"

Billy hugged Zhang. "Lucky that prick hates our asses. Now, all we gotta do is turn a profit on the emeralds."

"I say we give them to China," Jack suggested. "We're way over our heads on this one, Billy. They've been nothing but trouble."

Billy sighed. "Maybe you're right. It just pisses me off—"

Zhang quickly interjected. "Oh, I think I get you a sizable reward. That would be best." She looked at Billy. "*SD* said three million dollar, American, is authorized and waiting in Singapore if you give all the emeralds to China right now. Not as much as selling them, but *SD* not look for you forever." She looked back at Jack. "And they would come after you. Forever." Zhang pressed.

Billy and Jack exchanged glances, Billy nodded. Jack acquiesced with a smile.

"You got a deal, Zhang," Billy said.

"Leave to me," Zhang said with an excited air. "We do it in Singapore. Beijing or Hong Kong no good, they might arrest you. Singapore good." "But how we gonna make the trade?" Billy asked.

Zhang, very excited, gushed, "I told them you say it must be Singapore. How you say, neutral? My superior agree. He was ver' excited." "How d'we know they're not gonna screw us?" Jack asked.

"No screw. This'll be big coup for Second Department. Much honors for all politicians. It'll be huge news in China. The return of the *Concubine Emeralds*."

"Sounds good." Billy looked at Jack. He nodded.

"Just one thing," Jack said. "We can't be dragging millions of dollars around. We'd need a wheelbarrow. I want the money in one hundred thousand dollar bearer warrants. That'll be thirty warrants."

"What the hell's that?" Billy asked. He uncovered the pile of gems, grabbed a handful. "I want cash I can spend."

"Trust me, bro. Warrants are what we want. We can put them in our bank account at Hong Kong and Shanghai Bank in Singapore." Jack hoped it would be as easy as it sounded. He wanted to be rid of the jewels. He regarded the sparkling, light-capturing, burning emeralds, remembered what the old monk on the island temple in Quetta had ordered him to do:

"Remove the emerald shield, keep it safe until its rightful owners claim it." He wondered whether taking a reward would violate the old man's directive. He wondered how he would ever know who the rightful owners were. He felt a chill pass through his body.

Chapter 35

Exiting the Lear jet, Mara Bhutto ordered the Bosnians to board two white Ford Expeditions parked on the side of the asphalt runway. Southern Iran's heat was a huge change from Tajikistan's highlands—the group hurried through the super-hot, mid-day atmosphere to the air-conditioned vehicles.

In the front seat of the first vehicle, Mara pulled down the mirrored visor and checked her appearance. Her tired green eyes stared back, confirming her stunning, bronze-complexioned beauty. She noticed lines in the corners of her eyes and shuddered. *My second meeting with Rama Razi as a woman. I wonder whether he has totally accepted me as Mara Bhutto? What if he shuts off funds? But he sent his jet. He must still be committed.*

Mara glanced down at the clean but wrinkled khaki uniform she had pulled from her pack, donned in the jet's bathroom. She wanted to look a little like her old persona, Yassar Ahmoud, to ease the shock for Rama. He had never seen through her male disguise, had been shocked when she showed up as Mara Bhutto at his compound, after her defeat and loss of the biological warhead last year.

The big vehicles sped through the alluvial wastelands: they passed no trees, no bushes, no flowers, no grass or weeds. The SUVs topped a rise, beyond it was a white-stuccoed warehouse on a bluff hanging over the bluewatered Gulf of Oman.

Climbing out of the Expedition into the oppressive atmosphere, Mara and the others hurried to the cooled air of the warehouse. Inside, two armed Palestinian guards flanked the door. In the middle of the structure, she saw Rama's Bedouin tent, about fifteen meters by twenty meters, erected on a wood platform. The sides were rolled up, Rama Razi was lolling on his double king-size bed. A woman played an oud—a pear-shaped lute—at the foot of the bed.

Rama was wearing a loose Arabian robe called an aba over a white shirt; he stared at Mara and her Bosnians, then spread his huge arms in a welcoming manner.

"Saddam Gandhi." Rama used the name Mara had gone by when she attended Cairo University disguised as a man. "Or should I call you, Yassar Ahmoud—your collegiate moniker?" Rama giggled. His massive head, covered by a red and white ghutra—an Arabian headscarf—tied up with an agal cord, and fashioned of traditional goat hair, bobbed over his colossal body. He offered a half-empty platter of mansaf, consisting of stewed lamb on rice.

Mara approached, scooped out a handful, smiled. "Mara Bhutto will do for now."

Rama glanced at the pistol on Mara's hip. Large blue eyes twinkled in his handsome face. Curly black locks dangled across his forehead in an appealing fashion, made him look like a ballooned-up Clark Kent from an old American comic book. She remembered him as having grey eyes, wondered whether he was wearing tinted contacts.

As Mara's eyes swept below Rama's chin, she steeled herself to prevent revulsion from showing at the sight of his huge body.

"So, Mara Bhutto, you escaped your hated American persecutors," Rama Razi frowned, fear filled his face. "What if they followed you?"

"Rama, the Americans know everything they want about you. Quit worrying. If they wanted you, you would be dead. Now, everything is ready. Your pilot can take us to Tehran where we'll catch a flight to Frankfurt, then Canada. Across the ocean to the heart of the Beast. And then we'll strike!"

"*Saladin's Fist* is ready?" Rama asked. He again looked at the shuffling about blond Bosnians, didn't look like he trusted them. "They look so Western, even in their Afghan garb." The men returned his stares with awestruck expressions.

"Don't worry about the *Fist*, they appear as we want. All we need is the rest of the funding," Mara said. She held her breath for a few seconds. "I told you this would be the first grand gesture that will fulfill my dream of bringing America to ruins, and make you the most famous Arab since… well, Saladin, himself."

Rama laughed, under the concealing Arab robe—his gelatinous body bounced and writhed with an impossibly huge life

178

of its own. Mara shuddered. Wished she didn't have to beg for money from gross Rama. Rama grabbed a handful of jellybean candies from a bowl at his side, stuffed his mouth, mumbled, "You must have more than these few."

"I do," Mara said. "I have supporters in America. Potential jihadists who are waiting to join us. And KEGYA has an explosive mission for the *Fist*, after we complete the forest fire attacks. Just watch the news. I guarantee you'll be impressed."

Smirking, Rama regarded his female partner.

Chapter 36

Like the lobby furniture in the Singapore Raffles, the old hotel's twobedroom suite furniture was all quasi-antique English. While the lobby floor was bamboo, the room suite's flooring was dark polished mahogany with a large Afghan rug covering it. A ceiling fan slowly rotated from the extra-high ceiling, pushing cigarette-smelling air around the room.

To celebrate their successful trip to Singapore in the general's eagerly supplied military C-20 Lear jet, flown by two friendly civilian pilots who were Hindu Indians, Jack and Billy ordered room service, even though it was nine PM, local time. A Malay boy brought a meal on a cart consisting of steaks, baked potatoes, garden salads, and another serving of Zhang's beef stew.

Zhang called her superiors, arranged a meeting to pick up the warrants and left.

An hour later, she returned with China Mist, the boat girl. Both were dressed in shorts, halters, sandals. Zhang, her eyes sparkling with excitement, was carrying a black leather briefcase. She put the case on the table, next to the bag of emeralds.

Noting Jack's curious stare, Zhang admitted, "China Mist has been my colleague. She is *SD and* a member of *SDMCP*—the Malay Communist Party. I put her on the old Baba's tongkang—the sailboat—to help me keep an eye on you guys. That was before I know you and trust you." She smiled candidly, looked truthful.

After opening the briefcase, Jack shuffled through the warrants: issued by the Overseas Chinese Banking Corporation, they were all payable to bearer, looked genuine. *Better call and verify,* he thought.

"Now we party?" Zhang asked with a nervous smile. "Celebrate. You're rich now." She sounded overly insistent.

"First, I want to call that asshole, Farley, thank him for the ride," Billy said.

"Don't do it, Billy. You'll just piss him off even more," Jack put away the warrants, thought, *No reason to be suspicious—she brought the bearer bonds. She coulda taken 'em and ran.*

Billy laughed. "You didn't see what I put on the mirror in that jerk's jet. I wrote: *Thanks for the lift, General Dumbass.* I'm just afraid he won't figure out he's been tricked. If I call him, I'll make sure he got the message."

"You gave him enough message last year when you broke his jaw," Jack said. "Let it ride."

Zhang's stew was sitting in a covered pot with a candle under it to keep it hot. Bowls and spoons were beside it.

"Sorry, Zhang," Billy apologized. "Only your stew is left. We were too hungry to wait."

"I grab noodle dish at Hawker Centre food stall," Zhang replied. "But my stew'll be good. You two must try it, compare difference to Pakistani stew. Malay Chinese stew much better." She said to Jack, "Open a bottle of red wine from the bar."

He opened the wine, poured two glasses, which he handed to the women. Billy picked up a glass, but Jack shook his head slightly. "We need to keep a clear head, Billy, so we can keep an eye on the warrants." He turned to Zhang, asked, "When're you completing the exchange?"

"China Mist along to keep an eye on emeralds," Zhang said. "We drink wine, eat stew—I'm still hungry—then I go to *SD* with The Concubine's Emeralds."

Zhang took the stew into the small kitchenette, dished up two plastic bowls, returned and served the stew. "I eat later," she said as she put the bowls on the table.

The brothers tasted the stew, then consumed it. They each had only a half glass of wine with the fiery hot stew, but after fifteen minutes, Jack noticed Billy was exhibiting drunken behavior. His speech volume rose. Jack felt dizzy, disoriented.

For a half hour, Zhang told stories to China Mist, who was sitting next to Jack, about the trip to Shangri-La. China Mist grabbed Jack's thigh in mock terror, then did not let go. Soon she was casually, almost absentmindedly stroking his leg; he realized he was getting tremendously excited by the beautiful Malay girl's actions, but the room was spinning.

Billy suddenly grabbed Zhang, pulled her, laughing, into their bedroom. China Mist immediately turned, kissed Jack, climbed into his lap, began pulling off his shirt. Jack responded, picked her up and went to his bedroom. In minutes they were enjoying passionate, clothes-ripping-off, sprawling, tumbling on the floor, incredible sex. Jack quickly had a shattering orgasm but did not lose his erection. He briefly wondered why he was ready for more sex.

His body rapidly became disconnected from reality. China Mist climbed on him, took him inside. The rest of the room disappeared into an out-of-focus never land until he could only see China Mist.

A period of time later, maybe minutes, maybe hours—he couldn't tell —he dreamed Zhang entered, pushed China Mist aside and nestled next to him. Instead of complaining, China Mist continued to kiss and fondle Jack and the three rolled around the bed, onto the floor. He was in a dizzy state that he could not leave. Faces, limbs, torsos, appeared and disappeared. Time stretched out in an unknown place where he was trapped in the dream state. He slept.

Chapter 37

After taking a shower in a tiny hotel room in Frankfurt Airport, Mara put on new clothes she had purchased in an airport haberdashery. Tan cotton slacks, a blue silk blouse, a pale green scarf around her neck, white high heels. She checked her new Piaget watch; she had two more hours before the flight over the North Pole to Vancouver, British Columbia.

Mara ran her fingers through her straight black hair, unfolded the email she had accessed and printed out in a cyber café off the main airport lobby.

After she decoded the email, she looked at *Saladin's Fist*'s new itinerary:

Frankfurt, Germany, to Vancouver, Canada. A ferry ride to Vancouver Island; a bus to the city of Victoria, where an al Qaida agent would give them new Canadian papers, then another ferry to Port Angeles, Washington, where they would enter the U.S. as Canadian tourists. She hoped her new American mentors, *God's Purpose,* had planned adequately and was ready. She wondered for the twentieth time why KEGYA had connected her with the fanatical group, why the Christian group had offered to give *Saladin's Fist* their guidance and support.

Mara ached for a nap, looked forward to sleeping on the flight across the Pole. *A forest in the U.S. is waiting like a trussed-up virgin in a Bedouin tent,* she mused. *And I'll be the one to violate her with a burning hot, vibrant, pulsating, screaming organ of fire.* She smiled.

Chapter 38

"Jack, wake up!" Billy yelled. "Someone's kidnapped Zhang. The emeralds, the briefcase—all gone!"

"Gone?" Jack struggled to wakefulness. Stupefied, he stared at his naked brother, rolled out of bed, noticed it was daylight outside, stumbled to the living room. He stood over the dining table, gaped at the empty surface. Glanced at his watch—it was 0830 hours.

"What're you looking at? There's nothin' there!"

Brushing his hands over his face, Jack lurched to his bedroom, took a hurried cold shower that shocked him into a wakeful state, dressed in cargo pants, a polo shirt, sneakers. Went into the kitchen, poured water from a carafe.

He inspected the soup tureen, carefully sniffed it. "Opium," he muttered. "The bitch drugged the stew!" He noticed two small plastic capsule wrappers on the counter. Picked one up—a "V" was imprinted on it. Laughing, he returned to the living room.

Billy, now dressed in similar attire, glared at him. "What's so goddam funny?"

Jack tried to stop, kept chuckling. "I don't know about you, but I got high, then I got laid over and over. I couldn't stop."

"Yeah," Billy said. "One-sys and two-esys. Over and over."

"Look around, Billy. If there was a kidnapping, how come no signs of a struggle?" He held up the plastic wrap from the kitchen. Debated telling Billy he thought that Zhang had seduced him. Decided telling would do no good, suppressed guilt. He added, "We're probably the first guys ever to get slipped a Mickey Finn made of opium *and* Viagra."

"What's Mick got to do with it?"

"Not Mick—a mickey—old gangster term for when—never mind. Zhang slipped us a zinger, she an' China Mist screwed us to sleep, then split with the loot and the gems."

Billy, his face contorted, shouted, "No! She loves me! She wouldn't run out on me."

Jack started to laugh. "Only a girl as zany as Zhang Poon t'ang could come up with a scenario like this." Suddenly, Jack thought of the Chinese who had paid for the emeralds. "Billy," he asked, "D'you think she returned the gems? Or did she take them with her? Wherever she went."

Fears exploded when someone pounded on the door. He glanced at it —looked solid. No one was going to knock it open without a major effort.

"It's probably the *SD* dudes."

Billy wildly looked around the living room. "They're here for their gems. They'll never believe us."

"We gotta get outta here. Now!" Jack ran to his bedroom, grabbed his money belt containing his wallet, his bankbooks, and passports.

When he returned to the suite's living room, his brother was standing in the middle of the room, legs spread, aiming an M-9 at the dark mahogany door. "Screw 'em," Billy said with a strained voice. "I say, bring on the pricks."

"It's not their fault. Don't shoot." Jack grabbed his brother's arm. "Get your stuff. Let's haul ass."

"We're on the third floor. You plan on flying?"

Jack ran to the balcony's glass door, slid it open, looked out. "C'mon, we can jump to the next balcony."

Billy relented, dropped his aim on the shaking door and ran to find his papers and wallet. The knocks on the door increased in volume and intensity. Jack climbed on to the balcony safety rail, swung around the short wall separating rooms and jumped into the next balcony, tried the door— locked! Leapt to the next balcony— sprawled over a table, banged his elbow and hand. Flair of pain in his Leavenworth stab wound.

Billy jumped to join him, then picked up a teak chair, smashed the glass door. He reached in, twisted the handle. They rushed through the bedroom; an older white man and a young Malay girl in the bed peered at them, yelled and pulled the covers over their heads.

They left the room, saw no one in the hall, moved down it, in the direction of their suite.

A corner: they peeked, saw a man in a dark silk suit, realized it was the Pakistani renegade, General Hammar. He was turning away from their door. "General!" Jack shouted. The hard-looking man, about forty five years old, turned. He had the same hawk face with a big nose, intense wrinkles around black eyes. Tall, shaved head, with a mustache and goatee, he looked like an Oriental villain in an old movie.

Jack and Billy strode forward. Jack and the smiling general hugged.

He glanced at the pistol hanging in Billy's hand. "Young Jack, Billy. It's good to see you boys. I almost missed you." Billy looked up and down the hallway.

Jack said, "You scared the crap outta us, is what you did." The general looked like he had gained twenty pounds since his imprisonment in Bharakan Prison, but he still looked fit.

General Hammar watched Billy put his pistol in his pocket, smiled. "You're in trouble again, boys. Why am I not surprised?" He glanced up and down the hall. "You must come with me at once. I would've sent someone, but I was afraid you wouldn't listen, so I came myself. We must hurry. The police are after you."

Jack and Billy exchanged glances. "We'll get our stuff," Jack said.

"Not time!" Hammar beckoned and they followed. He added, as they hurriedly moved towards a fire exit sign, "I wish we had another catapult, Jack. Like the one we built to escape Bharakan Prison."

"We could make like Icarus and Daedulus and sail over Singapore,"
Jack laughed. "At least to the parking lot."

"No, fly straight to my villa in Punggol." Hammar cackled as he led them.

Billy opened the fire exit door, the elevator chimed behind them. The three rushed into the stairwell, Jack paused to watch through the cracked open door. Four Chinese men in black suits exited the elevator, looked at the room number signs and turned towards Jack and Billy's suite.

186

Suspicions confirmed, he thought. *Goddam Zhang grabbed the gems, too.* He eased the door shut, hurried to catch up to Billy and the general.

In the two-story lobby, they passed the Long Bar, original home of the *Singapore Sling*, saw three police cars and a SWAT van skid to a stop on Beach Road.

"This way," Hammar said. They moved through a service area, outside to an employee parking lot. "My car's in front. I'll leave it for now. The driver'll bring it home, eventually." The three hurried through the lot, reached the street and hailed a White Cab.

"What's going on?" Jack asked. "How'd you find us?" The taxi was small and the three had to crowd together. The Thai driver flashed a smile and u-turned, at Hammar's direction, and sped east along car-crowded Seah Street.

"You were reported for a disturbance in the Singapore Hotel a while back." Hammar explained. "Someone here at the Raffles Hotel must've recognized your name when you checked in. Called the police."

Jack and Billy, sitting on each side of the general, exchanged glances.

"No," Jack said. "That couldn't have been it."

"Because Zhang registered," Billy added. "The suite was in her name. She probably called us in to the police." Billy looked crestfallen, his dreams shattered. Hammar glanced at Billy, quoted,

"O Zeus, why did you
plague mankind With the
trickery of women?
If you wanted us to propagate,
Couldn't you have found a better way?"

"If I gotta listen to poetry an' history lessons, let's cut the crap an' get a bigger cab," Billy said.

Jack sat down and said, I'm guessing Sophocles."

"Euripides," Hammar corrected. Then the general added, "It's a ways to the Johor Strait. We need a larger cab." He directed the driver to find a cabstand.

Chapter 39

When the big Hummer taxi finally stopped in front of the general's villa, an hour before noon, Jack recalled Hammar's words the year before: *"I have a nest egg in Singapore. I'm too well known in Pakistan to stay around as long as Bastard Zardari's the president. I want to retire to a tongkang—a sailboat—in the Malay straits. I'm tired of living in dust, dirt, sparse weeds, and impossible mountains."*

Two tall Pakistani guards, dressed in tiger-stripe utilities, and holding pump shotguns, confronted the cab, then stiffened to attention when they recognized the general. A third dark-skinned man, also tall and looking like an officer of the guard, spoke into a walky-talky. Jack wondered whether the Chinese *SD* guys or the police had followed them. He had watched behind, had seen nothing suspicious.

The house was long, low—about three meters high—with a flat roof. It spread along the Strait's brown waters, barely visible beyond the house. Constructed of bamboo, mahogany, and teak, its front elevation had clean, stark lines.

"Some nest egg!" Jack exclaimed as they approached the elegant but simple house.

With the heat and humidity, the atmosphere outside the cab was stifling. Another guard, armed with a pistol on his hip, opened the front door. Inside, the floors were light bamboo; the walls overlooking the strait were all glass. The aquatic scene was refreshing, the air-conditioned environment was cool. Lush flower fragrances filled the air. A sleek, allwhite cabin cruiser was tied to a concrete dock in front of the house.

"Not exactly a sailboat," Jack commented. "But fabulous."

Hammar smiled. "You remember my dream—retirement on a boat. Back then, I had a small nest egg. Now, I have money beyond my wildest imagination, after—"

"A life on Pakistani Army pay?" Jack asked.

Billy looked at the expensive furniture, the fine wood paneling on the walls, asked, "Drugs?"

Hammar smiled, his hard face softened. He took off his expensive silk suit coat. "But of course. After Zardy threw me in Bharakan Prison, took away my command, my freedom, my pension, I— well, I'm sure you can fill in the blanks."

Jack thought, *Sounds like us: the Marines took away our pay, our ranks, our freedom.*

"General," Jack asked, "We need you to clear me on the issue of stealing that Caribou airplane last year. I was charged and convicted for stealing government property."

A houseboy appeared, Hammar stopped and ordered a pot of fresh coffee, then continued, "I've already written a statement a week ago at General Harmbruster's request. I've cleared you of the airplane charges. I was the person responsible for the theft." He smiled. "Of course, it was really a requisition. You know we needed it to haul supplies to the Afghan attack zone."

Jack was shocked that Harmbruster was actually trying to exonerate him.

"At any rate," Hammar said, "I have excellent local Intel connections, and after Charlie Davis called and said you were coming back this way, I put the word out to look for two young American tourists. When I was tipped that the Singapore police were looking for two Americans staying at Raffles Hotel, I hurried to your hotel to warn you. After all, we are comrades."

"Saved our asses." Billy felt for non-existent braids.

"We could use your Intel network, General." Jack sat down on a bench in front of a baby grand piano. He softly hit a couple of keys. "We were robbed by this Chinese woman, Zhang Poon t'ang."

Hammar smiled. "As I remember, a beautiful girl got you in trouble last year, in the caverns of the Hindu Kush. This one is attractive, no doubt?"

"Yes," Jack replied, "but this one belonged to Billy." He glanced at his brother, who again self-consciously reached for his missing braids.

"What'd she take?"

"Everything," Billy grunted. He still looked shaken by Zhang's treachery.

"We never told you 'cause we didn't see you again," Jack explained.

"We found some jewels in a cave in Afghanistan last year. Turns out some of them were stolen from China long ago." "Famous rocks," Billy added.

Jack laughed. "Yeah, pebbles. Anyway, we made a deal to return them to China, to Chinese *SD* agents. This *SD* babe was gonna—"

"Make the exchange," Billy interrupted. An expression of anger crossed his face.

"She betrayed you," the general guessed.

"Exactly! She drugged us and—"

Billy exclaimed, "Took the gems *and* the reward!"

"So now, China's *SD* is after us big-time," Jack concluded. He banged his hand on the piano keys. The sounds echoed through the room.

"You know," Billy said, "Last night, she mentioned something about having relatives in Canada: Victor or Victory—something like that. I remembered the name, 'cause it sounded old-timey."

Hammar said, "Victoria? The queen? She's been dead for over—"

"Over a hundred years," Jack interrupted. "No, that's not it. Not the Queen. There's a city in Canada named after her. On an island, like just across the straits from Seattle or Olympia, somewhere in there. And British Columbia has a huge Chinese expat population. From Hong Kong and Mainland China."

Billy observed, "Maybe she figures she can blend in there. Or maybe that's her entry to the U.S."

"Yeah," Jack continued, "an unobtrusive, low-key border crossing, where she can sneak into the U.S. But dude, we gotta go back to Pakistan, head into China, chase down Robert Arses. I need a statement from him about the source of the money he gave us last year. You know I'll need something from him if I hope to get the pardons."

"Yeah, but he's not goin' anywhere," Billy said. "We need to go to

Canada. Chase Zhang down."

Jack admitted, "It'd seem the only way to get the Chinese off our backs. They're probly seriously pissed at us."

"But the police," the general pointed out, "they'll be watching the airport. It'll be almost impossible—"

"We've got much bigger problems than that." A new voice uttered the words.

The three turned to see General Andrew Jackson Harmbruster enter the living room.

"General!" Jack said. He quickly looked beyond the Marine— no General Farley in trace. He relaxed slightly, but was still shocked to see the Marine general.

"General Hammar was kind enough to temporarily quarter me."

Jack looked at the general's shaved head, his smiling eyes framed by deep wrinkles, asked, "Did you know General Farley was sending us here?"

"Not until he called me." The general frowned. "I'm afraid he's in big trouble for trying to turn you over to Chinese agents. Anyway, he called me in Tokyo two days ago. I decided to come ask you boys to help me out." The general flashed his famous Eisenhower-like smile.

"We thought we were escaping General Farley's clutches," Jack observed. "Now, we're—" *in your clutches.*

"Yes, well, in our line of work, sometimes we get lucky." The general grinned, flashing an insincere smile. "Congratulations and well done for the cavern attack, Marines. Forty-eight Taliban, dead or wounded."

The general shook Billy's hand, then Jack's. "Your action and Intel were outstanding pieces of work. I'm sorry I can't award you Purple Hearts or other medals for heroism. And I'm sorry we couldn't bomb the rat bastards when they ran out their hidey hole and escaped into China." He grimaced. "If only you'd recovered the LIIT package."

"General, I'm more sorry we're not active," Jack responded. "I'm not even getting paid for this cluster-fu—" He stopped himself, added, "But Mick is active duty. He did a great job, even if we didn't recover the LIIT thingy."

"I'll want a detailed report on his actions. I can reward him."

"Yeah," Billy snarled. "He's not a criminal."

"So you caught all the bad guys, General?" Jack asked.

"Unfortunately, Homeland Security didn't put much stock in Bruno Utecht—your Russian FSB agent—and his warnings about *Saladin's Fist*," the general took a coffee from General Hammar's houseboy, smiled a thanks. "I yelled, I cursed, I almost jumped up and down, but it did no good. Until this morning."

"What changed, General?" Hammar asked.

Harmbruster put a photo of two men on the table.

"The passport photo you boys found in the Chinese cavern training camp? That same individual crossed from the Canadian border on a ferry two days ago. In Port Angeles, Washington. Computer matches caught his image from security camera reviews but it was too late. He'd already disappeared."

Jack looked at the picture: the man was blond, had a severe, sculptured face that reminded him of Bruno Utecht's—they could've been related. The man behind him was Mara, dressed as her male half, Yassar Ahmoud. "That's Mara Bhutto!" Jack punched her mustachioed image with a finger. "You'd figure she and the rest of *Saladin's Fist* are there with the blondie guy," Jack concluded.

"That bitch!" Billy exclaimed. "The Bosnian pricks're with her. Like ticks on a mule deer."

"Exactly." The general blew on his coffee, took a sip. He looked at the handsome blond Montanan and his striking, dark Indian half-brother, added, "I understand now that it's true what they say about her—she's a master of disguises. You two know her better than anyone else does." The general spilled coffee on his blouse, mumbled a curse. "I wonder why she's so intent on harming the USA?"

"Long story, General," Jack said. "The real question is how did she convince those *Fist* dudes to cross the ocean to America?"

"Hey," Billy pointed out. "Same as us. We've got a volunteer army. No shortage of American guys willing to come to Asia and the Middle East to whack Arabs. Same for them on us."

"So, are you boys ready to visit our magnificent Northwest? It sounds like you need to head that way, anyways. I overheard you tale of woe about the *SD* broad. Victoria is opposite Port Angeles. An hour by ferry. I wonder if the two bitches are connected, somehow."

"General," Jack exclaimed, "why in hell would we go back to the States, help you when General Farley and probly half the FBI're trying to arrest us at every turn—"

"An' send us back to Leavenworth playground," Billy concluded.

"I don't think you going to have to worry about the general much longer," Harmbruster said. "He may be forced to retire for—"

Men's shouts, an argument. The crackle of gunfire shattered the atmosphere. A man yelled, distinctive, booming bursts of fire from a shotgun responded.

Chapter 40

Rushing to narrow windows flanking the front door, the brothers and the two generals saw a guard sprawled on the drive circle in front of the house, his shotgun at his side. Two blue Toyota SUVs abandoned in the drive. Doors left open. Gunfire sparkled, flashed from the dense jungle growth on the far side of the driveway. The crash of return fire sounded from the corner of the house.

"Police?" Jack asked.

"Don't know," Hammar responded. He grabbed a walky-talky, yelled harsh, questioning words in Pakistani, received a shouted, short reply. He said to General Harmbruster, "No uniforms, no warning, no search or arrest warrants—must be Jack's Chinese." He swung around, pointed a finger at Jack. "They're after you. You three—take my boat. Head downriver, you'll hit the strait. Turn right, you'll reach the city." He grabbed a float key ring off a pegboard next to the door, tossed it to Jack. "There're weapons in the cabin. Loaded. Good luck." Hammar pointed at a door facing the river.

"Hurry, before they kill all my guards."

The three ran to the patio door, Billy in the lead with his M-9 drawn. He dove, rolled on the patio, shot a Chinaman in civilian clothing, near the side of the door. Guy grunted, dropped a machine pistol. Jack grabbed it, fired at another *SD* guy rounding the end of the house, man yelled, ducked away. Sound of gunfire rose in volume, opposite side of the house.

The general in the lead, they dashed to the dock, jumped on the 30-foot cabin cruiser, with Billy hanging back and providing cover with quick double shots.

Jack inserted the key in the ignition, didn't wait for the diesel ignition to warm, started the engine. Billy emptied his pistol at men rounding the house, Jack yelled at him, tossed him the machine pistol. The general unloosed the mooring line. Jack gunned the turbo diesel engines, raced into the river, turned downstream, Billy emptied the weapon: short bursts slowed the pursuers.

Out of range, Jack curved the boat downriver, reduced the throttle to seventy-five percent, trimmed the boat, wiped sweat from his face, heaved a sigh of relief as the boat settled into a smooth plane.

The general, with a huge grin on his face, also wiped away perspiration, joined Jack. "Action—I love it!" He glanced at Jack, "What'd you say about avoiding trouble?" Without waiting for a response, he added,

"Seems to me, I'm your best shot at getting out of Singapore."

"He's right, bro," Billy yelled. He tossed the empty machine pistol into the river. "We got cops—probly at the airport—we got Chinese maniacs at every turn. We gotta get goin'. Greasy Grass, Montana, is lookin' real good right now."

"Yeah," Jack agreed. "But the general wants us to go where real cops are lookin' to arrest us—"

"Not wants you to go, Jack. Needs." The general said.

"You must have other teams—"

"Son, we got dozens of teams operating Stateside, but you have a special connection to this group." He pointed a finger at Jack. "You boys're our best chance to stop a terrorist force with God knows what plans for the western United States. And you sent a message that the LIIT warhead is still in enemy hands. Millions of lives could be at risk."

Overcoming a feeling of dread, Jack mentally pushed aside a snap vision of being stuffed and pounded into the sump back at Leavenworth. A sensation of pain swept through his body. "You got me there, General. We'll do whatever we can." He glanced upriver, saw no craft following them. Looked back at the general. "We could use help. Can you get Mick to join us?"

"I'll send him directly from Islamabad. He said he could also ID Mara Bhutto. I'll get elements of a BCT assigned to Homeland Security standing by at Fort Lewis, ready to go for you. There'll be other *EA* teams in the area, as well."

"EA?" Jack asked.

"*Eagle's Aerie*—a post 9/11, multi-agency group. It was formed to coordinate activities and intelligence: CIA, NSA, FBI,

NIS. Homeland Security is just too cumbersome. So a couple other military agencies, not to mention Echelon, informally set it up. Off the radar screen. They were going to call it Eagle's Nest. Eagle for America and nest because it was a collection of agencies. I guess Aerie sounded less tangled, more elegant. It's where I hang my stars these days." The general glanced at the shore, back at the brothers. "I feel you boys are going to solve this terrorist incursion. Track down the illegal entrants. Young men plunge where middle-aged men hesitate to go. I have to admit, my star'll shine brightly. And then—"

Jack watched the heavily vegetated banks rush by. "I guess you don't follow T'ai Kung, General."

"Huh? How's that?"

"As I remember, he said: *A good general shares labor and suffering with his troops.*"

Harmbruster smiled. "Good one, Captain. But I lean toward Wu Ch'i: *Bearing a sword's not a general's affair.* And remember, none of Shih Huang Ti's terra cotta statue officers bear arms. Now get out there and kick some Moo-slim ass while I sit back and take all the credit."

"Hey!" Billy laughed. "I thought I was the only one around here with a
Chinese connection. You an' the general sound like you're ordering *Kung Pow Chicken* take out."

"I don't hear you dangling any offers to get us pardoned," Jack pointed out. But I'll guess you'll send *Care* packages to Leavenworth. Maybe some arsenic to ease the pain?"

The general looked out at the water, shook his head. "I'm not going to lie to you. After this affair is resolved, you'll have to return to Leavenworth until I can get you freed. But *Serva me, servabo te*—Serve me and I'll serve you."

"That ain't gonna happen, General," Billy said. "We ain't goin' back there. Guys in Leavenworth Prison wanna kill my brother."

The general nodded, "I checked—the leader of that element is out. Dawklings, the tattooed man, supposedly escaped. But really, he got a pardon in exchange for working undercover for Treasury's ATF. Infiltrating an outfit called *God's Purpose*, somewhere in Oregon. Tillamook, I think." "You mean, Tattoo?" Jack asked.

"Yep. His selling of stolen weapons to them was what got him sent to Leavenworth. Now he's been turned against the group by ATF."

"That guy's as incorrigible as he is terrible-lookin'."

"Maybe so, but he's in a vital spot. We've intercepted *God's Purpose* emails that suddenly show a link to your *Saladin's Fist*."

"He's a racist asshole an' now he's out of prison, but we can't get a pardon," Billy snarled.

"I'm afraid General Farley has fought your pardon requests every step of the way. At least you're not behind bars," General Harmbruster concluded.

Jack pounded his fist on the gunwale. "Pisses me off, General. But I have to work for you. We can't let a buncha ragheads—"

"And white supremacists—"

"Billy's right. We'll give one hundred percent, General. I've been reactin' too long. We're goin' proactive. Those pricks think they can waltz in to the U.S. and raise hell? Okay, let's show them what hell's all about. All I ask is that you keep the fibbies off our back." Excited by his own words, he pushed the throttle forward, raced down the brown-watered Johor Strait towards Singapore and America.

Chapter 41

When the JAL 747 banked to the east, leveled towards Seattle-Tacoma International Airport, Jack woke up, looked out the window of the Tourist Class cabin. Instead of tropical jungles or dusty Afghan highlands, he observed familiar conifer forests spreading across the landscape. It felt great to be home until he wondered if he was destined to return to Solitary. To the right of the airliner, he spotted mutilated Mount St. Helens, still showing the devastation of its 1970's eruption, it's snowcap still illuminated by the late afternoon sun. The sight made him sing to himself:

We have fought in ev'ry clime and place
Where we could take a gun.
In the snow of far-off northern lands,
And in sunny tropic scenes...

He went to the bathroom, checked out every Asian man, wondered if each was a *SD* agent. They all looked like hardened spy-types, except for one man who had a chubby body and a smiling, round Buddha face. Not reassured, he retreated to his seat. He wished he had more back-up than Billy, someone dependable like Mick Nakamura or Bulldog Mahoney.

Bulldog, he thought, *the meanest drill instructor at Marine Corps Officer Candidate School. Half Irish, half Choctaw Indian, half-starving crocodile. Big: six-foot-five, raw-boned man, beak-nosed, black-haired— meaner than a Yellowstone Park mama grizzly bear chasin' tourists.*

Dead. Killed in action serving with Jack and Billy against Taliban forces the year before. Brave beyond belief, loyal beyond...

Jack glanced at his brother, followed his gaze, saw a gorgeous flight attendant in the aisle. She was Asian, very beautiful, and was responding to Billy's blatant gapes with smiles and extra attention. She was carrying a bottle of champagne she had swiped from the First Class section, handed it to Billy with a smile. Jack introduced himself. Her name was Ishey. Her large eyes were rounded on the top half, flat on the bottom and very slanted over prominent cheekbones—the eyes looked mean. Her lips were full and bright red, her skin was yellowish-tan, her complexion was flawless.

When she moved up the aisle, he asked, "Dude, how could you fall in love during my nap? Another Chinese babe?" Jack asked. "Got something against American chicks?" He thought of Caylynn. Her final yell when the rope snapped on the icy serac: *"No-o!"* Savagely suppressed the memory at once.

Billy opened the champagne bottle. "Ishey Murolta. She's Japanese-American, like your pal, Mick. And does she have a lip lock!"

"Kissed her already!" Jack glanced at his half-brother, whose black hair was still too short to form his beloved missing braids.

"She'd been flirtin', I caught her alone in the galley, wanted to make a major move." Billy chuckled. "For a second, after I did, figured it was a toss-up whether she was gonna call 911 or drag me into an empty bathroom. As my old fire team buddies used to yell, OohRah!" He popped the cork, filled the two plastic stem glasses Ishey had brought with the bottle.

Jack gulped his drink down—the champagne was sweet. "Dude, here I'm worrying about saving America from dastardly villains and you're tryin' to get laid. This picture's gotta change—maybe reverse." He held out his glass for more.

"Hey, you've got a pregnant girl back in Shangri-La. You can't mess around."

"Yeah, but she's not my girl—she's a power-mad queen of a two-bit tribe in the mountains. Definitely crazy!" He added, "And who wanted to keep me in her playpen by force. And she's prob'ly just imagining she's pregnant. Anyway, I already screwed up by dallyin' with China Mist." He avoided mentioning that Zhang might have crawled into his bed with China Mist, wondered for a second what Penel was doing.

"China Mist didn't count. You was drugged, bro, just like me." Billy slugged down his glass, grimaced, poured two more drinks. Pulled out a baggy and took two Oxy tabs just as Ishey arrived with an opened bottle.

Jack frowned at the action, tried to ignore his brother's addiction. "I'm happy that we're flying government-class on the general's dime."

"You got it, bro. I met a real babe and there prob'ly ain't no bad guys on this plane, fixin' to shoot us or blow up the plane." Billy looked around, added, "I hope."

"I *hope* she works out better than Zhang did." Jack gulped down the wine, held out his glass.

Billy poured, shifted uncomfortably, "Yeah, man. Sorry 'bout the Zhang mess. But you know me when it comes to the skirts."

Jack laughed, remembered and murmured a verse to dead Bulldog Mahoney's favorite military ditty, the centuries old Garryowen:

We'll beat the bailiffs
And shout for beer,
We'll make the lasses and widows fear,
Our cocks are huge,
We'll get much fame.
Where'er we go, we'll raise such Cain,
We're Garryowen in glory.

"What'd say? The Garryowen?" Billy asked.

"Oh, I was just rememberin' Bulldog Mahoney. What a guy."

"That he was," Billy responded. He picked up his glass, toasted the dead Marine, bellowed out the next verse, Jack joined him:

"Instead of water, we'll drink champagne,
And grab a girl by her mane.
Without cash, we'll still get lain,
We're Garryowen in glory."

Other passengers, startled by the raucous song, peered at the yelling brothers. Before an attendant could arrive to shush them, the *"Fasten Seatbelt"* sign flashed on, the big jet dropped flaps and gear, descended on final approach for Sea-Tac Airport.

Jack, with sparkling wine surging through his body, pulled out the State of Washington map a steward had given him earlier, tried to concentrate. "While you go to Victoria to flush out Zhang, I'll take my rental car, go over to Bremerton, swing up and catch the 101 to Port

Angeles. I'll watch from there. Hopefully, we'll get Mick to monitor the Seattle ferry terminal."

"I didn't tell you the rest of it. Ishey's taggin' along to Victoria," Billy said. "She's gotta one-week vacation layover."

"I musta slept a *long* time. You sure you want to bring a civilian? Can't you just get laid in the lav and be done with it? She might get hurt. Like..."

Billy ignored the jibes, gulped the last of the wine from the bottle. A steward frowned at him, so he put his seat up, handed over the empty bottle. "Screw it! We're not even sure Zhang's in Victoria. I may as well have a little fun." He glanced at Jack. "After all, remember where we're headed when this gig is over."

Jack frowned, ground his teeth, clinched his fist. "I'm gonna get a pardon and get us out. That's it. End of story." He shut his eyes, felt the wine coursing through his body, partially overriding the dismay he felt over his brother's new partner.

After the JAL flight landed and taxied to the terminal, the two exited and waited at the gate area for General Harmbruster's contact person. Arriving passengers milled about, looked for friends and relatives.

While they lingered, Jack used his cell phone, got the voicemail for General Harmbruster, left a message about their arrival, then called his father in Montana.

Bill was delighted to hear his sons were back in the States, working for General Harmbruster. He confirmed that the Chinese jeweler had fed-exed a cashier's check for three hundred fifty thousand dollars, and that he and the senator were using the funds to work on a Pardon program. He asked for Billy, and while the father and son were discussing ranch and reservation news, a stunning, heart-stopping redhead arrived, introduced herself to Jack as the FBI special agent assigned to the Seattle Division of Homeland Security.

"I'm Special Agent Tucson Luvabrest." With her voice, she should've been working for a 1-900 number.

He noticed tons of freckles covering a beautiful, fair-skinned Irish face, a smile that could melt an ice sculpture in a puff of steam, a perfect nose, wide-set hazel eyes—level with his own—they had to be enhanced by tinted contacts. Great kissable lips—no lipstick. He glanced at her hands— no nail polish, clipped short like a man's. His eyes dropped to her chest, restrained and concealed by a pants suit and a white shirt, decorated by a man's regimental blue and red striped tie. He concluded sadly, *Long and lean, but only a lesbian would wear such a masculine costume over that wonderful body.*

"Me, too," Jack responded. When the FBI agent gave him a sharp look, eye to eye, he said, "Love breasts, I mean." Imagined his head between her breasts, realized he was drunk.

After giving him a dirty look, and exchanging a cold, firm handshake, the gorgeous FBI agent handed Billy a key chain just as Billy handed him the cell phone. He said goodbye to his dad.

Tucson frowned at the delay, then said, "As requested, an SUV, compliments of DEA Seizures. At the temporary parking lot. In the vehicle you'll find new IDs—in your own names. Also, weapons and ammunition. Two 9 millimeter Berettas and two Heckler and Koch Mk 23 .45 caliber pistols, and two 12 gauge six-shot Benelli M10 Tacticals with shortened barrels." She smiled faintly, like her face was ice and she was afraid to break it. "Two prepaid walky-talky cell phones, PRRs with 500-meter range, credit cards and cash."

"Hey, the headset radios we used in Af-gone-stan," Jack exclaimed. "I like 'em. Good range. Maybe I'll call Uncle Santa—I mean Uncle Sam, and thank him for your gifts."

Ignoring his drunken attempt at humor, Tucson added, "Also, pictures of Mara Bhutto and the blond suspect with her when she entered at Port Angeles." She looked at each, added, "I'm assigned to this case because I work under the Northwest WMD Response Coordinator, and although I'm not a field agent, I'm the local duty expert on *God's Purpose.*" She looked at Jack, sniffed his breath, said to Billy, "Your brother is in no shape to drive. Neither are you. You're both drunk!"

"So, luckily, it'll be you driving or a taxi for me," Jack said. "Billy's to be picked up an assistant, and they're runnin' up to Victoria for a day or so." He was immensely attracted to the outrageously beautiful, long-legged redhead, despite her repressed femininity. Hoped he was wrong about her leanings, figured he wasn't. Wondered if she was going to hinder their search for Zhang. He glanced at his brother, added, "Is Mick here yet?"

Luvabrest looked into his eyes, sniffed his breath again and frowned. She was so beautiful! Jack felt his knees shake.

She continued, "Mick Nakamura, the Army major? He'll arrive in two hours—2100 hours. We have a second SUV for him, and an agent from the Seattle office will meet him. Do you two have checked luggage? And you don't have time for side trips to Canada."

"No luggage, we had to get outta Dodge in a hurry," Jack said. He smiled, resisted an urge to lean into the FBI agent, kiss her beautiful, lush lips. "And you're probably giving Mick a cell phone, as well? D'you have that number?"

Luvabrest sniffed his breath, frowned and leaned away. Shifted her attention to Ishey Murolta, who was approaching the trio. Tucson's eyes narrowed, she frowned with a knowing air.

Jack took the paper-wrapped Khyber knife and sheath from Ishey. "I had to check my sword with the Head Steward."

"Sword?" Tucson asked. Her eyes widening, she suddenly looked interested. "I collect knives—let me see it. What is it?"

"A Khyber knife. It's a long story—skip it." Ignoring her request, Jack introduced the two women when he realized that his brother wasn't going to make an effort. The two shook hands, exchanging impersonal smiles. He noticed again that Tucson had very long legs, imagined thong panties with a K-bar knife stuck under one hip strap, a pistol under the other, tattoo on her maybe fabulous breast—of a FBI badge. Wondered why she collected knives. *Another factoid in figuring this weird babe out.*

"Let's head out," Jack said, restraining a drunken giggle. "Go rent a car and call, me later, Billy." He took the SUV keys from Billy and picked up his bag. "According to the schedule on my map, the first ferry'll arrive in Port Angeles tomorrow at 1000 hours. So you can do some trolling through the bars and restaurants tonight. I'll watch for Zhang in the morning."

A half hour later, a silent and fuming Luvabrest drove an almost new maroon Porsche SUV towards Bremerton. She finally asked Jack, who was checking out black body armor vests lying in the tan leather-covered back seat, "What's your plan? What'd you mean when you mentioned trolling? Who's Zhang? Is she part of the terrorist cell?"

Jack turned and grinned. "We have a little side mission before we start looking for *Saladin's Fist*."

"What!" the FBI agent glared at Jack.

"Keep your eyes on the road, lady," Jack suggested. "A Chinese babe in Singapore stole some very important items from us. She also happens to be a pal of Mara Bhutto, the terrorist leader." *Sort of a lie,* he thought. *Zhang is terrified of Mara.* "We think Zhang fled to Victoria—it has a Chinatown. Strange coincidence that the two both left the Far East and traveled to the same town." *Stretching it again,* he thought. "So Billy's gonna slide through every bar and restaurant in Chinatown, ask for her, see if he can flush her and maybe Mara out. Make 'em run for it. I'll watch the ferry from Canada, we'll get Mick to watch the Seattle ferry dock."

"The Bhutto woman is already in the States! This is nothing to do with your mission objective!" Luvabrest protested. She slammed a fist on the steering wheel.

Jack regarded the fiery redhead, mentally debated, then decided to tell all. For the next hour, while Luvabrest drove, he related the story of the treasure, the Second Department spy connection, and how its renegade agent, Zhang Poon t'ang had stolen the gems and the reward, and had probably fled to Canada. How the Second Department was hunting he and Billy. He left out the Leavenworth history.

His cell phone rang, interrupted the end of the tale. When Jack answered, Omar Johnson, Green Beret 2nd Lieutenant, and his former college roommate, yelled, "Hey, bro, my MFA—was I happy to get your voice mail? And you're in Seattle? Thought you were in Leavenworth the last six months. The hell you doing up here, bro?"

"Hey, what's up, dude? I'm temporarily assigned to… well, I'm working for General Harmbruster again." He glanced at Luvabrest, worried that she might have overheard the mention of Leavenworth. She was staring straight ahead, still looking pissed. He didn't want to mention his prison sentence, didn't want to tip her off. "How're you doin'? Mick told me you got whacked real bad servin' with Task Force 121."

"Yeah," Omar responded with a subdued tone, "MFA Baathist prick. He's dead but I'm still sufferin'. Lost my leg, got mustered out with seventy-five percent disability."

"How're you doing?" Jack asked his former college roommate again.

"Not great—but I got a prosthetic leg—really amazin'. I'm gonna work for my uncle Natrone, during the fire season. Over in Kingsville. Unofficial and unpaid, but maybe it'll lead to something besides an office job. I'm on my way there tomorrow. My sister, Melody, she's already workin' for him."

Jack saw a road sign that read: Kitsap 12 miles. "I could really use your help, Omar. The general's got a very bad… situation goin'." "Something like last year?" "Remember Mara Bhutto?"

"Are you kiddin'? She's got a special place in my nightmares. Her and that giant Chinese cannibal, what's his name."

Jack thought of the ugly giant, Mo Poo. "I know what you mean, dude. Well, hang on to your ass—she's in Washington State with a group of Islamic terrorists," Jack's grip tightened on the cell. He forced himself to relax. "And she may have the LIIT warhead. That's why I need your help. I need you bad, to cover my six."

"Man, where's my team when we want it!" the former Green Beret exclaimed. "But see, my uncle is running this program for disadvantaged kids. Got a grant to build this fire-fighting school for ghetto-bashin' black kids in Kingsville. Teaching them fire fighting. Tryin' to turn their lives around. He wants me to help with the first class."

"That's great, Omar, but maybe you could report in, like, a month late. I really could use you. I know I can trust and depend on you." He glanced at Luvabrest's breasts again, sighed.

Omar responded, "Hey, bro, that's' good to hear—I've had a hard… well, I'll tell you what. I'll check in first thing in the morning. Kingsville's about a hundred miles west of Portland, in the coastal redwoods. Natrone'll understand—he's a patriot. Served in the Air Force as a firefighter. I'll call you after I meet with him."

"Okay, Jack said. "I'm gonna work my way down the coast road, looking for signs of Mara." He glanced at the FBI agent again, added, "The fibbies're keeping the terrorist threat secret, I guess, but it's real, buddy. Billy and Mick'll come down the inland freeway. We should be in Oregon in a couple of days. And you remember what Mara looks like as a guy? Keep an eye out. You carryin'?"

"No," Omar answered. Jack glanced at Tucson, said, "I'll mech you up when I see you."

When he finished, Luvabrest stretched—Jack's heart rate spiked—then she observed, "Your chances of finding this Zhang Poon t'ang—is that name a joke? You're talking a long shot way beyond the laws of probability. She could've gone anywhere."

"True. But she slipped up, left a clue to her whereabouts—it's our only chance right now. We didn't have time to explain to the Chinese agents how we got screwed by her. *SD* wasn't asking questions. They're pissed and were shooting bullets." He picked up the new black metal M-9, checked its load—it was empty. "And they won't give up. I gotta feeling that *SD* is a lot closer than I'd like. Maybe they chased us all the way to the States."

Luvabrest drove in silence, Jack's thoughts wandered back to ShangriLa: *Penelope. I wonder what she's up to? What if she actually is pregnant? I must not love her, this babe is really turning me on—and Zhang was gettin' me going. I gotta simplify my life, starting with this woman.*

"There's a K-Mart. I need a change of clothes," Jack said.

"K-Mart? Yuck!"

Jack looked at the redhead. She didn't look like she shopped at KMarts. "No choice this time of night—we can't shop on Rodeo Drive in Beverly Hills. If you care to snuggle up to me, you'll know I smell, too. I need clean clothes, a shower, otherwise, I'll never have a shot at you."

Luvabrest gave him a scathing glance, exclaimed, "Fat chance!"

When she stopped the Cayenne, he added, "You're wearing a very austere suit," he said. "Is that typical Stateside FBI issue?"

Luvabrest glanced at him. "Stop staring at my breasts or I'll turn you in for sexual harassment."

Jack stared at her breasts. "Great, do it. Maybe they'll send me back to Afghanistan to fight terrorists." He added with a softer tone, "I guess I'm used to the FBI guys overseas. They're pretty casual, pretty friendly. I had a pal, former FBI. Dave Holland, got whacked pretty bad in Singapore. You know him?"

Tucson rolled her eyes sideways. "Did you hear me?"

Jack shut up. Looked out the window. Wondered where Zhang and *SD*'s emeralds were: what Mara the terrorist leader was up to at this moment.

A half hour after they were back on the road, a bag of casual clothes at his feet, Tucson slowed, hit a right turn signal.

Roused from a doze, Jack asked, "What's up?"

Tucson turned onto a two lane asphalt road. "I live in Port Ludlow. I'm going to stop and feed my dog."

"So you're taking me to your home?" Jack asked.

"Don't get your hopes up—you stay in the car."

"Why don't I just drive on from here?" Jack asked, wanting and not wanting to be free of the FBI babe.

Tucson regarded him with an unfriendly face, then forced a slight smile. "My car is back in Seattle. You'll take me to the ferry in Port
Angeles, where I can take it back to downtown."

They wound through the small seaside village and stopped in front of an old-fashioned Craftsman style, one story, bright yellow house with brown trim. The cottage sat on a hill that had a wonderful view of the local marina.

"Nice place," Jack commented. "FBI must pay well."

"My folks loaned me the down payment," Tucson admitted. "It was a real fixer. My dad and I worked on weekends. He scraped peeling paint and replaced dry rot, I painted." She gestured at the

207

yard. "Mom planted all the flowers." Vibrant red gladiolas were blooming along the front porch.

"Can I see your knife collection?"

"Stay in the car," she ordered. A moment later, she returned.

He wished he could inspect her dwelling, see what she was all about. *Forget it,* he thought. *Tucson's a lesbian—and I gotta work with her—what a waste!*

Chapter 42

Penel Kong, True Hunza tribal queen of Shangri-La, held up a British fifty-pound note, one of two bills Dickey had given her when she determined to take the cavern from Shangri-La to China. The Pakistani bus driver examined the bill, looked at the burqa-clad woman, sniffed at the thought of a woman traveling alone. He finally nodded his head, after peering closer and wondering about her barely visible pale skin, her blue eyes.

Penel climbed aboard the crowded bus, grateful to be out of China— she had avoided the Chinese border station thirty miles north of Pakistan by riding a cantankerous gelding around it in the dark of night. She was grateful to be off the ill-trained horse she had ridden out of Shangri-La after guiding it through the caverns—she had been unwilling to take her favored palomino, for risk of losing it.

She stepped onto the ornately-decorated bus, even though she was very fearful of the magical, horseless mode of transportation. She had heard of similar vehicles visiting Shangri-La during the brief Soviet occupation in the 1970s, before they blew up the tunnel into the valley. Dickey had said it was the only sure way to get to Islamabad, short of riding a horse or walking three hundred miles.

Penel expected to exchange one of her gold necklaces for cash once she reached Islamabad. Then she would go to the British Embassy with a letter from Dickey Arses to a friend of his. Once she had a passport, she could catch an airplane to Montana, America, by way of India or Europe. At the frightening thought of flight, she patted her flat tummy, drawing comfort from Jack's silently growing baby.

She pulled out the letter and looked at it again:

Jasper Hedgerunning
British Embassy, Islamabad
Jazz, old fellow,
This letter accompanies MS Penelope Kong. Her father, Alexandre Kong, was awarded a British passport in 1892 (yes, that is the correct date— you can look it up) for services to Lord

Durand when he established the boundary between India and Afghanistan. Please issue her a passport. She must travel to America and needs formal citizenship.
Bugger on, and up Worcester College,
Dickey Arses

Penel put the letter away, thought of her father. King Alexi had died a hero at the gates of Haartgard the year before, knee deep in dead bodies, fighting off Taliban attackers. She glanced out the bus's window at the steep, snow-covered mountains arcing up from the narrow road—at least the terrain was familiar-looking—returned her gaze to the seatback in front of her, fearful of the rapidly moving scenery. She pulled strength from her dead father, tried to imagine she was riding in a rapid moving carriage, wondered what it would be like to fly around the world. She had already traveled fifty times the entire length of Shangri-La.

Penel knew much of the outside world, but all of her knowledge consisted of long studied history and geography books that had been packed into the valley over the years. She still dreaded having had to read The Rise and Fall of the Roman Empire. Her father had forced all his children to study the seven volume work, written in the Eighteenth Century by Edward Gibbon, and given to him by Lord Durand in 1900 A. D. Her practical knowledge, garnered from long tales by Dickey Arses, was of far more value. Still, riding in a carriage without horses seemed impossible. She wondered if she would survive the trip to the great city of Islamabad.

Chapter 43

Zhang parked her rental car outside the seedy waterfront motel on a side street just off the 101 Highway, two blocks west of the ferry landing at Port Angeles. She stroked her ponytail, looked at the building—decrepit even in the faint lights of the town's distant streetlamps—but it was where Jack was staying for the night.

When the tiny GPS transmitter she had glued into the lining of Jack's travel bag had moved into range of her receiver, it had shown him traveling from Seattle-Tacoma Airport towards Bremerton, Washington. Excited, Zhang had grabbed her few personal items, the gems, and the bond-bearing briefcase. After taking an elevator to the hotel entrance, she had jumped in the first cab, left the huge old Empress Hotel, turned onto Victoria's Wharf Street and nervously rode the two blocks to the Port Angeles ferry.

Zhang, thrilled that Billy and Jack had figured out her hints and had caught up with her, was determined to reach Jack and Billy before Chinese agents picked up the *SD* transmitter's signal.

By the time she walked on the crowded ferry, climbed the steps and seated herself on the upper front deck, the boat to Port Angeles was passing to the right of the Ogden Point lighthouse just outside Victoria Harbor. The lights of the Canadian city gleamed on the receding waters. A glance at the map-filled small screen of her PDA showed that Jack was past Bremerton and heading west on the 101, about thirty miles short of Port Angeles, Washington.

An hour later, she nervously passed through U.S. Customs. The uniformed agent asked her where she was born. She responded in the Orange County accent she had picked up the year before, "Newport Beach, California." He waved her ahead with a smile, and amazingly, didn't ask for her fake American passport.

Looking at the waterfront motel, Zhang slowly walked across the faintly illuminated, asphalt-surfaced lot that stretched from the ferry landing, and moved around to the waterside of the building. Watching the PDA, she stopped, back-tracked to where the signal showed Jack's position. The lights were out in his room, but the sliding glass door was open to the warm sea air over Juan De Fuca

Strait. Still, she trembled with excitement in the damp atmosphere, listened to a mournful foghorn, a distant barking dog.

Silently stepping inside the room, she glanced at the television. A late night weatherman was pointing at an offshore storm, approaching the Northwest United States. When he called the tropical depression, Draco, Zhang looked more closely: the storm, pictured onscreen by satellite photos, did look like an uncoiled dragon, heading for Oregon. The man was saying, "—suddenly swung north, bounced off a Hawaiian high, and is approaching the Pacific Northwest at a speed of twenty miles an hour. It's a category 3 storm with winds up to one hundred twenty miles an hour."

There were two beds: one was empty, in the other—a sleeping man, Jack or Billy. She listened: Billy snored. It was Jack, breathing slowly, in a deep sleep.

Exhausted from the long flight, she thought, *his loss.* Saw the open travel bag on the dresser top. Pulled a small knife out of her purse, felt inside, found the lump that was the transmitter, sliced it free. Pushed the power button three times to turn it off. It beeped, she looked at the sleeping man, held her breath. No movement.

Checked her receiver to confirm her action. She took a deep breath, tried to relax. Now, *SD* agents would lose the trail unless they were already here.

Zhang moved to the door, looked at the area between the motel and the water—no movement, no agents. Fog was creeping towards the shore. She left the door ajar.

Back to the sleeping man. A sudden thought entered her mind. *Maybe not his loss—maybe his gain.*

She smiled and pulled two plastic restraint strips out of her purse, then her 6mm Tokarev semi-auto, prodded his foot with the barrel. She wondered how angry he would be when he realized who she was. She prodded him again. "Wake up, Jack," she commanded.

Chapter 44

As Mara watched from behind a screen of small pine trees, Mikhail al Slovenly, the Bosnian leader of *Saladin's Fist*, silently climbed the ladder to the fire watchtower. Tall, slender, and athletic, the man quickly ascended the ladder. He was barely visible in the faint illumination from a canopy of brilliant stars. He disappeared from sight when he passed into the shadow of the tower, then reappeared at the top. She worried about this first real test of the Fist's resolve.

When al Slovenly stepped onto the tower's deck, a voice challenged him. Mara listened, heard a woman's voice, loud, almost hysterical, shout, "Who are you? You're not allowed up here. Uncle Natrone!" A man's voice, more commanding, "What the hell do you want? Go back down at —" Mara heard the thud of a silenced pistol. The man grunted, the woman screamed, but stopped after a very short outcry.

Al Slovenly called down in a quiet voice, "I have a woman." The other six of the Fist hurried up the fifty-foot ladder, giggled, joshed each other, sounded eager to enjoy their first reward in America.

Mara heard a moan of terror, a hard slap. When all had reached the top and disappeared, Mara caught a flash of movement on the tower deck. A silent body plunged to the ground, hit with a loud thump. Above she heard a laugh, a stifled cry of excitement, another of encouragement. She checked her watch, swallowed disgust and saliva-moistened pleasure, waited.

While the Fist members amused themselves with the woman in the tower, Mara thought: *I must focus on our goals. These men're weak. But they'll destroy Kingsville, kill every human in it before we start the fires that'll reduce the redwood forest park to ashes. The double blow will inject terror into every American's soul. Fear and trembling into the heart of every American town, into the heart of every American coward.*

Mara's thoughts turned to *God's Purpose*, the fanatical Christian group that was guiding her. A strange name for aiders and

213

abettors to Islamic jihadists, but modern-day politics made strange bedfellows. And her KEGYA contact had insisted that she work with the American group.

Mara waited for ten slow minutes, checked again. *Surely enough time,* she thought. She waited a couple more minutes, then blew a short blast on a whistle. Seconds later, another body plunged to the ground, made the same distinctive thump when it hit. She approached the two bodies, realized that both were black.

Saladin's Fist climbed down the ladder, assembled in front of Mara. The youthful voices quieted.

"The radios?"

"Destroyed," sculptured, hard-faced al Slovenly responded. "Just like the telephone lines to the town."

"Now it's time for the village," Mara said. The *Fist* nudged each other, shuffled their feet. "Remember," she added. "No looting. We don't have time. Our intelligence source at *God's Purpose* states there are approximately thirty firefighters and forty family and friends living in the village. We start at this end, on line, work eastward. No unsilenced gunfire, allow no screams. Silence will be the hallmark of our success. Silence is golden."

Al Slovenly stood in front of his six young men, spoke in American accented English. They were dressed in American clothes: ragged blue jeans, t-shirts, sports shirts, baseball caps, sunglasses on one member, worn even in the dark. "Remember, don't violate any Infidel women. We don't have time. You had your turns up there." He pointed at the silent tower looming above them. "We must be finished by dawn. Discipline is the key to excellent work, praise Allah," he continued. "Help each other, support each other. Work together. We're a team. When we're finished, we'll have a celebratory breakfast, prepare for the fire. We're at the end of a long, hard ordeal. Now, Allah willing, we can reap the rewards of our hard efforts."

Mara was impressed with al Slovenly's speech. She tried to discern the men's mental state—she couldn't see their faces. But most of them were bouncing or swaying with excitement. At least, she didn't have to worry about their commitment to violence. She marveled, and tried to understand —as a Catholic—how the Muslims' God, shared with Christians and Jews, could inspire such hatred.

Mara started the huge, second-hand Ford Excursion she had purchased in Vancouver, waited for the Fist to board. She drove slowly, followed by al Slovenly in a smaller Ford SUV he had stolen from the tower's shed when he discovered keys in the ignition. The Bosnians in the Excursion's back seat joked and talked in their incomprehensible language.

The two vehicles moved along the narrow one-lane road to the larger paved road that connected the village to the coast highway, ten miles to the west. Huge redwood trees flanked the road, hid the stars—she had to turn on her parking lights to see anything.

She turned left on the paved road. Up the grade of the narrow, two-lane asphalt road. *They even pave tiny roads to nowhere,* she marveled. *Oh, to make this country as poor as our world.* She felt a flush of enthusiasm, a surge of anticipatory pride.

Chapter 45

Jack woke from a deep sleep, in the dim light filtering through the window, he saw a woman's form at the end of the bed, wondered if it was Tucson, but heard a vaguely familiar man's high-pitched voice. An unmistakable voice from his nightmares of the last year. With a shudder of fear, he exclaimed, "Yassar—I mean, Mara!"

"Don't move, Jack," Zhang commanded in a workable imitation of Mara's fake male voice. "I don't want to shoot you…"

"What d'you want? Why're you still pretending to be Ahmoud?" Jack's heart was in overdrive, he felt horror from being trapped, sweat popped out of his skin. He had trouble getting enough air. He stared, trying to see her face.

Zhang tossed the two plastic hand restraints on the bed. "Handcuff your wrists to the bedpost."

Jack tried to see her face but could only see a dark form. "No way!"

"Don't worry, it's just a safety precaution. I don't want to hurt you. Do it, or—"

Jack still hesitated, thought about taking a chance, jumping into an attack. The woman's fist moved into the faint light from the window. Jack saw the small pistol, it was steady, unwavering.

"Mara, we're pals. Don't shoot me. I spared your life in the cavern. Hey, I'll do anything—I'll take you to a chick flick and not whine."

"Shut up with your stupid jokes! You're right, I won't shoot you," her high-pitched voice growled. "But I must secure you so I can question you. Now, do it!"

Reluctantly, quelling feelings of terror, Jack handcuffed his right hand to the bedpost. He held the other restraint on his left wrist but didn't attach it. He balled his free fist, waited.

The woman moved closer, he peered but could not see her face, read her intentions. He readied himself. She aimed the weapon directly at his head, but stayed out of reach; he gave up and snapped the second plastic strip to the bedpost, got ready to kick her.

"Hah!" she exclaimed in triumph. "Now I have the unbeatable Jack Flashhardt!"

"What's going on, Mara? What're you doing in America?" He hoped he could get her talking.

"Shut up, Jack."

He watched her put the gun on the dresser, start removing her clothes. Astonished, he watched her take all her clothes off, approach the end of the bed. *Kick her, maybe get lucky, knock her unconscious, but can I break the bedposts and free myself before she recovers? What the hell is she doing?*

Maybe reading his mind, she fell forward, grabbed his legs. "Now, Jack, perform, if you want to live."

"What? Are you crazy?"

"Big white man. Lord of the mountains, get it up."

"Mara, this is ridiculous—what're you trying to prove? Let me free. I couldn't possibly—"

"Maybe if I gave you some Viagra."

Jack's mind raced for a second, he asked, "Zhang?" She greeted his question with a peal of laughter.

"Are you crazy?"

"You already asked me. Or should I say, you asked Mara." She laughed again, ran her fingers over his ribs, up to his chest.

"Why're you doing this? What the hell were you thinking?"

"I was worried," Zhang answered, "that you might shoot me on sight. I wanted to give you a chance to cool down." She teased her fingers down his sides. "Admit it. Haven't you always wanted me?"

"Wanted you? I've had dreams about you. Ever since I met you. But not like this—let me loose."

"Not until you promise," Zhang said. She began stroking him—despite his anger, he started to become aroused by the unreal but provocative situation.

"Promise what?" Jack asked. Desire surged through his body, replacing terror.

"That's what I want." Zhang climbed on top of him.

"Zhang, you—"

"Shut up, Jack," she murmured, "We'll talk about emeralds, bonds, promises, *SD*—all that—after." She began to move faster. He rose to meet every thrust of her fabulous body. Billy's image flashed through his mind. He flushed it.

Chapter 46

Mara saw the sickening sight as soon as she reached the store: a baby lying in the doorway of the 7-Eleven store on the main street of Kingsville. The mother, who had probably made a late night run to the convenience store for baby formula, was as black and as dead as the infant, whose brains had been splattered all over the door frame.

The dead night clerk: black. Another corpse next to the rear door: black.

Suddenly worried, Mara hurried to the small house next to the store—a man, a woman, sprawled across their bed: black. A frightened Labrador puppy, upset by its unresponsive, blood-drenched owners, crawled towards Mara, hopefully wagging its tail. Distracted by the horrifying scene, she bent over, patted the whining puppy.

She left the house, the puppy scrambled to keep up to the long-legged Pakistani woman. The next house: all blacks. The next: the same.

She realized that the entire village was inhabited by blacks. *God's Purpose*, her American supporters, benefactors, had targeted a minority village. They had used *Saladin's Fist* to implement their hatred of American blacks. *Nothing good can come of this,* Mara thought.

She pulled out her walky-talky, called al Slovenly and said, "Abort. Abort the mission at once."

She heard a woman's cry, then men's cheering at the end of the five building commercial district. On the street, she saw a person run through the lit-up area from a house's windows, disappear in darkness, reappear in the lights of the next house. Members of *Saladin's Fist* were trotting like a pack of confident wolves behind the white woman, who wore only an open shirt over panties. The woman was grossly overweight and slowing. Her huge breasts swayed in front of her.

One of the *Fist* darted in, tripped her. The woman screeched, tumbled to the street. Mara wanted to stop the men, but feared their emotions were too high. She stepped into darkness and watched. Despite her initial anger at their reckless disregard for orders, she felt stimulated by the scene. She swallowed excess spittle, watched the men—who had totally forgotten their mission objectives—circle the woman like jackals surrounding fallen prey. One man turned her over, kicked her legs apart. Dropped his pants, fell to his knees between the woman's massive thighs. He raped her—finished in seconds—stood, laughed. Another man took his place.

Mara swallowed bile rising in her throat, listened to the victim's keening wails, an encouraging Bosnian chant from the *Fist* members, saw another man drop to his knees. No villagers responded to the victim's screams. They were either hiding or dead.

Chapter 47

A ringing cell phone woke Jack. Zhang was asleep, her head on his thigh. He grabbed the cell—it was Billy.

"Bro, I hit every Chink bar in Victoria. Don't miss the first ferry at ten hundred hours. I'll cover the Seattle boarding."

"Hold on a sec," Jack said, "someone wants to talk to you."

He shook Zhang, handed her the cell. He checked his Timex—it was 0730. A heavy odor permeated the bed.

"Hello?" she answered with a sleepy voice. She rubbed her eyes.

Jack heard his brother's shout from three feet away. Zhang winced and held the cell away from her ear for five seconds, then said into it, "Billy, I'm sor-ry!" More shouting. "I'm here to start my new career. In Hollywood."

She held the phone away for a couple of seconds, then said, "I told you where I was going. I knew you guys would follow me." She listened again. "I want to sing." Zhang listened to more shouts, responded, "I'm famous in China, but I want Holly—"

More shouts came from the cell, she said, "Whatever!" threw the cell to Jack, got up, retreated to the bathroom.

"She showed up in the middle of the night," Jack explained. "Turns out I was carryin' a transmitter she'd planted on me in Singapore. Her receiver thingy picked it up when we landed in Seattle. Zhang caught the final ferry last night, tracked me down." He listened to Billy's next question about the gems, then yelled, "Where're the emeralds, Zhang?" he held out the cell.

From the bathroom, over the sound of a flushing toilet, Zhang yelled in a screechy voice, "In my bag."

"Got that?" Jack asked his brother. He took a deep breath, wanting time before he had to face his brother. "She was on her way to L.A. when she decided to drop in. So you catch the next ferry to Seattle and head down the Five freeway, like we planned. Stop at gas stations and restaurants, show the photos. You know the drill. Zhang an' I'll do the 101 down the coast, then cut over to Portland.

We'll meet there. And you track down Mick; his number is programmed into your phone. Tell him we'll meet in Portland."

Billy asked, "What about the fibbie? She looks like trouble. She could arrest our asses if she found out we're escaped cons. You ditch her yet?"

Smiling, Jack responded, "Nope, she's still hangin' around." He hung up before Billy—he could tell his brother was royally pissed—could object, pulled on underwear, a pair of cargo pants. Zhang, still naked, came out of the bathroom, at the same time as a knocking sounded on the door.

Before Jack could respond, Tucson Luvabrest, the redheaded FBI agent, walked into the room bearing two coffees. She checked out Jack's bare chest, thoroughly inspected Zhang's perfect naked body. "My," she said in a cold voice, "I didn't realize you had friends in this part of the country." She looked back at Jack. "And here I thought you were exhausted last night."

"Yeah, I was pretty bushed, but when one more pretty bush grew near…"

Tucson's beautiful hazel eyes narrowed, shifted back to Zhang, who was standing between the two Americans, showing the unconcern of a naked woman who knew she had a glorious body. Tucson, dressed in tight blue cotton slacks, a t-shirt with the words Shoot a Tree on it, held up two Starbucks coffees. "I'm sorry I barged in here—"

"No, you're not," Jack guessed. "I thought you were taking the ferry back to Seattle."

"My superior is out of town. I went home, left a message. I want to come with your team." Tucson glanced at Zhang, looked at Jack with a hopeful expression.

Ducking the issue, Jack said, "Anyway, meet our Chinese connection —the girl we were lookin' for, Zhang Poon t'ang. She's my banker, my mobile safety deposit box. She's just getting dressed, right, Zhang?" Back to the FBI agent: "Did you bring cinnamon rolls or muffins?"

Tucson looked at Jack, back at Zhang. "The name's a joke, right?"

Zhang said, "Whatever!" grabbed her bag, walked into the bathroom, started the shower.

Still looking uncomfortable, the redhead handed him a coffee, sat in the armchair. "So you caught up with Zhang. I'm impressed— you work fast. Interested in joining the FBI when you're done with your service obligation?"

Jack chuckled to himself as he thought about nineteen-plus years in Leavenworth. He tried not to sound ironic when he said, "Sure, get me an application."

"Seriously, how did you find her so quickly? And if she stole something from you, how come..." she broke off and pointed at Zhang's pile of clothes.

Jack thought of the shadowy woman standing over him hours before, the semi-auto, the handcuffs. "Some people are just irresistible, but don't believe everything you see."

Tucson suppressed a smirk. "You or her?"

Jack waved a hand in dismissal, smiled. "Anyway, we can get about the business of finding *Saladin's Fist* without delay. Zhang'll come along— she knows Mara Bhutto. They're old pals. They went to school together."

"I know, Hainan—" Tucson stopped, started again, "Hey, now how long have they known each other?"

Jack thought about Tucson's apparent slip and changed wording for a moment. He looked at the FBI agent out of the corner of his eye. She appeared flustered, then she covered by inspecting her bluntly trimmed fingernails.

"I guess... yeah, maybe they went to Beijing University Extension classes—at an arts and crafts and terrorism school on Hainan Island," he responded, enunciating the Chinese name carefully. Tucson did not flinch. He thought, *What the hell's goin' on?*

"How do you know Mara?" Tucson asked.

"I met her when I worked for the UN," Jack responded. "She was... actually, she was many things. She was a professor, a dead prime minister's daughter, an assassin for China, and—"

"Busy girl!" Tucson exclaimed. "How *well* did you know her? As well as you know *this* woman?" She nodded her head towards the bathroom.

"Why're they both in the same part of the world at the same time?"

Jack stared at the flamboyant redhead. Her eyes appeared angry. *Maybe I was wrong about her.* He responded, "I'm gonna clean up. You watch the news."

Tucson put the coffee down and left the room, slamming the door as she went. He sipped the coffee—it was bitter but great-tasting after too many cups of Asian coffee full of unappreciated sugar. He tried to flush the image of Tucson's tight-fitting pants, her impressive breasts under the tshirt. He took the hot drink into the bathroom and shaved while Zhang showered. When they exchanged places, Jack asked, "Ever see her before?" "N-no," Zhang muttered as she grabbed his coffee off the sink top.

Ten minutes later, carrying the weapons bag and a backpack, he opened the door. Tucson was driving across the asphalt parking lot in the Porsche. She stopped, got out.

Jack bent over, inspected the empty interior. "Look, we're all gonna be traveling together, you okay with that?"

"Where's Zhang?" Tucson asked over the noise from a squawking seagull that was flying overhead.

"She's buyin' some muffins and more coffee by the Port Entry. We'll pick her up."

"She's very beautiful," Tucson observed. "Very cool."

"Yeah, well, so are you. Let's go."

Jack threw the weapons and the hiker's knapsack in the back seat.

"Zhang's?" she asked.

"Yeah," Jack said.

"She smuggled the jewels across the border like that? And she trusted you to not ditch her now that you have them?"

Jack mentally kicked himself for being stupid enough to tell the FBI agent about the emeralds. "Smuggled what?"

"Your missing gems. If she didn't declare them—and I'm guessing she didn't—that's a federal crime." Her voice grew eager. "I'll have to arrest her."

Jack started the SUV as Tucson settled into the passenger seat, pictured himself twisting into a human pretzel and kicking himself again. "You got time for a search warrant? I thought this terrorist business was pretty important."

"Probable cause," Tucson announced with satisfaction. "A righteous bust—"

Jack's cell rang. It was Omar, returning his call, and he was talking too rapidly to understand.

"Slow down, Green weenie."

Ignoring Jack's jibe, Omar rattled, "My sister, Melody—my uncle— dead! My God, Jack, half the town. The Sheriff's Department's here. Bodies all over—like, one whole side of Kingsville. All dead!"

"Omar, I'm sorry!" Jack exclaimed. "Hang on a minute." He parked in front of a donut shop and Zhang, a small pack on her back, carrying the bank warrant briefcase, drinks and a bag of food, climbed in back. He glanced at the black leather briefcase from Singapore, up at Zhang. She nodded. Returned his attention to Omar. "You think these killings have anything to do with Mara?" Jack U-turned and headed west on the 101 Highway. He noticed Tucson sit up, look at him. He held the cell in the air between them.

"No, 'cause the words *God's Purpose* are scrawled on the window of the 7-Eleven," Omar's words carried through the Cayenne. "In blood. Sounds like a hate group thing to me, 'cause this whole camp and village are brothers and sisters, bro."

Jack felt a cold weirdness flush through his body. "Dude, General Harmbruster told me some *God's Purpose* crowd is Mara's Stateside connection. But why would they admit to killing…"

"Doesn't make sense," Omar sobbed, stopped himself. "Sheriff already called the FBI. *God's Purpose,* whatever they are, is goin' down. They've gone off the deep end. Melody, Natrone— dead. Jack… she was raped, left like garbage. An' I saw a baby…"

225

Jack's mind raced. "Unless Mara's trying to double-cross her benefactor for some reason."

"But… how would Mara know about a tiny village in the redwoods? Melody and Natrone. They shot him… dumped my uncle off the watchtower like a sack of goddam trash! Melody, the same. No bullet wounds on her. And they're still pulling bodies out of houses."

"Half the town is dead?" Jack asked. "How do we get there?"

"Don't worry," Tucson interrupted him with a touch on his shoulder.

"I've got my iPhone."

"Omar, we'll be there in…" he glanced at Tucson who was staring at her cell, held it out.

"Less than four hours to the Oregon border. Maybe another hour to wherever." She checked her watch, added, "One PM if we speed."

Jack patted the dashboard. "This turbo Cayenne costs over a hundred grand. I'll bet it can speed." He spoke into the cell, "Got that, Omar?"

"Let me drive," Zhang said. "I took a racing course on Hainan Island."

"No," Tucson said. "I'm the only law enforcement agent in the car." She glanced at Zhang. "American, anyway. I can conduct a pursuit. And I took a racing course at Las Vegas Speedway. Pull over, Jack."

He jammed to the side of the two-lane highway. "It's so nice when you guys, like, let me at least wear the pants around here." He got out, ran around the front of the car while Tucson climbed into the driver's seat. "I'll bet this thing can fly. Just don't get us in an accident," he cautioned.

226

Chapter 48

Opening her eyes was impossible. Penel Kong had shut them when she saw the ground fall away from the airplane. It was as though she was a child again, flying into the air as she had done when her father used to throw her as high as he could. But this rapid ascent was horrifying. She clenched her fists and waited for the craft to fall back to the earth.

"Are you alright, sweetie?"

She peeked through one eye, saw a Chinese woman in a pants uniform of sorts, who was clasping her shoulder.

"Never flown before?" the woman added. "Can I get you something to drink?"

Seeing the unconcerned woman helped calm her. "Thou art not afraid this craft will crash to earth?" she asked.

"Heavens, no! Relax, honey, I do this all day. They hardly ever set down where they're not supposed to."

Penel felt a pang of nausea in her stomach. She beckoned the uniformed woman to lean closer. "I need to…"

The woman asked, "Can you wait a few minutes?" She looked at Penel, answered her own question, "No. Come with me."

Chapter 49

Mikhail al Slovenly, the *Saladin Fist's* Bosnian commander, shuffled his feet during Mara Bhutto's rant. Since he couldn't look her in the eye, she knew she still had control. Satisfied, Mara switched topics. "This morning, we'll overcome last night's disaster at the village." She glared at the other men, who were looking down, around, and anywhere but at her. She tried to soften her words with a half-smile. "Mikhail, you were brilliant to think of leaving a clue pointing to *God's Purpose.* We earned our propaganda victory. Unfortunately, we can't take credit because of the white racist gang's trick."

Mara spread a map across the hood of the Ford Explorer they had stolen from the fire watchtower, then beckoned granite-faced al Slovenly closer, pointed at a spot on the map. "This redwood forest appears tinderdry from the drought. The winds are favorable."

With a marker pen, she made an X an inch in from the coastline. "One man will start a fire at the outskirts of this village called Necanicum, on the 26 roadway. Another man will penetrate the forest for ten kilometers directly to the south and start fires." She made another X.

Mara looked at the Bosnians. "Another man will head ten kilometers north from the intersection of the Wilson River and the 6 roadway." She stabbed that point on the map, also an inch in from the ocean, with the marker.

"A fourth man will start a fire at the intersection of the river and the road. A fifth man will head ten kilometers south from that point. The sixth man will move ten kilometers north of the junction of the 22 and the 18." She marked those points, looked up. "These fires will all start at noon, when the winds are freshening, and the dryness is reaching its highest point of the day. The resulting sixty kilometer long firestorm will be unstoppable. I'll wager there has never been a fire this big in dense foliage like this. It could burn all the way to Portland. These high winds are a deserved plus after our fiasco in the village." Mara pointed at the wind-blown branches in the forest's trees.

Al Slovenly observed, "Just to move through the tangle will be difficult."

"Make sure your compasses are functioning. If you start now, you should be able to travel ten kilometers by noon."

The Bosnian looked at the north-south line and nodded again, then looked at the dense forest on all sides. "What will you do?" he asked.

"You and I will pick up the *Fist* at the checkpoints and meet in Eugene at the Holiday Inn, just off the Five Freeway, where I have rooms reserved." Mara looked at the sculptured-faced Bosnian. Wondered what their chances were of starting a fire that might burn all the way to the city of Portland. Prayed they were good chances. Hated the over-confident Bosnian.

Chapter 50

Tucson Luvabrest, the redheaded, freckle-faced FBI agent, took over driving duties on the outskirts of Port Angeles, the U.S. ferry port for Vancouver Island, Canada. A half hour later, she raced along a forest-lined two-lane road, slowed briefly in a village a sign identified as Ruby Beach, drove south along the Pacific Ocean.

A strong wind was bending weeds, shrubs and trees. The wind was also catching the top of the huge waves crashing against the shore, tossing sprays of white foam in the air. Jack lowered the window: the smell of the sea was strong, with a tang of salt, a hint of decomposing fish.

The sky was blue overhead, but to the southwest, a huge storm front, towering to at least sixty thousand feet, and covering a third of the horizon, was soaring towards land. By noon, as they crossed into Oregon, the leading edges of the storm were hitting the shore and torrential rains and high-powered winds slowed their progress to a crawl through a forest of giant redwoods along the coast.

"It's *Dragon God!*" Zhang Poon t'ang exclaimed from the backseat of the rocking SUV.

Superstitious and alarmed, Jack stared at Zhang. Tucson asked, "What're you talking about?"

"The man on the television said the storm's name is Draco," the former *SD* operative explained with a woeful tone.

Jack relaxed. "Just a name."

An hour later, Jack's cell phone rang. It was ex-Green Beret Omar Johnson. "Jack, it has to be the Bhutto bitch!"

"Omar? What're you talking about?" Jack checked Zhang in the back seat. She appeared to be sleeping, using the pack of gems as an ultraexpensive pillow.

"Two fires started. Responding fire trucks got fired at by ambushers." Omar's voice rose with excitement. His words were rushed. "Trucks couldn't get to the fires. More fires reported. The terrorists musta started them."

Jack looked at the slashing wipers try to clear the pounding rain off the windshield. "Fires! Omar, how far are you from the coast?"

"About fifteen miles, but the point is—"

"Dude, don't worry about fires. Way it's raining on the beach, no fire in the world'll survive. Head for the coast. Call me when you get to Tillamook. We'll arrange to meet."

Tucson was bent forward, trying to see through the cascading downpour. She continued at a slow pace that frustrated Jack. Zhang slept, unperturbed by the weather, with the gems bag still under her head. An hour later, they pulled into Tillamook, passed the cheese factory, stopped at the Sheriff's station. Two helicopters were tied down in the howling wind: one a Bell Jet Ranger with State of Oregon State Police markings, and the other a white unmarked MD 500. When Tucson saw the unmarked helicopter, she muttered, "Oh, shit!"

Jack glanced at her, then at Zhang before he opened the door. She was still sleeping on the gem bag. He smiled. *Wonder if our antics last night exhausted her. Billy—wonder how pissed he would be? Should take the gems inside. But what if the cops question what's in the bag?* Sheets of rain instantly drenched Tucson and Jack when they climbed out of the SUV.

Tall, lean Omar Johnson, who had been watching for the Porsche Cayenne, held the door open as Jack and Tucson ran into the one-story building. He yelled a greeting, turned and led them inside, showing no signs of a limp, despite his artificial metal leg—which was visible because he was wearing shorts. Out of the driving rain, Omar, dark and thinner than the year before, hugged Jack, smiled at Tucson, then the three hurried to the sheriff's office. The room was spare, with linoleum floors, beige walls and gray metal cabinets. Two men, one uniformed, one in civvies. A short fat woman in uniform. A blown-up picture of Mara Bhutto, appearing as a man, and the blond *Fist* member, taken at Port Angeles border entry, was taped to a blackboard on the end wall. An arrow pointing at the photo and written words: FIND HIM/HER.

Omar introduced Jack to Sheriff Bjorn Jansen, a heavy-set, balding man with a blond walrus mustache, calculating blue eyes, rosy cheeks, and a big, disarming smile. He wore a khaki uniform.

Jansen said, "I've already heard from your boss, General Harmbruster. Said to expect you. Said you're a good man. One of his best." He shook hands with Jack. "I'm surprised you're so young. You must have some special talents. Thanks for coming."

Tucson also shook the sheriff's hand and introduced herself, then presented Jack to her superior, Kenneth Yarmouth, the regional WMD Response Coordinator who had flown down from Seattle in the late morning. He was dressed in a blue windbreaker like the one Tucson was wearing, that spelled FBI over the left chest and on the back. Yarmouth was tall—almost as tall as six-foot-four, long-legged Omar. He was a thin man, with short, sandy hair, scars from a lost battle with adolescent acne, and protruding ears. He frowned at Tucson until Jack shook the agent's hand. Jack wondered, *What if they figure out who I am? Do I get a medal before I get out of here? Or do they slap me in handcuffs?*

The last person in the room was introduced by the Sheriff as the US Forest Service, Northern Division Fire Administrator for northern Oregon and southern Washington. She was a heavy-set, grey-haired woman named Clara Nielson, who stood five feet two inches tall, had a harried look, accentuated by wisps of dirty hair that kept falling in her face. She ignored an offered handshake. Jack wondered whether she had ever actually fought a fire.

The sheriff started the meeting by welcoming all present to Tillamook. He pointed out sandwiches and a coffee urn to Jack and Tucson. The others were already devouring food.

Jack, more interested in checking Zhang out than feeding her, grabbed a sandwich and a coffee. He excused himself and took the victuals to the SUV, shielding the food and drink from the downpour.

"You okay?" he asked as he climbed in the Porsche. "We haven't had a chance to talk."

"Get rid of Love Tits," Zhang declared with a hostile tone. She sipped, then gulped warm coffee. "She wants to throw me in the darkest American prison."

"We don't have dark prisons," Jack grinned. "Here, you get work-out rooms, Medicare, TV." He thought of his cell in Solitary back at Leavenworth. *Yeah, right.*

"I'll pass," Zhang said through a mouthful of cheese sandwich.

Returning to the building, he heard the gray-haired woman say, "— three firefighters wounded by gunfire, two seriously. All three were medevac'd to Portland by ambulance. Too stormy for helicopters." He helped himself to a sandwich and a cold coffee.

"Luckily," the sheriff interrupted, "it appears their weapons misfired in the middle of the attack, or there woulda been more casualties."

The Fire Administrator frowned at the sheriff's interruption, finished with an officious voice, "There were actually twelve separate fires started. We were able to get to three of the fire sites. But we pulled back after ambushes by unknown assailants, at the junction of Highways 22 and 18, and at a point on Highway 6, just east of the town of Necanicum."

"If they're A-rab terrorists like the General thinks, it's like Japan's fire attacks on Oregon by balloon in World War II," the sheriff mused. "Like the Japs, they got no idea of how big this country is— Anyway," he continued, "it appears the perps used old, poorly-functioning, military M-16 rifles. At least, they were firing military ammo. They disappeared, but we have roadblocks on the 101, the 22, the 18, and the 6. We're searching every vehicle— although there's not much traffic in this storm. And we can't use aircraft until the ceiling lifts and this goddam storm passes."

"Still, it looks like the weather saved your asses," Jack observed.

"No one can expect firefighters to operate under combat conditions," Clara Nielsen, the short Fire Administrator protested. "We could have had a fire holocaust. The fires were spread along a north-south line, twenty plus miles long in a tinder-dry forest. The storm snuffed out the flames better than a C-130 chemical dump."

The sheriff agreed, "We got lucky. This Pacific storm, Draco, hit our coast at a most opportune time. We've had a year-long drought in these parts. We coulda had a firestorm."

At the mention of the storm's moniker, Jack and Omar exchanged glances. Both thought of Dragon God, shook their heads at the coincidental name. Jack had an image of the golden dragon roaring across the skies, breathing water instead of fire. He checked out Tucson—she looked very nervous.

The sheriff continued, "The question in my mind is, did these terrorists kill the folks up in Kingsville? The strange thing is, *God's Purpose* called and reported hearing gunfire in the village."

"There's been a lotta conflict in the past," Omar said. "My uncle, Natrone Johnson, told me about numerous verbal confrontations he had with those racist beasts. Why would they now try and save people in Kingsville?" Jack said, "We know there've been communications between *Saladin's Fist* and *God's Purpose*."

The sheriff glanced at Yarmouth, the acne-scarred FBI guy. "I'm familiar with the *Purpose* folks. Buncha racist nuts live on a farm east of Manzanita—that's a small village about twenty miles up the coast. But they're fundamental Christians—at least, so they claim—why d'you think they'd be connected to Islamic terrorists? Seems like they'd be at each other's throats."

"Maybe they are," Jack observed.

"What d'you mean?" Yarmouth asked. He took off his blue FBI jacket.

Tucson sipped coffee. "Sir, he means, what if *God's Purpose* misdirected their supposed ally? Used them for their own reasons. The terrorists would be pretty clueless, would've—"

"Depended on the whackos for their Intel," Omar interrupted. "And my Uncle Natrone's school could've—" "Paid the price," Tucson finished.

"So maybe the terrorists painted the name *'God's Purpose'* on the store window," Jack speculated, "as a payback."

Yarmouth and the sheriff listened to the guesswork, both laughed.

"Too many conspiracies," the sheriff said. "Buncha damned ragamuffins."

"These Bosnian guys are tough, dedicated," Jack pointed out. "There were thirty-plus candidates, narrowed down to ten. Our team raided their headquarters in Afghanistan and ran into a vicious firefight. We managed to kill three of the *Fist*, twenty-three local Islamics and Taliban militia. They suffered two dozen wounded. When we catch them here, we'll finish the job."

"Hold on there, son," the sheriff protested. "I'm runnin' any operations in this county, not you. You can't be going around shooting folk just because—"

Jack raised his hand, interrupted, "You don't understand the magnitude of the problem, Sheriff. They're militant Islamic jihadists who want to kill all Christians and Jews. They'll never give up. We'll have to kill every single one of them. They're like a disease."

"Jack's right," Omar added. "These aren't a bunch of street punks or Mexican Mafia. These guys *want* to die for their cause. And we'd best make sure the bastards meet their destiny."

With heavy sarcasm, Yarmouth said, "Well, thanks for fluffing out our profiles of these so-called terrorists. But do we know that they're not American citizens? We're not even sure whether *God's Purpose* or your *Fist* people are responsible. And we can't go shooting American citizens just because we don't like them. Sounds too much like Waco or Ruby Ridge. So just hold onto your horses, Flashhardt. The FBI is running this operation, not a kid from the military. And if they are Islamic terrorists. We have to suppress that news."

After a dirty look at Yarmouth, the sheriff asked, "When you had that terrible fight with these feisty salad fist folks, how many casualties did you suffer?"

"None," Jack admitted.

"Son, that sounds like you were shootin' fish in a barrel," the sheriff scoffed.

Omar immediately stood. "That's because you don't know Jack. He planned and executed a rescue of me from the Taliban last year, his force killed fifteen enemy with zero KIAs. Then later, he led a combined force that wiped out a force of 115 Taliban with one friendly KIA, then he and his brother dropped an avalanche that destroyed a force of over two hundred attackers with no KIAs. This man is a… killing machine like no other man you've ever met."

When Omar finished, the two agents and the sheriff were staring at him, open-mouthed.

Jack said, "Any PR guys present?" He held up three fingers. "That's Flashhardt—double h. Anyway, spare us the history lessons, Omar. These folks're gonna think I'm bloodthirsty. I'm not. Sheriff, I'd be happy to back out of this, but I have very specific orders from General Harmbruster of EA —that's—never mind. Suffice it to say, my orders supercede your office and the FBI as well." He smiled. "I'll be happy for any assistance you can provide. I have a feeling," Jack continued, "that we're goin' to need all the help we can get. You guys dodged a bullet, but the *Saladin's Fist* guys are still at full strength. The question is, what're they gonna do next?"

"Listen, kid," Yarmouth said, "the sheriff and I are running this, not you."

Jack looked at the sheriff, Tucson, then Yarmouth. He asked, "Has anybody in this room actually killed a bad guy? I mean besides Omar, who is absolutely fearless in combat. And myself?"

The law enforcement agents looked at each other, looked down, kept quiet.

"Well, that's good. It's a horrible experience. Killing people, I mean. I think I'll pay *God's Purpose* a visit. I have a contact there."

"Son, you don't wanna mess with those crazies," the sheriff said.

"They make David Koresh of Waco look like a Sunday School teacher."

Just, then, the dispatcher, a short, overweight blonde woman about twenty years old, burst into the room. "Sheriff, two SUVs just ran the roadblock on south Highway 101, There's no response from deputies after the initial report of contact."

Chapter 51

The first thing Jack noticed when he, Omar, and Tucson ran through the downpour to the SUV and opened the car door, was the empty back seat. Emeralds: gone. Warrants: gone.

"Damn that woman! Give me the keys," he snarled.

Tucson triumphantly grinned at him. "What made you think you could trust her? Your performance in a one-night stand?"

"Are you kidding?" Jack scoffed. "She's Billy's girlfriend, not mine. It's just that she was overwhelmingly persuasive last night."

"You cheated on your own brother?" Tucson sounded offended.

Jack thought: *the pistol, plastic cuffs, Zhang lying on my body, stroking me. Wish I could tell what happened.* "I guess you'd had to be there before you could judge."

Tucson opened her laptop. "We have to head north to the *God's Purpose* headquarters." She looked up. "You're heading south." "Yeah, north's the direction," Omar agreed.

"Omar, I'm heading south because I need to round up Zhang," Jack said. "Goofy broad thinks she's gonna get away to Frisco or L.A. She can't have gotten far. I haven't forgotten your uncle and sister."

Tucson pounded the dash with a fist. "You can't put your personal affairs before the mission!"

"Oh, yeah?" Jack retorted. "If I don't find those gems and get them to Second Department, there won't be a mission, 'cause I'll be room temperature."

"China won't put operatives on US territory," Tucson sneered. "They know we'd apprehend them at the border."

"Right!" Jack scoffed. "Then I guess I don't have to worry that I can't reach Billy, warm him that a Second Department agent—called Ishey Murolta—is traveling with him."

Aghast, Tucson looked at him. "*SD*? How do you know?"

"Because Zhang *is SD*. She ratted out Ishey when I gave her a description. She's Zhang's Chinese stand-in. Billy thinks she's Japanese— well, they all look alike to me. And he's not answering his cell phone." He looked at Tucson. "See the problema? She'll string him along until she figures out he can't deliver the emeralds. Then she'll dust him. My brother'll die."

"I'll have her arrested." Tucson dug into her purse for a cell phone.

"No!" Jack exclaimed. "Billy an' Ishey might blow away a cop or one of your agents. Then where'd we be?"

"Sounds like I've got a lotta history to catch up on," Omar observed.

"Dude, you can't imagine what you've missed, lying around some VA hospital ogling the nurses," Jack replied. "We'll catch up later." Nurse Candy of Bethesda Hospital jumped into his mind. He regretfully brushed her wonderful image aside.

As Tucson put her cell away, it rang. She answered with a hello and listened for a moment. Then she put the cell on speaker.

"I was upset with your continuing on with the military punk from Port Angeles," Yarmouth's voice said. "But I want you to stay with him. He and his pals are loose cannons. Keep me up to speed." The cell went silent.

Jack, who was driving through the downtown district of Tillamook, slowing in front of every roadside business, suddenly swerved in front of an eighteen-wheeler that was leaving a restaurant parking lot.

Jack didn't move the SUV, even when the huge truck hit its air horn. After another thirty seconds, Zhang climbed down, wearing the backpack and carrying the briefcase. Soaked, she got in the backseat of the Cayenne without a word. Jack backed up, let the truck gain the highway and leave.

He glanced at Zhang. "What? I forget to brush my teeth? Wrong deodorant? Didn't ask for your phone number after you crawled out of bed?
By the way, Omar, this is Zhang."

Zhang peeked at Jack, looked away.

Tucson Luvabrest asked with a sneering voice, "So what'd you promise the truck driver—a blow job?"

Zhang returned Tucson's look with a withering glare.

Tucson snickered. "Hope he didn't make you prepay."

Zhang fixed her frown on the downpour outside, did not respond to Tucson's taunts.

Jack made a U-turn, headed north on the 101 highway, along the beach and its storm-tossed waters. When he saw a post office, he stopped, took the briefcase containing the warrants, went into the post office, put them in an overnight envelope and sent them to his dad in Montana.

He tossed the briefcase in a trash barrel by the exit, rejoined Tucson, Omar, and Zhang.

Driving north along the ocean, the clouds were so low, the top twothirds of the closely packed pines along the road were invisible. The trees looked like they had been beheaded by the gray mists. Jack breathed deeply of the ocean's salt air, glanced at Omar.

"The Hunza," Omar guessed, referring to the trooper beheaded in the caves of Afghanistan the year before.

"Yeah, you got it, pal," Jack agreed. "Lucky these beheadings're just trees."

Driving at a speed of twenty miles an hour, through sheets of water that splashed up like waves from a racing boat, they reached the seaside village of Manzanita an hour later, at half past three in the afternoon. The rain continued to sheet from the sky.

Omar said to Jack, "I really want to meet up with these Purpose dudes, but I think you'd better check it out first. I don't think it's a good idea for Zhang and I to go to *God's Purpose* with you. Snoop Dogg gangsta rap won't mix with Country Western. But I left my car at the school. Why don't we rent a hotel room here on the coast and wait for you."

"I guess you're right," Jack agreed. He pulled into one of the many seaside lodgings. It was named The Sunshine Motel. "Take the emeralds. You good to go on cash? I'll fund you later."

"I'm cool," Omar said. "Be careful."

"I think we should all stick together," Zhang said.

Jack looked at her. "Right. Don't take any cookies or drinks or nothing from Zhang. And when she seduces you, make sure her hands are empty." He said to Zhang, "Give me the .25. Or better yet, give it to Omar."

Zhang gave Jack a dirty look, did nothing. She and Omar got out and Omar waved goodbye.

Following Tucson's instructions, Jack returned to the 101 and minutes later, turned inland on a gravel road that headed into heavily wooded hills. The blackberry underbrush on each side looked like an impenetrable jungle. Twice they had to drive off the road and crush their way through the brush to skirt washouts, and once they had to drive partially around and then over a fallen tree.

The Cayenne, with the ability to automatically direct power to the wheels with the most traction, bumped over seemingly impossible obstacles. The rain, which continued to pour down, made the two feel like they were isolated in a watery capsule, winding through the verdant forest.

Tucson asked, "How'd your friend lose his leg?"

Jack looked at the lush undergrowth on each side of the road. "He was second in command on a Special Forces team in Iraq. I don't have the details yet. It's just such a shame—he was a real athletic guy." "I'm sorry," Tucson said.

"We were pals since we were at Stanford. Drawn together, I guess, 'cause both our families had a long military tradition. And I was a country hick from Montana—I'd never met anyone like Omar. He was the first black guy I ever really talked to—I mean I had met blacks in Africa when Dad and I were climbing Kilimanjaro."

"You climbed it?"

He glanced at the agent, then back at the mist-filled, rain-soaked forest lane.

"I was born in a hurricane
And I howled in the driving rain,
But it's all right now, in fact, it's a gas!
But it's all right. I'm Jumpin' Jack Flash."

"That sounds vaguely familiar," Tucson commented.

Laughing, Jack looked at his companion. "You're too young, but so am

I. My dad used to sing it to me once in a while. Rolling Stones."

Tucson smiled. "You're right."

"It was sorta like Jackie Chang meets Chris Tucker in *Rush Hour,* the movie. Anyway, we were real close in college, then I ended up investigating his guerilla force when I served with the United Nations in Pakistan. He got captured by Taliban during the investigation an' me an' some other guys rescued him…"

Jack bumped over a fallen tree, added, "Last year, Omar and some of my other buddies helped me save my girlfriend when she was kidnapped in the same area of the Hindu Kush."

Tucson, sat up, asked, "Where is she?"

"She's…" *I don't want to say Ashley bailed on me when I got convicted.* "…gone on down the road. We parted company."

Tucson looked at him and asked, "Your choice or hers?"

Jack glanced at the redhead. "Hers."

"Do you miss her?"

Ashley: brilliant, tall, smoky hazel eyes, pouty lips, tangled blonde hair: gone. A baby miscarried.

"I try not to think about it. Been over six months."

"It's hard to imagine you having a sensitive side, Jack Flashhardt. You come off as a cocky, wise-cracking, militarist punk."

Jack smiled, "Hey, I aim to please an' I'm an expert marksman." "See? It's impossible for you to be serious," Tucson fumed.

After turning onto another one-lane dirt road that was muddy and slippery, they soon entered an overgrown grass clearing strewn with trash, discarded tires, run-down vehicles. Across the clearing was a large log structure: a square, two-story building, with one-story wings flaring to each side; the building was almost invisible in the rain and fog.

Jack stopped in a gravel parking lot. Suddenly two gunshots, muffled by the rain, barked. Both side mirrors clanged, ripped away from the maroon Cayenne!

The two ducked low, heard loud roars: two Harley motorcycles shot across the lot, skidded to a stop behind the SUV.

Jack turned off the engine, watched the riders aim lever-action saddle guns at the Cayenne.

Chapter 52

Four men in biker garb, also carrying weapons, walked through the downpour, stopped in front of the Cayenne. "Get out of the truck!" one yelled as he aimed a short-barreled shotgun. He was overweight—his bulging belly hanging over his pants—long-haired, wet.

Jack slowly got out.

"What in hell you doin' here?" the fat bewhiskered guy yelled. "This's private property. Get the fuck outta here!"

Tucson lowered her window. "We want to talk to Joshua Trumpet," she shouted over the noise of the rain drumming on the Cayenne's roof. "You fired on a federal vehicle!"

Fat Guy approached the window, peered through the rain streaks, looked at her blue FBI jacket. "Get the hell off our property!" "I'm a federal agent!" Tucson shouted.

"You got a search warrant, lady?" the first guy with the shotgun.

"No," she admitted.

Jack asked, "I'm not FBI. How about if she stays in the SUV?"

"No. Last chance to drive away, trespassers," the man stated. He pointed his shotgun at a tire. "Go now, or you'll walk."

"I'm lookin' for Bobby Ray Dawklings. He here?" Jack asked.

"He's an acquaintance of mine." *Might say Tattoo and I used to be real tight. Him squeezing the life out of me.*

Fat Guy stared at Jack, turned and walked. "Leave the fibbie here," he directed. "You come." He looked back. "An' you better not be bullshittin' me."

Jack followed across the lot. The big log lodge, nestled in the redwood forest, solidified in the mist and rain.

Its logs were cut flat on the exterior, so the building looked like it was made of one-foot-square beams. Two three-foot-diameter redwood trunks in front were pillars that supported the overhung entry. Large redwoods majestically stood on all sides of the building.

Jack and the bikers entered the dark and gloomy lodge. An unlit deerantler chandelier hung in the center of the room.

"Mister, you gotta lotta nerve comin' here with that fibbie bitch," fat guy muttered. "Wait over there until Bobby Ray calls you." He pointed at a row of chairs by a big window. Jack walked across the plank floor of the big room, sat down on a plain straight-back wood chair. The others moved to a bar across the almost empty room, poured and drank coffee, ignored Jack.

Ten long minutes later, short-legged, long-bodied Dawklings entered the huge room, stopped in front of Jack, rubbed his shaved head. His massive limbs were bare, showing the devil face tattoos repeated all over his thigh-sized arms. His giant neck carried the same motif of devil's faces —one on each side of his neck and one centered under his chin. He wore a dirty muscle undershirt, faded black jeans, muddy biker boots. The left eye was covered by a patch.

Jack saw movement, inspected the tattoos: they were definitely snarling, snapping their jaws: he hadn't imagined it back in the prison. He stared at the patch over Dawklings' left eye. "Nice seeing you, Bobby."

Dawklings snarled, touched his eyepatch string. "How'd you get out, traitor?"

"I escaped from the naval hospital I had to visit after our last soiree."

"I lost my eye, fucker!"

"Yeah, well, sorry about that. I wasn't a traitor. I was framed. You oughta be able to see that—uh, scratch that last."

"I can't see shit, thanks to you."

"Well, forget visions of the past, that is to see—I mean say— you guys know what's the deal with *Saladin's Fist?* I need help."

Dawklings stared at Jack with his one eye, stroked his chin whiskers. "This way." He turned and stomped to a hallway, turned into the first office, slammed the door behind Jack. The floor was littered with motorcycle parts, several ammunition boxes and a sawed-off double-barrel shotgun leaning against the bulkhead in the corner. On a wall, a metal picture about twelve by eighteen inches carried the image of a trout jumping out of a stream. On a side table, an old computer's oversized monitor showed lists of names. More names had been scrawled on the monitor case with ink markers. The rain continued to crash against a wood frame window.

"So," Jack said. "How's working for Alcohol, Tobacco and Firearms?"

With a shocked expression, Dawklings returned to the door, looked outside, closed it again. "Shut the fuck up about ATF! You could get me killed, asshole!" His demon tattoos opened their mouths in expressions of surprise.

Amazed at the sight, he wondered how Dawklings controlled his muscles so precisely. "That's good to know," Jack said. "I mean, okay. Now, tell me everything about *Saladin's Fist*."

"The people that started the fires? What d'you care?" Dawklings asked. All the tattoos scowled.

"I'm mired in alphabet soup, just like you. You're working for ATF on *God's Purpose*; I'm working for... another government entity against Islamic terrorists. So where's *Saladin's Fist* going?"

"I don't know much about them," Dawklings admitted. "That's Joshua Trumpet's undertaking. They were referred to one of his websites. He fed them misinformation, used them. He tricked them into attacking this firefighting school next door, because they're all black. He hates anybody who isn't white. He's a real case study for some budding psychologist."

"So introduce me," Jack directed. He noted Dawklings' improved grammar and vocabulary, wondered about it.

"I can't do that, he's in his main office in Lake Arrowhead."

"What's the story on Joshua Trumpet? That's not his real name, is it?"

"He's a double amputee. The old fucker lost both his legs in Vietnam. A landmine. His best friend, a black man, stepped on it, set it off, then abandoned him. So now he hates blacks. He floundered along, basically a street corner beggar, but when the Internet got up and running, he found his true path. He has these hate websites—calls himself Trumpet. Collects money from disaffected whites. Money just flows in to *God's Purpose*. But *God's Purpose* is mostly show. A money scam."

"So why're you here?" Jack asked.

The man dubbed Tattoo shook his head. "You're right, I'm ATF. I was operating undercover, sold weapons to the *Purpose*. Over-used, burnt-out junk, I might add. Then we arranged a conviction and I was imprisoned in Leavenworth. I selected you for a show fight. I didn't know you were a mass murderer—a combat specialist that would almost kill me." Dawklings glared with his one eye.

Jack felt shame sweep over him. "Hey, I didn't know either. I'm sorry about your eye—I thought you were trying to kill my brother and me. And the bad thing is we were using you guys as an excuse to get to a hospital and make a break."

Dawklings glared, finally smiled. "Well, we're a couple of fuck-ups, but here we are. I say, let's make the best of the situation." He held out his hand.

Jack took the man's massive appendage, shook. Dawklings' grip was gentle, but the many demon faces frowned with hideous expressions.

"You certainly look the part," Jack commented. "I'd pick you for a radical dude out of any line-up. Does FBI know about your thing?"

Dawklings grinned, his face still looked mean. "No, but since you do, I guess somebody does. Anyway, let me give you Joshua's address in Arrowhead. Maybe they're planning on paying him a visit. Here's Joshua's telephone. I've Mara's cell phone number as well." He opened a file on the desk computer, wrote numbers on a sheet of paper.

"Great!" Jack took the paper. "I'll head out."

Dawklings said, "I'll give you an unfriendly goodbye. I'll remember my eye—that'll help." He glared, his head cocked to the side.

"Dude, I'm sorry about that."

Jack left the *God's Purpose* lodge, hurried through the rain to the Cayenne. After he climbed in, drove away, Tucson asked, "How'd it go?"

Jack glanced at the freckle-faced, redheaded agent, returned his attention to the narrow road through the woods. "My guy didn't know much, 'cause his boss is the contact point for Mara."

"While you were gone," Tucson said, "I checked agency files for your background." She stopped and jabbed a finger at his chest. "You have none. Just that you joined the Marine Corps. We ran a profile on you back then, for the Marine Corps. We do it for every potential officer. We later updated it for a Top Secret clearance, which you got. Then a couple of medals, including a Silver Star, a Purple Heart, and an award from Pakistan. Then nothing. There's a block on the rest of your file by *Eagle's Aerie*. You said something about Leavenworth. What gives?"

Jack peered through the windshield, checked the empty road behind them. Memories flooded his mind: *slick General Harmbruster, hateful General Farley, the ceremony when President Zardari awarded him, the leper prison he had escaped in Pakistan, and finally, Leavenworth Prison.* He said nothing.

Tucson glanced behind. "Pull over for a minute." When he did so, she reached over, turned off the ignition key.

He looked at her beautiful freckled face, she grabbed his jacket. "What's going on, Jack? Who are you? And how come you're pals with members of *God's Purpose?*"

"I'm from Red Lodge, Montana. I'm with *Eagle's Aerie*. That's all you need to know."

Tucson leaned closer, searched his eyes, suddenly he kissed her. She tried to pull away, he put his hand behind her neck, grabbed her hair, held her tight. Her lips were flat, then slowly responded with increasing passion. After a long moment, she pulled back, said, "What about Zhang?" Without retorting, he kissed her again. Within a minute they were tugging each other's clothes off. When they were half-undressed, Jack said, "I do."

Tucson Luvabrest giggled. "Do what? You're proposing marriage?" "Love your breasts." He reached back, lowered the back seat.

Tucson unbuttoned his pants, yanked them down while he was stretched out, rubbed her white breasts against his legs, his groin.

He crawled in back, pulled her next to him, undid her pants, stripped them off her long legs. He kept his t-shirt on, sensitive and ashamed about the long knife scar on his back and left side. The rain drummed on the roof, danced and cascaded over the windshield. Jack kissed Tucson again, lost himself in her wonderful lips, felt her breasts push against his chest. He pushed his thigh between her legs, she spread them, wrapped around his legs, thrust her tongue in his mouth.

Chapter 53

Jack's cell phone rang, he removed one hand from the steering wheel, answered.

"Hey," his brother said, "it's me."

Jack gripped the phone. "Billy, where the hell are you?"

"Comin' up on Portland. It's rainin' like crazy. And I hear the bad weather's all the way to the California border. What's the story on Zhang?"

Trying to keep his voice level, Jack asked, "She's in a motel with Omar. We're on our way to meet them. Is your friend—Ishey, with you?"

"Yeah, we're pretty tight. She wants to spend the rest of her vacation with me, what d'you think? And d'you got the—you know, stuff?"

"That's a great idea," Jack answered. He thought about what Ishey might do to Billy if she found out the gems were missing. "I still have the... I've got the stuff. I'll meet you in Portland, later today. The weather's real bad, so it might take me all day to get there. You get a hotel, an extra room for us and call me, let me know where to go in Portland." Jack squeezed the cell phone tighter, tried to think of a way to warn his brother about the *SD* agent. "And, Billy, don't trust anyone. Understand? Anyone."

After Billy disconnected, Jack looked at Tucson. She was trying to untangle her hair. "I've got to get to Portland ASAP. Billy's in terrible danger."

"Call the local authorities," she suggested. "We have to continue with the mission."

"No way!" Jack shook his head. He started the engine, raced through the forest, sliding and skidding along the muddy, rain-swept road. "She could resist the cops, even Billy might. Then he's up for copkiller!" He glared at Tucson. "Not takin' a chance on that kinda bullshit. I have to get there at once." He looked up and saw the road open to a view of the stormtossed ocean.

Five minutes later, the clerk at the shabby motel gave Omar's room number to Jack. When he reached the first floor room, he found the wellworn door ajar. He pulled his M-9 out of a jacket pocket, pushed the door open, peeked into the room. Furniture knocked around, spotted an artificial leg jutting out from behind the bed.

Omar was lying on the blood-drenched floor. Rushed over, checked Omar's pulse, felt a weak but rapid heartbeat. The black man's skin was cool to the touch. Tucson went to the room phone, dialed 911, requested paramedics.

They pulled Omar to the center of the room. His right side was soaked in blood.

"Where's Zhang?" Tucson asked.

Jack probed the blood-soaked area, felt a bullet wound. "Maybe she did it, and escaped with the emeralds. I can't believe I didn't take the gems with us." Physically sick, he went to the bathroom, discovered the window over the shower was open, the screen knocked out. *What a disaster! Of his own making. Omar down, Zhang and the bag of emeralds gone.* "The windows are broken out. If she'd shot him, why would she go out the window?"

"Maybe it was the *SD* agents," Tucson said. "If she was *SD*, maybe they had a transmitter on her. Like the one she had on you. Tracked her here."

"How could I be so stupid! I should've thought of that." *Omar, my college roommate, friend, fearless fellow warrior: what a disaster!* He prayed Omar would pull through. He grabbed a towel, hurried back to his friend, pressed it on the wound.

Scrawled on the wall, about twelve inches above the floor where Omar had fallen, were three letters: MOP.

He stared at the letters written in blood. A message from Omar.

Tucson spoke to an operator and then a deputy at the Sheriff's station. She hung up, looked at the bloody letters, asked, "What do you think it means?"

"MOP. I don't know. Clean up—head of hair—maybe mope—maybe the getaway vehicle was a moped… it's hard to say."

Tucson removed her cell from her purse, took a picture of the scrawl.

"It's obvious he was trying to say something about his attackers."

An ambulance's muted siren approached, grew louder. The vehicle skidded to a stop in front of the room.

"Let's get out of here," Jack said. "There's nothing we can do. I have to get to Billy."

Tucson glanced around the room, opened the door for the ambulance team, who rushed to Omar. One of the members replaced Jack's pressing hand. He looked up with a questioning air.

"Gunshot," Jack offered. "Take care of him." He rose and headed for the door.

In the SUV, she asked, "Aren't you going after Zhang?"

Jack gunned the Cayenne, skidded onto the road. "I can't worry about her. Billy's in severe danger. We have to get to Portland."

He drove south on the 101, through the villages of Rockaway Beach, Garibaldi, Bay City. Each hamlet hunkered down in the gray fog, appeared and disappeared in the downpour. In Tillamook, Jack sped through the larger town, turned onto Highway 6 and headed east through intermixed forests and farmlands. The word "MOP" raced through his mind. He noticed the dried blood on his hand, wiped it on his pants leg. *Poor Omar trying to send a message. Knew I'd failed him, and must've known he might be dying. Omar, still worried about me. Wanted justice. He'll get it.* His thoughts shifted to Mara. He wondered what she hoped to accomplish with fires. Forest fires burned thousands of acres practically every day. So what?

Chapter 54

Mara Bhutto brushed her long black hair away from her copper-colored face, studied the AAA map of California that she had spread across her hotel room table in Eugene, Oregon. The size of the areas intimidated and depressed her. Western America had been just a place on the map in Pakistan, but it's actual size was unbelievable. The rains, occurring all the way south to Grants Pass, Oregon, had stymied her efforts and were influencing the weather in Northern California. On the television's weather channel, intermittent rain cells were showing across the upper parts of the state.

Her options were now limited to the area south of San Francisco, starting in a good-sized town called Santa Barbara.

Hard-faced, blond Bosnian Mikhail al Slovenly came out of the bathroom, still looked respectful. "Have you decided on our target?" "Los Angeles," she responded.

"Long ways," he commented.

"That is our mission objective. There is no option."

The Bosnian shrugged. "Many trees here. One forest is like another."

"I control the purse and I say Los Angeles." The Bosnian had asked very specific questions about credit card practices and customs of usage. She felt like a midget riding a tiger. "There's a drought and a dead forest in the San Bernardino Mountains, east of Los Angeles," she continued. "With luck, we'll burn the entire city."

"A dead forest?" The terrorist leader sat down, frowned.

"A Japanese beetle infestation has killed large elements of the forest throughout the range. And environmentalists have prevented the dead trees from being cut away, because that would cost the loss of habitat—"

"For the bugs?" al Slovenly laughed. "What a country!"

"We have the added bonus of tracking down the evil man who subverted our efforts: Joshua Trumpet. And he never told us the Americans fight fires even in remote areas."

"He's in California?" al Slovenly asked, a gleam coming into his blue eyes. "That will be good." He clasped and unclasped his big hands. "But when will we reach Hollywood? I've heard there are many beautiful women in Hollywood. From all over the world."

Mara snarled, "You had your fun with the girl in the tower. And the fat woman in the street in Kingsville. *And* the girl on the roadside—the one trying to fetch a ride. Where is she?"

The Bosnian smiled, did not answer. It was not a pretty sight. His blue eyes, cold and narrowed, gave Mara the shivers; she looked down at the map to conceal her sudden fright. "Where is she?"

"We took her for a ride," al Slovenly smiled again.

"Where is she now?"

"We let her off. Solved her problems. Turned her loose." Mara felt a chill of dread go through her body.

"We need money for refreshments," al Slovenly demanded. He flashed a hateful cold grin.

Mara took a handful of fifty-dollar bills out of her bag, resisted pushing the money on the frightening man, but then handed the money to him. "We divide tomorrow," she said. "You'll pick up several volunteers that're waiting to join us here in Portland."

"Local Muslims? Arabs?" al Slovenly asked. "We don't want al Qaeda wantabes—they're too visible. All the al Qaeda are good for is to hide in caves and send messages to each other on the Internet."

Frowning, Mara looked at the handsome Bosnian. "Yes, true," she responded, "but these men are native Americans, sympathetic to our cause —the destruction of America."

"What if they're government agents?"

"Kill them." Mara stared at the Bosnian. "And dump the stolen vehicles right away. The American volunteer jihadists have two vans. You split your men between the two vehicles. One group will take the Five south towards Los Angeles. The second group will take the 140 Highway to the 395 in eastern Oregon and also head south towards Los Angeles." Mara traced the already marked-in-red routes on the map. "Both roads eventually cross Highway 14 near our target. We will rendezvous at another Holiday Inn in Palmdale, a city in the desert, just east of Los Angeles." She pointed at an X on the map. "I will take a bus down to Sacramento, then rent a car and meet you." She handed al Slovenly two prepaid cell phones she had purchased in Portland. "We will communicate with these."

"How long will it take to reach the target city?"

"I'm not sure. California's a large state. It's 1600 kilometers from north to south. But the roads appear to be excellent. Their remote country roads are better than the Grand Trunk Road, for God's sake."

"What's that?"

"It's the main road from India, through Pakistan, all the way to Kabul, Afghanistan— Never mind. We'll plan to reach the destination three days from tomorrow morning. Call each day and report your progress. Tell the other team the same."

Al Slovenly grinned, "A road trip."

"Do not indulge in alcohol or frivolities," Mara cautioned. "Speak only English. Remember, you are Canadian foresters heading south for possible work. And the American volunteers are fervent Muslims. They are excited about joining you."

"Allah will protect and serve us," the Bosnian smiled confidently. "The stupid Americans'll never know what hit them until it's too late. Just like those police we killed at the roadblock. Just like the young Christian girl on the road. God is most great."

"Don't think they're stupid. Remember, they almost killed all of us in Shangri-La. And remember, we must be in Death Valley in six days. Without fail."

"Pure luck in the Afghan cavern," al Slovenly scoffed. "Americans are decadent, weak cowards. They have their advanced weapons to use from high altitudes over the Muslim world, but they can't use them here. Man to man, we will crush the cowards. God is most great." He looked into Mara's exotic green eyes. "Why is it so important to be in this Death Valley?
Sounds ominous."

"Just be on schedule," Mara ordered.

"We'll try," the Bosnian muttered.

Mara contemplated her Bosnian ally. *I hope you do,* she thought. *Putting up with your arrogance is almost more than I can take. And I must spread fire from horizon to horizon. From the mountains to the ocean. Yes, we'll destroy the mountains all the way to the sea. Los Angeles will be a shattered memory. Then the world will know our power and fear us. Then I will be...* she blocked off her thoughts, looked into the Bosnian's glacial blue eyes, wondered if those eyes would ever fix her with a last deadly glare before he struck at her.

Chapter 55

Penel Kong, the Shangrilan princess, waited in the Customs area in the Los Angeles terminal, her British passport in one hand, her bag in the other. It contained two changes of clothes, eight thousand US dollars in American Express cheques, a heavily engraved, silver-plated, ivory-handled Khyber Knife, and four quart bottles of tarn waters of long life. The knife's handle was wrapped with dirty, tattered scraps of leather. Dickey had told her that she could not bring ivory into America and had told her how to wrap and thereby camouflage the knife's handle.

A steward had explained that Los Angeles meant *the angels*, but she saw none as the line moved forward.

When it was her turn to speak with an agent, she nervously smiled and handed the black man her declaration form and placed her new suitcase on the counter. When the man saw a knife listed, he opened the bag and pulled out the knife.

"Whoa!" he exclaimed, "This is some pig-sticker. Almost two feet long!" He turned and showed it to a female supervisor. That person looked at Penel's passport, then at the knife.

"What's that for, honey?" the fat woman in a dark blue uniform asked. She glanced eye to eye with the tall, strong-looking blonde.

"It's a family heirloom. A work of art," Penel responded as Dickey had instructed her. Amazed at her first sight of a morbidly obese person, she stared, wide-eyed, at the supervisor.

"What'cha gonna do with it?" the young black woman asked. Her dark eyes stared into Penel's blue eyes. She cocked her head, listened to Penel's English accent. She smiled, revealing round cheeks with big dimples, a beautiful face with a wonderful smile.

"A present to the family I will be staying with in Mon-tan-a."
"Don't hurt yourself, honey," the supervisor cautioned.

"What you carryin' in the bottles?" the inspector asked.

"Mineral water," Penel said.

"Better pour it out, honey. You'll have grey hair by the time Customs verifies the contents," the fat supervisor said.

Penel blanched at the thought. The supervisor noticed her reaction. Her voice toughened. "Something you want to tell me, miss? You got opium or heroin dissolved in that water?"

"No," Penel said. "But I must retain the tarn waters… for health reasons. They must not be contaminated. Thou mayest take a tiny sample. How long before thou mightest release my waters?"

The fat woman relaxed, perceiving that strange-talking Penel was truthful. "A few days, honey. You sure you don't want to pour it out? No, I can see not."

"Please ensure they do not contaminate the waters," Penel pleaded. She added, "Can thou directest me to accommodations, an inn? While I wait?"

The black woman looked at the beautiful, strangely dressed woman. The tall blonde was wearing vibrantly blue silk pants, a silk wrap around her waist, a light brown cashmere sweater with a pale yellow silk scarf draped over her blonde hair, and over her shoulders. With a quizzical air, she asked, "You never traveled in the U.S.? There's a bank of hotel phones in the main terminal." The woman looked at Penel's confused expression. "I'm due for a break. Come with me…" She glanced at the Customs declaration and said, "Penelope Kong. I'll buy you a cup of coffee while Sam here closes down and prepares a receipt for your exotic waters, Penelope." She said to the inspector, "We'll be at Starbucks."

"Thank you," Penel said. She followed the hugely fat, waddling woman through a throng of travelers and people who were meeting them. Penel looked around. She was amazed that there were more people within her sight than she had ever met in all her life. All seemed to be hurrying in one direction or another. She tried to remember how many times she had hurried in her life. She smiled, relieved that a friendly official was helping her.

"I'm Beauty Walker," the woman said with a twinkling smile. "Where you from? You got an English accent, but you talk sorta funny."

Penel was about to say Shangri-La when she remembered how strangely people reacted when they heard that name. "I am a True

Hunza. From… Kafiristan," she said, using the disparaging Muslim term for all the highland Animist infidels.

"Strange, I've never heard of it," Beauty said. "Sounds like one of those war-torn *stan* lands we're continually sticking our noses into." She smiled again. "Even though we don't know where they are or even know how to spell them. Let's get a cup of coffee and talk about your future travels in America." She turned into a small restaurant off the wide hallway and walked through a line that passed a glass-covered table laden with breads and fruits. A board on the wall listed coffees and teas. The odors of fresh ground coffee filled the air. Penel stared at the first urn—it proclaimed: *bold, robust, powerful*. The next urn's label said—*sweet, pleasing*. The third said—*tantalizing, fun*.

Penel asked, "Does the coffee include drugs? Can I just get a plain coffee without an experience?"

Beauty laughed, paid for two cups. "You're fightin' a West Coast trend, sweetie," she said as she handed Penel a coffee.

Penel stared at the paper cup, wondered if it would disintegrate when filled with liquid. She sat with the black woman at a small marble slab table. She speculated that the flimsy metal chair would collapse under the strangely-built woman, but it did not. Looking around the shop, she noticed many of the people were overweight, an unknown condition in Shangri-La.

"Honey, why're you goin' to Montana?" Beauty asked. "Let me guess—gorgeous girl like you—must be a man in the picture."

Smiling, Penel sipped the coffee; it was thankfully bitter, and without the emotions advertised on the signs. "I'm with child," she said with a contented smile.

Beauty's big eyes widened. "Did your man send for you? Is he an American soldier?"

"No, and yes," Penel answered. "I know where his land is, and I will go there to have his child. He said that he would want that if I truly became pregnant."

Beauty blew on her coffee. "Did he get shipped out?"

"No, he was in pursuit of enemies of America."

"That's tough. Seems like the best ones are always running off to war. I lost my man… in the latest combat shindig in Iraq."

Penel looked at the black woman, touched her hand, resting on the table. "I'm sorry."

"Thanks. Do you love him? Does he love you?"

"We've not been together enough for that. Our lovemaking is intense, wonderful… but he does not love me. Yet." Penel looked into Beauty's soft and beautiful brown eyes. "But I bear his child— I have a responsibility to tell him. I did tell him, but he scoffed."

"You came all the way here on that?" Beauty stared. "There gots to be more to this."

"There is," Penel admitted. "I've always wanted to see the outside world. I've known an Englishman who lived in my land. Listened to his stories—I've always wanted to leave my homeland. But the valley has been isolated since the Russians blew the tunnel to the outside world. We've been cut off until the Americans—first, Jack, then others dropped into our valley… our world."

"You know, you don't have to stay pregnant."

"What do you mean?" Penel sipped her coffee.

"I know an abortion clinic in Manhattan Beach. It's close by."

"Abort the baby!" Penel was shocked at Beauty's casual tone.

"Happens all the time, honey. All over the country—maybe a million times a year."

Penel mused out loud, "I've heard they kill female babies in China, but I can't imagine—"

"You own your body, honey. No one can make you have a baby."

Penel shook her head. "Not in my case. Life is too precious," Penel responded. "A baby is so rare, such a gift is a sacred trust. When Drag— when God bestows pregnancy, one must fulfill the sacrament in every way possible—"

"Rare!" Beauty glanced around, reached across the table and took Penel's hand. "You been listening to too many old men. Pregnancy is the easiest thing in the world to catch. All you need is a hard man an' a soft pussy, honey."

Penel looked around the café. "Maybe things are different in America. But in Shang—but where I come from, it is very difficult to…" she broke off and thought for a moment. *Maybe Jack was right. Maybe, the tarn waters do prevent pregnancy.* She glanced at Beauty's body, changed the subject. "Why are thou so big?"

Beauty stared. "I wasn't always this way. I started eating when my Leon was killed."

"You mean you ate until thou were this big?" Penel asked. "It doesn't seem possible. Stop!"

"Easy to say, honey," Beauty responded. Her eyes shifted downward.

"Thou hast helped me," Penel said. "I will help you."

Beauty sighed, looked at Penel's slim, muscular body. "Wish you could, honey. But they ain't no way. I gots a huge hole in my heart that I can't fill."

Chapter 56

Driving south over Portland's Willamette River on Interstate 5, Jack turned off on the first off-ramp after the bridge, and pulled into the Willamette Embassy Suites, the hotel where his brother, Billy Howling Dog, had instructed them to rendezvous with Mick Nakamura. The storm had reduced to a misting rain, the visibility had increased until at sunset, the western sky was clear.

Jack glanced at his watch—2000 hours—eight PM. He swallowed a yawn, looked at redheaded Tucson Luvabrest, remembered for the hundredth time, her apparent slip up: the mention and cover up of Hainan Island. Was she a double agent? Like in the movies? Another Yassar Ahmoud? That would make three devious women having crossed his path. No one was that unlucky.

He glanced at her again—she was asleep. He hoped she remembered their plan to separate the *SD* operative from Billy. He picked up his cell phone, auto-called. When his brother answered, Jack said, "We're here."

"Hey, come to room 716. I'll give you a keycard. You're stayin' right next door."

"Billy," Jack added. "Omar's hurt bad."

"You're shittin' me! What happened?"

"I just checked with the hospital. He's gonna make it. I'll tell you when I see you."

Ten minutes later, Jack, with an M-9 shoved in his belt in the small of his back, Tucson at his side, knocked on Billy's door. His heart was in overdrive.

Ishey Murolta, the *SD* agent, opened the door, smiled a friendly greeting. Jack was struck by how beautiful she was. He wondered how, like a King Cobra snake, she could look so beautiful and yet be so deadly. He suddenly realized she was for sure the third woman, maybe the fourth, counting Tucson.

The brothers touched fists, the four moved to the living area. Billy and the *SD* agent sat on barstools at the kitchen bar, with Ishey sitting on the far side of Billy, to Jack's left. Tucson took a seat in an armchair by the window, to Jack's right. He sat on the arm of the sofa against a wall, across from the bar. Tucson held her purse in her lap.

Ishey Murolta was wearing a yellow raincoat, her hands were thrust in her pockets. Her very slanted eyes, rounded on top, flat on the bottom, had a calculating squint, but when she noticed Jack's attention, she smiled, transforming herself from an evil Chinese agent to a beautiful young woman.

"What about Omar?" Billy asked.

Jack forced himself to not look at Ishey. "Somebody shot him in a hotel room. He'll be okay, I checked with the hospital. That's all I know."

"The emeralds," Billy said. "Where the hell are they? Where's Zhang?"

"Zhang took off again. The emeralds are in the SUV," Jack responded. "Don't worry, it has an alarm," he added when he saw the sudden fear on Billy's face.

"Bullshit!" Billy exclaimed. "So what if a thief sets off the alarm?
He'll be gone, the emeralds'll be gone."

"Alright, alright." He threw the keys to Billy. "Go get the bag. Tucson, you go with, show him where the Cayenne is parked. Don't worry, Billy, I found a buyer in Vancouver, Canada. We'll have them sold by this time tomorrow."

"I need some exercise," Ishey said, "I'll go, as well."

"That's alright," Tucson said. "I have some Bureau questions for Billy. He'll want to keep them private. We'll get the gems, stop and pick up cups of coffee."

Ishey sat back down, Jack heaved a sigh of relief. *So far, so good,* he thought.

Billy and Tucson left the room, Jack raised his arms over his head, stretched, then put his arms behind his back, groaned with pain. "Too much driving," he said. He carefully pulled the M-9, held it under his thigh. When the door shut, he ignored his pounding heart. "So, Ishey, how long you on vacation?"

The frustrated-looking woman stared at the door, looked back at Jack, smiled smoothly. "A week left."

"You and Billy must be getting' along real good."

Ishey smiled. "He's the furthermost." She kept both hands in her rain jacket's pockets. He wondered whether she had a gun, whether she would fire at the first sign of trouble. He prayed his headstrong brother wouldn't come charging in when Tucson revealed the *SD* agent's true identity.

"You mean greatest," Jack responded.

"Yes, of course." Ishey crossed to a CD player, turned on crashing music—it was an Outkast CD. She swayed with the music, hands still in her pockets. Looked over her shoulder, flashed a wondrous smile. "He's the greatest," she said.

"I know what you mean. I love him. He's loyal, trustworthy—sounds like a Boy Scout. Do you think you have a future? Will *SD* let you settle in America?" Cursed himself for slipping up! Cursed his talkative mouth.

Ishey's eyes widened. Without hesitation, she fired a small-caliber pistol from inside her pocket. The bullet missed Jack, hit the lamp on a small end table next to him. He dove behind the armchair. She fired again, charged towards the chair.

Jack pulled his M-9, returned fire. Hit her in the arm, her gun flew. Disregarding her injury, Ishey threw a lamp, a pitcher of water that momentarily blinded him, picked up a chair, rushed. He dashed the water from his eyes, stood and focused—shot twice, knocked a leg off the chair. It flew through the air, entangled his legs as he stepped back from her charge. He fell. She smashed the chair over his head as he rose, stunned him.

Jack fell again, dropped his pistol. Ishey raised the chair, hit him over the head once more. He saw stars, consciousness started to fade, his vision tunneled, darkness grew around the edges. Ishey, a wild look on her face, raised the chair again, swung it—he rolled and she missed. Jack feebly kicked and caught a foot between her legs. She fell on top of him, their faces were an inch apart. She pushed an elbow against his throat, wrapped her other arm around his back. He swung wildly, hit her in the ribs.

Wet air exploded into his face. He wrapped his arms around her, hugged as hard as he could, but felt weak. She spat in his face, opened her mouth, tried to bite him. He gasped for air, turned his head to protect his nose, she nuzzled his ear, whispered, "I'll kill you!" bit down, he jerked, pulled his ear out from between her closing teeth, felt flesh tear. He jabbed her. Her mouth flew open, releasing his ear.

Ishey tried to grab his hair with one hand—it was too short. Her entire body was pressing against him. She pushed her knee between his legs, forced them apart with impossibly strong leg muscles.

Jack clutched harder, she moaned and coughed, he felt her hot breath on his neck. He twisted away as she savagely bit into a neck muscle. Intense pain flared, he felt blood spurt onto his shoulder.

Ishey's hand groped towards his crotch, reached for his groin, wrapped the fingers of a hand around his testicles. She squeezed, more a caress than anything else, then wrenched.

The painful shock frightened, then snapped his mind out of their almost passionate embrace. He shoved her away, pushed his back against the floor, punched her on the jaw. She flew backwards, her hand released his burning groin.

He rolled behind the bar, pushed himself erect. Ishey rose on the other side of the bar, jumped over it, attacked his face with her fingernails. He ducked, she slammed onto his back, began hitting his ribs. He heaved her over his back, held onto the bar, kicked back as fast as he could. She responded with grunts and screams.

Jack threw himself over the bar, dove for his pistol. He grabbed it, turned and fired while still on the floor: missed.

Ishey ducked below the bar. Came up throwing—he ducked under a liquor bottle. More followed, each crashed and broke against the wall behind him. Whiskey, vodka, brandy, splashed over him. She dove for her weapon, he shot her in the midsection. She began panting, making a keening sound with each breath. He shot again. The Chinese woman's eyes widened, she rose to her knees, gasped. Reached for the small, black semiauto lying just beyond her grasping fingers, he shot a third time; she held her breath, sighed, fell forward.

Panting from fear and exertion, his ear, neck and face burning, Jack crossed the room warily, heard the door click open.

Tucson, then Billy entered. He cursed when he saw his girlfriend sprawled on the floor, blood, liquor, furniture, splashed all over the floor and walls.

Tucson asked, "Is she—"

"Dead?" Jack responded. "Hope so."

"You just shot her?" Billy demanded, his face twisted with anger.

"Why?"

Tucson spotted the dropped semi-auto pistol, went to her knees and sniffed the gun without touching it. "Been fired," she said, then she looked up at Billy. "I told you—she was an enemy agent. For China."

Jack slumped against the wall. "Bro, I screwed up."

Tucson crossed to him, touched his bleeding neck. "Are you alright? You look like you lost the fight."

"Yeah," he responded. Then he sagged to his knees, clutched his aching groin.

Billy's dark face grew darker. "How? Why'd you shoot her?"

"I asked her about *SD*. It just slipped out accidentally. She instantly shot her weapon. I had to defend..." he looked at Billy with a pleading expression. "I'm sorry... but she almost killed me." Billy's face was still dark with rage.

Tucson rose, picked up the fallen lamp. "There's a bullet hole."

Billy Howling Dog joined her, inspected the lamp. He turned to Jack.

"I—I'm sorry. I guess you had no choice. It's just Ishey and I—"

"I know, Billy, but you didn't realize she was *SD*. I was afraid to tell you, in case she overheard. I tried to warn you, but—"

"He was afraid she'd kill you, Billy," Tucson interrupted. "He dropped everything: Zhang, the emeralds, the terrorists, to come to your aid." "But why'd she shoot at you?" Billy demanded.

"I don't know, bro, I guess because I screwed up an' let her… know— know that I knew she was in *SD*."

"Unless she planned on killing us all," Tucson said. She went to the bathroom, returned with a wet towel, and wiped blood off Jack's neck. "You're too old for a hickey," she said with a slight smile. She wrinkled her nose. "And you smell like the town drunk who missed his mouth."

Billy shook his head, lashed out, "I can't believe you let Zhang get away!"

"Dude, I didn't. Omar is hurt bad. *SD* agents shot him, I figure. Zhang probably barely escaped with her life. Does MOP mean anything to you?" "Your friend Omar scrawled it on the motel wall with his own blood," Tucson elaborated. She crossed to Ishey's body.

"Mop?" Billy shook his head.

"Means something," Jack observed. "He spent his last moments of consciousness trying to tell us something."

"I need to call the police," Tucson said. She pulled out her cell phone.

"No!" Jack and Billy protested in unison.

"Look, I'm a law enforcement agent. I have a duty—"

"Police come, they'll lock our asses up," Billy snarled. "First thing they'll do."

"This isn't television drama, Tucson," Jack said. He threw the towel in the bar sink, ran water on it, dabbed his burning ear. "We don't have time to deal with the cops. What happens if an FBI agent shoots someone in the line of duty?"

"We're put on administrative leave or duty until all the facts are in."

"Exactly! No time for that—we need to get out of here," Jack responded.

"We need to get to L.A. I gotta feeling all the answers are in L.A."

"I hate to slow you down," Tucson said with a sarcastic tone, "but we have a dead body here. This isn't Afghanistan. We can't just leave corpses lying about."

"She was a dangerous illegal alien, an enemy agent, carrying a weapon and a false ID," Jack pointed out. "We'll dump the body, get out of here. When the authorities find her, they can deal with it."

"Fuck that, Jack!" Billy lurched forward, shoved Jack with an angry thrust to the chest.

Dump the body!" Tucson looked shocked. "That's tampering with evidence. Not to mention how despicable that would be."

"You just don't get it, Tucson," Jack said. "We have terrorists heading God knows where. We were sent here from Singapore by *Eagle's Aerie.* We work for them. Because we're the only Americans that've dealt with Mara Bhutto and her gang. And if you think she's an everyday criminal, check this out." Jack bared his back, showing the knife scar that traced from high on his left shoulder blade, around his back to his lower ribcage. "Mara gave me this. Almost killed me. She's a trained *SD* assassin, just like Zhang. They're both ruthless."

Billy admitted, "An' they don't worry about no rules of engagement."

Jack added, "D'you want to be responsible for pulling Billy and me out of action during this crisis, even for a few days?" He picked up the general's cell phone. "But you're right—she doesn't deserve to be dumped. She was just doin' her job. I'm sorry. What I just said was stupid. Hey—I'm not an expert at body disposal or respect for the dead. I'm only good at killing people. We'll report the event to *EA,* let them deal with it."

"Are you finished moaning and complaining about your lot in life?" Tucson asked. "And we'd better hurry, before someone reports gunshots to the police."

Billy leaned over the dead young woman, pushed away a lock of hair that was falling across her very white face. He said, "What about Zhang?" He looked up at his brother. "She really got the emeralds?"

Jack stared at Ishey's body, sighed, said in a low voice, "I don't know for sure. All we know is someone whacked Omar big-time, left him for dead. Zhang and the gems are gone."

Billy stroked Ishey's cheek, brushed more strands of hair to the side. "If *SD* has 'em, maybe they'll lay off us. Maybe Ishey... didn't get the word to quit."

"More importantly, I wonder what the hell Mara hopes to accomplish?" Jack said. "I mean, like, a forest fire? Big deal. It'll make local newscasts, maybe a mention on back page news."

Tucson regarded him. "The fires were quite widespread here. What if she created a line of fires twenty, fifty, even a hundred miles long? Say during a Santa Ana windstorm in Southern California. The television images, the fear could be like nothing Americans have ever seen before. Especially if Islamic terrorists took credit again. That would mean they can enter and operate in this country with impunity." "Still, there must be something else up her sleeve." Billy bent over to straighten Ishey's legs.

Tucson exclaimed, "Don't touch the body!"

Billy ignored her, straightened Ishey out, put her hands at her side.

"Bodies," he said as he rose. "It seems we gotta superabundance of bodies. I wonder how many more we'll litter the landscape with before we finish?" He pulled a baggy out of his pocket, gulped an Oxy tab.

Chapter 57

A knock on the door. Jack, gingerly drying his head after a quick shower, peered through a tiny peephole—it was Chopstick Mick Nakamura. He opened the door, slapped hands. "Dude, good to see you."

"Hey, Pilgrim," Mick responded with his characteristic John Wayne accent. He grinned, his eyes disappeared in his wide Japanese face. His wide body filled the doorway. "What happened to you?" "Hey," Billy said.

"Hi," Mick greeted Billy. They bumped fists.

"Major Mick Nakamura, this is Tucson Luvabrest, FBI," Jack waved at Tucson.

Mick stepped forward, staggered when he saw the sheet-covered body on the floor. "What the hell—?"

Jack looked down, explained, "We had a problem. She was *SD*. Tried to pot me. We're about to clear out for L.A., turn this mess over to *Eagle's Aerie* and the fibbies."

"Man, I can't believe it!" Mick exclaimed. He glanced at Jack, grinned. "Jack, can you go anywhere without spreading corpses about? You're worse than an English butler in a murder mystery. You're not a litterbug, you're a goddam litterbody!"

"Hey, I aim to please. And in this case, my aim was—" Jack broke off, glanced at Billy with an apologetic expression, quelled his excitement and relief at still being alive.

Billy stared at Ishey's body.

Tucson remarked, "You look conflicted."

"I am," Billy said. "She was good to me, a lot of fun, supportive, beautiful... and the whole time everything was a lie. Just like Zhang. What is it with broads? Can't they ever be real?"

"You've just had bad experiences. But consider where you are,"

Tucson said. "If you were back on your ranch in Montana, you wouldn't—"

"Be exposed to women like Ishey and Zhang," Jack interjected. "We're livin' in an unreal world, bro. This ain't suburbia or—"

"Greasy Grass, Montana," Billy admitted. "Let's get outta here. Mick, you ride with me, catch some z's—I'm too shook to sleep." "Mick, did Billy tell you about Omar?" Jack asked.

Mick frowned. "Yeah, unbelievable. All he went through in Asia and somebody wings him in a sleazy motel in the States."

Jack, struck by a sudden thought, asked, "Hey, Mick, does MOP mean anything to you? Omar wrote it in blood on the motel bulkhead. It was a message."

"Yeah, I know," Mick responded. "I figured it out on the road from Seattle. It's not mop—it's Mo Poo. He just couldn't finish it."

Jack felt a flush of fear course through his body, looked at Tucson and the others. "That's it!" he slapped his forehead. Thought of his first encounter with the hideous Chinese giant on the slopes of the Hindu Kush. Mo Poo had growled in a basso voice so deep it made Jack's body resonate like a tuning fork: *I smell you, fan gway. I am Mo Poo. You killed mine daughter, foreign devil. Now I never rest until I kill you.*

"What about my vehicle?" Mick asked Tucson, breaking Jack's racing mind train.

"Leave the keys on the table," she ordered. "I'll tell my supervisor after…" she hesitated, then added with heavy sarcasm, "we've made our *getaway* to Los Angeles."

Jack looked at the beautiful redhead. "Only tourists and weathermen call it Los Angeles. Anyway, we're going to Lake Arrowhead—that's almost eighty miles from L.A. Where's Mo Poo? More importantly, why's Mo Poo here?" *That's easy, stupid. He's here for me.*

The center of the Pacific storm known as Draco, originally a Category 1 hurricane (winds at 74-95 mph), crossed the eastern Oregon border; high pressure began to build as it headed toward the Rocky Mountains and the Great Basin. The storm system was pushed by a southward diving jet stream and headed towards Four Corners, the point where Utah, Arizona, Colorado, and New Mexico meet, at a storm speed of twenty miles per hour, or approximately five hundred miles per day.

The morning after Jack and Tucson had left the Tillamook headquarters of *God's Purpose*, Bobby Ray Dawklings and ten rough and ready members, ranging in age from seventeen to forty five, climbed aboard an old, chartered DC-3, bound for Big Bear Lake, California, the closest airport to the Lake Arrowhead headquarters of Joshua Trumpet's white supremacist force. Each of the men, some brawny—like ex high school jocks gone to fat— others scrawny—like mean-looking wannabe geeks— proudly carried a bag containing pistols, assault rifles, and ammunition.

Bobby Ray Dawklings carried a map of Death Valley.

The weakening storm, transformed to a high pressure system with a barometric pressure of 30.22 inches, and formerly known as Draco, crossed the Texas coast and increased to a speed of twenty-five miles per hour as it was pulled southward by a low pressure system hovering in the corridor of warm water between the Cape Verde Islands and Central America.

The U.S. government agency, NOAA, dispatched a WP-3D Orion aircraft to the tropical depression, loaded with radar, sensors, and cloud particle probes. Forecasters predicted a potential of the converging patterns turning into a Category 5 hurricane (155 mph winds and above). National Hurricane Center decided to rename the new storm, Draco, as it contained the remnants of a unique tropical storm, which had originated in the Northwestern Pacific, after picking up massive energy when it swung south to Hawaii, and after it had pounded the west coast of the United States.

The renegade Chinaman, Mo Poo, the leader of the surviving escapees of
a decades-long Second Department program to produce giant warriors for the Chinese army, sat in the Cadillac Escalade, watched the little Second Department agent drive south on the 101 Highway towards California at a reckless and terrifying speed. The puny man had predicted an eight-hour drive to the California province.

Mo Poo shifted around, trying to get comfortable. He decided to try to take a nap. He wasn't fully recovered from the seasickness he had experienced in the smuggler's boat that had taken him and the *SD* agents across from Vancouver, Canada. His first trip across open seawater had been frightening. The sea was the biggest thing he had ever seen, save the mountains of Asia. He had always considered the mountains to be most representative of an over-world deity, with the far-off stars serving as a close second. But the surging, changing, ever-moving ocean: it was colossal, grand, powerful… fitting to be Mo Poo's God.

He glanced at the nameless little man—he seemed so self-confident. Mo Poo felt very nervous. He wished he could've taken time to finish and cook part of the black man the *SD* agent had shot in the coastal village. The comfort of human flesh would have righted his soul and settled his stomach. But the *SD* worms had insisted that they hurry after the female, Poon t'ang.

Mo Poo wished he had stayed in China. Wished he had never been taken prisoner by the Chinese border guards on the Karakoram Highway as he tried to lead his people to safety from Shangri-La to Tibet. Wished he and the last of his people had not been forced into the choice of either serving the hated Second Department in the pursuit of the American, or dying on the plains of Kashgar, short of their destination in the southeastern foothills of the Himalayas.

The flight to Tokyo and then to Canada had been terrifying—he had never flown through the air in machines.

He fell asleep and woke when the *SD* man stopped for fuel. He looked at an auto in the next stall and noticed a little boy staring at him. The boy pointed at Mo Poo and broke into tears of terror. The driver, probably the child's parent, looked at Mo Poo's giant head—the horrible tiger scars on his face, the sunken dead eye. The man blanched and quickly drove away. Mo Poo wasn't surprised. He had always been looked upon with horror by the little ones. He cursed his oversized body, wished for a thousandth time he was normal. Thought of his daughter, beautiful, wonderful Chin Bit—she and his son had been the only bright spots in his entire existence: Chin Bit, dead at the hands of the American. He thought of Herotmere, his retreat, his safety, his home in the caverns of the Hindu Kush: destroyed by the same vicious, relentless American.

His thoughts turned to his son: he wondered where Sun Pin was. The boy had sent a message—a message saying, "Come to our new homeland in the headwaters of the Nu River." Mo Poo sighed. Would be ever leave these strange, hostile shores, see his people, his beloved son?

The clever and deadly American had a home, as well, to which he would go after he defeated Mara Bhutto. The American would want to relax. His guard would be down. Mo Poo sighed again, glanced at the tiny *SD* man getting behind the wheel.

His deep voice rumbled, overpowering in the confines of the vehicle. "It is a waste for me here. I want to go to the mountains. Mara Bhutto told me my daughter's killer lives in Montanastan. She will fail to exterminate him. We will go to Montanastan and wait for him. It is better for me in the mountains."

The Chinese *SD* man glanced at Mo Poo's horrible face. "We don't know where his home is."

"Your computing machine will search out that answer. Ask it. Why chase all over this vast land? He is bound to return to his home."

The little man, with a fearful expression, looked up at the giant. "We have a mission. We only have three teams. We cannot afford to divert one. Our mission does not include Montana. Now we must also catch the traitorous bitch of a thief, Zhang Poon t'ang, and regain the emeralds."

Mo Poo put a huge hand on the driver's tiny leg. "You'll fail. You say the traitor's with the American. He's too smart to keep her around. We must go to his home, catch him with his guard down. That's where he'll go after he has defeated the Bhutto woman. Take me to Montanastan. Now."

Chapter 58

The center of the Pacific storm known as Draco, originally a Category 1 hurricane (winds at 74-95 mph), crossed the eastern Oregon border; high pressure began to build as it headed toward the Rocky Mountains and the Great Basin. The storm system was pushed by a southward diving jet stream and headed towards Four Corners, the point where Utah, Arizona, Colorado, and New Mexico meet, at a storm speed of twenty miles per hour, or approximately five hundred miles per day.

The morning after Jack and Tucson had left the Tillamook headquarters of God's Purpose, Bobby Ray Dawklings and ten rough and ready members, ranging in age from seventeen to forty five, climbed aboard an old, chartered DC-3, bound for Big Bear Lake, California, the closest airport to the Lake Arrowhead headquarters of Joshua Trumpet's white supremacist force. Each of the men, some brawny—like ex high school jocks gone to fat—others scrawny—like mean-looking wannabe geeks— proudly carried a bag containing pistols, assault rifles, and ammunition. Bobby Ray Dawklings carried a map of Death Valley.

The weakening storm, transformed to a high pressure system with a barometric pressure of 30.22 inches, and formerly known as Draco, crossed the Texas coast and increased to a speed of twenty-five miles per hour as it was pulled southward by a low pressure system hovering in the corridor of warm water between the Cape Verde Islands and Central America.

The U.S. government agency, NOAA, dispatched a WP-3D Orion aircraft to the tropical depression, loaded with radar, sensors, and cloud particle probes. Forecasters predicted a potential of the converging patterns turning into a Category 5 hurricane (155 mph winds and above). National Hurricane Center decided to rename the new storm, Draco, as it contained the remnants of a unique tropical storm, which had originated in the Northwestern Pacific, after picking up massive energy when it swung south to Hawaii, and after it had pounded the west coast of the United States.

Chapter 59

The renegade Chinaman, Mo Poo, the leader of the surviving escapees of a decades-long Second Department program to produce giant warriors for the Chinese army, sat in the Cadillac Escalade, watched the little Second Department agent drive south on the 101 Highway towards California at a reckless and terrifying speed. The puny man had predicted an eight-hour drive to the California province.

Mo Poo shifted around, trying to get comfortable. He decided to try to take a nap. He wasn't fully recovered from the seasickness he had experienced in the smuggler's boat that had taken him and the SD agents across from Vancouver, Canada. His first trip across open seawater had been frightening. The sea was the biggest thing he had ever seen, save the mountains of Asia. He had always considered the mountains to be most representative of an over-world deity, with the far-off stars serving as a close second. But the surging, changing, ever-moving ocean: it was colossal, grand, powerful… fitting to be Mo Poo's God.

He glanced at the nameless little man—he seemed so self-confident. Mo Poo felt very nervous. He wished he could've taken time to finish and cook part of the black man the SD agent had shot in the coastal village. The comfort of human flesh would have righted his soul and settled his stomach. But the SD worms had insisted that they hurry after the female, Poon t'ang.

Mo Poo wished he had stayed in China. Wished he had never been taken prisoner by the Chinese border guards on the Karakoram Highway as he tried to lead his people to safety from Shangri-La to Tibet. Wished he and the last of his people had not been forced into the choice of either serving the hated Second Department in the pursuit of the American, or dying on the plains of Kashgar, short of their destination in the southeastern foothills of the Himalayas.

The flight to Tokyo and then to Canada had been terrifying—he had never flown through the air in machines.

Chapter 60

The fell asleep and woke when the SD man stopped for fuel. He looked at an auto in the next stall and noticed a little boy staring at him. The boy pointed at Mo Poo and broke into tears of terror. The driver, probably the child's parent, looked at Mo Poo's giant head—the horrible tiger scars on his face, the sunken dead eye. The man blanched and quickly drove away. Mo Poo wasn't surprised. He had always been looked upon with horror by the little ones. He cursed his oversized body, wished for a thousandth time he was normal. Thought of his daughter, beautiful, wonderful Chin Bit—she and his son had been the only bright spots in his entire existence: Chin Bit, dead at the hands of the American. He thought of Herotmere, his retreat, his safety, his home in the caverns of the Hindu Kush: destroyed by the same vicious, relentless American. His thoughts turned to his son: he wondered where Sun Pin was. The boy had sent a message—a message saying, "Come to our new homeland in the headwaters of the Nu River." Mo Poo sighed. Would be ever leave these strange, hostile shores, see his people, his beloved son?

The clever and deadly American had a home, as well, to which he would go after he defeated Mara Bhutto. The American would want to relax. His guard would be down. Mo Poo sighed again, glanced at the tiny SD man getting behind the wheel.

His deep voice rumbled, overpowering in the confines of the vehicle. "It is a waste for me here. I want to go to the mountains. Mara Bhutto told me my daughter's killer lives in Montanastan. She will fail to exterminate him. We will go to Montanastan and wait for him. It is better for me in the mountains."

The Chinese SD man glanced at Mo Poo's horrible face. "We don't know where his home is."

"Your computing machine will search out that answer. Ask it. Why chase all over this vast land? He is bound to return to his home."

The little man, with a fearful expression, looked up at the giant. "We have a mission. We only have three teams. We cannot afford to divert one. Our mission does not include Montana. Now we must also catch the traitorous bitch of a thief, Zhang Poon t'ang, and regain the emeralds."

Mo Poo put a huge hand on the driver's tiny leg. "You'll fail. You say the traitor's with the American. He's too smart to keep her around. We must go to his home, catch him with his guard down. That's where he'll go after he has defeated the Bhutto woman. Take me to Montanastan. Now."

Chapter 61

The uniquely merged and vastly strengthened storm system, renamed Draco by the National Hurricane Center, left the Gulf of Mexico and swept across the Mexican coast with a barometric pressure of 930 millibars, rapidly headed towards Guadalajara, Mexico. The Center predicted that the renewed hurricane would dissipate to the level of a tropical depression as it crossed the mainland of Mexico, east to west. Nevertheless, twelve to fourteen inches of rain were predicted in its path.

Jack, sleeping in the backseat of the Cayenne, awoke at a gas station in north central California. It was still dark outside but he saw an off-ramp sign that read: *Chico Next right 32East*. He glanced at the white Dodge van in the next bay, it was much longer and sat higher than the Cayenne. He noticed that the driver and front seat passenger were both young, athleticlooking blond men.

When Tucson returned from the truck stop café with a cup of coffee in her hand, he said, "You've driven for hours. I'm rested—I'll take it from here. And, Tucson, check out the van next to us."

Tucson discreetly studied the big Dodge. It had windows in front, but the rear part was windowless. Three men were standing next to the van, a fourth man was pumping gas. The thin blond youth finished and walked around the vehicle, glanced at Tucson, stared intently, as the others got in the vehicle. "All blond, all young. Maybe surfer refugees from So Cal?"

"I can't imagine a man looking at you without smiling," Jack suggested.

"That guy looked at you like you were a snake in the grass."

"No," Tucson responded. "Trust me on this—he wanted me, but not in a nice way."

"Might be our guys," Jack concluded. "They had a certain look, you know? Kinda like two Bosnians I dusted in Afgoneland." He thought of the incident: *two men in the tunnel, flashes from gun barrels, dropped both with a long burst. They were blond!*

Tucson, startled by Jack's casual mention of having killed two men, stared at him with wide open eyes.

Jack smiled, leaned over and kissed her.

She distractedly kissed him. "I wish we weren't in gas stations looking for terrorists. I'd like to revisit a quiet, rain-soaked glen in Northern Oregon right now."

"Let's see… chasing bad guys or you and a woodside glen. H-mmm. Ya think?" Jack grinned. "But first we gotta save the world. Maybe tonight we can find time for ourselves. I almost can't think of anything else, truly." Hoped he was right, hoped she wasn't an enemy agent, like Mara, and Ishey, and Zhang. Kissed her again, then got out and moved to the driver's side of the Cayenne. He spotted Billy's black Cayenne at the next gas pump to the rear. Billy was pumping gas.

"How you doin', bro?"

Billy frowned, put away the gas pump. "I'm hurtin' and pissed."

"Billy, you're the best. I can't tell you—"

"Let's move on," Billy growled.

"But I feel so—"

Billy looked at his brother. "If this is gonna be a long guilt whine, I gotta take a piss."

"You're one tough hombre, bro," Jack wished he could break through his brother's hard exterior. He slapped Billy on the back, then walked to Mick's window and knocked until Mick woke up. "We might have run into Mara's gang," he said after Mick lowered his window. "A white van with a bunch of men inside. With Oregon plates. Headed south a couple minutes ago."

"Let's go get 'em!" Mick exclaimed.

Jack shook his head. "No, let's hang back. Don't worry, we'll catch them if they're our guys. This freeway runs straight for a long stretch through nothing but farm country. If it's them, they're going someplace a long ways away."

"So what's the plan?" Tucson, who had joined the huddle, asked. "Call CHP? Set up a roadblock?"

With scorn in his voice, Jack said, "Yeah, right! That'll go over big with CHP if these guys are just tourists. Let's get our weapons out, ready to go. We'll catch up, hang behind them until they stop again. There're several rest stops between here and LA. Out of a bunch of guys, someone's gonna have to take a piss. When they stop, I'll block their front if I can isolate them from civilian activity. Mick, you block their rear. We cover them from the sides. Mick, you cover from the rear. That way we don't shoot each other. Then we establish their identity. If they're just tourists, we back off. Remember, if they're the Bosnians, they're really bad guys. Don't hold back."

Five minutes later, after a toilet run, the two Cayennes pulled back on Freeway 5 and headed south, like a pair of race horses, for Sacramento. Jack noticed a white Crown Victoria hanging behind Mick's vehicle. When he slowed, it also slowed and fell back until it was out of sight.

Fifteen minutes later, he saw a sign for San Francisco. It was strange to ignore it, not turn west on the 80 Freeway, head to law school. Thought of the old song, sang a couple of lines:

"If you're goin' to San Francisco, better wear some flowers in your hair…"

Old friends were going about their scholarly duties—he was carrying guns instead of law books. Wearing night vision goggles instead of flowers in his hair. It seemed an eternity since he had been yanked out of law school by his reserve unit, transformed from a part-time soldier and full-time scholar to an unending death-dealer.

Now, a lifetime of experience since he had eaten a wonderful hamburger in the old campus favorite, *The Oasis,* on El Camino Real in Menlo Park. Now, he was chasing potential terrorists in a lawman act.

Thinking about it, he realized he was crossing more than the upcoming freeway to Frisco. The dream of returning to law school was fading. He could see himself driving on, pursuing the bad guys ahead. He couldn't see himself ever standing in front of a judge and jury, pushing paper and legal points. That life was history. He'd been dealt too much action, turmoil, upheaval. He'd dealt too much pain, sorrow, destruction, death. Hundreds of dead enemy stood over the shadow of his soul, comrades now, judging his actions. He shook his head, trying to free it of mystical, depressing musings, increased his speed until he saw the distinctive white van in the distance.

The potential terrorists did not turn onto the 80 Freeway to San Francisco in the west or Lake Tahoe in the east: the off ramp to San Fran slipped past, did not yank him back.

Tucson and Billy switched vehicles on the side of the road just after the sun rose over the Sierra Nevada Mountains.

The rejoined brothers calmed their nerves by talking about growing up in Montana, hunting prairie dogs and snakes when they were young, deer and elk when they were in their later teens. Billy getting stalked by a grizzly in the Bitterroots. Jack catching a monster cutthroat trout next to a hot spring in Yellowstone Lake.

A light tule fog blanketing the countless farms of the flat San Joaquin Valley, burned off after the sunrise revealed its ghostly presence. Billy fell asleep.

Jack could only find a San Francisco radio station playing blues music. He listened to Howling Wolf, Ma Rainey, Janis Joplin, Lead Belly, Dizzy Gillespie, and Big Joe Turner perform the art form for an hour. When B.B. King sang a song of the Old South, crying for fair treatment, blind justice, equal opportunity, he thought of Omar, felt tears form in his eyes. But the singer's last shouted song, *Rock me baby,* brought a thrill of carnal delight that flushed Jack's down mood.

He was further amped when a San Francisco FM rock station played a Strokes album, *Is This It,* with simple songs about love, sex, and getting drunk in New York's East Village.

He contemplated a huge water canal on the left side of the freeway. He noticed that the sign identifying it as the California Aqueduct had been taken down, probably to forestall terrorist actions.

He passed countless laser-flat, graded cotton fields, scattered almond groves and more cotton fields. The contrasts with the worn-out farmlands of India, Pakistan, Afghanistan, and even the African plains surrounding Mount Kilimanjaro, were amazing.

He sped up and caught the Dodge van again, fifty miles south of Sacramento. He studied it from ten car lengths, but realized there was no way to tell how many people were inside. He jolted to complete wakefulness when the Dodge, now a half mile ahead, turned off at a rest stop surrounded by knee-high cotton fields fifteen miles south of Los Banos. He poked Billy and tapped his brake lights several times to signal Mick and Tucson.

His heart hammering, Jack slowed while Billy put the Benelli shotguns, loaded with double odd buckshot rounds, in the front compartment.

Slowing, Jack saw the Dodge park between two family-filled vehicles. He drove into the one-way access road that serviced the rest stop, drifted past the target, parked beyond the last car in the parking lot, just before the onramp. Checked his watch: 0745.

Mick parked next to him, lowered his window. Tucson, in the passenger seat, stared, her eyes wide open.

Jack instructed, "I'll move along the on-ramp, wait. When the van approaches, I'll block the exit, just like we planned. You fall in behind, make sure no one else passes."

Mick exposed his canines, concealed his eyes in a wide grin. He pumped his fist in excitement. "I gotta feeling about this," he exclaimed. "I gotta feelin' it's gonna be goo-od!"

"Give them a chance," Jack cautioned. "They might be tourists. If they're not—it's *hasta la vista—*"

"Ba-by," Mick interrupted with a mean grin on his face. Tucson was still staring, Jack hoped she would be up to the action.

"Hook up your PRRs." He strapped his radio on with a velcro headband, turned it up. Backed away from the curb, moved along the onramp towards the freeway, looked back, surveyed the rest stop. An oasis in the farmlands: mowed grass, scattered trees, a toilet complex, a pet-walking area, trudging travelers stiff from sitting in cars. A cotton field to the right, eighteen-wheelers roaring southward on the left. A pile of decorative boulders between the on-ramp and the freeway, another on the other side of the on-ramp, about thirty yards away. The group of van guys exited the toilet building, moved to their vehicle.

"Here they come," Billy whispered. He climbed into the back seat and sat behind Jack, waited for the action.

Jack looked around, ordered, "Go to that rock pile. We'll set up crossing fire." He pointed at the western side of the on-ramp.

Billy rolled out of the SUV, ran to the rocks and settled. "I'm ready," he said into his microphone. Jack drove forward fifteen meters until the blocking Cayenne was the southern high point of a triangle with the other ends being the two rock piles.

The oversized van backed up, moved towards the one-lane freeway access road at a very slow pace. Impeded by Jack's Cayenne, the Dodge driver impatiently honked.

"Showtime," Jack muttered. He put the Cayenne in reverse and suddenly backed into the bigger vehicle. Jack jumped out, ran five steps towards the freeway, leaped behind the eastern rock pile, covered the van.

"Police! Get out, hands up!" Jack shouted.

The front and back windows slowly descended, startled eyes stared.

"Get out at once—FBI!" Tucson shouted from the rear.

The van driver smashed into the front Cayenne, reversed. Slammed into Mick's vehicle, pushed it backward, its wheels screeching on the pavement as Mick slammed on his brakes. Jack saw a man in the back seat raise a pistol and snap a shot. He re-aimed the Benelli, shot out the front tire. Billy took out the right-side tire. The Dodge slumped forward.

A hail of pistol shots rang out from inside the van, ricocheted off the boulders. Ignoring the fire, Jack and Billy responded with crossing fire, blew out the windshield, rear windows, shredded the door panels. Driver slumped out of sight. Men jumped out of the vehicle. Mick and Tucson cut down one man; he sprawled on the grass.

The others ran toward the western rock pile until Billy rose and shot one man down. Another man fired. Billy yelled, flopped backwards, fell out of sight.

"Billy!" Jack shouted. He jumped up, ran towards the remaining terrorists. He and Mick fired simultaneously, an Arabic-looking man was jerked in several directions by impacting rounds.

Jack scrambled after another Arab, knocked him down with the butt of his shotgun, kicked the fallen man's pistol away. Saw Billy sitting up, holding his left wrist. Vivid red blood was seeping through his fingers, dripping on the green grass. Two men dodged around Billy, ran into the field to the south, disappeared over a rise.

"How bad?" Jack asked, kneeling next to his brother.

"Fuckin' bullet went up my sleeve!" Billy exclaimed. "Ricocheted off the body armour. Hurts like hell."

Helping his brother shed the ceramic and titanium-infused shirt, Jack saw that the bullet had bounced off the instantly hardening cloth armour several times. Billy had three flesh wounds. Jack forced Billy to release his grip on his wrist. The bullet had penetrated the top of the wrist and exited on the underside, shot up his sleeves. It had freakishly passed between the ulna and radius, without breaking either bone.

Tucson threw herself to her knees next to the brothers, tore her black vest open, pulled out a green package of QuikClot, ripped it open and poured the hemostatic agent on the wound, then pressed a compress bandage on Billy's forearm. "Put his head down, raise his legs," she ordered. "Prevent shock."

Ignoring her, Billy forced himself to his knees, then stood, fighting to maintain his balance. "I'm okay. Check out the bad guys."

Jack walked to the semi-conscious man and an obviously dead man sprawled on the grass. He kicked the wounded man's pistol farther away, leaned over, peered into the man's blue eyes. "Where you guys headed? What're you up to?"

The man spat in Jack's face, uttered a curse in an unrecognizable language.

Billy, observing, hurried over and kicked the man directly on a bleeding leg wound. The man screamed.

"No!" Tucson looked horrified, was in shock. "You can't torture this man. What if they're just civilians defending themselves?" she babbled.

"What if they're innocent? What if—"

"Shut up, Tucson!" Jack exclaimed. "Every one of them had a weapon. They shot first."

"You said they were all blond! Some of them have black hair."

"They musta picked up some pals. No way these guys are civilians," Billy added, still clutching his wrist. "An' look what they did to the rear of the Porsche and the front of Mick's. That'd be reason enough to road-rage these pricks." He leaned over, grabbed the terrorist by the hair, jerked his head up.

"What's up, Dude?" He kicked the man on his wound again.

"Please!" Tucson said. "The man's wounded. You can't—"

"Shut up!" Billy exclaimed. "This guy talks right now or he's dead. What if'n they are headed to commit another attack? You want more innocent civilians killed, maimed by these scumbags?"

Jack grabbed Tucson's elbow and lead her towards the terrorists' SUV. He exchanged glances with his brother, nodded his head once.

"Don't you understand?" Tucson, tears in her eyes, pleaded. "We can't lower ourselves to their level. We'll be the same as them!"

"Give it up, Tucson," Jack said. "I'm not gonna give you a long speech about right and wrong, justify our acts. Screw that! We've been doing what we need to do. To accomplish the mission we've been given. And let the chips fall. You wanna arrest us later, go for it." He released her elbow.

"Right now," he added, "let it rest."

In the background, the wounded man howled. Tucson flinched, began crying again.

The rear bumper of the Cayenne was stove in where the oversized van had smashed into it, and the front of the second Cayenne was badly damaged, with a fender crushed into the left front wheel.

Mick was inspecting the man in the front seat of the van. Multiple gunshot wounds, blood, gore, and shattered glass all over the cab: guy was dead. Blood was dripping from the van, onto the pavement. They looked at third and fourth dead bodies—numerous wounds were still pulsing with bright red blood. Jack turned, hurriedly checked out the backseat of the terrorist vehicle. He found a briefcase on the floor. He grabbed it, saw no other papers, backed out.

"They gotta be the Bosnians," Mick concluded. He high-fived Jack, hugged Tucson, who was still in a post-combat stupor.

Jack returned to his Cayenne, called the general's voicemail, gave a detailed report of the action. Tucson snapped out of her reaction, then entered the SUV and listened to the last words of his dispassionate account. When he was finished, she asked, "How can you describe it like it was a TV show you were watching?"

"Hey, Tucson. This is my current occupation. I was gonna be an attorney arguing for the rights of rapists and criminals like all good trial lawyers. Now I'm just an ordinary grunt working for my country. If I couldn't take it, I'd be long gone." He shut his eyes, thought of his first close-up action in Shangri-La: *drew his pistol, knocked a young turbaned guy over with his horse. Boy screamed, fell. Second one grabbed his reins, drew a Khyber knife. Jack shot him, guy flew backwards. Shot the first guy when he struggled to his feet.*

Jack shook his head, thought of his first case of remorse. He'd responded to the monk in the Hindu Kush high temple, who had observed:

"You're confused, filled with pain."

"Well, yeah! I killed two men and a woman. Human beings with their own hopes, dreams. I ended them. What d'you expect?"

"You're a warrior. It's your duty to fight. You'll fill lakes with blood before your end."

"Maybe you're more bothered than you let on," Tucson broke into his thought train. "I'm calling my Sacramento office, I have to report this to my superiors."

"That's fine, Tucson," Jack said. "But we're not sticking around. We work for *Eagle's Aerie*. Don't have time to get embroiled in local issues."

286

"Local issues?" Tucson indignantly pointed at a body sprawled on the ground. "You call this a local issue? We can't just leave corpses strewn about the San Joaquin Valley!"

Jack looked at the abandoned vehicle, the visible bodies. "You're right." He got out, approached Billy and Mick. "One of us has to stay until the authorities get here."

"It can't be you or me!" Billy exclaimed.

"Yeah, that's so." Jack glanced at Tucson, who was still in the SUV, speaking into her cell. His cell phone rang—it was the general.

"Hey, Jack, you whip-ass SOB! Your news is sensational!" the general shouted. "You said no casualties? Any prisoners?"

"One, General," Jack responded. " And Billy took a round. He'll survive. Two bad guys ran into the fields. Should be easy to track down. And no collateral damage. We'd track them down but we've got a shot-up SUV and lotsa bodies. I imagine there's been about a hundred 911 calls from civilian bystanders horrified by the gun battle." He saw a state trooper vehicle with flashing lights on its roof enter the rest stop, park at the restroom area.

"You guys are a war machine! Tell Major Nakamura to hold in place," the general directed. "But tell him not to claim responsibility—tell him to point to the fibbie lady, what's her name?"

"Agent Tucson Luvabrest. But she's not a field agent and—"

"Doesn't matter. We got a JAG lawyer snooping around our offices, mumbling about violations of the *Posse Comitatus* laws. I'll send a helicopter, give Major Nakamura a lift to Los Alamitos Army Airfield down in Orange County, and he can catch up later after he forms a rapid response team out at... no, maybe I'll send him straight to Camp Irvin. Tell him to call me at once. Same number. I'll have my aide call the Highway Patrol, explain the situation, tell them to cordon off the scene."

Jack thought about mentioning the briefcase, but he wanted to inspect the contents and he knew that the general would insist that he leave it with Mick. "Yes, General. One more thing. See if your aide can requisition an XM-199. I need a non-lethal weapon. That

199 rules. And by the way, General, you'd better give me a contact number, in case this preprogrammed cell goes dead."

The general grumbled about tracking down the experimental weapon, but agreed to assign the task to an aide. He gave Jack a Virginia area code and telephone number. Jack wrote it down, then entered it in the cell, put it away, and relayed the general's message to Mick.

Mick sighed, "Okay, I'll stay. When I'm done hosting the mobs, I catch a flight out?" He glanced at the briefcase in Jack's hand, at the Highway Patrol's black and white with rooftop flashing headlights. "You'd better boogie," he cautioned.

Tucson joined them. "I'm staying with Mick. I have to go to our Sacramento office and debrief. My supervisor, Special Agent Yarmouth, is waiting for me."

Jack looked at the beautiful girl. She appeared to be hyperventilating.

"You did all this, the general says. You can come clean with your supervisors. But take care," Jack said. "We got Comitatus issues at the general's office. Until he gets that cleared up, we gotta lay low. An' Mick has gotta get outta here. We're heading south—same direction these assholes were going. I'm bettin' Mara'll answer this cell." He held up a cell phone he had found on the front seat floor.

Tucson seemed torn by a hard decision. "I want to go with you. Follow this to the end. But my supervisor is yelling at me because I'm not a field agent—"

"No sweat," Jack said. He resisted an urge to hug her. "We'll hook up down the road."

He and Billy slowly drove onto the freeway. In the rearview mirror, Jack saw Tucson standing in the middle of the service road, waving empty arms at the slowly approaching patrol car. Jack hit the first lane and quickly accelerated. Soon, he couldn't see Tucson's slender figure or the rest stop in his mirror.

Chapter 62

Glancing at her cell phone, Mara Bhutto resisted the urge to call Mikhail al Slovenly, her Bosnian subordinate. As usual, his young Islamic terrorist gang was late. 0600 hours—al Slovenly had called the previous evening and left a message that *Saladin's Fist* would rise early and arrive in Palmdale at 0600 hours. He had said the words: "The other *Fingers of the Fist* had serious trouble—got burned hands, I fear." She wondered and worried about what he meant.

She glanced at the newspapers on the passenger seat of the used Chevrolet SUV she had purchased for cash in Sacramento, the first city in which she had noticed the string of sex crime articles in local newspapers. The Sacramento Bee listed the crimes in Sacramento and Fresno that had occurred by the time Mara reached the first city.

The police or the media in Sacramento had tabbed the crimes the *Fattie-Babe/Moslem-Wave.* Fresno, Bakersfield, and the Los Angeles papers had picked up the term and each article headlined the moniker.

After noticing the crimes, Mara had turned onto the 99 Highway that led to Fresno, then had followed the crime trail to Bakersfield. A dead woman had been found in all of the three cities: in each case, the victim was thin and had been beautiful. Each body had been repeatedly raped, left naked on a roadside with a crude crescent and star carved on the victim's abdomen.

Also, in each city, a grossly overweight woman had been abducted, and dropped off unharmed in the next town on the highway. The released women, apparently traumatized, had refused to render accounts of their treatment by the kidnappers.

Mara smiled. *The stupid and fat bitches are probably standing on the side of the road, hoping for more Bosnian rapists to come along.*

The last news article linked the crimes to a dual rape-murder in Oregon. Based on the interstate nature of the crimes and the apparent kidnappings, the FBI had been called into the investigations.

Mara had no doubt that the Bosnians were guilty. They had abandoned her planned routes, had traveled the 5 Freeway and then the 99 Freeway to Los Angeles. They were conducting their own version of a terrorist attack on the United States. She remembered the scene in the middle of the street in Kingsville, Oregon, shuddered. She mused out loud, "I've traveled around the world, spent Rama's money, and I promised a huge conflagration that would destroy an American city. That was preposterous. Their resources outweigh any possible firestorm. I should've known rich America would have the resources to stamp out fires that would burn for months in Asia. It's hopeless. And the sex maniac Bosnians are missing."

She tried to suppress her anger, tried to see things from the *Fist's* viewpoint: they were in America, a land they hated; they were outside the law, trying to instill terror, hoping to burn down forests and cities; they were outside Islamic law, and anyway, were doing no wrong in their own minds by killing Infidel women. She remembered the grade school admonition taught to every child in Muslim countries around the world, *"Pick up a rock. If you find a Christian or a Jew under the rock, kill them in the name of Islam."*

Nevertheless, she had to regain control of *Saladin's Fist*, or they would be eventually apprehended for the *Babe* murder-rapes and Fattie kidnappings. Then the mission would fall apart. All her work of the last year would've been for nothing. She thought of her contacts at KEGYA in Shangri-La. They had instructed, Go to KEGCILT after the fires, or if you have problems. The treachery by Joshua Trumpet: what did it mean? Could she trust the ultra-secret organization, KEGCILT? Was it just a FBI front?

She dropped that line of thought and imagined a fire sweeping over Joshua Trumpet's compound and smiled. She would make sure that no one would escape from the villainous Trumpet's fortress. Her scouring, cleansing, killing fires would first be set on all sides of Joshua's temple. Then she could go to KEGCILT in the mysterious Area 51 for her next assignment. Then on to Montana.

She remembered Jack's words to her the year before, when he tried to help her: "People are not the same everywhere, Mara. People in America are good. We're about good, truth, justice—it's the American way. We help each other. Leave this miserable country. This land's all about hate of women, misery, poverty, religious intolerance. Go stay at my ranch in Red Lodge. We have plenty of room at the Flying Eagle." She thought, *Right! Open your arms, America. Open your arms and cuddle me to your good and true breast—just like you cuddled my father to his hanging death. You fools think you can act without consequence.*

Red Lodge, Montana. Right next to a national park. Two objectives with one act. She fantasized devastation of a national landmark, the destruction of Jack's home and family. She wondered for the thousandth time why Jack had become the focus of her hate for white men and America instead of a love interest. She had been tremendously attracted to him when she had first met him. He was a typical American: upbeat, wise-cracking, confident, handsome. Everything hateful about America. And she had not been able to kill him with a knife when she had the chance. She shook her head to free it of doubt. He had to die. But first—Los Angeles.

An hour later, after repeatedly reviewing a map and affirming that a fire line along the eastern mountains would inflict the most damage to the forests overlooking the Los Angeles basin, she heaved a sigh of relief when she saw the Explorer, with al Slovenly driving, turn into the hotel parking lot. She flashed her lights at the oncoming SUV.

Mikhail al Slovenly grinned when he saw the beautiful, bronzeskinned Pakistani woman. He and the last two surviving members of *Saladin's Fist* climbed out of the SUV and joined Mara on a walk to a restaurant in the hotel. On the way, in a low voice, Mikhail told Mara about the disappearance of the other four *Fist* members and the volunteer jihadists.

She felt dismay flush through her body. "I have heard nothing on the news," she offered.

"Just a tiny mention of a disturbance south of the province's capital, Sacramento." Mikhail replied. He looked around the parking lot, saw nothing suspicious. "Something about a carjacking at a rest stop. Mostar, Zenic, Luka, and Magic have disappeared and do not answer their cell phone."

In the air-conditioned restaurant, Mara looked at the three blond men sitting in the booth. Mikhail, with white blond hair, was on her side, the other two men were across from her. One had handsome features, but his skin was marred by heavy acne, the other had a rat's face, with a receding chin and forehead, and a big nose with nose hairs protruding in abundance, squinting eyes. Mara was amazed that a man could look so much like an animal. She thought and recalled his name was Brod.

The four ordered breakfast from a fat waitress, then sipped rich coffee that a Hispanic waiter served. The Bosnians added spoon after spoon of sugar to their drinks.

Mara began, "I have recruited local men in Los Angeles. Five Islamic Pakistanis that are in the U.S. on student visas and six Egyptians who crossed the Mexican border without papers. There's no shortage of volunteers. Unfortunately, they are not as highly trained as you three are. But we needed more men; now we have them. They will meet us after we start the fires. More importantly, there's an unusual weather pattern occurring right now that will greatly aid us."

The others looked at her, then were distracted when their food arrived. She impatiently waited several moments while the three men ate, then began again. "The weather is expected to blow from the deserts to the sea. The high velocity winds will cause a fire to spread rapidly in tinder-dry brush lands and dying forests."

"Allah has granted our prayers," rat-faced Brod exclaimed.

"We'll destroy the American city," Mikhail chimed in after sipping coffee.

"But hopefully not Hollywood," he added. "I've heard it's full of beautiful women."

"All Infidels to your Faith," Mara pointed out. "Worthy only of death. We'll rent two piloted airplanes, fly over the mountains and drop road flares from the sky. We should easily create a catastrophic fire line of two hundred miles."

Al Slovenly asked, "I saw an accident on the road. Policeman putting down small fire flares. That the kind you mean?"

"Yes!" Mara exclaimed. "I asked a servant at a gas station and he told me we could buy them at an auto parts store. They appear to weigh very little."

"Won't we attract attention when we buy a large quantity?" Rat Face asked.

Mara responded to Mikhail, "Take a list from a telephone book. Go to several stores. Tell each we're buying safety equipment for our trucking company, if anybody questions the quantities."

The fat waitress brought the green tea Mara had ordered. She sipped the hot brew, felt calmness wash through her body. She put a hotel access card on the table in front of Mikhail. "I have this room for you. Two beds and a pullout sofa. Freshen yourselves and go shopping for the flares." She spread a state map on the table, over the dirty plates. "I'll go to the airport in the next town, Lancaster. The weather condition started yesterday. It'll last for several days. We must strike today, while the winds are getting strongest. We'll fly at 1100 hours."

Mara traced lines with a pen as she spoke: "One airplane will drop flares on the eastern side of the mountains and head north. I'll start fires at the junction of the Fourteen Freeway and the Five Freeway. And head south towards and past the western flank of the San Bernardino Mountains to San Gorgonio Mountain. I'll require one of you to drop the flares while I ensure the pilot fulfills his duties."

"Then Brod and I'll drop fire from the other airplane?" al Slovenly enthusiastically asked. His smile was open and sunny.

Mara regarded the Bosnian. "Yes, you'll start at the same Fourteen Freeway, on the eastern flank of the same mountains you see to the west, and fly north for one hundred kilometers. That line of attack is your mission objective. After you land back in Lancaster, kill your pilot. We'll rendezvous here tonight with our new recruits, assuming no unexpected difficulties."

"Untrained," Rat Face pointed out.

"We will take them to the mountains, between Death Valley and Area 51. Train them there on a ranch KEGCILT owns."

"Death Valley?" al Slovenly asked. "An ominous name."

"A tourist area. A very hot desert valley," Mara responded. "Nothing else."

Chapter 63

The flat San Joaquin Valley, a farmer's paradise and California's breadbasket, irrigated by snowmelt waters from the huge Sierra Nevada Mountains that rise along its eastern flank, swept southward to the east-west Tehachapi mountain range on the northern border of Los Angeles, hundreds of miles to the south. Unrelentingly flat, the valley was close to one hundred miles wide, and was bordered by low rolling hills on the west. The north-south freeway cut through it like a straight sword swipe in the dirt.

Busy with eighteen-wheeler traffic in both directions, Jack was only able to maintain an average of seventy miles per hour on the four-lane highway. As he drove south, the cotton fields gave way to huge nut orchards on both sides of the freeway.

He stopped at a rest stop at 1100 hours, and then stopped again for lunch in the tiny town of Buttonwillow, five miles south of the rest stop.

After filling the gas tank, he pulled into a Jack in the Box restaurant and the brothers ordered huge burgers with fries and coffee. Billy offered a string of remarks about the restaurant's name, Jack laughed at the lame jokes.

The hamburgers and fries were delicious, but the coffee was weak. A black and white Highway Patrol car cruised through the parking lot. Their food sticking in suddenly dry throats, they tried not staring at the cruiser—it passed the restaurant, continued under the freeway, turned north.

"About thirty miles ahead," Jack said, "the freeway climbs into the mountains, and an hour more, the 210 cuts off, just past the Fourteen Freeway. We could take the 210 to the 15 Freeway in San Bernardino. Then it's up the mountain to Lake Arrowhead."

"What about Zhang?" Billy asked. "Remember? She has relatives in Orange County. In Newport Beach. Or she'll go into Chinatown in L.A. and try to sell the gems. We've gotta catch up to her." "Right," Jack reluctantly agreed.

"She mentioned a couple of places," Billy said. "If we can find her in Newport Beach and get the emeralds back, we can get the Chinese off our backs."

"We've already lost Omar, we don't want to add to the list," Jack concluded. "Let's get going. The sooner we get to Newport, the sooner we can go after the fizzled-out gang—that is, the *Saladin Fisties*."

The two continued south on Freeway 5, but as they started up the grade to Tejon Pass, a large flashing sign over the road stated that twenty miles ahead the freeway section known as the Grapevine was closed due to a fire north of Castaic. Jack checked the map, saw that the tiny town was halfway through the mountains to Los Angeles. "Get off on the next exit," he said. "Let's go back to the last town we passed through—Gorman—then take a road west to Ventura, pick up the 101 Freeway to Los Angeles."

Fifteen minutes later, Billy sped the Cayenne over a narrow two-lane asphalt road, through rugged brush-covered mountains, dotted with spreading old oak trees and small vineyards. After sixty miles, they crested a ridge and saw the blue Pacific spread out before them.

They turned south on the 101 Freeway and raced towards the San Fernando Valley in northern Los Angeles County. In Thousand Oaks they encountered a band of smoke that turned the sky a dirty brownish-gray. The smell of smoke was faint but the sun was a red ball in the sky. Jack turned off the air-conditioning and kept the windows up. He peered up at the red sun.

"Looks like we're too late. Mara and her crowd—"

"Fires might just be from run-of-the- mill arsonists," Billy scoffed.

"Too convenient. I smell Mayhem Mara," Jack responded.

In Encino, Billy turned onto the 405. The sky turned clear and stayed that way as they listened to radio reports that told of increasing road closures and school closings in the fire areas rapidly spreading through the eastern mountains flanking Los Angeles.

High winds whipped the Cayenne as Billy inched through a massive traffic jam south of Beverly Hills, then ground past LAX

Airport and Long Beach. The skies turned smoke cloudy again as they crossed the Arches bridge over Coast Highway and drove onto Newport Beach peninsula. Billy pointed at a waterfront restaurant, Woody's Wharf and turned into the restaurant's parking lot. Groups of people were standing around, staring at the eastern skies.

Inside, the two stood at a high table and ordered mugs of Sam Adams beer from a big-breasted waitress that Billy shamelessly ogled with *Hillbilly Heroin* eyes. Suspended televisions showed flashes of houses burning in the mountains.

Jack shoved down his anger at his brother's continued drug abuse.

"Think they're just normal crazed arsonists, or is it really Mara's gang?"

"Seems like they always have fires in Southern California during Santa Ana wind storms," Billy said.

"Santa Ana winds're blowing the smoke offshore," Jack pointed out.

"Nothing we can do if Mara's already struck. We're too late." Suppressing a sense of failure, he went to the toilet, then glanced through an Orange County list of t'angs on his iPhone. He spotted a t'ang with a Newport Beach address. He rejoined Billy, who was staring at a burning house on an overhead TV screen. As he sat down, he said, "We've got two hints on where Zhang likes to hang. Especially at sunset which is coming up. We'll check them, and if we strike out, we'll pay a visit to the t'ang residence, which is on the bay front on Lido Isle. At least people of that name live on Lido Isle, according to the iPhone information. We'll split up, then meet back here. I'll walk out on the pier." He looked into his brother's spaced eyes, worried that he'd get pulled over by the cops. "You continue down this street to the end. There's a rock jetty at the harbor mouth. Walk out on the rocks at the south end of the peninsula." Jack paid for the two beers after the waitress put them on the little round table. He glanced out the window at the sailboat masts and water beyond. A gray haze hung over the wind-rippled bay waters.

They gulped down their beers, left the restaurant and took the SUV, with Billy driving, to the pier, where he let Jack out.

Jack stopped to let a skinny redheaded girl in a sexy white thong and brief halter-top rollerblade past him, then dodged a surfer dude in baggy faded red shorts on a fast-moving skateboard, carrying a short surfboard. He passed an old fishing dory on display and stopped at the sand, looked across the very wide beach, then walked onto the long pier. He looked to the front, trying to spot Zhang. He suddenly felt like it was ridiculous that he could hope to find the Chinese girl.

He dodged a silvery mackerel dangling from a line that a young boy pulled over the handrail. An admiring old Asian man clapped his hands in delight.

He reached the restaurant at the far end of the pier and stopped at the rail to watch the reddish sun settle into a smoke bank.

"No green flash tonight," Jack declared out loud. Frustrated, he returned to the beach.

Just off the pier, almost on the sand, he booked two rooms in a small beachfront hotel called the Doryman's Inn, paid for one night and collected the door access cards.

His phone rang: it was Tucson. "Hi. I'm in L.A. Miss me?"

"Absolutely," Jack responded.

"I was reassigned, but I convinced my supervisor, Kenneth Yarmouth, to let me rejoin you."

Jack walked outside, stood on the sidewalk, watched the ocean waves advance on the beach. "You must have been persuasive."

"Actually, I think your boss, the General, had more to do with it. Something about 'If it ain't broke, don't fix it.'"

"Sounds like him." Jack walked to the old fishing boat leaning on a post, acting as a monument of sorts. "Where are you?" he asked.

"Just crossed the bridge, coming down Newport Boulevard. Can't imagine what you're doing here. I was flown down from Sacramento to John Wayne Airport. An agent is driving me. I've never been treated so… special."

"How did you know where we… never mind. I'll see you in a few." He disconnected, walked past the Doryman's craft, sat on the sand, wondered how he would ever escape the surveillance the entire world seemed to so successfully use to constantly keep track of his movements. His cell phone immediately rang again.

Billy said, "Bingo, Red Ryder."

"She on the jetty?"

"I see her just sitting at the end of the bay, watching the tide roll away."

"Fun-ny!" Jack felt his heart hammering in his chest. "You excited as me?"

"You know it, bro."

"You need help?"

"Naw, I'll wait at the land end of the jetty, collect her, round up the emeralds—if she still has 'em. Meet you at Woody's."

"Make it the Crab Catcher, just as you're comin' back this way."

"A restaurant?"

"Yeah, it's chow time. We'll have a reunion meal." Jack laughed. An old Asian woman turned, looked at him with unfriendly eyes, swore as a car swerved to the curb.

Tucson got out of a brown sedan, walked to Jack. She was carrying a black satchel.

"Hey," he called.

"Hi," Tucson responded as she stopped next to him. She turned and watched the sedan swing around, depart. Jack put out his arms and she kissed him. Hard.

He pointed at the hotel. "I've got a room."

"I'll bet," Tucson laughed.

They hurried up to the room, burst into it and threw clothes on the floor as they rushed to the four-poster canopy bed. They grabbed each other in a frenzy of lust: kissed, fondled each other, made love on the bed.

They slowed after a few minutes and stroked each other, settled into a leisurely, pleasurable rhythm until, after fifteen minutes, first Tucson—now half out of the bed—and then Jack, gasped with delight.

After sharing a mutually enjoyed scrub-down session in the cramped shower, they dressed and hurried out of the tiny lobby and began walking north on Newport Boulevard. When they entered the Crab Catcher, a crowded fish restaurant, they sat under a huge twelve-foot-long shark, mounted and suspended from the ceiling, ordered a bottle of house white wine from a slender, attractive blonde waitress with short hair and a smiling, well-tanned face.

Jack and Tucson sat across from each other, beamed as they stared into each other's eyes. Tucson's face still carried a high color as she reflected on their passionate interlude.

Sitting against the wall, Jack spotted Billy and Zhang enter the restaurant, walk past the host's desk. Billy was carrying the small backpack. Zhang Poon t'ang was wearing tight, low-cut jeans and a white halter. She looked fabulous, excepting a sheepish, pouting countenance. The two sat across the table after Tucson moved to Jack's side. Billy put the pack between his legs.

"Hi," Zhang said. She noted Tucson's skin tone, smiled knowingly. Seeing that she gave the tiniest of nods to Tucson, Jack wondered again about their pasts.

"I see you two're getting along," Zhang commented.

"I got the emeralds," Billy added in a low voice.

Before anybody could respond, the blonde waitress delivered a basket of bread sticks, put down an open bottle of wine and four plastic glasses. After she had taken food orders, she left the table.

"I sent them to my uncle by UPS," Zhang said. "Then I caught a ride to Eugene, flew to John Wayne Airport here in Orange County to wait for the emeralds." She glanced at Tucson, then ignored her. "I barely escaped Second Department henchmen. What took you so long to catch up with me?" she asked with a straight face.

"How'd you get away from the *SD* guys?" Jack asked. He looked into her eyes, waited for her to make up an answer.

"I saw them enter the motel parking lot. I warned your friend, then went out the bathroom window. But the black man was too big to follow me. I ran like a spanked Mongolian camel calf." She looked around, added,

"I'm *sor-ry*."

"That's good to know," Jack said with a bitterly sarcastic tone.

"*Especially* since they were following you."

"I searched myself before I left Singapore," Zhang protested. "I'm clean. There's no bug on me."

"Then how did they track you?" Tucson asked.

"Unless you're still working for them," Jack added.

"No!" Zhang looked at Billy, back at Jack.

"What if the bug's inside you?" Tucson wondered.

The waitress brought salads on paper plates, slid them across the table to each of the four.

Billy said, "It should be easy to give them the emeralds when they catch up to us."

"Yeah," Jack agreed. "We'll spend the night here in Newport. I got us a hotel. After din-din, let's go buy some changes of clothes. Hopefully, we can contact *SD* and give them the emeralds before they kill us. Over some stupid gems I wish I'd never seen!"

Chapter 64

Penelope Kong, after instructions from Customs Agent Beauty Smith, called a hotel and took a shuttle bus to the nearby Airport Hilton Hotel On Sepulveda Boulevard, where she checked in and was eagerly escorted to her tenth floor room by a bellboy. When he showed her the television remote, she asked what it was. Amazed at her ignorance of television, he demonstrated how to use it.

He led her into the bathroom and answered her questions, explained the room service menu and the telephone, then left, wondering what exotic part of the world could produce such a clueless though beautiful woman.

Ignoring the bizarre machine with living pictures, Penelope took a hot bath in a comfortable tub, and after the bath, she looked out the window at a huge road with six lanes in each direction to the east of the hotel. She wondered whether Jack was traveling in one of the thousands of amazing vehicles that were flowing past the hotel like a molten river of steel. She ordered a steak dinner from room service and fearfully settled down in front of the television to wait for the Customs Service to release her tarn waters. After she figured out how to change channels, she realized that almost every channel carried news reports covering a large fire east of the city. Images of countless burning structures and fleeing citizens filled the screen. She worried that it would reach her part of the immense city that seemed to stretch on forever.

Chapter 65

After leaving the hotel the next morning, Jack, Tucson, Billy, and Zhang, drove over the Arches Bridge to the 55 Freeway, then to the 91 Freeway East towards the smoke-covered mountains. Tucson rode with Jack in the front seat, while Billy and Zhang rode in the back. Ashes, looking like huge snowflakes falling in a forest, smashed and disintegrated against the windshield. The reddened sun peeked through heavy smoke clouds; their eyes burned from the smoke leaking through the AC system.

"It's like the end of the world," Tucson said with a hushed tone.

"Huge fires are pretty common in So Cal," Jack responded. "But this is over the top." The westward side of the 91 freeway was a creeping parking lot, inching towards Orange County and Los Angeles through murky mountain canyons. He glanced at his brother, who still looked sleepy. "How was bunking with Zhang?"

"Ever slept with a venomous snake?" Billy asked.

Jack thought of handcuffs, stupidity, anger, embarrassment, sex in the motel in Port Angeles. "I think I know what you mean."

Zhang laughed triumphantly. "Hogwash! Billy's so easy."

The four stopped for breakfast at a *Denny's* in Yorba Linda. Billy and Zhang sat across from Tucson and Jack. No one looked rested and the mood around the table was irritable. The cheerful Hispanic waitress poured hot coffee and fresh orange juice.

"So what's the plan, Fearless Leader?" Billy asked. He patted his hair, searching for non-existent braids.

"I called Dad, asked him what we should do with these stupid gems. He suggested we send them to him. He'll have Senator Jensen give them to the State Department, have them turn them over to the Chinese government.
What d'you think?"

Billy glanced at Zhang. "Sounds good to me. Let's get rid of a major headache. We've been paid for them—a damn fair reward. Truth be told, I woulda given them to China for free. If the idiot broad here hadn't stolen them—and our reward—we wouldn't be dodging *SD* creeps." Zhang shrank back on the booth seat.

"And your friend Omar wouldn't be severely injured," Tucson added, after a glance at Zhang.

"Too true," Jack said, wondering how Omar was doing. He made a mental note to check on Omar after breakfast. "On a different subject, I heard from Mick. He's moved from Los Al here in Orange County to Fort Irwin in Barstow. The general got him a rapid response unit and they'll arrive after our recon of Joshua's headquarters. Lookin' at the gunk in the air, we're probly too late but we may as well check the area out, try an' figure out what's going on. Hopefully, we can get some Intel from the Joshua dude. I studied the maps: we'll stay on the 91 Freeway east to Highway 30, take that to the 18 and then up the 189 to Lake Arrowhead.
Should only take a couple hours, depending on traffic."

He checked a list of notes. "We have to stop at a sporting goods store. We need a compass, several other items." He pulled out a folded map and added, "Oh, and there's this. I found it in the SUV after we dusted those Saladin dudes."

Tucson peered at the map. "It's a road map of California. No big deal—every tourist has one."

"Yeah," Jack agreed, "but I wonder what this means?" He pointed at a word scrawled across the Death Valley portion of the map.

Billy leaned forward. "*KEGCILT*. What the hell's that?"

"I dunno," Jack responded. "But I remember a similar word from Shangri-La: *KEGYA*."

"Not the same," Zhang pointed out. She unconsciously stroked Billy's forearm.

"Too similar to be coincidental."

"*KEGYA* and *KEGCILT*," Tucson said with amusing tone. "The one sounds vaguely familiar. Something about an old cult. I wonder what they mean?"

"Code words," Jack answered. He saw Billy pull his arm out of reach of Zhang's hand, give her a dirty look. "The names of places." "Keg of beer, powder keg," Billy said.

"A barrel, a cask," Tucson suggested.

"But why's it written with a different spelling on your American map?" Zhang asked.

"Different place," Jack pointed out. He felt a touch on his leg, glanced at Zhang as he felt her foot rub and move up his leg. He sensed blood rushing to his face. She regarded him with a coy expression and a small, satisfied smile.

"*KEGCILT,*" Billy said. "Killed the keg. Must mean they drank all the beer. It's a party scene."

"I doubt it, knowing the Saladin and Mara crowd," Jack said. The Bosnians're Muslims. Not supposed to drink."

"Yeah, *right!*" Billy scoffed. "They're boozers, an' maximum druggies. Opium at night, hashish for breakfast. Buncha damn cowardly hypocrites."

"Yeah, you're right," Jack said. "Strongest part of their fanatical religion is 'Get high, kill Christians.' Let's get outta here. Let's all think about Keg-whatever."

Two hours later, they traveled up the 18 Highway, a narrow, traffic free two-lane asphalt road rising into the pine forests that capped the San Bernardino Mountains. Jack rounded a bend and encountered a roadblock.

He stopped and tensed as he watched a Highway Patrol officer approach. In the background, he saw a fire marshal's SUV. A CL 415 super scooper fire-fighting airplane flew overhead, disappeared over the high ridges.

"What's up, Officer?" he asked.

The man touched his baseball-type cap. "Road's closed, sir. Fires flaring all over these mountains."

Tucson pulled out her Bureau ID and showed it to the patrolman. "We're investigating the source of the fires," she said. "They may have been started by terrorists."

The officer stepped back, checked out her badge, then cautioned, "Be careful." He motioned them to proceed with an arm gesture. Jack gunned the engine and sped up the mountain. Two men, leaning on shovels, in yellow fire outfits with the letters CDF on their backs, watched them pass.

Tucson asked, "Are we all going to barge in?"

"Last time we split forces, it was a disaster," Jack responded.

"I just wish we were a little more weaponed-up. Pistols and shotguns don't constitute overwhelming power."

Tucson smiled. "Guess what I've got in my bag? A Heckler & Koch MP-10 with a silencer."

"Oh, babe, when you talk guns, you really turn me on," Jack said.

"Only one? I guess I'll have to settle for sloppy seconds."

Tucson punched him in the arm. "Let's call my Los Angeles Division for back-up," she suggested.

Jack frowned. "Maybe later. Let's check out the situation first."

"Why're you so wary of formal law enforcement?" Tucson asked. She stared at his face. "What is it with you *Eagle Aerie* guys? You're driving my supervisors crazy."

"Jack," Billy warned from the back seat.

Looking at Tucson, Jack thought of telling her about Leavenworth, remembered all the times he had been open with women and had been stung. Decided to keep his mouth shut, listen to his brother. "Maybe later," he mumbled.

"I'll go there, question him," Tucson said in a firm voice. "I'm not a member of *BAM*, but I can hold my own." "*BAM?*" Billy asked.

"*By Any Means*," Jack answered. "David Holland was a member of it —an informal FBI group—their name speaks for itself. Before he transferred to CIA."

"*BAM, BAM*—I like it." Billy laughed. "Need recruits? I could go for some safe boom boom."

Zhang whacked Billy on the arm. "That's BAM, you jerk!"

Jack laughed, then said, "Tucson, you can't go without back-up. Mick'll be bringing soldiers from Fort Irwin after my recon. I'd rather rely on them than bureaucratic fibbies worried about rules of engagement and who's the boss. Right now, let's focus on the terrorists. Where are they, what're they doing?" He suddenly remembered he had Mara Bhutto's cell number. He pulled out his wallet, handed the slip of paper to Tucson. "There're a couple of numbers. The second one is Mara's cell. Why don't you call and ask her where she is? What's she up to? Pretend you're an enabler. Who knows, she might tell you. Let's call you… Fatima—that was Muhammad's daughter's name. There's a terrorist group in Singapore—*Jemaah Islamiyah*. Say you're with them."

"How do you pronounce it again?" Tucson asked.

"I don't know. Just call it J-I. She'll know who you mean. Give it a try—what've we got to lose?"

"Let me do it," Zhang offered.

Ignoring her, Tucson turned on her BlackBerry, entered Mara's number. Held the BlackBerry in front of her.

"Hello?" Mara answered on the third ring.

"Where are you?" Tucson asked.

Jack's heart raced when he heard Mara's voice.

"Who is this?" Mara demanded.

Tucson took a deep breath. "I'm Fatima, praise Allah. I support J-I. I've been contacted, ask to supply any help you need."

"By who? Rama… J-I?" Mara asked. "Why would *Jemaah Islamiyah*…"

"Are you near Los Angeles yet?"

"Soon," Mara answered with a vague air.

Tucson quickly asked, "How can I help *Saladin's Fist?*"

"How do you know… tell me what Riduan Isamuddin's last name is."

Tucson stammered. Mara yelled, "It's Hambali, you idiot."

Jack grabbed Tucson's wrist, pulled it close and said, "Hey, Mayhem Mara, it's me, Jack."

There was a pause, then Mara asked with an astonished air, "Jack?"

"Hey, I'm glad to see you survived the Afghan cavern, Mara. Welcome to America. See the sights, spend your hard-earned tourist dollars, them go home or I'm going to send you—" She disconnected.

Jack swerved around a rock that had tumbled off a rocky cliff looming over the constricted asphalt road. Seeing a sign, he turned left onto Highway 189 to Lake Arrowhead.

Jack glanced down the cliffside at the valleys to the west. Smoke and haze blurred the details. "Call Joshua Trumpet, tell him you're Mara. See what he says. It's the other number."

Tucson called the leader. An elderly man answered, "Trumpet."

Tucson said in as close an imitation of Mara's European-sounding accent as she could muster, "This is Mara Bhutto."

"What d'you want? Lost again?"

"I want to meet with you. Do you have any new recommendations?"

"I'm busy," Joshua Trumpet disconnected.

Patting Tucson on the thigh, Jack said, "Not bad. We now know they're both prob'ly in the hunt. You're a helluva a spy and interrogator. Now we need to find *God's Purpose* location on the lake."

"I can access from my laptop," Tucson said. She opened it and went to work.

He returned his attention to the winding woodland road until they saw the smoke-darkened sheen of Lake Arrowhead's mile-high waters. They turned into a shopping center on the lakefront and parked in front of a McDonald's restaurant. Jack got out of the SUV, studied the lake's windrippled waters: it looked about a mile across, surrounded by houses—he wondered where Joshua Trumpet's place was. Tucson went to the real estate office next to the restaurant to look for a rental house. Jack took the bag of gems to the post office, two doors down, boxed them and sent them to the Flying Eagle Ranch in Red Lodge by Express Mail. The guy at the counter asked if he wanted insurance, Jack laughed to himself when he wondered what the guy would say if he asked for fifty mil as a value.

"Sure," Jack responded. "About fifty mil will cover it." He immediately regretted the joke.

The clerk glanced at Jack, then laughed. "Yeah, right." He shook the box and heard rattling sounds, looked at Jack again.

"Been rock-hounding," Jack said.

"Found diamonds in Big Bear?"

Jack forced a smile. "Something like that." He paid with cash and left the post office for the restaurant across the parking lot.

The four met at the fast food restaurant and ordered Big Macs and Cokes. The hamburgers were hot and tasty, the fries were salty, soggy, and cold. The view from the deck of the Golden Arches, hanging over the lake, was good. It looked like thousands of other American lakes, but it was surrounded by dull greenery, the water was gray in the smoky atmosphere. A roaring speed boat arced across the wind-tossed lake.

After eating, the four drove around the south side of the heavily forested lake to the house Tucson had rented which proved to be made of logs with a carved lintel, log beams, pine floors and a modern kitchen. Jack paused on the doorstep, looked across the gray waters. *Where was Trumpet's house? What was waiting there?*

Chapter 66

Dressed in black clothes purchased in a Sears store in San Bernardino the day before, Jack and Billy, with Zhang sitting in the middle, paddled across night-darkened Lake Arrowhead. They were in an aluminum canoe from the rental house's garage on the south side of the lake. The craft's dark green color disappeared in the night light as the canoe ghosted across the water. Zhang rode in the middle.

Jack illuminated his watch-compass: 0300 hours. He was on a heading of 010 degrees, and they had at least a half mile to go to the *God's Purpose* lodge. There was a strong scent of smoke in the air.

For a second he thought of a poem from his childhood. He sang in a low voice that the other two could barely hear over the soft splashes of the paddles:

By the shores of Gitche Gumee
By the shining Big-Sea-Water…
Northward, northward,
Hiawatha paddled
Under the fiery skies.
Sailed into pulsing bloodshed,
From the shores
of Gitche Gumee,
In the fire-lit Big-
Sky-Waters.
Into pounding Death,
Into the Big-sky Forest.

"Cheery," Zhang whispered

"Hey," Jack said. "I hope—what was his name, you know—the Indian boogey man? The giant fish guy? Hope he isn't under the canoe, waiting to swallow us."

"The sturgeon monster, Mishe-Nahma," Billy responded.

Jack asked, "I didn't know you were a Native American scholar. Your braids growing faster?"

"You got it, White Man," Billy responded. "The Song of Hiawatha makes me wanna scalp a white… a bad guy."

"Yeah, Bro—you're ready to rape and pillage—just don't blunder."

"That's plunder, White Man. Rape, pillage and plunder."

"Okay, Billy," Jack smiled. *So much for the scholar,* he thought.

"Anyway, it feels good to be back in action after hauling ass across three states."

"And hauling my ass all over the world," Billy complained.

"And like chasing my beautiful, rounded—some would say—perfect tush all over," Zhang pointed out from the bottom of the canoe.

"Why don't we just leave the FBI woman to her own devices and get *so* out of here. Why'd she leave, anyway?"

"I told her the truth—that Billy and I are fugitives from Leavenworth. She lost it: yelled about lies and deception, then shut up until I fell asleep. When I woke an hour ago, she was gone. I figure she went to the Joshua guy's place. She's way over her head—she's not a field agent, not even an AIC—Agent In Charge." He impatiently glanced at his watch again, shielded it, touched a button. When it illuminated, he noted it was 0330 hours.

"You're better off being rid of her," Zhang said in a low voice. "She'll arrest your asses. Mine, too."

"Hey, she's a fabulous woman," Jack responded as he dipped his paddle into the dark water. "How's the arm?" he asked Billy.

Billy did not answer, just continued to paddle.

The brothers bent to their task and fifteen minutes later, they began paddling silently, keeping their paddles in the water after every stroke. The canoe slowly, effortlessly glided toward the shore. An east wind rippled the reddened, fire-lit waters.

The canoe slid onto the beach next to a wooden dock that was entirely out of the water. Evidently, the water level of the lake had dropped a great deal during the current drought cycle. Jack checked his compass again, hoped that this was the *God's Purpose* compound.

Billy, his face, neck, and hands blackened with cammo paint, hissed, then pointed at a guard lighting a cigarette fifty meters from the water. Jack idly wondered why anybody would feel a need to smoke in the foul, smoky air hanging over the lake, then mentally kicked himself for being distracted.

The brothers climbed out of the canoe, stepped in the cold mountain water, moved slowly onto shore. They circled to approach the guard from opposite sides. Zhang stayed by the canoe.

Five minutes later, Billy stabbed a knife an inch into the guard's back.

"Drop your weapon. Don't make a sound."

The man gasped in pain and shock, his rifle thudded on the grass. Jack stood up, ten feet in front of the guard, who had not seen either man approach his position. He jabbed his Beretta into the guard's ribs, said in a low voice, "Is Joshua in the house?"

"Who the hell're you?" the man sputtered.

"Billy, if he doesn't answer in ten seconds, kill him."

Petrified, the man tried to free himself. Billy dropped his knife, threw his arm around the man's neck, choked off a scream. The man kicked, struggled, gurgled through his throat, slumped into unconsciousness.

"Damn! I was bluffing!" Jack exclaimed.

"He ain't dead.," Billy whispered. "Can't leave too many bodies lying around. This ain't Afgoneland or whacked Iraq." He bent to the grass, found his knife, put it away.

Zhang moved to their position, the three pulled the body into nearby bushes, turned and headed toward the house, about another fifty meters from the shore. The eastern, fire-lit sky cast a faint, reddish glow to everything.

Black tree masses in the night, gloomy pines surrounded the house. Smaller trees on the sides and rear of the spacious lot.

Moving from dark spot to dark spot until they were at the side of the big, two-story house, they circled it, smelled smoke, then saw another guard smoking on the upper deck at the back of the house. They retreated to the side of the house, tried a window—it was locked. Tried a second—locked.

"We need to take out that guard, go in through the door," Jack whispered.

Zhang felt on the ground, found a big pinecone—at least six inches in diameter, lofted it like a pitched horseshoe towards the back corner of the house, it landed on the ground below the guard's perch. He walked towards the sound. They saw him lean over the rail, backlit by a wall light. After a moment, he moved away and Billy lofted another pinecone, then moved to the other side of the door, filled a sock from his pocket with rocky soil quickly scooped from below a rose bush.

The guard retreated, and a minute later emerged from the back door. Jack, behind a tree, whispered, "Psst. Over here."

The guard turned to look and Billy sapped him on the side of the head. He motioned for Zhang to guard the slumping, semi-conscious man.

Quietly moving into the house, the brothers searched every room. The first floor was empty. Billy maintained a position of dominance while Jack crept up the stairs. It turned out there was no need for caution; the guard had been the only occupant of the house.

Outside again, the first light from false dawn illuminated their faces. They returned to the unconscious guard, shook him awake.

The groggy man looked at the three cammo-painted faces looming over him. "What the hell?"

"Where's the woman FBI agent?" Jack asked.

"Where's Joshua Trumpet?"

The man, still spaced, mumbled, "Get fucked!"

Billy pulled his knife, barely jabbed it into the man's crotch, between his legs.

The guard jumped, grabbed his crotch and screamed. He scooted back until Jack grabbed him.

"Don't hurt me again. Don't hurt me!" the man pleaded.

"The Refuge —they're gone to the Refuge. After they took her prisoner, everybody split."

"What is it? How do we get there?" Jack asked.

The man gasped out directions to *God's Purpose* stronghold in the wilderness east of the lake.

"Let's finish him," Billy suggested.

"He'll rat us out to the horn blower guy."

"No-o!" the man screamed.

"I suggest you run home before your toes get singed. Get the hell outta here," Jack said.

"Before we change our mind."

The man scrambled to his feet, ran into the woods.

"Comic relief," Jack whispered. "Let's head back to the cabin, see when Chopstick Mick will get here."

"Be sure and tell him to bring aerials of this Refuge place," Billy said.

"We'll need them—I've no doubt you're bent on saving the fibbie babe."

Chapter 67

A television weather announcer, wearing a fire helmet and goggles spoke into the camera. In the background, a raging fire was finishing off a large house. "Long-lasting, robust Draco, the storm, has re-entered the Pacific Ocean south of Cabo San Lucas, and is being pulled north and westward by a low pressure dust storm system that originated in Southeastern China, three weeks ago." The announcer looked over his shoulder at the inferno, then continued, "Draco's storm front has now been caught up by the Pineapple Express from Hawaii, and is being watched with amazement by the National Hurricane Center's forecasters. An Air Force Reserve WC130, a Hurricane Hunter, out of San Diego, California, reported that barometric pressure is now 965 millibars in the eye of the Category 3 storm with winds of 111-130 miles per hour."

The Anchorman asked, "This is the storm that hit Northern California just recently? How is that possible?"

The onsite man answered, "Beats me. Several forecasters state that Draco's unique second West Coast landfall could produce torrential rains and flooding in Southern California's coastal and deserts areas. As you know, we're in the middle of a Santa Ana condition that has helped spread thousands of acres of fires in coastal mountain ranges, but could also prevent a landfall by Draco, the "*I'll be back*" storm. National Hurricane Center—"

Jack turned off the television, looked at Billy.

"What's up with that?" Billy asked.

"Yeah, the same storm that hit us in Oregon—and called Draco. Dragon God's come to America again, Billy. Dragon God's Blowback. Too weird!" He looked at his brother again, tried to search his eyes.

Billy avoided his brother's searching gaze. "I dunno. I think the dragon's comin' after me, Bro."

"Come on, Billy. Get your head out of your ass! That statue is just a hunk of metal. And speaking of weird, I need ta be able to depend on you. It's gonna get tight. Can you go clean of the *Hillbilly* crap?"

"I'm tellin' you, the dragon—I keep havin' nightmares every time I—"

"You have to shape up—you could get us killed if you're not on top of your game."

"Yeah, I know—I'll try."

The sounds of an approaching helicopter drew them outside, and they watched a CH-47D Chinook helicopter settle onto the beach in front of their rented house. An east wind that had been freshening all morning was blowing at a steady fifteen miles per hour, and the mist kicked up by the huge helicopter's props felt like a light rain as it spread across the lawn.

"Good thing the lake's way down." Billy observed, "Or they'd have a tough time finding a landing spot for that big sucker."

"You know," Jack observed, "like it's great to see the Army come in. Somehow, it makes me feel everything's gonna be alright."

"He-y," Billy punched his brother in the arm. "Those are like U.S. soldiers—they'll kick ass on those overweight, overblown militias like there's no tomorrow."

Chopstick Mick Nakamura led a squad out of the rear gate and over to Jack and Billy, who were sitting on a nicely mown lawn in front of the rented log house. The helicopter lifted and left.

"Hey, guys, how's it going?" Mick greeted them as his soldiers spread across the lawn and fell into relaxed but guarded positions, as only trained soldiers knew how to do. He grinned, his eyes disappeared in his fleshy Asian face. "Guess what? The pilot let me take the left seat in that big sucker. I flew it all the way from Fort Irwin."

An older staff NCO accompanied Mick, who introduced the soldier, "Captain Jack Flashhardt, this is Sergeant First Class Bart Savage."

Jack shook hands with the bush-hatted soldier. He had a hawk nose, very dark, rosy-hued skin, short black hair. Stood about five-feet-ten, one hundred eighty pounds. Looked deadly, had brown eyes that were slightly more open than normal, a bulging forehead. The eyes gave the E-7 a slightly crazed look. Jack immediately dubbed the man "Crazed Gaze Gunny" in his mind.

Mick added, "Sarge, this is Jack's brother, Corporal Billy Howling Dog—don't ask me to explain the last name, except Billy's one-half redskin, one-half kick-ass Marine, an' three-quarters wildcat who loves to scalp bad guys."

The sergeant grinned, flashing white but crooked teeth. His eyes opened even more. "My kinda Marine."

"Major," Jack asked Mick, "Did you bring the special ammo? Do you have aerials of the area I requested? How about the M-199?"

"Yeah, I got the ammo and the laser gun," Mick said. "And MilSat real-time images." Mick pulled a small laptop out of a bag slung over his shoulder, and all four men sat while he booted up the satellite images. "I've looked, there're three candidates for Joshua's compound."

"So we're gonna have to check 'em out, find the exact location," Billy observed.

"Unfortunately, we have several problems," Jack added. "The first is, Tucson Luvabrest went to God's *Purpose* and was taken or went away with them when they left the lake house. Another is, they probably know we're coming because Billy and I reconned the lake house, asked questions that'll tip them off."

"You probably're happier now," Mick exclaimed. "Gives you a chance to lay waste—like a Montana Cossack. What Bruno the Russian used to call you."

"Poor Bruno," Jack said, reminded of the Russian's partial castration.

"I wonder if he's recovered?"

Mick turned to Savage. "He got one nut cut off during an interrogation."

Savage grimaced, looked at Jack. "So, Captain," the rosy-skinned E-7 asked, "how do we conduct a recon?"

"Tourists. We're bikers—that's our cover," Jack said. "We'll go to the village, you two buy some sports clothes, we'll rent mountain bikes and head out." He glanced at the squad of soldiers.

"Tell your men to set up and plan on staying the night, Sergeant."

"Works for me," Mick said. "Get cold at night?"

Jack thought of the canoe expedition before sunrise. It had been cool, not cold. "It's okay. It'll get pretty warm today. Lotta smoke, but the fire line to the east is still quite a ways off."

"Sarge, your guys are soldiers," Billy pointed out. "You can hack it."

The team drove to the village and Jack rented four mountain bikes while the sergeant and Mick selected shorts, shirts, sport shoes, and small backpacks in another store, then discovered they had no money. Jack paid their bill after the sergeant fetched him. Billy purchased water bottles.

They regrouped on the McDonald's deck, over-looking Lake Arrowhead; Jack went inside and returned with four cups of coffee. The table had ash and soot on the surface—he ignored the debris. The sun was an angry orange color and the sun's path of light on the lake carried the same sullen colors.

A very attractive woman and her young teenage son, both wearing colorful biking apparel had sat at the table next to the soldiers and Billy. She was a sun-streaked brunette, slender and athletic, her son was tall, very skinny, had piercing blue eyes.

After Jack put the coffees down, he glanced at the woman, she smiled back. Her hazel eyes were intense.

"Hi. I'm Susan. Going biking?" she asked. "We were going around the lake. But it's too smoky to exercise. How about you?"

Jack regarded her—she was older, close to his former boss's age: Elle, the UN babe in Islamabad. He wondered if this woman was as great as Elle had been. Broad shoulders, big boobs, slim, real slim body—she looked wonderful. He sighed, wished he could explore the chance encounter. Wondered if his mother looked like this beautiful woman. Instead, he forced a rude expression, pointedly turned his back, hoping she and her son would move away.

Rebuffed, the woman collected her son and left, a hurt expression on her face.

Watching the woman's attractive rear, Billy growled, "OohRah! I'll take some of that with my coffee and donut."

"I woulda thought you're too busy with your Chinese spy babe or maybe you're still in mourning over your other Chinese spy chick—the dead one—the one Jack iced," Mick jested.

Billy gave Mick a dirty look, said nothing.

The four drank their coffee, discussed their planned reconnaissance, then rose and biked the narrow asphalt road that skirted Lake Arrowhead. A half hour later, they encountered a dirt road that headed northeast. The narrow road descended from the mountain plateau towards the desert highlands to the east through a pine forest that was heavy, very aged, and sprinkled with many standing dead trees. Some of the expired trees, hundreds of years old, were up to five feet in diameter. The red-barked Manzanita undergrowth was light and scattered widely. Huge granite boulders, big as houses, arose like monolithic sentries throughout the forest.

Pausing on a ledge overlooking a small valley, the team eliminated, after minutes of observation, the two working ranches on each side of the basin. They biked through the wooded valley, climbed another ridge that was five hundred feet higher than the bottom of the valley. The sandy trail narrowed to the width of a bike trail, ended on the next ridge.

The four dismounted, Mick pulled the laptop out of his backpack; they climbed a granite ledge, peered around a VW bug-sized rock sitting on the granite ledge. In the eastern forests, columns of smoke filled the air.

"Hey, this's a *Bell Rock*!" Billy exclaimed.

"Wha's that?" Crazed Gunny Bart asked.

"Talking Dog—my grandfather, the chief. He told me once, Indians used to employ them to signal each other," Billy explained.

"You hit it a certain way and it produces a sound that travels. For to signal your pals." "Indian version of cell phones, huh?" Jack observed.

"Musta been damned big Indians!" Bart joked.

"Whatever happened to smoke signals—like in the movies?" Mick kidded.

"Second generation innovation," Billy answered with a grunt. The others laughed.

The four settled behind the *Bell Rock*, took turns glassing the next valley. It was about a mile across. A small hill, cleared of a majority of trees, sat in the middle of the valley. A one-story log house, with a cedar shingle roof, multiple patio walls, hedges, and rock outcroppings around it, sat on the center of the hill. Three large SUVs and two white vans were parked in front of the house.

As they watched, Jack recognized and pointed out Bobby Dawklings. The tattooed man, who had come out the front door with another man, pointed at the smoky eastern horizon, then one of the vans, and talked for a few minutes.

"Wonder what he's doing here?" Jack observed.

"I've spotted two lookout posts," Bart said. He pointed at a near location and one across the valley.

"I've seen enough," Jack declared. "Let's go back to the lake."

The four retraced their steps, the hot east wind pushing at their backs as they biked up and down the dusty trail and road on the way back to the lake. Scrub oak leaves and pine sprigs, knocked loose by the increasing wind, blew past them as they worked up and down the rocky trail and dirt road.

At the lake house, they went to the kitchen, refilled their water bottles and sat outside. The rosy-skinned E-7 called the squad leader up and a Polynesian soldier, squat and wide like Mick, with short black hair, dark brown skin, an infectious smile, joined the four on the lawn in front of the house. Unlike Mick, he had wide-open eyes.

"This's Sergeant Robby Tanoe, like canoe," Gunny Savage said. He introduced the sergeant to the others.

"So, Fearless Leader," Chopstick Mick asked Jack.

"What's our plan?" He grinned, did the disappearing eye thing, flashed his canine teeth, appeared eager to do battle.

"You don't wanna just call the local sheriff, do you?"

Jack looked at his friend. "That'd be nice, but a backwater like this, they don't have experience. And the fibbies would take days to get organized. No, it's up to us."

He leaned back on the grass. "Okay, guys, it goes like this. Your teams have four men, and you have four fire teams, right, Sarge? How'll you move to the objective?"

Tanoe frowned "We'll go by Bounding Overwatch, fire team by fire team moving forward, one at a time, the others covering."

"Great!" Jack agreed. "Then one of your teams will set up and stay outside the front door and one team will cover the rear entrance. Those two teams will be responsible for setting charges on the doors and blowing them open. As the other teams progress through the structure, the outside covering teams will collect and secure any surviving prisoners. The attacking two units will have two "A" members and two "B" members. The "A" men will throw two flash-bangs into a room, fire a burst. They hit the deck, the "B" men, in a position of dominance, will be ready for any remaining lethal response, disarm any survivors. Tanoe, you direct traffic for the team going in the front. Sarge, you handle the team going in the rear."

"Sounds good, sir."

"Mick, you hang with the radioman, direct overall traffic, control air back up."

Jack drew an arrow on the map, looked at Mick. "You have two Blackhawks available?"

"Right," Mick nodded his head. "They'll be on station. But I hate—"

Jack patted Mick on the shoulder, "I know, Mick, you wanna take the place down by yourself. So predictable. I'm really sorry you don't get to create havoc and destruction. It's the painful price of leadership."

He continued, "Billy will handle the prisoners. I'll be responsible for securing the captive woman. Her name is Tucson and she's a tall redhead. Can't miss her—very flashy hair, although, I don't imagine she'll look like she just came out of a beauty salon."

"What time'll this soiree kick off?" Savage asked.

Jack glanced at his watch. "I have 1904 hours, 1905 hours on my mark." The others readied their watches. "Mark: 1905 hours." He glanced at the others—they looked upbeat, eager. "You barely have time to get ready. Go ahead and create your order. Practice the attack now that you know the lay of the land. We'll leave at 0030, march to the ridge—should take a couple hours—we'll make a final reconnoiter and take out the posted guards. We'll blast the doors at

0400." He glanced at SFC Savage. "Sarge, d'you have night visions for Billy and me? The M-199 I requested?"

"Affirmative, sir," the E-7 went to a gear bag on a pile under a nearby tree, returned with the goggles and the M-199 laser rifle.

Jack received the items. "That's it." He hefted the non-lethal weapon. "Now I don't have to worry about leaving any dead bodies lying around." He glanced at the others. "Any questions? Let's eat, issue a warning order, run through some practice drills, then secure until kick-off."

After a dinner of cold turkey sandwiches, while the soldiers practiced their structure invasion, Jack and Billy tried quick-kill methods with a BB gun and ping-pong balls Jack had purchased the day before.

"Shooting by a yard light is tough, but this goofy shit helps accuracy, doesn't it?" Billy exclaimed after a turn at shooting flung balls. He had missed a dozen before he hit three in a row.

"Gunnery Sergeant Tensht put me through a week of this stuff in Okinawa," Jack said. "I would've never believed I could hit flying pingpong balls, shooting from the hip."

"You think the fibbie's okay?" Billy asked.

"I hope and pray she is."

"You like groove on her, huh?"

"She's the real deal." Jack sighed.

"But there's no future. I'm a fugitive and she's a federal agent."

Billy threw a ball on the ground, said with a disgusted tone, "I gotta believe they'll pardon us after all this."

"All what? We haven't accomplished shit!" Jack exclaimed.

"And I killed Ishey!"

With a scornful tone, Billy added, "She was, like a—what d'you call it—foreign agent. An' we got those guys in the van."

"Bottom line is, we haven't done much. But once we get Tucson out, I gotta feeling, Mara's gonna raise her lovely head."

"Deadly cobra head's more like it. Hopefully on the way to becoming a deadhead."

"Yeah, but I fear Tucson's gonna compete with Mara to chop our heads off."

Hey," Billy objected, "don' forget. We dusted those *Fist* guys. Turned 'em into dead pinkies."

"Big deal. Just a few ragheads," Jack responded.

"Question is... will we be able to stop the *Fist*'s brain—Mara."

Chapter 68

Too miserable to sleep, Tucson Luvabrest huddled on the hardwood floor in the corner of the room where she was being held prisoner. She glanced at her watch: 0355. She felt pain all over her body, and sharp pain was radiating from her groin. She dimly remembered being raped multiple times by Joshua Trumpet's men. The wheelchair-bound man had sat through the many rapes, gasping and grunting with pleasure, shouting questions or blaring his vile propaganda and ridiculous belief structure whenever his men rested.

He was certifiably insane: was convinced that blacks had taken over the country, were going to kill all whites. After the first rape, Tucson had mentally shut down. Everything else that had happened had been a blur. Joshua had only left when a strange, exotic, bronze-skinned woman had stalked into the room, leaned close, gazed into Tucson's eyes with complete indifference to her horrible quandary. The woman had spoken Joshua's name, turned and left the room. Joshua had quickly followed, rolling his wheelchair by himself.

Her body ached where she had been beaten, her vagina felt like it had been ripped out and stuffed back in sideways, her head was pounding, her throat was hoarse from yelled protests and cries of pain. Her throat was also burning from the smoky air. She prayed Jack Flashhardt would ignore her stupid posturing back at the lake house. She bitterly regretted her threats of arresting him and his two cohorts before she had stormed out of the rented lake house.

An ear-splitting blast at the front of the house! A second at the rear. Multiple crashing explosions, assault rifle fire—full auto: it sounded like a full-scale battle raging through *God's Purpose*. Hope surged: it had to be Jack and a thousand Marines.

Her door flew open, the hugely-muscled tattoo man dashed in, a pistol in one hand, a combat knife in the other. Shots rang out behind him. He slammed the door shut. Hit the light switch. Crossed to her, pulled her up. Patch on one eye, shaved head, short in stature. She remembered the demons. She had imagined that every tattoo had silently howled with delight when the man—one of many—had raped her.

Snarled in her ear, "We're gettin' outta here, bitch. You're my ticket."

"Jack said you're with ATF," Tucson protested. "Why did you—"

Bobby Ray Dawklings grimaced. "Exactly! I was stupid to jump you.

Thought they'd waste you, couldn't resist." He waved a hand in dismissal.

"Too late now. I'm not goin' down on a rape charge."

Tucson pleaded, "I won't burn you. I—"

Bobby Ray barked a nervous laugh. "Yeah, right!"

"You're not thinking clearly. You—"

He scowled. "Just shut up, bitch!"

Soldiers moved in waves, running and throwing flash-bang grenades into every room, then emptied a magazine at the occupants, who fell or threw themselves to the floor in abject terror at the shocking violence of the attack.

Jack followed in trace behind the wave of attackers as the men shouted "Clear!" after cleaning out each room. The attack was working exactly as planned: complete surprise. Dazed, crawling men being herded to the entry. He cautiously moved down a smoke-filled hall. Into a room: empty guest toilet. Next room: a man trying to crawl under a bed, two soldiers pulling his feet. Next room: old guy in a wheelchair: dead! A hole in his forehead, a stain of blood across his face and white beard. Last room: Tucson!

Tattoo Dawklings was standing in a corner, the FBI agent held in front of him. He was wearing a shirt, no underwear. Knife at her throat, he aimed a handgun at Jack, fired twice, the gun emptied. His good eye was shut, he'd fired wildly, missed when Jack ducked away.

"Give it up, Dawklings," Jack shouted from the floor. "Don't hurt her. Spread them!" Tucson stared at him. Both eyes were blackened, swollen almost shut. Her lips were puffed out, showed dried blood. A silent scream on her bloated face. He activated the laser gun, aimed the weapon at Tucson.

"Out of my way, asshole!" Dawklings screamed. He cowered behind Tucson. "I'll kill her. Move!"

"Go ahead," Jack said. "I don't like the fibbie bitch anyway."

"I'll kill you!" the tattooed man screamed.

"With that pigsticker? Give me a break! Now, spread them!" Jack repeated. He thought, *Ping-pong balls.*

Tucson blinked, looked at his weapon, quickly spread her long legs. Without hesitation, Jack shot the laser from the hip, between Tucson's legs, into the tattooed man's barely exposed crotch.

Dawklings screamed, dropped the knife and empty gun. Fell to the ground, curled into a fetal position. Jack maintained his aim on Dawklings' writhing body. Dawklings' hands grabbed his burning flesh but when the laser targeted his hands, he jerked them away.

Jack redirected his aim at the ugly demon tattoos on Dawkling's neck. Steam, then blood spurted out of his neck as blood vessels evaporated and released bubbling fluid. Gore poured across the hardwood floor.

Tattoos on his arms and neck silently howled in pain, finally fear. As Jack and Tucson watched, riveted by the horrible display, the tennis ballsized demons on Dawkling's arms and neck all continued to silently scream, then disappeared as blood sheeted over them.

Tucson turned and threw her arms around Jack. "Oh, thank you, it was terrible," she murmured into his neck. "Those horrid men—"

"Shhh. I'm so sorry we failed you—came as soon as possible," Jack whispered. Noticed silence of arms. Commanding shouts still rang out. Lack of gunfire and explosions. The battle was over. "Let's go outside."

"What was that weapon? What'd it do to him? I've never seen—"

"Secret weapon, Tucson. Sposed to be non-lethal, but I guess I proved different." The image of the melting, steaming flesh burned into his mind. He bent over, felt for a pulse, weak and fluttering. "I'd better get help to drag him out."

What'd you bring? A regiment?" Tucson asked as he helped her through the door.

"Could've. But they're U.S. Army—I only needed a squad. Hey, Tanoe—way to go, man!"

The Polynesian, wide and squat, grinned, lifted his assault rifle in the air in triumph. "No casualties, sir! We kicked ass!"

She stopped in the hall, clutched his arm. "Jack, I figured it out."

"Let's get outta here," he commanded. He seized one of Tattoo's arms, Tanoe grabbed the other; they hauled the monstrous man across the house floor, outside, left him next to about fifteen men who were sitting on the ground, their hands behind their heads, illuminated by the headlights of an SUV.

"They're all alive!" Tucson exclaimed as she limped out of the front door.

Mick, a triumphant grin on his face, said to Tucson, "Jack's a genius! We had teams. The first guy fired blanks. The second man was ready with real ammo if there was resistance, but the militia guys panicked and they all gave up without a fight."

"Captain Flashhardt figured we'd best not—we couldn't kill fifteen Americans," Savage added as he skirted the captives and approached.

Jack declared in a fake-solemn voice, *"Silent leges inter arma.* During war, the laws are silent. But that doesn't apply here in the States." He glanced at those around him, tried to suppress a triumphant grin.

"Flash-bangs and blanks. Like an electronic shooting gallery in a fun zone," Billy laughed. "Nobody was even wounded. Buncha cowardly assholes—they all gave up without a fight."

Jack thought, *No, Bobby Ray Dawklings cashed in some painful chips. And all his tattooed demons: tears at the end.* He said nothing, exchanged a glance with Tucson.

Tucson looked at the eastern sky. Billy joined them, followed her gaze. She asked, "Is the sun coming up already?"

All turned and saw the entire horizon lit up by a red glow.

"That's not dawn's light—that's fire!" Jack shouted. "Mick, call in the Blackhawks. We gotta get out of here."

Chapter 69

"What about the prisoners?" Mick asked as he saw the first flames flare on a tree behind the house.

"Let 'em shift for themselves, Major," Billy yelled. "If the helicopters can't land cause of the winds, we gotta get outta here." More flares flew through the air and landed on all sides, exploding into flames like exploding white phosphorus shells.

"We got the hostage, sir. The prisoners'll just slow us up," Bart Savage shouted. "We gotta haul ass! Screw 'em, form up an' let's high diddle diddle."

The column ran towards the ridge that formed the valley's west side. Jack carried Tucson piggyback, her long legs dangling over his forearms. In single file, they reached the crest five minutes later. Jack had started at the head of the column, as they topped the ridge he was in the rear.

At the top, they regrouped and paused to watch the rapidly spreading fire head towards Joshua Trumpet's Retreat. Flares of fire were blowing from tree to tree. The freed prisoners had taken the van and the SUVs and were already gone. The smell of smoke was strong, the visible smoke was whipping through the trees.

"Look!" Billy shouted.

The cloudless sky was filled with a towering smoke column that was bent westward by strong Santa Ana winds.

"Hey!" a soldier shouted. "To the west."

On the southwestern horizon, a gigantic, soaring cloudbank, at least 60,000 feet high, was rapidly moving eastward, and the Santa Ana winds, which were still blowing at the fire line, were being met by the approaching storm front. Tremendous lightning bolts were flashing throughout the colossal cloudbank and a rainsquall line was already rapidly moving across Lake Arrowhead in their direction. Impossibly long, twisting, dancing, miniature tornadoes—thousands of feet above their heads—marked the collision of the two storm fronts.

The Army column resumed the march into the next valley, pounding rain slashed into them—they were drenched in seconds. Lightning flashed around them like artillery explosions.

They made the paved perimeter road on the east side of Arrowhead in forty minutes of forced marching. The faint sounds of sirens from several directions sounded, perverted and warped by the howling winds vying for supremacy far over their heads.

Several early rising local inhabitants looking into dawn's first light and the heavy rainfall, were amazed to see the group of heavily armed military men marching around the lake on Highway 173.

Hurried 911 calls prompted the San Bernardino County Sheriff's Department to dispatch four two-man vehicles. The sheriffs arrived just as the tired but happy group entered the rented lake house.

A deputy chief warily stepped out of his vehicle as the soldiers filed into the house to get out of the rain. Flashing vehicle lights seemed to reflect the almost constant lightning from the overhead storm.

The deputy, wearing a yellow rain jacket, looked like he didn't want to approach the log house. Three sheriff SUVs pulled up and parked in a line by his car; the deputies remained in their vehicles.

Mick Nakamura emerged from the house unarmed, dressed in his cammo outfit, slowly walked towards the deputy chief.

The deputy chief spoke into a loud hailer, "Raise your arms above your head, Approach slowly."

Mick ignored the order to raise his hands, continued to walk towards the deputy. He stopped about ten feet from the very nervous sheriff.

"Halt! Identify yourself," the lawman demanded.

"Major Mick Nakamura, US Army," Mick announced in a firm voice.

"I'm the leader of a joint-force Homeland Security operation against a paramilitary outfit, *God's Purpose*. Our mission, which we've completed, was to rescue an abducted FBI agent."

"We heard nothing about an abduction or an unauthorized military operation in our jurisdiction," the sheriff's official responded. His voice sounded slightly less strained, a lot more belligerent.

"Security reasons," Mick said in a patient voice.

"*God's Purpose* has law enforcement ties and we figured they monitor the police radio networks. We needed total surprise to minimize casualties."

"Where did this so-called "minimized casualty" operation take place?" the deputy asked. "Where's the FBI agent?"

"She's being treated inside. Why don't we get out of the rain? Let's go in the house and talk it over."

The sheriff put his hand on his pistol butt. "Don't move. You're in violation of *Posse Commie-whatever*, at the least."

Mick smiled, his eyes disappearing. "Chill, Sheriff. I don't serve you. You're not in my chain of command. I'm getting out of this rainstorm. You want to stay here, talk to us on your loud hailer, go right ahead. You want to ignore my invitation and play hardball, get a warrant and come on back. We may still be here. And the word you were searching for was *comitatus*. Doesn't apply to Homeland Security forces." He turned and walked slowly back to the house, paying no attention to the deputy's demands to stop.

Unsure of what to do, the deputy chief retreated to his vehicle, called the Sheriff at home for direction. The Sheriff put in a frantic call to the Federal Bureau of Investigation offices in San Bernardino, and the Governor's office in Sacramento. As he feared and expected, no one accepted his calls, so the Sheriff called his deputy back and instructed him to go ahead and meet with the joint force.

Reluctantly approaching the two-story log house, the deputy chief knocked on the front door. It opened and he saw over twenty young, physically fit men and two women sitting and lying on furniture or the floor, cleaning assault weapons, sawed-off shotguns and black pistols, eating food from packages, relaxing. A loud hum of conversation ended, all stopped, glanced at the man in the doorway, wearing an old-fashioned drill instructor's brimmed cap, a yellow rain coat. Most of the men returned to their tasks.

Not used to being ignored, he said in a loud voice, "I'm Deputy Chief Don Reading. Who's in charge here?"

All eyes returned to the medium-sized but overweight man, who was nervously stroking moisture from his walrus mustache, his fat cheeks. No one responded. He looked at the two women, trying to figure out which was the supposed FBI agent. One, a black woman, had a superior smile on her face; the other, a redhead, wore a large bandage on her forehead, was lying on the sofa. He surmised she was FBI. "Ma'am, are you a government agent?"

"Yes, I am. Tucson Luvabrest, Federal Bureau of Investigation." Her voice was weak, she put her head back down on a pillow.

"She's in no condition to answer questions, Officer," said a young soldier with a medic tag on his tan BDU blouse.

Mick and Bart Savage rose together. Mick directed, "Let's go in the kitchen, Sheriff. We'll brief you on our operation against *God's Purpose*."

"And you're saying there were no casualties?"

Mick and Jack looked at each other. "No," Mick responded. "I'm saying I and my Army force didn't inflict or suffer serious casualties. But there's a major fire to the east that forced us to abandon the fifteen uninjured prisoners we took an' run for our lives. I don't know what happened to them after we secured Miss Luvabrest and left."

Jack, Billy, and Zhang exchanged glances, watched the deputy follow Mick and Savage to the kitchen. The three rose and headed for the bedroom wing.

Chapter 70

Penel Kong, the tall blonde princess of Shangri-La, broke into a huge smile when she entered the Customs testing area at LAX Airport and saw her four tarn water bottles sitting on a countertop. She carefully packed the bottles in a large leather bag she had brought, secured a flap to close it.

Beauty Walker waddled around the counter and hugged the thin athletic-looking Shangrilan, who was dressed in a grey pants suit, accented with a red leather belt and a red scarf. The two had become fast friends in a very short time, and Penel had purchased a new wardrobe in a Torrance shopping center Beauty had taken her to the night before. Beauty glanced at her watch. "I can take a lunch break, let's go have coffee."

In the tiny restaurant, Penel picked up her coffee and an empty cup, took the cups to their table. She said, "I have two presents for thee." She reached behind her neck and unclasped a gold necklace, handed it to Beauty. It was a choker of gold incised with complex patterns that made the metal twist and weave as Beauty turned it in her hand.

"It's gold. Very valuable. It's quite old. Modeled on the Brosinga mene."

Beauty tore her eyes off the wondrous gleaming necklace, asked, "What's that, honey?"

"*The Brosinga mene of Beowulf.* The infamous Brising Necklace. *Goddess Freyja*, beautiful as the sea in sunlight, the mountains at dawn, slept with four ugly, misshapen dwarfs for four days and four nights in exchange for the necklace."

"Four days! She musta been one sore puppy when they was done," Beauty laughed.

"They had made the necklace in a cavern near the gates of Hel. Then Loki, The Trickster God, stole it from Goddess Freyja, Goddess of War, at Odin, the Terrible One's command." Penel, looked up and recited:

'Get that necklace, Sly One,' roared Odin.
His one eye was burning,

Reflecting the flames of Hel.
'Until you steal it
From whoring-about Freyja,' he bellowed,
'Proving her guilt,
Let me never see your sly Shape-Changer face
In wondrous Asgard again.'

"Heavy!" Beauty exclaimed. "The verses, I mean." She looked at Penel.

"I thought you were from Asia. Vikings're from Scandahoovia."

"My people are descendants of five Northmen who deserted from an ancient army and settled in Kafiristan."

Beauty fingered the weighty chain, held it up to her neck and sighed. She looked into Penel's beautiful widespread blue eyes. "Sorry, honey, I can't take this. It could be construed as a bribe."

"I did not mean it that way. It is a store of wealth for my travels. As you can see, I have others around my neck. I consider you a friend. Anyway, my second present is more valuable." She held up a hand to silence another protest, then poured about four ounces of tarn water into the paper cup and placed it in front of Beauty. She smiled again. "What I mean is that the people of Shangri-La have discovered that consumption of these tarn waters prevents illness, including excess weight, I presume."

Beauty smiled. "Makes you lose weight—stay healthy? So it's just mineral water? Honey, you hung around waiting for a friggin' watery weight-loss product?"

Penel smiled, pointed at the water. "Drink, doubter. Visit me in six months, your body in balance with nature, wearing a new wardrobe on a slender body. And contain your anger at having to purchase a new wardrobe." She stood and watched Beauty finish the cup of tarn water. "Now, I must travel Northwest Airlines to the city of salt water, transfer again to Montana."

Beauty finished the mineral water, grimaced. "Tastes yucky." She stopped when she felt a livening sensation slowly progress through her body. She looked at the empty glass, up at Penel. "City of… you mean Salt Lake City? Okay, honey. Remember, when you get to Billings, stay in a hotel—you don't want to bust in on folk in the middle of the night. In the morning, you hire a taxi to take you to your boyfriend's ranch." Beauty took Penel's hand, put the necklace in it and added, "Weird water. Anyways, I'll catch a shuttle with you to Northwest Airlines terminal. You stay in Salt Lake tonight. Billings tomorrow night, if need be. Call me when you arrive safely. I'm transferring to Homeland Security and movin' to Nevada for an undercover operation, but I'll be in L.A. for a couple more days."

"Undercover? What means that? A spy?"

Beauty smiled. "I'll be working as a maid in a whorehouse. In Pahrump, Nevada. We think some crazies next door to the cathouse're plannin' a terrorist attack."

Penel searched her friend's face, asked, "Hard to understand your meanings," Penel said. "Do you think Jack—my man—will welcome me?"

Beauty appraised her new friend: wide-set, intensely blue eyes, high cheekbones, a wonderful, rosy-cream tanned skin, thick blonde hair. "Honey, if he knew you were comin', he'd have a brass band and dead Elvis greeting you."

Chapter 71

Mo Poo, the giant Chinaman, emerged from the trees bordering the eastern Idaho highway. He had fallen asleep and the little *SD* man had pulled a weapon from under his car seat, aimed it at Mo Poo.

One flip of his giant fist—the man was unconscious. The bullet from his pistol had gone through the windshield.

After pushing the car fifty feet into the brush, Mo Poo had carefully questioned, then easily strangled the little driver.

Now, an automobile approached. It slowed, then sped up again when the driver realized how big and how ugly Mo Poo was.

Having questioned the *SD* man, Mo Poo knew where he was going in Montana—the Flying Eagle Ranch, northeast of a village called Red Lodge. With a map and directions in his bag, he continued eastward on the asphalt road. Occasionally cars slowed, sped up again when they drew near enough to see him clearly.

Realizing that it would be impossible to convince anyone to stop, Mo Poo lay down in the middle of the road, hid his face in the crook of his arm. The next vehicle to approach was a battered pickup. It screeched to a skidding halt just ten feet short of Mo Poo. A man and a woman got out of the truck.

"Guy's a monster!" the woman driver exclaimed. She was large, overweight, had a big head, bulging eyes, dirty blonde hair. She looked at the hitchhiker she had picked up earlier. He was undersized, short and skinny. "Wonder if he's hung as big… maybe we can load him in the bed, take him to a doc in town."

The little man prodded Mo Poo with a boot. "No way we're gonna lift this guy. Need a fuckin' forklift. He's the biggest dude I've ever seen.

Makes Shaq O'Neal look undersized, I'll bet. Guy's eight feet tall!"

Mo Poo opened his good eye, saw a man's legs standing by his head. He wrapped a huge hand around the man's boot, jerked him to the ground and broke his neck as if it was a twig. Stood and threw the dead body into the ditch.

At the crunching, cracking sound, the woman jumped and staggered back, horrified. Mo Poo looked down at the woman. She had greasy, stringy yellow hair, pale blue eyes, looked like an overstuffed white Shangrilan.

When the monstrous, hideous-faced man loomed over her, she froze, paralyzed with fright, urinated. Liquid slowly crept from her foot, trickled across the asphalt. "What... what do you want? I'll... I'll give you anything—"

Grabbed her forearm, dragged her to the passenger side, pointed at the cab. "Take me. To Montanastan."

Chapter 72

"You will meet a shepherd at two thousand hours, at the Chicken Ranch in Pahrump, Nevada. Tomorrow night. Thank God you're on schedule. Do you know where Pahrump is?" the voice asked.

Mara answered, "I have no idea. Is it here in Death Valley? I'm near a tourist site, Scotty's Castle."

"No, just a few miles east," the voice informed. "You will go east out of the valley to Beatty, Nevada, then take Highway 95 to the 160, then south to the Chicken Ranch in Pahrump. Go to the Ranch, you will be contacted by Mr. Homer. Identify yourself as MS Marge. Do not be late."

The voice asked, "By the way—your appearance?"

I have short black hair," Mara offered. "And I'm told my skin has a distinctive copper-like hue."

"Copper-like? Appropriate," the voice responded.

"Why?" Mara asked. The line disconnected.

Mara hung up left the restaurant and stepped into the blast furnace atmosphere of Death Valley. She cursed herself for assuming that she would meet the *KEGCILT* people in Death Valley itself.

Inside the Explorer she started the engine, turned on the AC to high, glanced at her road map. Quickly realized she had several hours of driving to go before she would reach Pahrump, a small desert town on the outskirts of Las Vegas. She had sent the *Fist* on to Las Vegas from Palmdale. They were staying in a cheap motel, a few blocks off the Strip. No doubt drinking and carousing. She would have to hurry to her *KEGCILT* meeting before they got in trouble.

Luckily, their blond, blue-eyed appearance would melt into the American scene. She prayed that they would stay motivated, stay on purpose, stay out of trouble.

Mara wore a western outfit: tight, stone-washed blue jeans that showed off her wonderful figure, a white t-shirt that displayed, *You Go Girl—Shop Til Ya Drop!* spelled out in fake rhinestones over her impressive breasts. On her head she wore a black, wide-brimmed cowboy hat. She carried her Tokarev pistol in a black leather purse.

Mara pulled onto the two-lane asphalt road unmarred by potholes even in this remote desert—just another example of her hated enemy's wealth as a nation—sped up and raced toward the rocky, desolate mountains to the east. As she drove, she thought of the futile attempts the *Fist* had made to burn the West Coast. She suppressed a feeling of despair as she reflected on their crushed attempts to attack America. Wondered for a minute whether her hatred for an entire nation was a symptom of insanity. Remembered the image of her daddy, hanging from the hangman's rope in the square. *America. Jack Flashhardt. They'll all pay, Daddy. If I could just get my hands on a nuclear suitcase bomb.*

She had heard that there were twenty such bombs in America, but she doubted that there were more than one or two devices, and they were hidden somewhere in Los Angeles and Chicago. She had heard whispers that the bombs had been snuck in on container ships from Europe. She speculated how much of Las Vegas, the essence of Western corruption, could be destroyed with such a bomb.

Chapter 73

Skidding down the mountain at a reckless pace, Jack's FBI Cayenne quickly outdistanced the pursuing sheriff's SUV. It had turned and chased Jack, Billy, and Zhang, when a deputy spotted them circling around the lake house, then quietly driving away from the confrontation of the soldiers and the sheriffs.

The all-wheel-drive Cayenne hugged the rain-slicked two-lane road, enabling Jack to drive at a pace that quickly sent the pursuing deputy's Japanese SUV skidding into a ditch.

"We have to get off this mountain road, reach the freeway before they call ahead, set up a roadblock down the hill," Jack said. He was already below the pine-growing elevations, and the hillsides—barely visible in the rain—were covered with scrub oaks, twisted aspens, grayish-green sage brush.

Peering through the rain-splashed windshield, Billy observed, "Nothing in sight, except falling-down, long way down cliffs. Don't slide off the road, Flashy."

"No sweat," Jack responded, skidding around a corner.

"And why did we run, you stipids?" Zhang asked. "We were surrounded by your friends. Now we are alone."

Jack laughed. "That's stupids. Try an' get your insults pronounced correctly." Billy joined his laughter. Jack added, "Anyway, Tucson might delay and obfuscate, but she'll eventually tell the sheriffs and her superiors our story. And I left Dawklings—the tattoo guy—dead or semi-dead at Joshua's. I need to call the general and get the locals and the FBI off our backs."

"So we can get on with runnin' down Mara and her gang?" Billy asked. "Who gives a shit about them, anyway? Especially since nobody gives a rat's ass about us!"

Jack glanced back, returned his eyes to the road. "So you're sayin' let these terrorists have their way just 'cause the government has been jerking us around? Crapping all over us?"

Billy paused, responded. "Oh, all right! I don't want these pricks like runnin' free an' having their way any more'n you." He tapped Jack on the shoulder. "So, I guess we gotta do our thing.

Whack the bastards. As my DI used to say, *Kill 'em all, let their seventy two virgins sort it out.*"

"Exactly," Jack responded. He rounded a sharp corner in the road. "Look! We made it. There's the freeway." He took a long onramp onto the four-lane highway, sped north. When he reached an off-ramp sign that read *Las Vegas*, he turned east on the 15 Freeway.

"Where we going?" Billy asked.

"Vegas," Jack said. "If the rain lets up, we'll make the Nevada border in two hours."

"Why don't we dump this car?" Zhang asked. "Why don't we let me out so I can go to Hollywood and become a rock star?"

Jack turned his head, peered at Zhang. "Everybody'll expect us to drive to L.A. So we'll go to Vegas. You're with us until we know the gems have been returned. Then you can go your way. But you bring up a good point."

"What's that?" Billy asked.

"We'll dump our cell phones in Victorville—it's just up the road. The cells have transmitters in them that continuously broadcast their positions to the nearest cell towers. That might be one of the reasons we got out of Arrowhead so easily."

"You mean they just *let* us go? Hoping we'll do their thing? Then, you're right! Send the cells to L.A.," Billy cackled. "I love it."

Jack drove east, up the Cajon Pass grade, through the San Bernardino Mountains. The three wondered at the dying brush fires that spread north and south of the freeway. The storm was doing its thing again, almost as if it was a thinking, rational force. Many fire-fighting vehicles and numerous helicopters were parked on both sides of the freeway, but the fighters were standing in groups, watching the storm drown out the flames.

At the top of the grade, they left the mountains, started across the cactus-covered high desert. Tacky commercial buildings and relentless billboards masked the views of the spectacular Joshua Tree Desert. In the distance, rugged blue mountains spread across their path like looming castle tower guards.

Fifteen miles farther, Jack got off on the main street of Victorville, passed a number of fast food and Mexican restaurants, five-dollar retail stores, and stopped at the Greyhound bus station. A dusty bus was parked in front of the station, its diesel engine idling. A block down the street, he noticed a white Crown Victoria Ford turn into a Circle K parking lot.

"Billy," he instructed. "If that bus is going west, you buy three tickets with a credit card. Get on and dump the cells. I'll fill up on gas, be back in a few minutes."

Billy and Zhang got out of the Cayenne, followed Jack's instructions. When he returned, they jumped in and he headed for the 15 Freeway. The Ford was nowhere in sight.

"How'd we do?" he asked.

"Zhang is gettin' her wish," Billy cackled, then added, "You, me, and her cell phones're on their way to L.A."

Taking prewrapped sandwiches and three Cokes out of a plastic bag, the Chinese girl handed the food and drinks around with a pouting air. "You guys don't need me—just let me go. I want go to Hollywood, not send my cell phone."

"Shut up, Zhang, you're with me 'til the Chinese're off our backs," Billy grumbled through a mouthful of food.

Zhang glared but said nothing.

Jack wolfed down his tasteless turkey sandwich in several huge bites while he drove through back streets of Victorville. On the eastern outskirts of the desert town, he pulled onto the four-lane freeway, increased his speed to over 100 miles per hour.

Fifteen minutes later, he slowed as they approached the town of Barstow, then increased speed again after leaving the city. A half hour later, they passed the one hundred-thirty-four-foot tall thermometer in the tiny town of Baker. A roadside sign said the tower's height represented the highest temperature ever recorded in Baker.

The starkly beautiful desert and the bare rock mountains swelled on each side of the freeway, with all the glory of a hugely talented artist's best efforts. The salt flats at the bottom of each valley were empty of vegetation and glistened pearly white. The brown jagged ridges and blue tinted peaks, stacked in layer after layer of deepening purple tones, looked tough but climbable.

The trio reached Stateline in less than an hour: a complex of mid-rise hotels huddled on the Nevada border, an architectural teaser for the neonsaturated city beyond the intervening ridges.

They stopped at Buffalo Bill's Hotel and Casino, had a barely adequate prime rib dinner, watched tourists riding small boats in a fake flume, shooting electronic guns at cute targets of bad guys with drooping mustaches and eye patches, and other targets of animals with horrifying expressions.

Watching the gamesters, Jack was reminded of Mo Poo and his giant cohorts. Felt Mo Poo was still on his trail. Wondered how close the giant was. Lost his appetite, pushed his food around the plate while Billy ordered seconds, put away another juicy prime rib. After dinner, they checked into two hotel rooms. Jack managed to relax after he unpacked, laid out the shotgun on the floor next to his bed, and the Beretta on the bedside table. He slept poorly, dreamt he was hauling trash uphill like the frustrated god, Sisyphus, doomed to push a rock up a mountain for eternity.

Late the next morning, they crossed the forty-plus miles of dried-up white lakebeds surrounded by brown and blue mountains on the way to the sprawling city of Las Vegas.

Huge subdivisions of houses sprawled across the valley, crept up the mountain slopes, and surrounded the downtown area of highrises that all together resembled a towering, multi-walled castle in the distance, surrounded by peasant villages.

The trio checked into the Bellagio, a high-end hotel casino on the Strip, with a view of a ten-acre artificial lake through the windows of a thousand dollar a night, two-bedroom waterside villa.

After they were settled, Jack said, "I think we need to make a methodical search for Zhang's bug."

"I have," Zhang insisted. "I drenched my purse, I even threw away all my shoes in case one was embedded in a heel."

"Where's that little .25 caliber pistol?"

Zhang removed the palm-sized weapon from her purse. "I checked it thoroughly."

Jack took the little black semi-auto gun, and with Billy and Zhang watching, quickly stripped it, removed the plastic grip plates on the handle, using a small knife from his SAS tin as a screwdriver. The skeleton frame was clean. He emptied the magazine, probed the inside: nothing.

"What about the shells?" Billy suggested.

Jack spread the five shells out, pried the lead pellet out of each round, poured the powder on a napkin. When he emptied the last shell, no powder fell out. He selected a needle probe on the knife, inserted it in the shell. A tiny black transmitter the size of a thumb tack popped out, fell to the napkin.

The three looked at each other.

"Only good if you didn't fire all the rounds," Jack observed. He pushed the transmitter around the table with his knife.

"What should we do with it?"

Billy glanced at his watch, suggested, "Post office's still open, mail it to the remotest town in Texas."

Jack laughed at the thought of Chinese spies milling around West Texas scrublands. Even Zhang smiled at the suggestion, her beautiful face turning from a hard, calculating appearance to one of rare beauty.

Billy and Zhang left to find a post office. Jack called General Harmbruster's personal number, got a voicemail and left a message updating their leader about their movements. Then he raided the granite countered kitchen, ate mixed nuts, potato chips, drank two Sierra Nevada beers. Went out to the patio, watched dancing waters in the lake, fell asleep in a wooden steamer lounge chair. As he drifted off, he wondered how Billy and Zhang had made up so quickly, thought of her muscular body, smiled. He doubted she had ever told Billy about the handcuff episode. He felt a momentary pang of guilt, hoped his short-tempered brother would understand if he found out about the episode.

He slept poorly, dreamt of fighting fires alongside faceless Chinese firemen, dancing for snow with giant mountain men, Chinese waist drum dancers leaping about with huge emeralds pasted on their necks in place of heads.

The phone rang at four P.M., pulling him out of dream-tossed sleep. It was General Harmbruster. "Jack, how the hell are you?" he asked. "It's good to hear from you. Strange, I gotta report that you are in downtown L.A. At the bus station. Update me on progress. What're you doin' in Las Vegas?"

Jack tried to ignore a bad mood, talked for ten minutes, telling the general everything that had transpired, and his suspicions that Mara and *Saladin's Fist* had started the fires. While he talked, he turned the television on to the Weather Channel and muted it.

"You're right about the *Fist*. They tried to claim credit for the fires with a fax to the *LA Times*. Luckily, we got the liberal bastards at the paper to squash the claims. We can't let it out that terrorists are running amuck, burning up our wild lands and cities. We have to get them before they realize we've hushed them up. By the way, you did great work on that Bosnian encounter up north," the general enthused. "I knew you'd come through with shining colors. I guess no chance of taking prisoners? And how the hell did you track down the terrorists so quickly?"

Jack thought of the chance encounter with the blond Bosnian terrorists, smiled to himself. "My brother's a natural-born detective."

"You got that right—I'm putting him down for a promotion to E-5." "General, he's a convict." *How clueless can one general be?*

"Not like you, Jack. Your brother is still a Marine. He just has some time to serve. But now we got *Posse Comitatus* issues. So you guys gotta stay civilian until this is over. But soon as he's out, bingo—he's an E-5 Marine. Don't worry about all that. I'm working on reversing everything that has happened to you boys. You just concentrate on the bad guys. I'll deal with these JAG ass—uh, investigators."

Jack ground his teeth, clinched his fist and mentally slugged the general. He exclaimed, "Talk is…" *Is cheap, General.*

"Obviously," the general continued, "there're still some bad guys out there, but outstanding effort by you on rescuing that FBI agent. Amazing that you pulled that rescue off with no friendly casualties. Major Nakamura is still singing your praises."

"Thanks, General. Mick is one great soldier. He kicked ass on the *Fist* in Sacramento. And his makeshift, thrown-together unit performed brilliantly at Arrowhead. Made me proud to fight for America. If I was," he added, trying to mask bitterness and sarcasm. "But I did pop the one guy who was holding Agent Luvabrest hostage—with the laser gun. Fried his… private parts."

"She made a report. Good shooting! What about the dead man in the wheelchair?"

"Dead when we broke in," Jack said. "Anyway, I don't have a clue on what to do now. I think we need to hold until we get some *INTEL*. I'd like to wait at my home in Montana. I can fly out of there and be anywhere in twenty four hours."

"I'd rather you wait in Las Vegas or Los Angeles, Jack. That way you're closer to the action. And you stay in a battle-mode frame of mind for the *GWOT*."

"General, I haven't been home since before the trial."

"Stay where you are, Jack—that's an order," the general insisted.

"*Saladin's Fist* will strike again. We need you to be ready. You've been best at stopping them. By far. So just bivouac up until we give you the word.
You could use a little R and R."

"Yes, sir, General." Disappointed, Jack glanced at the television and saw the storm, *Draco*, stalled on the west coast of California. "I'll wait here until I hear from you or acquire a hot lead. But I'll have to move. We can't afford the Bellagio for more than a day. And we're running low on cash. We can't use credit cards for everything. By the way, I need another weapon."

"Major Nakamura informed me you left Lake Arrowhead with two M16s and ammo, the M-199, two shotguns and two Berettas. Sounds like you've got everything you need short of an Abram's tank."

"Yes, sir, but I need a special weapon. For one of the bad guys. If you saw him you'd understand. He's almost eight feet tall—makes Shaquille O'Neal look like a middleweight boxer. I

want a Ruger revolver. A semicustom job. Shoots a .454 Casull—
a 260 grain bullet."

"That wheelgun's a cannon," the general said.

"Yes, sir, it has close to around 2,000 foot-pounds of muzzle energy. Just about the biggest handgun available."

"Why so much?"

"That big Chinaman, Mo Poo, is in America. The only reason I can think of is that *SD* is using him to go after me. He and I have personal issues regarding his daughter's death. And I think *SD* is just one step behind us."

"Can't stay away from the skirts, can you, Jack? That may be a weakness."

Yes, sir," Jack agreed. "But she tried—almost *did* kill me in Afghanistan last year."

"I don't recall an incident report. How do you know the Chinese father is in the hunt?"

"General, he whacked Lieutenant Johnson in Oregon." He thought of Chin Bit, was suddenly back in bed in Haartgard, the year before: he *caught a glimpse of bare skin moving through a faint shaft of moonlight shining through the castle's window. But who the hell was it? She leaned, settled, crushed her pelvis down on him— searing heat as she enveloped him. Leaned closer, panted against his ear; foul breath, nuzzled his neck, wrapped her hands around his neck, squeezed harder and harder with immensely huge, immensely strong fingers. "I hate!" she whispered. He desperately fought to stay alive.*

Jack shook his head to clear the terrible memory. "Also, I need a halfdozen ISRs—the palm-sized, intersquad radios. And a couple sets of NVGs."

"Okay, *Eagle's Aerie* has pre-po stock at Nellis Air Force Base right there in Vegas. Where do you want the gear, the laser gun, this Casull, and the cash delivered?" The general sounded impatient to end the conversation.

"I'll call your aide for a delivery of the pre-positioned munitions and gear once we get situated, General. And I need a contact number for Mick. I have a new cell phone." Jack shook his head again, hoping to flush the memory of horrible China Bitch out of his mind.

"I'll have Major Nakamura call you on this number. Oh, one thing you'll be interested to know, Jack. Your nemesis, General Farley was asked to retire."

Amazed, Jack asked, "Why?"

"For turning you over to the Chinese. The issue went all the way to the top dogs in the Army. They blew a gasket. Demanded Farley resign."

"Couldn't happen to a more deserving guy."

"I thought that'd be your attitude." the general laughed.

"Say, General, sir, do you have any info or background on an outfit called KEGCILT, or KEGYA?"

The general did not respond immediately, then said, "I've seen nothing in *EA* files. I'll have my aide check it out." He quickly said goodbye and hung up.

Jack heard Billy and Zhang returning.

Billy wandered onto the patio, watched sprays from water fountains shoot out of the lake, fall back. "Living the high life, huh, bro? I won five hundred fifty-some dollars playin' video poker."

"This high life beats overlooking Peckerwood Hill Cemetery at Leavenworth Prison," Jack admitted. He caught a mental flash of the concrete sump, quickly blocked it.

Snorting, Billy agreed, "You got that right. I just hope we don't end up owning two six-foot-long dirt patches of it."

"Yeah, Dude! And now Harmbruster wants us to hang here. But I'm thinking you were right. Mexico for me, back to Leavenworth for you.

You'll get off easy, serve your time, you're square with the system."

"Bullshit!" Billy exclaimed. He slammed a handful of chips on the table—they skipped in all directions.

"I'm telling you," Jack responded as he helped Billy pick up scattered chips, "the general is not going to get it done. He's just using us, holding pardons out like dangling carrots. I hope Dad and Senator Jensen can get the pardons. But I'm not going back to

Leavenworth, wait for government assholes to decide my fate. We've whacked most of *Saladin's Fist*. Seven out of ten. Let someone else get the rest. More'n six hundred batting average. That'd be great in the National League. If I'm pardoned, they can mail the paperwork to the beach in Zihuatanejo, Mexico." Jack smiled. "Oh, and your favorite general's no more."

"Farley?"

"Forced to resign."

Billy clapped his hands, did a miniature war dance. Whooped as loud as he could, "OohRah!"

Yawning, Zhang walked onto the patio. The sight of her stretching in a T-shirt was breathtaking. Billy noticed Jack's look, stopped dancing, scowled, said nothing.

Chapter 74

Mo Poo and his carjack victim, the terrified blond woman, stopped for fuel in West Yellowstone, Montana, a small mountain tourist village just outside Yellowstone Park.

The fat woman pushed hair out of her face. "I have to go to the toilet." "Said needed fuel," Mo Poo rumbled. "Get it."

The woman fed a credit card into the gas pump with a trembling hand, and filled her pickup while Mo Poo stood nearby. She thought about running or screaming, but was too afraid. The carjacker was so big! When she finished, she asked to go to the toilet. Mo Poo loomed over the woman. She drew back but he grasped her wrist, "Has to piss? Do here."

Terrified, the whimpering woman felt wetness trickle down her legs. She cried in frustration and terror as a puddle of urine flowed over her sandal, formed at her feet. She looked for a police car, saw no help, was too terrified to scream. Weeping, she allowed herself to be led to the car door. Mo Poo kept his huge hand on her wrist, climbed in first, yanked her into the vehicle. She banged her head on the car door, a sharp pain, blood flowed across her cheek, mingled with streaming tears.

Chapter 75

The three companions cleaned up, checked out, shopped, found an apartment-hotel with weekly rates. Moved into a two-bedroom condo in the Polo Club, a time-share hotel on the Strip that gave them a weekly rate almost the same as the one night rate at the Bellagio. Unlike the Bellagio, the furniture was all made of cheap wood veneers, but the place looked modern and was clean. The walls were painted in muted pastel colors and the drapes over the windows were a dark red that accented the tan carpets.

Jack had noticed a Verizon store a half-block away, so he took the elevator down and purchased three prepaid cell phones from a slender young man, then called the general's voicemail and reported their new address. Called the ranch—no one picked up so he left a voicemail message, telling Bill where his sons were staying.

By evening, he had received no callbacks, so when Zhang went out and returned with a bottle of expensive Stolichnaya vodka, he and Billy each took a double shot over ice from the apartment-sized refrigerator and the three moved to the patio overlooking the Strip.

It had been fiercely hot all day but the sun was behind massive Mount Charleston to the west and the shadowed desert air was rapidly cooling. The street and sidewalk traffic below was nonstop in both directions, as people were apparently searching for new places to find excitement.

"Everybody seeking thrills," Billy observed.

"I wouldn't mind tradin' our thrills," Jack responded.

Zhang poured fresh drinks. "Really?"

Jack thought. "Maybe not. Gambling seems like a poor substitute for real thrills like climbing or…"

"Substitution sounds good to me," Billy yawned.

"Everybody I see around here has a smile on his face. Unlike us."

Jack yawned back. "Thrills. Real and imagined are great, but I've had my share. I'm turning in early."

"I want to gamble," Zhang suggested.

"This is a gambling town, Billy, let's try our luck again. It's better than Macau—the gambling city back in Zhong Guo—I mean China."

The two left after sharing another round of drinks with Jack. He stumbled to bed and did not hear them return.

The next morning he showered, shaved, went out for breakfast at a nearby Carrow's Restaurant. The early morning air was fresh and clean, even in the crowded, bustling city. To the south, over McCarran Airport, he saw inbound airliners lined up for miles and miles, flying out of the early morning sunrise over Lake Mead.

After a leisurely breakfast of flavorful blueberry pancakes, intensely yellow scrambled eggs, crisp sausage, fresh, pulpy orange juice, and hot coffee, Jack read the Las Vegas Review Journal: terrorists were blowing themselves up in various parts of the world, just like self-exploding toads; French activists were marching in Paris for peace, trees, and longer mandated vacations; politicians were raising taxes and their salaries everywhere; rival African leaders were denouncing each other and/or eating their subjects; glaciers were melting in Alaska, Iceland, and Chile; whales were beaching themselves in Carolina—situation normal all over the world. In California, the governor had declared a state of emergency because of the fires, several hundred structures had been burned, tens of thousands of acres had been fire-ravaged. Crazy arsonists had been blamed, but there was no mention of *Saladin's Fist* or Arab terrorists.

Jack paid for his meal, took the paper back to the apartment for Billy to read. He turned on the television and watched more reports on the storm extinguished fires.

While Billy and Zhang slept through lunch, Jack went to the club's exercise room and pounded for an hour on a treadmill, then spent another hour on upper body exercise machines. After a Big Mac and a chocolate milkshake at a McDonald's next to the club, he returned to the condo, turned on the room computer and searched the Internet for the words *KEGCILT* and *KEGYA*. He found nothing on either name except three cross references to a secret fraternal organization: *(1) Knights of the Golden Circle, secret order of*

Southern sympathizers; (2) Confederate operatives during the Civil War who went on to form a secret society; (3) Golden Circle was a secret antebellum organization that sought to establish a slave empire. Its members were also known as Copperheads. When he looked at the word *Copperheads,* he remembered it had been the name for the Nineteenth Century Peacenik group that was against the Civil War and the Union.

He searched for *Copperheads* and found an article on the Copperheads:

In the pre-Civil War era, the Copperhead Movement spread like wildfire through the South and the Midwest. From harmless rituals they turned to violence and conquest when they tried to promote the extension of slavery by attempting the conquest of Mexico.

Secession from the Union was their goal before the Civil War. The separatist movement flourished and became a real danger to the Union Army after war broke out.

Not all the members knew the secret pro-slavery aims of the movement. Many solemnly went through the elaborate rituals, swore their oaths, believing themselves to be members of the Democratic Party, simply preserving the freedom against the new tyrannical party of Republicans. Only those who took the last two advanced degrees were told of the violent goals their leaders intended.

In Iowa, Copperheads burned the homes of men who joined the Federal Army of the Republic and a U.S. Marshall found evidence that the Copperheads were gun-running for Quantrill's guerrillas in Missouri. In August, 1862, the Chicago Tribune declared the movement had 20,000 members. Missouri membership alone was reported from 10,000 to 60,000.

He dumped that article and started to read another article about the KGC:

Rogue officials in the U.S. federal government dreamed of a golden empire to stabilize slavery. Their concept was that an imaginary circle be drawn, 16 degrees latitude and 16 degrees longitude, with its center in Havana, Cuba. The circle extended north into Pennsylvania and Ohio, including all the slave States, and South—to the Isthmus of Darien (sometimes called the Panama Isthmus). It embraced the West Indies Islands and those of the Caribbean Sea with a great part of Mexico and Central America. The idea was also to purchase Cuba or conquer it. They planned and executed many train and bank robberies, amassing a huge illicit fortune to finance…

Before he could further investigate the Copperheads or the KGC's activities in the U.S., Billy entered the living room, sleepily demanding that they go out and eat. Jack reluctantly shut down the computer, flushed copperhead snake images out of his mind.

At six PM, the three caught a taxi to the already busy Gordon Biersch microbrewery, sat at the circular bar, ate giant steak sandwiches, and drank tall glasses of specialty amber beer that was made on site in huge stainless steel barrels.

After paying, they took a cab to the Hard Rock Café, stood at the bar and ordered tall tropical drinks with tiny umbrellas sitting on the tops of the glasses.

A blonde entertainer finished singing a song, left the stage and sat on an empty stool next to Jack. Her face was tanned and beautiful, her hair was bleached white and was short and spikey on top, her eyes were large and blue, her lips were collagen-full, her breasts impressive, like over-sized spinnaker sails on a small sloop. She was only about five feet five inches in her platform shoes, and wore a skin-tight, white spandex pantsuit with a blue sapphire-dusted collar.

The girl, in her late twenties, ordered a drink, turned to Jack and asked, "I'm Lauren Titwel-Wilder. How'd you like my act?"

Jack had paid no attention but responded quickly, "Wonderful. I'm wild about tits, as well."

The singer nervously giggled, ignored his crack, then said, "Even an early gig here is a big break for me."

Not wanting to insult her to a greater degree, he tried to pass her off.

"Great!" he exclaimed. "I'm Jack. Meet Zhang Poon t'ang and Billy Howling Dog."

Startled by the strange names, Lauren looked into Jack's face, trying to determine whether he was putting her on. "I thought I had an original name."

"I liked your performance—I'm an entertainer," Zhang announced.

"I'm a Wayang singer—that's Chinese opera—and a waist drum dancer in a troupe."

"Really?" At first Lauren did not look impressed, but then she exclaimed, "Oh, my God! Opera?"

"Yes," Zhang affirmed, "but I've come to America to be a popular singer. Do you have advice?"

Lauren left her stool and stood next to Zhang. Billy shifted next to Jack, pushed his umbrella drink aside, ordered a beer from the female bartender, who was dressed in a cowgirl outfit complete with a black hat.

"So what do you think, big bro—dancing, drinking and wild behavior, or back to the Polo Club?" Billy looked around the crowded club. The patrons looked like young professionals.

"All of it. When was the last time we partied?"

Billy drank beer, looked up, "Not countin' our whirlin' soiree with the tattooed monster and his buddies in the hallowed halls of Leavenworth? Our bullet-dodging act in the caverns of Shangri-La? Our rest stop dance in the San Joaquin Valley?" He touched his healing arm.

"Ha, ha! You're a real comedian." Jack looked around. "Which reminds me: don't get any ideas tonight about baying at the moon over goblets of tequila. We need to keep a clear head until the Chi-creeps call off their party-crashing ways."

"Chi-creeps? Oh, what a poet!"

Lauren Titwel-Wilder turned to Jack. "Hey, what's a Chi-creep?"

Looking at the white-blonde singer, Jack said, "You don't wanna know."

Lauren's eyes widened. "Are you guys on the run? Are you bank robbers or something?"

Jack smiled, "Nothing so romantic. But Zhang has some jilted Chinese boyfriends we're having to deal with."

Lauren stared into his face, smiled, "*Whatever!* Men are *so* stupid sometimes. They just don't know when to let go."

Jack smiled. "My sentiments exactly."

"So," Lauren asked, a mischievous look in her eyes, "are you a hangeron or a let-her-go?"

Jack realized how ridiculous the conversation was getting, pushed away from the bar. "Neither. And hangin' here's made me tired. Nice meeting you." He waved at Billy and Zhang and left the noisy bar.

He walked the short distance to the Strip, strolled along the tourist filled sidewalk. Wondered at the number of throngs eagerly looking for new places to lose their money.

Seeing no dice- or grenade-throwing Chinese agents lurking at the entrance to the Polo Club, he took the elevator to their apartment, emptied the weapons bag and cleaned the laser rifle he had used on the tattooed man. After he reassembled the rifle, he took out the Dragon God's Khyber knife, wiped it clean with an oily cloth. Finished, he turned on the television and watched Wheel of Fortune until he dozed off.

Hours later, Billy, Zhang and Lauren burst into the apartment, giggling and laughing. Lauren walked to the sofa and sat on top of Jack. Her eyes widened when she realized an assault rifle and a huge knife in a plain leather sheath were lying in front of him on the coffee table.

"You said you weren't bank robbers!" Lauren exclaimed. "What are you, assassins?"

Jack woke in an instantly irritable mood, thought about pushing her onto the floor, but politely moved to the side to give her space to sit.

"We ain't bank robbers," Billy responded. He picked up the laser rifle and put it back in the weapons bag.

Lauren pointed at the bag. "Well, sugar, that weird-looking weapon wasn't a paperweight! And that sword isn't an envelope opener."

Zhang sat in an armchair, amused and smiling at the singer's reaction.

Ignoring the three, Jack got up, stumbled to his bedroom, stripped and went to bed. Much later, he sensed then checked: the singer had gotten in bed with him. He thought about waking her up, instead he rolled over, went back to sleep.

A knocking woke him. Jack glanced at the girl: she was naked, sound asleep. He pulled on a pair of cargo pants, stumbled through the living room, and looked through the peephole of the entry door. Tucson Luvabrest stood in the hall, carrying a small suitcase and a brown sports bag!

Astonished, he opened the door, stepped back. She walked in, her eyes masked by wraparound sunglasses, stood in the middle of the living room. She had masked her neck and facial bruises with makeup. She was wearing a blue linen blazer over a white shirt, tight grey slacks that revealed her slender hips. She looked wonderful.

"Happy to see me?" Tucson asked. "Your greeting is underwhelming."

Jack smiled, put his arms around her. "I'm just shocked to see you looking so great after your ordeal." Her lower lip was still slightly swollen.

Lauren, naked, walked out of the bedroom, on her way to the kitchen for a glass of water. The singer stopped when she noticed Tucson and Jack. She gasped and retreated, slammed the bedroom door.

Tucson stepped back, pushed Jack's arms away, declared with an angry tone, "Every time I take my eyes off you, a strange woman, naked as a jaybird, shows up. Why're you such a player?"

Jack glanced at Tucson with a look of dismay. "This morning shoulda come with a dimmer switch. Hey, I didn't invite her in. She's a friend of Billy and Zhang." He sat down, looked at Tucson. "What's up?"

She said with a cold, matter-of-fact air, "You requested Night visions and a weapon." She put the bag down on the coffee table. "And cash. Five thousand dollars. I was ordered by *Eagle's Aerie*, to which I'm now Opcon, to deliver it. Sign here." She took out a slip of paper and a pen, put them next to the bag, pulled the heavy revolver out of the bag.

Jack glanced up, saw a gleam of tears in Tucson's eyes. "I'm telling you, I don't know her."

She hefted the oversized weapon, sized him up like she was looking for a convenient place to ventilate him.

Lauren Titwel-Wilder, now fully dressed, emerged and stared into the huge .454 caliber barrel, pointing in her direction. "Oh, my God! What are you people?" she looked at Tucson.

"Jack's wife," Tucson said with a straight face. With two hands, she was still pointing the big gun at the blonde. "Who the hell are you?"

Jack interrupted, "This's Tucson Luvabrest. Federal Bureau of Investigation."

"Wife? FBI? I don't know him!" Lauren protested. "Anyways, I just met him last night!" she fixated on the huge pistol pointed in her direction, her blue eyes wide with fright.

"And you still slept with Jack?" Tucson accused. "Seems sudden, if you don't know him." She glanced at Jack, added, "Well, he is cute. Even so…"

Lauren looked at the big Casull, put her hand on her breast. "I didn't, I swear! I just passed… just fell asleep on his bed. I was with the other two.
We came here, he went to his bedroom. It was his bed or the sofa… I must admit, I expected… but I'm innocent of whatever they've done."

Jack smiled. "Lauren, don't worry about it. Tucson's a bully. Ignore her. She gets her… she likes to push people around. Typical cop."

Lauren grabbed her purse, a rhinestone-decorated red leather bag, hurried to the door. She glanced at Tucson's pistol with frightened eyes, rushed out of the apartment.

Chapter 76

Mara Bhutto drove over a crest on Highway 160, sixty miles north of Las Vegas, and saw the town of Pahrump spread out in a valley completely surrounded by conifer-covered, towering mountains to the east and stark, smaller desert mountains to the west and south. The town was spread out all over the valley and as she drove through it, she saw many house trailer homes and cheaply designed houses, surrounded by old cars, rusty machinery and piles of litter. Strangely, there was no downtown area in the shabby desert town.

After getting directions, and traveling for about 12 kilometers over an asphalt and then gravel street named Homestead Road, she saw a neon sign outside a building with a false front similar to buildings she had seen in old Hollywood westerns, and another structure with high pitched dormers. She checked her watch—she was fifteen minutes late. Mara parked the Explorer and hurried through the white picket fence's gate, passed under a sign proclaiming The Leghorn Bar and a mounted set of long bull horns. Inside it was dark, smelled of smoke and perfume.

An attractive woman was sitting at the bar with an overweight black woman with a very beautiful face. When the thinner woman saw Mara, she picked up a cell and made a brief call, then rose and approached her. The woman was attractive, dressed in a floor-length red dress with a low-cut top that revealed her swelling breasts. With dark hair, attractive dark eyes, she was older, maybe forty to fifty, but very slender and very beautiful.

"Sweetie, welcome to the Chicken Ranch. I'm Judith Ryan, your hostess." The woman appraised Mara's short hair, looked closer and said, "Honey, I can see you'll want a *special* lady."

Mara flushed, then looked at the red cloth-covered pool table, the bar with high-backed chairs along its rail, the low ceilings. Realizing that she was in a brothel, she shrugged off the Madam's hand, walked to the bar, and sat next to the fat black woman.

Beauty Walker gazed at Mara, flashed a grin, her round cheeks imprinted with big dimples. "Hey, Sugar, how you doin'?" Mara smiled faintly.

Beauty, in her new undercover role as a Homeland Security officer, suddenly recognized Mara as the masquerading terrorist who had crossed the border at Port Angeles, Washington; she pressed her hand against her chest, hoping to conceal her rapidly beating heart.

The Madam followed Mara, frowned at Beauty Walker. "The interview is over. Go to the kitchen and report to the cook or one of the shift managers." She pointed at a door on the side of the barroom.

Beauty scrutinized Mara's face, then left the bar.

Feeling that she had been recognized, Mara turned to the Madam and snapped, "This is a brothel? Is she an example of your women?"

Judith smiled, "She's a new member of the household staff, not one of our girls. If you want to step through to our parlor, I will send you a couple of our most beautiful girls for your approval. Your kind is especially popular with the staff."

Feeling trapped, Mara glanced at the low-ceiling and cheap furnishings. The bar was empty but she worried about the fat woman who was now gone.

"Come to the parlor," Judith Ryan urged. "It's more comfortable." She led the Pakistani terrorist into a room filled with overstuffed red velvet sofas and armchairs.

"You have a different accent," the Madam remarked. "We get visitors from all over, honey. Where you from?"

"I'm a British citizen," Mara responded. She checked out the empty room, looked for an escape route. The whole situation was turning into a nightmare. She squeezed her leather bag, felt the hard outline of her Makarov inside it. Reassured, she sat on a sofa, tried to relax.

A tall thin man dressed in a blue western shirt and weathered jeans, entered the parlor and crossed to Mara. Judith Ryan quickly left the room, her long dress swishing as she walked. Mara tensed, opened her bag.

The darkly tanned man stroked a thin mustache under a long, sharp nose, touched her on the shoulder. "MS Marge?" He waited for her nodding affirmation, then said, "I am Mr. Homer. Follow me."

Outside, he led her to a white, full-sized pickup. He directed her to sit in the rear seat next to an overweight, pimple-scarred young man, who grinned as he slipped a black cotton cloth bag over her head. His mintsmelling breath assaulted her nose as he gently tightened a drawstring around her neck.

Settled, Mara heard the truck engine start and felt the vehicle move onto the road. Dust inside the bag made her sneeze. Five minutes later she felt the truck increase its speed and after a fifteen-minute drive, it slowed, then pulled onto another road, which it followed at a lower speed. The men did not speak during the ride. Neither answered her when she asked, "Where are you taking me?"

Finally, the truck turned and rolled to a stop. She was helped out of the truck and someone said, "Inside. Follow me. His Exalted Eminence is waiting." He took her elbow and led her.

Inside a structure, her hood was removed by the man who called himself Mr. Homer. He led her through a traditional living room and stopped in front of a closed door. She recognized the six inch by two inch bird claw embossed on the door as identical to one she had seen on the gateway to KEGYA in Shangri-La. The sight somehow comforted her even though it was mystifying. Mr. Homer knocked on the door three times, entered. He guided Mara through, but did not accompany her.

"His Exalted Eminence will join you," he announced in a respectful tone as he shut the door behind her. A window had open drapes. She glanced and realized the building just a quarter-mile away was the Chicken Ranch. She had been driven around to confuse her. A curtain, covering one end of the room, slid open and two men, one an old man, the other a man in his twenties, were sitting on a high-backed velvet-padded sofa.

Chapter 77

When his cell phone rang, Jack said hello, smiled when he heard his dad's voice, said to Tucson, "Get Billy. It's Dad." Cradling the phone on his shoulder, he took the Casull revolver, checked—it was empty. He took a box of big shells out of the bag, loaded it while he conversed.

After exchanging pleasantries, Bill said, "I got the emeralds. Son, they're unbelievable! You told me all about the treasure, but looking at it's another thing. The senator's on the way from Washington. Wants to see the gems before he talks to the State Department. We'll need an armed escort to move them. I can't believe you sent 'em by mail!"

"I guess," Jack grumbled, "after hauling them all over, I consider the emeralds more of an anchor than a gross of valuable jewels. I'll be happy when we deliver them to the Chinese government." *And then hopefully I'll get the SD jerks off our backs.*

Tucson returned, stroked the back of Jack's head, quickly kissed his cheek, sat down next to him while he talked to his father.

"What else is going on, Dad?"

"We're getting a great rain," Bill added.

"It'll produce a wonderful summer grass crop. We'll have fat yearlings next fall."

"That's great, Dad." *The storm, Draco?* Jack wondered. *I thought it was stalled in California. Dragon God come visiting? Stop the superstition!*

"One more thing, son. A big surprise, for you have a visitor. I thought it was Ashley at first. Amazing resemblance, but this girl's from Asia. Said you told her to come to the ranch. Said she's pregnant. Name of Penel Kong. You didn't tell me I was gonna be a grandparent."

Shocked, Jack asked, "Can you put her on? I'd like to talk to her."

"She's asleep right now. Probably exhausted from her trip. I'll have her call you when she wakes."

Wearing only cargo pants, Billy walked into the room, Jack said, "Here's Billy, your good son. I love you, Dad. Be sure to have Penel call me ASAP." His head spinning from the news, Jack handed the phone to Billy.

"How's your family?" Tucson asked.

"It's raining in Montana. Dad's fine. Penelope Kong just showed up from Shangri-La."

Tucson whirled around, stared at Jack. "Shangri-La? Penelope Kong— who's that? Another jilted Chinese assassin or secret agent lady?"

Jack looked at the beautiful FBI agent. He felt a pang of regret at what he was going to tell her. He took a deep breath and began, "She... I met her in Asia last year. We helped her people—her tribe—fight off a muj... a Muslim attack. Then, a short while back, I was sent to Shangri-La on a mission to investigate *Saladin's Fist*. We... Penelope and I... got together. Now she has somehow turned up at our ranch. She said... she told my dad that I've impregnated her. I didn't believe her last month when she predicted it. Now she's at the ranch. Says... says she truly is pregnant."

The flamboyantly beautiful FBI agent said nothing, but her face turned red, tears formed in her eyes.

Billy, talking to his father, stared at Jack. "Damn! The telephone line just went dead!"

"Well, Dad said it was storming at the ranch," Jack responded. "Call him back."

Billy tried to reach the ranch, got no answer.

Jack stood. "I need a shower, some food."

"Never a dull moment around you, Jack Flashhardt," Tucson said from the armchair. Her voice was bitter. "Why'd you have to be a convict? Why do you have to have a pregnant woman in the closet?" "I'm cursed and I'm blessed," Jack responded.

Tucson pounded the armrest, stood up. "By the way, remember what I told you back at Lake Arrowhead? About the word, KEGCILT? That was written on the terrorist's map of Death Valley? About the code words?"

Jack stopped in midstride, looked at Tucson. "What?"

"They both say basically the same thing," Tucson said.

"KEGYA in Shangri-La and KEGCILT in Death Valley."

"How so?" Billy asked.

Tucson smiled triumphantly. "Keg sounds like K and G. And ya also could mean 'si'."

"'Si' means 'yes' in Spanish," Jack said.

"I still don't get it."

"Think about sounds," Tucson added.

"The word 'si' sounds like the letter C. So KEGYA is K.G.C."

"And KEGCILT?" Zhang asked.

"K.G.C. again," Jack guessed.

Tucson smiled again. "Right. K. G. C. But there's more than that to the word. There's a triple meaning. KEGCILT—cilt could be a version of cult—a secret society. And then there's kilt. A Scottish warrior's dress." Jack pounded the table. "Dad took me there when I was twelve!" "Where's 'at?" Billy asked, a frown showing on his face.

"Don't be pissed, Billy," Jack said. He glanced at Tucson. "That was before Little Willow told anyone you were my brother. Just like Penelope was before… anyway—"

"Scotty's Castle," Tucson guessed and finished his sentence.

"It's a huge old castle built in Death Valley, built about seventy-five years ago by a very wealthy, very eccentric man from Chicago. It's near Area 51."

"And he never lived there," Jack's voice rose with excitement.

"No one could figure out why he spent all that money building a fabulous castle —I mean a really huge castle—in one of the remotest places in the world— Death Valley. Remember, this was the 1920s. We're talking the far end of the world from Chicago, Illinois."

"So he was—how do you say? Eccentric and crazy—so what?" Zhang asked.

"You're Chinese—you wouldn't know," Jack said. "But don't feel bad—hardly anybody knows what the KGC is."

"What?" Billy asked.

Jack smiled fondly at his brother. "You're a victim of our country's wonderful public education.

"But it just so happens, I translated, for fun and practice, a proclamation that was discovered in the Vatican years ago—it was in Latin, of course—exonerating the Knight's Templars, who had all been arrested in 1306, by Phillip, King of France."

"Hey, I never dug history!" Billy exclaimed.

"What's the point? Who were these ten-purr guys?"

"Templars, dude. They were warriors. Like Recon, or Seals—Special Forces or Rangers. Maximum dudes who fought the—catch this—Muslims for the Holy Land in the Crusades."

"But the French were Catholic?" Zhang asked. "Why would they arrest—"

Glancing at the Chinese agent, Jack explained, "Politics. The Templars were busy taking over Europe. Church leaders feared and resented them. They were getting too powerful. But after most of them were arrested and thrown in prison to rot..." a snap vision of Leavenworth flashed through his mind and he shuddered. "Then they went underground and kept true to their mission," Jack finished.

"Which was...?" Billy asked.

Jack concluded, "It's speculated that they hold and guard the Holy Grail."

"Give me a break!" Billy said. "You mean the old 'Choose wisely' dude in the cave in Indiana Jones?"

"Exactly," Jack said. "But that was the European Templars. The American branch was also a secret society, known as the *Copperheads* in American history." He went to the bar and opened a bottle of water, drank. He continued, "They were pro-slavery and pro-States' Rights in antebellum days. They even turned to piracy, but their ships were destroyed by the British Navy. And after the war—bitter because their side lost—they robbed banks, built up a huge treasury." He pointed at the floor. "They buried the treasure in caves all over the U. S. in preparation for a new Civil War.

Supposedly, even Jessie James, the outlaw, was a member of KGC."

"So this's about a cup? Or about slavery?" Billy pressed.

Jack looked at the others. Scratched his head. "I dunno, maybe it's the South rising again… maybe it's about what the cup—you know the grail thing?—holds. Maybe the grail is full of tarn waters from Shangri-La. Why else would a bunch of cranks have a site in Shangri-La? Maybe they buy into the long-lived propaganda."

Chapter 78

"So what's the plan?" Tucson Luvabrest asked when Jack emerged from the bathroom. "I'm sure you have one. I must say, my superiors are in awe of you. All they can talk about. It's grinding on them that they can't figure out who you are. I wanted to tell them, but I decided not to after I talked to General Harmbruster."

Jack regarded Tucson, was amazed at her changed, friendlier attitude. But the news of Penelope—pregnant in Montana—was overwhelming him, even chasing the KGC thoughts out of his mind. "I thought you were pissed about the lies and deception."

Tucson touched his leg, stroked it. "I thought about it. You were dragged into all this. I understand. I just can't… I just wish I could…" she smiled ruefully. "Nevertheless, I've been ordered to get your fingerprints. I felt like telling my boss I already have them—all over my body."

"So it doesn't bother you, hangin' with an escaped con? What did your bosses say about Dawklings, the tattoo turncoat?"

Tucson frowned. "You're much more than an escaped convict, Jack. I have to believe that the general will do what he promises—get you a pardon and reinstatement in the Marines." She glanced at Billy, added in a low voice, "They think Dawklings died from the fires. It destroyed the building, burnt his body. I didn't report the shooting—or whatever you did to him with that weird weapon. And the coroner won't find a bullet, so you're clear on that. No explanations needed. I didn't want to relate all the details of what happened to me while in Joshua's company. I… I refused a physical. If the Bureau guys knew how I was treated, what really happened, I'd be viewed… be dealt with in a completely new way. I don't want that. I'd have to get out of the Bureau, disgraced."

"I'm sorry about all that." Jack tried to imagine the horror she had suffered from the multiple rapes. *Just like Amy. But Amy, the tree-hugging Arab lover couldn't take it and committed suicide. Tucson looks okay. Semigood to go.*

"Joshua Trumpet got his just desserts," Tucson declared. "He had a bullet hole in his skull. Shot in the head. But forensics said the bullet casing was of Chinese manufacture."

"You mentioned a bronze-skinned woman was at the Retreat," Jack responded. "That was undoubtedly Mara. She must've shot him. Probably with her Chinese pistol. She carries a nine millimeter. I wonder why she killed Joshua Trumpet?" He went to the refrigerator and pulled out a sixpack of beer. "Anyway, Tucson, you have to face the fact that you're not a field agent. You rushed off in an emotional state—left yourself vulnerable with no backup."

"Don't gloat, you asshole!" Tucson retorted heatedly.

"So you asked *What's the plan?*" Jack continued, ignoring her remark, "I'm' goin' rock climbing in Red Rock Canyon. Out by Blue Diamond. South side of Mount Charleston. While we wait until AE INTEL gives us the scoop. I could use some R and R."

"You ain't got any climbing gear," Billy pointed out.

Jack grinned, his blue eyes sparkled, his face lit up. "Won't need any. You guys can hang in the shade of an old oak tree or a big cactus—it's around sixty-two hundred feet up there between the town of Pahrump an' Vegas. I'm gonna do some free climbing. No ropes, no bolts, no belts. Just me and a coupla cliffs. Let's go!"

Billy laughed, caught up by Jack's new attitude. "Pah-rump? Sounds more like an elephant fartin' than the name for a town."

Jack chuckled with the others, then remembered, "Pahrump used to be an outlaw hangout. Strange, there's even a legend that Jessie James wasn't killed in the Midwest. Said he faked his death, hid out in Pahrump and died of old age."

"Go figure," Billy said over his shoulder as he walked into the bedroom. "He was KGC, you said."

Tucson interjected, "And Mara had the word KEGCILT written on her map. In Death Valley. Pahrump is on the eastern edge of Death Valley and right next to Area 51."

"Give it a rest," Jack concluded as he peered out the window. "Let's go up an' relax. Look's like a great day."

"You want the weapons bag?" Billy asked.

Jack glanced at Tucson. "Naw, we got a heavy-duty fibbie to protect us. What could go wrong in Red Rock Canyon? Nothing but wild horse and burro herds."

Chapter 79

"You're a long way from Shangri-La," the old man said. He was seated in a leather recliner. He was short, fat—looked like a merry Buddha, with a kindly smile on his youthful face, which looked out of place on his old man's body.

"You know of the valley," Mara acknowledged.

"After our American Civil War, a group of KGC stumbled into the valley, following an ancient templar map that purportedly led to the Holy Grail. They did not find the Grail but they found the magical—they thought —tarn waters." The old man grinned. I was a member of that team of explorers."

"You!" Mara stared at the old man.

"But that was—you would be…" His Exalted Eminence smiled in a beatific manner.

"But that's impossible!" Mara exclaimed.

"Those superstitious tribes and their tales of—"

"Are true. Certain glacial melt waters contain unique combinations of minerals and electrolytes, that completely balance the body's metabolic functions, make it work as efficiently as intended by our Maker. It's not so strange. Remember, from the same materials, some mountains produce coal, others produce diamonds." The old man smiled again. "I'm a diamond."

Mara looked around the room, suddenly dismayed that she had wasted her time on KEGCILT. Nothing but a bunch of eccentric kooks.

Sensing Mara's change in attitude, the old man pointed out, "Your fires did not work too well. It seems Mother Nature foiled your plans. Luckily you are here on time."

"My mission has failed miserably. I hoped…" her voice trailed off. She wondered how she could get out of this remote hideaway.

"Why do you want so desperately to injure America?"

Still irritated, Mara shot back, "Why do you? You're an American."

370

The old man smiled, with a rueful air, added, "My America lost the war. The Civil War."

Mara stared at the Eminence. "You want to bring back slavery?"

"Dead issue. States' Rights was the real focus, anyway. Now, we seek the destruction of the U.S. as we know it, so we can create a more perfect union. The Golden Circle is centered in Havana and is 2,400 miles in diameter. It includes northern South America, most of Mexico, all of Central America, Haiti/Dominican Republic and most other Caribbean islands, and the southern United States."

"You would burn, blow up, destroy American cities?"

His Eminence waved a dismissive hand. "My hero, Thomas Jefferson, said: *We cannot be translated from despotism to liberty in a feather-bed… rivers of blood must yet flow.*"

"So you have this secret society committed to the destruction of America." Mara doubted the old man had any fangs she could really use.

"Again, President Jefferson said: *As revolutionary instruments, secret societies are necessary and indispensable, and the right to use them is inalienable. Remember, rebellion against tyrants is obedience to God.*"

"Can you give me anything I can really use?" Mara asked with a scornful tone. "Like a nuclear suitcase bomb?"

His Eminence smiled. "Perhaps. But you will have to prove you are capable before you can play with serious weapons. Are you familiar with the effects of an ammonium nitrate bomb?"

Mara smiled, leaned forward. "Of course. Given a high enough percentage of the necessary ingredients, a massive explosion is relatively easy."

"Describe how you would make such a bomb," the old man demanded.

"Easy," Mara responded eagerly. "Cotton and diesel fuel on top of small-granule ammonium nitrate fertilizer, add a fuse and you have Timothy McVeigh's Oklahoma City bombing revisited as well as the Oslo explosion."

His Eminence leaned back in his high-backed, ornately carved chair. "Excellent!" he exclaimed. "I have prepared… we will give you three RVs, each already loaded with five thousand pounds of such explosives. Your *Saladin's Fist* will take them from Pahrump to Las Vegas, and detonate then under or next to three casinos." The old man smiled. "We will shut down that godless city for years to come."

"When will we do this?" Mara asked. Her heart began to race.

The old man smiled, his eyes twinkled with merriment. "Is your *Fist* ready to strike?"

"They are waiting in Las Vegas."

"Assemble them at the Saddle West in Pahrump. Tomorrow you will attack."

"We need to conduct reconnaissance, practice," Mara protested.

"Each RV has a GPS. Your drivers will be verbally instructed by the computer every inch of the way."

"I have never seen such a thing," Mara said. "I don't understand."

"Your men will practice with the system tonight," the old man explained. "Once they use the GPS command mapping system, you'll understand. It'll guide them to the parking garages as easily as a walk in the park. And then we'll see about your next objective. You went to school in the Middle East? If you succeed, you'll enjoy the next target we give you— oil."

Chapter 80

Tucson sipped a long-neck beer in the shade of a huge boulder, just fifty feet off the Blue Diamond Highway. She watched Jack scaling a vertical cliff as though he was slowly, methodically walking up a stairway. She was amazed at his rock-climbing talents. "How long has he been climbing?" She asked Billy, who was reclining with Zhang on an oversized towel.

"All his life," Billy responded. "An' Dad dragged him all over the world in his early teens, climbin' bigger, stupider rocks."

Tucson regarded Jack's brother. His words, his tone were wistful, slightly jealous.

"What's he doin'?" Zhang asked. She was wearing a white cotton halter and low-riding red shorts that totally revealed her wonderful, trim body. Looking at her, Tucson felt like a draft animal next to a sleek Arabian racehorse.

Tucson looked up at the climber through her hand-sized Tasco 8X25 binoculars. He had paused just below a ledge, was talking on his cell phone.

Jack dug the toes of his Montrail bouldering shoes into a crack and listened to General Harmbruster speak in an excited voice.

"Jack, you were dead on when you asked me to check out KGC. Dumbass ATF has been watching an event in Nevada, but neglected to put the Intel through Homeland or *EA* channels."

"What's goin' on with the alphabet soup crowd, General? They boilin' over?"

Ignoring Jack's gibe, the general said, "ATF was tracing seven tons of missing ammonium nitrate. Then they sent up a Pioneer UAV to monitor a loading dock northwest of Las Vegas, town called Pahrump. If they had used the *Eagle's Aerie* network correctly, they would have sent the data and photos to us. Your gal, Mara Bhutto, is in a series of photos we just received minutes ago."

Jack tightened his grip on a crack in the rock wall with his free hand. A tiny waterfall, trickling down, shifted and splashed on the hand. He squeezed tighter with his wet fingers, dug his toes in as hard as he could. Talcum powder, used to combat sweaty palms, had washed away. Jack stared at his straining white fingers.

The general continued, "The RVs have mixed in with a convoy of about fifty other RVs. They're headed towards Las Vegas."

Jack glanced at the whitewash trail of talcum powder draining past his face, which was just inches from the sheer cliff. He felt his grip was strong, but he wondered what would happen when he shifted positions. His shoe felt loose: glancing down, he saw it was untied.

"What d'you want me to do, General? Throw some ps and qs at 'em?

Don't like alphabet soup. Anyway, which way they going into Vegas?"

The general's voice began to break up on the cell. "Apparently, half are caravanning on 95 and half are moving down the 160. Where are you?"

Jack carefully looked over his shoulder. The 160 Highway was a halfmile away across very rugged highland terrain composed of huge boulders, red rock ridges, cactus and thick chaparral bushes. "I'm just north of the Blue Diamond cutoff, about sixty-five hundred feet. Just east of the summit."

After glancing at his photo overlays, the general said, "Great! You and your brother block the 160 group. If they get past you they can turn on a dozen different roads to the city. Then they'll get lost amongst hundreds of tourist RVs. Police'll never be able to stop them."

"Can't they just stop them all?"

"No, just suspicious ones. Probable cause issues."

"Yes, sir," Jack muttered. He contemplated moving but couldn't do it while on the cell. "Sir, call me back in five minutes." He jammed the cell in his pocket, stared at his wet hand, worried that it would slip. Finally, he looked down, saw a crack. He let go, dropped three feet to where he regripped the lower crack with both hands. His untied shoe slipped off, plummeted to the ground. A minute later, he had scrambled down the face and was running across the ridge.

His shoeless foot found every sharp rock in his path. The first encounters were painful, but then he kicked a barrel cactus and the shock numbed his foot.

"Jack's coming at a gallop," Tucson said as she watched him through her binoculars.

"Must be something important for him to give up on a rock," Billy pronounced. He stood and watched three wild mustangs, surprised by Jack, bolt to the south, scramble out of his path. "Hey! Check out the red mustangs," he called.

Scant minutes later, Jack yelled as he approached, "Let's go! Batter up.

We're done takin' the afternoon off. The *Fist* is comin'!"

The four scrambled into the Cayenne with Tucson at the wheel.

"What's goin' down?" Billy demanded as the FBI agent started the SUV and raced north after Jack pointed the way.

"Mara's headin' this way," Jack responded. "A convoy of RVs. The general and *EA* think they're haulin' explosives to Vegas. Comin' from Pahrump."

"This's the road to Pahrump and Area 51," Tucson pointed out. "How far are they?"

"I don't know, but real close, I fear."

Your foot! It's bleeding!" Zhang gasped.

Jack lifted it and rested it on the dash. The white sock was drenched with blood. A long cactus needle protruded from just below his ankle. "Lost my shoe on the cliff," he grunted.

Tucson glanced at his foot, said, "Billy, do something."

Jack swung his leg around and Billy extracted two needles.

"What are we doing?" Zhang asked. She winced at the sight of the mangled foot as Billy peeled off the drenched sock.

Jack bit his lip. "Our only chance to block 'em will be when they're comin' up the grade at a slow pace. Past us... they can take a dozen roads."

"We're gonna stop 'em in this puny SUV?" Billy snorted. "And no weapons?"

Jack pointed at a restaurant parking lot just over the crest. "Check out that eighteen-wheeler. Placed right, that could block both oncoming lanes and the shoulders."

Tucson veered off the highway, into the lot, slammed to a stop next to the pink cab of the huge truck.

"C'mon, Billy," Jack yelled. The two jumped out. In the distance, a long line of RVs were slowly grinding up the grade from the north.

The big eighteen-wheeler's motor was idling, the driver's head was bent over papers. Jack jumped on the running board, shouted, "We need your truck!"

The startled driver, a brown-haired man about fifty years old, looked up through the partially-closed window. Wide-eyed, he punched the door lock button.

"Billy, help!" Jack grabbed the window and pulled—it did not give. His brother climbed next to him and the two swung their fists as the driver raised it. The window shattered into countless webbed pieces, Jack pulled it away from its track in a crumbled mass.

He reached inside, unlocked the door. "Get out," he yelled.

Finally, the man managed to scream. "Are you crazy? Help! I'll call 911!" He leaned away, scrambled out the passenger side door.

Jack jumped behind the wheel, engaged the clutch as Billy jumped back. He released the hand brake, slammed the truck into second gear. Headed across the northbound lanes. Shifted, ground the gearbox, raced the engine, but picked up speed.

Glancing at the southbound lanes, he saw a RV—a tan Winnebago— grind past. Jack hit the grass-covered median, shifted and accelerated. A second RV passed. He slammed down a small bank onto the shoulder. Saw the panicked face of the third RV's driver just before he t-boned the rear half of the thirty-foot-long vehicle.

The eighteen-wheeler jolted to a stop. Jack, who had not had time to engage the seatbelt, was thrown forward and sidewards, under the dash. His head hit, he smelled lilac flowers, blacked out.

Chapter 81

Slowly regaining consciousness, Jack opened his eyes. The heavy odor of diesel fuel filled his nostrils. He opened his eyes wider, saw only whiteness. He realized he was staring through the windshield at the side of the crumpled RV.

His legs jammed under the dash, he tried to move but it had buckled after the impact, pressing down on his knee, pushing his already injured left foot into the floorboard.

"Jack, you alright?" Billy yelled as he jumped up to the door.

"Stuck," Jack mumbled. He but his lip to avoid crying out from the pain.

"You crazy sumbitch! You wrecked my god-lovin' RV! Now it's burnin', you bastard!" A strange voice outside, yelling and cursing.

Billy tried to open the door—it was wedged shut. "Help me," he yelled at the RV driver.

"Help you? I'm almost dead!" The man swiped at a bleeding cut.

"Hurry!" Billy insisted. "He's trapped."

Oh, shit! Jack thought. *I could come up roasted marshmallows.* "C'mon, Billy—before I'm crispy critters." He pounded his stuck knee sideways, it did not move. Pain intensified.

"What's wrong?" Tucson's voice.

"The door's jammed," Billy shouted.

The odor of diesel quickly changed to a smell of smoke.

"Zhang!" Tucson yelled. "Help!"

Billy and Tucson tugged on the door, the driver pulled on Billy's waist, Zhang arrived and pulled on Tucson. The door, screeched, slowly shifted, flew open. All four fell backwards.

Jack looked down at them, saw smoke leak from under the cab. He pounded his knee again, nothing. Refusing to give up, he balled his fists, swung sideways: the knee popped loose. Billy jumped up, pulled him down and out of the cab. Tucson grabbed his other arm, they dragged him away.

Seeing Jack free, the driver walked next to the group as they crossed the lanes, again yelling down at Jack, "You asshole! What'd you do that for?"

"Stop the bombers," Jack mumbled. He slowly waved his hand at the screaming man. Suddenly aware, Jack pulled free, looked at the stalled line of RVs. "If they're not the first two that got through, they'll come after us." He looked up at Tucson. "Got your weapon? Cover us—"

He stood up, swayed with dizziness. A blue SUV pulled out from behind the next RV and raced forward.

"Look out!" Jack yelled. Tucson, her arm around Jack, froze. He glanced around. Billy, the driver, and Zhang were already on the highway shoulder.

Jack shoved Tucson out of the way, pain forgotten. Leaped as high as he could. A glimpse of a copper-colored face, short black hair—Mara! He landed on the windshield, felt it give, then he bounced away as the SUV sped down the road.

Crashed onto the hard surface of the road, felt a shock to his collarbone, one elbow, his left knee.

The wail of approaching sirens drowned out his words. One Las Vegas police car, then another, skidded to a stop on the northbound lanes. Tucson pulled out her FBI ID and held it aloft as she pushed through the long brown grass in the median, towards the police cars. After a quick huddle with two policemen, she returned and announced, "They stopped the first two RVs—just tourists. No bombs."

"You real traffic jam, Jack," Zhang said as she helped him to his feet.

"Yeah," Jack said as he stood, rubbed his bloody elbow, carefully tested his left ankle and bloodied foot. "Hey, Tucson—tell the cops to stop the SUV heading towards Vegas. The one that hit me—it was Mara." Pain shot through the injured joint, up his leg, but he could put weight on it, figured it wasn't broken. He felt blood drain down his calf, onto his bare foot. He lifted a pants leg, saw only a trickle of blood; relieved, he looked at the stalled line of RVs.

"Let's get outta here before the cops decide to hold us for questioning."

A police officer approached. Jack wiped blood off his forehead. Said to the cop, "I'm okay, but you better check out the RV driver." He waved at the two vehicles. Smoke and flames were now gushing skyward into a cloudless blue sky. The officer hurried across to the wreck.

"Let's go," Jack ordered.

Tucson joined them at the Cayenne, slid behind the wheel. "I'm learning. Lie like hell, run like rats. Let's get out of here. After I retire from the Bureau, I'm gonna be a bank robber trainer."

Laughing, the others slipped into the Porsche. She started it, drove across the road, across the median, turned left and headed for Las Vegas. Two minutes later, Jack said, "The Blue Diamond cutoff is just ahead. Take a left and let's go around any roadblocks."

When Tucson saw the sign, she skidded into a hard left, raced into Red Rock Canyon.

Jack's cell beeped, indicating a missed call. He keyed the instrument, it called the missed number.

General Harmbruster answered with a shout. "I see what you did, Jack.

Outstanding! Anybody hurt?"

"Just bruises, General," Jack responded. He wiggled his foot—it still worked. "Did we stop them? Or did they go the other way?"

"I pray you did, but the police have shut down Highway 95. The second convoy will reach the roadblock in about a half-hour. Police helicopters are tracking overhead. We'll soon see, but you did all I asked. Good work, Jack. Get back to your apartment and write up an after-action report. Text message it to Major Broyer. No, he's giving me trouble. Text message to me. Same number."

"Trouble from your people? What's that all about? What about the bad guys, General?"

"They escaped east into the pine forest at the summit. Sheriff's Search and Rescue teams from Clark County and Nye

County are organizing to chase the terrorists. 'Course, we can't call 'em that. Don't want tourists fleeing Vegas."

Jack hesitated, then asked, "Did the police catch Mara? In the SUV?"

"Not that lucky—she slipped the noose," the general responded. "But you stopped the RVs. That was the important issue. You'll catch her later."

"She probably was passed through—she looks like a guy now. They were probly looking for a woman. She has cropped hair, a fake mustache." An hour later, Tucson and the emotionally-drained group had wound through surface streets, turned onto the Strip from Tropicana Boulevard .

In the hotel suite, Jack swallowed three aspirins, hobbled to the sofa, fell asleep. He awoke five hours later. His foot felt cold. He looked and realized an ice pack was straddling it.

"Let's look at your foot and ankle," Tucson said when she saw him move. She knelt on the floor, felt his ankle, then pushed his bloody pants leg up. Just above his knee, she saw the bandaged wound from his impact with the truck's dash. She went to the kitchen alcove and returned.

"Do you still have Mara's number? Remember I gave it to you?" He winced as she ripped off the bandage and applied fresh antiseptic on the mushy injury. Tucson searched her wallet, found the slip of paper, handed it to Jack.

Looking at the number, he saw a watermark had blurred two digits. "Damn! I wanted to talk to her. He concentrated, hobbled to the kitchen, picked up a cell phone. "I'm good with numbers. I think I can remember." He entered a number and waited: no service. He entered another variation: wrong number. He tried a third.

Mara Bhutto answered, "Hello?"

"Mara, how you doin'? This is your cave-spelunking pal, Jack." He winked at Billy, who was standing near the window.

In a shocked tone, Mara responded, "Jack! What do *you* want?"

"Remember when we were hangin' with the Chi-creep, Lotta Shit? I mean, Mo Poo? Remember when we were apple-bobbing for the LIIT bomb? When I saved your beautiful ass?" Jack paused, recalled the two last times he had seen Mara. The first: *Splashing through the underground lake, he caught up to Mara, just when she slumped forward, gave up in exhaustion. He hesitated, but he couldn't abandon her to the giant Chinese brutes. He grabbed her by the arm.*

"I certainly do, Jack! You threw me to Mo Poo. Sacrificed me to save your own skin."

Jack thought of those frantic moments a year ago: *An eager yowl behind them. He glanced into Mo Poo's ripped-open, bloody face. The giant Chinaman stretched his long arms.*

"Not to save me, Mara. It was you or Ashley. I chose Ashley." *Heaved Mara between Ashley and the ogre.* "But remember, I turned back—I still can't believe I knocked the wind outta him when I head-butted him." "The American—that bitch!" Mara exclaimed.

"Hey," Jack interrupted. "At least she had never tried to shish-kabob me like you did, but in the end she turned out to be a poor choice. She dumped me. I guess she didn't like my vacation choices. Anyway, I figured you and Mo Poo were pals and he wouldn't hurt you. I guess I was right."

"I'm sorry your love life's in tatters, Jack," Mara said in a sarcastic tone. "Just count yourself lucky I ran out of bullets in the training camp and that I didn't run into you today."

"That was cold, Mara. And after I let you escape in the cavern."

"Thank you, Jack," Mara said with an overly-sweet, sarcastic tone.

"Whatever, Mara. Hey, *Saladin's Fist* rocks. I enjoyed meeting your arsonist fiends—I mean, friends. Up in Sacramento. Sorry they had to like depart this sad vale."

"That was you?" Mara swore an oath in Urdu, yelled, "I hate you. You've stymied me at every step!"

"*Mara,* don't be that way," Jack taunted. "We've been through so much together. Say, how's your campaign to destroy

America? Do you feel a little bit like a flea on a camel's hump or a mosquito on an elephant's ass?"

"Jack," Mara retorted with clipped off words, "I admit I had misconceptions, but I will prevail. I have new mujs. American recruits who flock to my aid," she added triumphantly. "I have sent them on a mission already. America and *you* will burn. In more ways than one."

"Big deal, Mara. You sign 'em up, we'll knock 'em down. How'd you like what I did to your convoy? Happy to mess up your planned fireworks." "You bastard!" Mara hung up.

Jack looked at the others, held up a fist, gave a thumb's up. "I think we got the right convoy. Mara sounds, like, totally pissed."

"Alright!" Billy exclaimed. He crossed to the refrigerator, pulled out a six-pack of beer. He twisted off a bottle cap and drained the beer in one long, gulping pull.

Tucson selected a beer, thirstily drank. "Problem is, what's she going to try next? Think she'll quit?"

Zhang shook her head, stretched, thrusting her breasts out. "She no give up. Hate has destroyed her life."

"What's her problem?" Tucson asked.

Zhang stared at Tucson with cold eyes, finally decided to respond, "Her father was hanged by Pakistani government. For being Communist.
She blames America."

"Yeah," Jack agreed after swallowing three aspirins. "She has serious issues. I can't blame her, but get over it! Question is, what'll she try next?" He uncapped a beer, tried to wash down the aspirins stuck in his throat. "It's strange," he mused out loud. "How we seem to be in a minuet of action with Mara's gang. Like the whole thing is preplanned. We're always in the right place."

"Man, you kiddin'?" Billy scoffed. "The general dragged our ass all the way from Singapore. Then sent us haulin' ass all the way down the West Coast. That's why we're in this box waltz. Ain't no plan to it 'cept his."

"Remember," Tucson added. "Our superiors have the high ground. With spy sats and GPS, they can see everything if they know where and when to look, and they can send us anywhere in immediate response. That's why terrorists are reluctant to attack American soil, now that we're up to speed."

Finishing his beer, Jack aimed at a wastebasket and made the shot. "I dunno," he said, "I don't call that mad crash we just pulled off nothin' more than a successful cluster—" he broke off and limped to the bathroom.

"Question is," Billy said to the two women. "What're these maniacs gonna try next?"

Chapter 82

After a short soak in the Jacuzzi tub, Jack limped to his bed, fell asleep almost immediately. He did not hear Tucson enter the room, slip out of her clothes, take a long shower. Nor did he awake when she crawled into his bed and snuggled up next to him. She stared at his unshaven, lean, sculptured face, inches from her own. His sweet breath brushed her face. His muscular arm moved over her, pulled her closer.

Still asleep, her presence nevertheless affected his slumber and finally he dreamed. He was back in Shangri-La: *Wantonal dried him with a large wool shawl. She accidentally— playfully?— brushed her full, bare breasts against his chest while she toweled his hair. He inhaled a hint of saffron, fought an urge to embrace her. Still nervous, he restrained himself until she looked into his eyes with an inviting smile, gorgeous blue eyes. Her look, her hand, slowly stroking his hip with the shawl. These girls must be bored stiff. Shortage of guys in Shangri-La? No wonder it's called Paradise. Stick around awhile? Pull her closer, stupid. She softly kissed him, thrust her tongue in his mouth. He felt passion engorge him.*

Jack awoke already inside Tucson. She was slowly moving against him, kissing him on the neck. Her hands were running up and down his sides— she grabbed his arms with fierce grips. When he realized what was happening, he jerked, started to pull away, but couldn't. He released himself to the wonderful pleasure, the passion of their lovemaking. He put his head down, nuzzled her breasts.

Suddenly, an image of Penelope shot into his mind. Passion shot out of him like spurting blood from a fresh wound.

Abruptly, his cellphone rang and rang and rang. Jack and Tucson were frozen, arms around each other. Finally, Tucson sighed in exasperation, picked up the cell from the bed stand and put it against his ear.

"Hello?" he gasped.

"Last year," Mara spoke with deadly intensity, "You invited me to your ranch. Thanks, I've accepted."

"Mara! What d'you mean?" Jack stalled, a sudden fear rising in his throat. "Mara. I'm in Las Vegas. Let's meet here. Stay away from my family!"

"Stay away?" Mara asked. "Why would I do that? They welcomed me with open arms. Your father and the Shangrilan woman. The fools!" The phone went dead.

Chapter 83

Glanced at his watch: almost 1200 hours. "We need to get to Montana!" Jack sat up, exclaimed, "Mara's at the ranch!"

"The general's aide told me to remind you to stay in Las Vegas," Tucson pointed out. "No matter what." Frowning, she sat up on the edge of the bed. A bitter note entered her voice. "You sure this isn't just a ploy to join your pregnant girlfriend?"

Jack regarded the naked redhead next to him. He rolled away, passion now far from his mind. "You don't understand—this is hot pursuit." He called the general's voicemail number, spoke into the cell, "We've a lead on *Saladin's Fist*. We need to get to Montana immediately. And we need Mick's—er, Major Nakamura's rapid response unit. The terrorists are at my dad's ranch. And I think their next target is Yellowstone Park."

"You might not get a response," Billy cautioned. "EA might think you're bullshitting them so we can go home."

Jack turned to Tucson, held out his hands in a pleading gesture. She pulled out her BlackBerry while Jack updated Billy, then cleaned up, dressed, and packed. Finished, he joined Billy in the living room, where they donned their cera-flex armour shirts.

Ten minutes later, Tucson proudly announced, "I've got a ride waiting at Nellis Air Force Base. To Billings." A hint of smugness in her voice.

"That was fast. You're great, Tucson!" Jack exclaimed. "Let's go."

Billy grabbed the weapons bag, Jack took their personal bags and the four, with Tucson driving, took the Cayenne to the 15 Freeway, north on the 95 Freeway, and turned onto Craig Road, passing countless commercial stores and strip centers, to Nellis Air Force Base. The ride to the front gate, which was guarded by two armed Air Force types, took twenty-five minutes.

An hour later, they lifted off in a small Air Force Gulfstream jet flown by two friendly Air Force captains. The jet swung over the city, accelerated towards the mountains that surrounded the valley. Tucson pointed at the Las Vegas Speedway, sitting between the base and the 15 freeway. "I took a racing course at the Penske School last year."

"No wonder you drove like a maniac in Washington and Oregon," Jack said.

Tucson studied Jack's face. "If I was as fast with cars as you are with women, I'd be a superstar NASCAR driver." She leaned over and kissed him on the cheek, made a small humming sound in her throat, then walked forward to talk to the pilots.

"You've got it all wrong. I—" Just then, Jack's cell rang. It was the general.

"Jack, what's this harebrained idea of yours. I told you to stay in Vegas until we had solid INTEL."

"General, the terrorists are at my ranch!" Jack exclaimed.

"There's no way, son. Calm down. This is how you got in trouble last year—not following orders."

"With all due respect, General—get screwed!" Jack closed the flip phone.

Zhang said into the silence, "It looks like the harshest, driest parts of Gobi Desert down there." She leaned over the others. "I thought America was the land of milk and honey. Why's there a great city in this wilderness?"

Billy glanced at the stark landscape. "The land of lots of slots, where tourists travel great distances to build fabulous casinos with their voluntary donations to the gambling gods."

Jack looked at his brother. His mind was tumbling with possible plans of action, intermingled with confused fear and anger. He decided to say nothing until he had calmed himself.

The jet turned northeast for Montana. Jack stared at the pilot's compartment, worried that the general would track them down, order the pilots to turn back. He glanced at Zhang, said to all, "Don't use a cell phone. I don't want us tracked and stopped. We have to get to the ranch." The four read magazines, cleaned weapons, dozed, then buckled up two hours later when the pilot announced a long downwind approach to Billings Airport.

Gusting rain sheeted on the windows as the jet descended. Wind turbulence bounced the light aircraft around but the touchdown was smooth.

It was 1600 hours—four PM.

Tucson rented a Ford Expedition in the airport and the four hurried through Billings, stopped at a Hardee's on Montana Avenue for burgers, fries, and drinks. The coffee and meat aromas filled the vehicle's interior as they gulped down the food.

Jack directed Tucson to head west on Highway 90 for fifteen miles, then they turned southwest onto the 212. Rain continued without let-up. The wind died down, but lightning slashed through the clouds, striking and sending crashing thunder that rattled the windows as they drove across High Plains' terrain towards the town of Red Lodge and the Flying Eagle Ranch. Jack and Billy peered through the storm-smashed countryside for familiar sights.

Ten minutes after the four turned east off Highway 212, they turned and passed under an entry monument that read: *Flying Eagle Ranch.*

They continued across a flat prairie and after twenty minutes, began to climb into a north-south range of juniper-covered heights. The gravel road narrowed as it wound into the hills.

Minutes later, Jack and Billy, their excitement increasing as they neared the ranch house, were shocked to see a mud and rockslide completely blocking the passage on the road.

"Now what?" Tucson asked.

"I don't like this," Jack said.

"Shouldn't be a landslide here," Billy agreed.

"I'll go check it out, Billy," Jack ordered.

"You stay with Zhang and Tucson." He grabbed a small backpack.

"How far is it?" Zhang looked up, flinched as tremendous lightning flashed through the late afternoon sky.

"Too damned far to go alone!" Billy exclaimed. "A couple of miles."

"Hey, you guys'll be dry. Just keep an eye out. Something's wrong. Assuming everything's okay at home, I'll come back in a ranch truck." He flinched at a nearby lightning strike, added, "It's almost six. Hour there, ten minutes back."

"Too long!" Tucson protested.

Jack shook his head. "Too risky for all of us to tramp around before we have more INTEL," he said. "I'll call you on my cell, update you."

"Bullshit, Flashy!" Billy exclaimed. "I'm not letting you go alone."

Jack held up both hands. "Don't sweat it, I'll just do a recon—one person will be stealthier. Give me a couple spare clips for my M-9," he ordered. "Wish we had a UAV—an unmanned airplane—to check out what's going on over there." He pulled a cammo stick out of the gear bag, painted his face, neck, and hands. "Prob'ly couldn't fly in this weather anyway."

Finished, he climbed out, took the sheathed Khyber knife, an M-16, and two mags out of the gun bag. He put a first aid pack in the backpack, added a liter bottle of water. He stepped into the howling, rain-lashed storm.

Lightning flashed repeatedly as Jack clambered over the slippery rocks and through the mud, brush, and uprooted tangle. Cold rain pounded him as he regained the road. Water ran in rivulets across the gravel road and a new stream flowed along the side of the road. He reflected that Penel was waiting at his destination, and he was bringing another woman, just like he had done back in Afghanistan. He wondered what would happen when the two women met.

Penel being pregnant hit him: a baby. His. The thought was almost overwhelming. But the baby and Penel were in mortal danger.

Keeping his head up, he refocused on action: jogged up the road until he broke out of the hills, reached a pine tree-covered plateau sprinkled with meadows bound by old-fashioned split-rail fences. He spotted sections he had helped his dad and the ranch hands repair over the years. Remembered driving a skip loader for the first time. Slowly passed a loading corral and after a half-hour, he saw the giant trees that grew around the ranch house: his pulse quickened. Thought of a verse from an old poem:

Chasing down my foe,
Through the woods I go.
Through the bogs and mire,
To save my heart's desire.

He left the road, plunged into the forest, scared himself and a small herd of deer that were lying in long grass. The deer herd bounded away like rivulets of dark, flowing silver; they quickly disappeared.

The sky was bleakly gray and darkening, rain pounded the dark green forest. Lightning continued to flash, crackling thunder smashed through the air.

A figure startled him when he stepped out from an abandoned shed. Lightning revealed Talking Dog—Billy's maternal grandfather. The old man, his weathered face showing his mid-eighties age, wore old jeans, patched beyond recognition, a familiar calico shirt made from an old feed sack, a leather vest with fringe strips across the chest and silver buttons down the front. He was carrying a saddle gun—an old .30-30 lever-action Winchester.

Touching his black Stetson, the old man smiled, nodded a greeting, spoke in a formal tone. "It is good to see you, Jackson. How is my grandson, Billy Howling Dog?"

Jack hoped the old man wasn't looking for a long conversation. "Talking Dog, Billy is well. He's become a great warrior. We have experienced memorable battles. I thank you for sending my brother to me."

The old man smiled again, wrinkling his time-furrowed face. His voice was old but firm. "You are welcome, Jackson. The senator an' your papa have confirmed your bravery. They been told by your military superiors that you an' Billy're brave warriors. That is well, for there be trouble on the F E Ranch." Talking Dog stepped back in the shed, Jack followed. The rain drummed on the steel roof paneling.

The old man's odor—that of a man who took one bath each spring in a local pond—and overlain with a strong hint of saddle oil, gun cleaning fluid, and smoke from countless fires, flooded back, carrying countless childhood memories of stories around campfires, work on fencelines, herding and branding cattle.

"What kind of trouble?" Jack wiped the rain out of his face, thankful to be out of the downpour. "What about Dad? Penel, the blonde woman. Is she here? Is she okay?" Swallowed his fear. Stared into the old man's eyes.

"They're holed up in the safe room. An' Senator Jensen, who was at the ranch on some matter or t'other. Your papa and the senator fought bravely. There is seven bodies stacked in the barn. I snuck out the back door, then watched the false visitors carry their fallen out of the house."

"Seven?" Jack asked. "I thought there were only three, maybe four of them. There were ten, I killed two in Afghanistan, we killed four in Sacramento."

"No prisoners? You two are truly deadly warriors. Perhaps these bad men got more help."

"Local ragheads? I doubt it. Maybe they brought fellow travelers from California." Jack looked at the old man. "How many are there?"

"At least twenty, 'cluding the copper-skinned female. She come first, alone. Your papa welcomed her, but figgered his mistake when the sand niggers showed up. He fought bravely, then they had to retreat upstairs to the safe room. I was in the tool shed, I crept away."

"Weapons?"

"The bad men got small arms only." The old man removed his hat, wiped his brow. "They be waiting to ambush someone. You?"

"I'm sure they expect me. Any ideas, Talking Dog?"

The old man looked into Jack's eyes. Lightning flickered, making his face appear and disappear. "Call the Sheriff. I was on my way to the highway when I spotted you. You saved me a long tramp."

Jack shook his head. "What if the locals screw it up? No, I don't want outsiders who could give a shit whether anybody survives. We have to keep this from the local authorities. Dad always said the Sheriff is a complete idiot, anyway. Guy's a political. Are there look-outs?"

"I saw no one, but there was a small fire in the barn, mayhaps from a careless smoke. Only a city-type stranger'd smoke in a hay barn. And pigeons're avoiding the granary." The old man looked outside. "And there's one other. A Big Foot of the mountains has appeared, is lurking nearby. A monster of a creature. I never seen such a big man. Scared the crap outta me."

Jack grimaced. "Mo Poo. Just what I need." He called Billy. When his brother answered, he said, "Mara and the bad guys're here. Dad might be hurt—I don' know how bad. I'm gonna check it out. Call Mick, get him and his unit here ASAP. Let's rendezvous on the entry road a mile west of the house in two hours, around midnight. There's a shed—remember? We used to play in it. Talking Dog will meet—" the cell went dead.

He cursed, put the cell away, stepped to the doorway, looked for signs of activity, saw none. The rain had increased in intensity. He shivered—the evening air was cooling and his clothes were soaked.

Talking Dog sat down on the hard-packed dirt floor, asked, "What'll you do?"

Jack thought of his dad, injured. Penel—probably terrified. *No,* he decided. *She's one tough broad. She'll hold up. But what am I gonna do? I can't make a mistake. It's Dad. And Penel carrying my unborn child. Not just me—much bigger stakes.* Jack suddenly felt overwhelmed, terrified.

Talking Dog looked into Jack's eyes. "I knew you would come if you could. We must prepare for the battle. We'll set up a Spirit Summons: this ceremony'll calm and strengthen your soul. Ready you for the battle." He looked up, sang in a warbling monotone above the thunder and rattling rain:

The ground trembles
As I am about to enter
My heart fails me
As I am about to enter,
The spirit lodge.

"Sounds great!" Jack agreed. "Better yet, got any tequila? But I gotta go, Chief."

Ignoring him, the old man shut the shed door, pulled out an old Zippo lighter, pushed a small pile of straw together on the dirt floor, lit it. He removed a bag suspended from a leather thong hung around his neck. Took a pinch of weeds and dropped them into the fire. He handed the bag to Jack.

"You must consult your ancestors. How many will you call?"

"Uh, can I just email or drop a text message note? I'm in a hurry and I'd rather not see dead folks in person—"

The old man shut his eyes and said with a strong voice, "I begin the Steam Lodge Song." He sang:

A voice I will send to the Afterlife.
Hear me Ancestors!
To the dead lands, a voice I
am sending! Hear me!

"We'll summon three," Talking Dog's voice sounded younger.

"Throw in the first pinch. I warn you, the mixture contains ver' powerful summoning agents."

"Oh, great! Now, I'm adding drug abuse to my list of wrongdoings." Impatient to be done with the ceremony, Jack quickly drizzled the weed mixture into the fire. The flames shot up, smoke filled the shed.

Talking Dog pulled Jack down next to him on the cool dirt with a strong grip. Cupped the herbs-scented smoke, wafted it to Jack's face. Jack copied his actions. Smelled marijuana, locoweed, prairie grass, Indian tobacco, fennel, sage. He shut his eyes for a moment, breathed deeply, opened them. Nothing happened for several long minutes. Talking Dog hummed a chant in a singsong, gravelly voice.

Suddenly, the shed walls receded, the smoke from the fire bent and twisted into the shape of a young woman dressed in a full-length pale blue dress. She wore long white hair in a tight bun.

"This woman be your ancestor," Talking Dog explained.

"She and her daughter were trapped while visiting the Alamo. She survived battles between the Mexicano beaners and the

American ranchers after the Alamo was overrun. Her name be Eunice Waggoner. Her husband, Squire Damon, was one of the Immortal Thirty Two, and died in the Alamo conflict when he went in after her. The Mexicans spared the women and children, and after the war, she moved north in a wagon train that was destroyed by Cherokee in Oklahoma. Eunice died in a burning wagon, but her daughter Charlotte was raised by the Tribes, eventually lived in Montana. Charlotte married a French-Indian trapper and her daughter was your grandmother seven times removed."

"Hey, Eunice," Jack asked. "How's it going? Uh, you don't have to answer that." He felt giddy, wanted to be serious, suppressed a giggle, worried that he would be too drugged-out to function.

"What do you want?" the smoky apparition asked. "Why hast thou called me?"

Jack swallowed another giggle. "Advice," he blurted out.

The woman stared into space. "At the Battle of the Alamo, my first husband lamented being tied down by place and emotion," the ghost spoke, then dropped her eyes, fell silent.

"That's it?" Jack asked. He felt silly—realized he was high from the pungent smoke. "Say, as long as you're here, got any hot lotto number picks?"

The smoke wavered, the frowning apparition disappeared.

"Another pinch," Talking Dog commanded with a firm voice. "Larger."

Jack threw in two smidgens of powder and weeds. The smoke blossomed, Talking Dog wafted more smoke to Jack's nose and Jack emulated him, then breathed deeply. The new smoke made him feel even sillier, but his eyesight seemed to improve. He noticed an axe and an old shovel in a corner of the shed, tried to not laugh.

An apparition formed in the smoke from the fire, drew his eyes back to the rising smoke: a young man dressed in a khaki uniform.

"You have ancestors that have fought in every war since the French and Indian Wars," the old Indian stated. "This be Reiner Flashhardt, a paternal ancestor, five times removed. He worked for Teddy Roosevelt on his Dakota ranch as a bronco buster, later served as an aide to Roosevelt, and participated in the charge on San Juan Hill."

The soldier pointed upward. "Once you decide to charge the heights, do not waver, do not hesitate. The power in your heart will defeat your enemy."

"Charge the hill? Maybe we could just level it first with a couple of Daisy Cutter bombs?" Jack asked, suppressing another cackle.

The apparition disappeared. Talking Dog held out the bag, Jack took a bigger pinch, tossed it in the fire, eager to finish with the ceremony.

The smoke expanded again, Jack breathed deeply. Suddenly, Grandpa appeared: the old man looked as he had last seen him in the Honduran jungle just before he was murdered, a big man in his seventies, showing a strong visage. He was wearing jeans, a gray and white checkered shirt. His hair smoky white, his eyes reddish rather than kindly blue. The old man's visage took Jack back to Custer's battlefield in an instant: he and Grandpa tramping the Montana hills overlooking the Little Big Horn River, the blue and brown water cutting through the High Plain's greasy grass hills, meadowlarks calling, a bald eagle's white head flashing in the sunlight every time it wheeled about, bluebell flowers reaching for the sun in an impossibly clear blue sky, a hawk being harassed by two black and white magpies, prairie dogs whistling alarms. The two discussed Custer's decisions, Reno's retreat, Gall's overrunning the rearguard, and Crazy Horse's attack up the gullies—the death of 197 cavalrymen.

"Hello, Jackson," the familiar deep voice. He felt a chill sweep through his body, sobered instantly.

Talking Dog said, "Your granpapa—Frank Flashhardt. Served in Vietnam and Laos in 1961 and '62. Died in Honduras, three years ago."

"Grandpa…" Jack was overwhelmed by emotion, fell silent. For the first time, he took the confrontation seriously.

The image spoke, "I view your warrior's life with pride. You are strong, smart, fearless. Our times tramping and discussing the

Battles of Greasy Grass, Valley Forge, the Civil War battlefields in Virginia were well spent—"

"No time for reminiscences," Talking Dog ordered.

Grandpa's red·smoky eyes glared at the Indian. He snarled, "I only wish to remind Jackson that there are many ways to win a battle." His face and voice softened again. "The conflict is decided before the first shot is fired. Lay the groundwork, plan well, most importantly: instill fear and trembling. Then strike with overwhelming force. Shock your enemy." His voice strengthened, he added, "Jackson—you must save your father, the senator, your woman, and my unborn great-grandson. Then you must come get my body…"

Jokes and silliness were washed away by sadness and love. Jack said, "Grandpa, I love you. Tell me, will I succeed?"

Frank Flashhardt gazed at Jack's face, as though he was trying to memorize it. He slowly looked up. "I summon my Volva, now Odin's seeress." He faded away and was replaced by a tall Nordic-looking woman dressed in a long medieval-looking white robe. She sang in a harsh, wailing voice:

Jormungard—the dragon serpent
Spews venom,
The earth splashed with his poison.
But storm will conceal.
Sons of sand approach from the south,
Spreading fire and mayhem.
Your worlds will burn,
If you fail, you will die.

The apparition faded, disappeared—still screaming soundless words.

Chapter 84

Rising from the hard-packed dirt floor of the small shed, Talking Dog opened the door, inhaled fresh air in the darkening landscape. The old Brule chief beckoned Jack to step outside.

The rain, which had faded away in Jack's mind, still drummed on the metal roof, continued to pound outside. He looked at Talking Dog. "Well, she was cheery, wasn't she?" "So, it was successful?"

"Either that or I gotta stop eating those peanut butter and anchovy sandwiches before bed. Don't you recall what happened?"

"I saw nothing, said naught. This was your Spirit Summons, not mine.

It took place in your mind, not mine." The old man gazed into Jack's eyes.

"More important, now I see hard flint in your eyes."

"Well, yeah! But that last Viking-type broad was all, like, gloom and doom."

"Perhaps she meant to flush fear from your mind."

Jack clasped the old man's hand. "Don't sweat it, Chief. Thanks." He checked the time: just minutes after 2300 hours—little time had really passed. Another mystery. He thought of his grandfather again, shuddered. Wondered how he could have conjured such images.

His cell vibrated—he had switched it to silent mode earlier: it was Mick Nakamura. "Hey, buddy, Billy called me. You got something goin'?"

"I'm pretty sure I have *Saladin's Fist*, Mick. Can you bring your team?" The cell went dead.

Seconds later it vibrated. "Jack, the unit scrambled. They got a report *Saladin's Fist* started a fire in Mogollon Rim high country, down at the Arizona-New Mexico border. The Savage took the team. I'm in Colorado Springs, just picking up a Super Cobra gunship for fire support."

Jack gripped the cell so hard he was afraid he would crush it. "Where'd the Intel come from?"

"*Saladin's Fist* claimed credit for the fires."

"It's a smokescreen, Mick. I talked to Mara Bhutto on her cell. She told me *Saladin's Fist* was going after my family in Montana. We came up and one of the ranch hands said a group attacked last night. Kidnapped my dad and the senator…"

"Holy shit!" Mick's voice rose with excitement.

"Jack, it's probly about five hundred miles. If I leave now, I can make it in 'bout three hours, depending on winds aloft, plus a fuel stop in… Cheyenne. I'm on my way. Tell me where to go."

Jack gave Mick instructions and directions from Red Lodge. Turned to Talking Dog. "Enough visions. Time to get on with my to-do list: I need to get in, take a look, assess the situation."

Talking Dog watched a lone black and white magpie. Illuminated by lightning flashes, the bird beat its way through the rains and winds, disappeared in the night sky. "When you were young, you and Billy used to practice your skills. Sneaking up on me and the other cowhands. Pounding on the walls of line shacks, middle of the night, scaring the crap out of us. Now's the time to utilize those talents again."

Talking Dog's mention of his brother and their childhood friendship prompted him to ask, "When we were small, why weren't we told we were brothers?"

The old man stared across the night-darkened meadow, avoided Jack's eyes, shifted from one foot to the other. "Billy's mama. She always hated Whites."

"Then how'd she get pregnant by Dad if she hated—?"

"Life is full of irony and mystery. He was lonely, hurt by the loss of your mama, maybe he caught her in a weak moment, either for him or for her. But she told no one who Billy's father was until her deathbed, over ten years ago. I always suspected. But only then did we learn the truth." He looked at Jack, added, "But now it's good again. I mean between you and my grandson, Billy. You are family."

Jack thought of his brother. The old man was right—it was good between the two. He completely trusted Billy, save the Oxycontin addiction. It was a good feeling when working in a world of lies, distrust and denial. Jack patted the Dragon God's Khyber knife on his belt, checked the M-16, stepped into the downpour towards the ranch center.

He left the meadow, entered the pines. There was very little undergrowth; the trees were mostly mature. Scattered groves of smaller sixto ten-foot trees, hand-planted over the years, provided cover. As he walked, he mentally reviewed the layout of the buildings surrounding the house: all were laid out like the four endpoints on a cross. At the top, to the north, was the large two-story house. The big barn was one hundred yards to the south, the smaller granary fifty yards to the west, and the tractor shed fifty yards to the east.

He cautiously crept into the cleared, mowed area that contained the outbuildings and the house. An old split-rail fence overgrown with weeds and brush that served as cover for wild pheasant flocks crossed the meadow and terminated on the blank sidewall of the granary.

Jack placed the M-16 in a fire-created cleft of a large cottonwood tree where he had hidden secret treasures as a child. The irony and danger of the present circumstances flashed through his mind as he fed a round into his M-9, patted the long Dragon God knife for reassurance. He cautiously crawled to the fence, the drenched grass cold on his lower legs, then moved along the three-foot-high brush line growing on its path until he finally reached the granary.

There were two entrances: one was a shuttered opening just under the eave of the one-story frame shed that served as an inlet for grain unloaded from harvest machinery—it was four feet square; the other opening was a sliding shed door at the end of the fifty-foot-long building. Jack stumbled on an old two-by-eight board lying next to the shed. He listened and watched, his heart beating in his ears. Saw no movement, leaned it against the wall, crawled up to the shutters. Rain pounded on the metal pitched roof. He carefully opened a shutter and dropped into the pile of grain inside. Noise of the rain blasting off the roof was almost deafening. Felt small animals scamper over his feet: remembered the rats or mice that he and Billy had chased as children. Barely audible hiss from one of the many feral cats on the ranch.

Silently waded across the mound of grain until he topped the last crest and saw the red embers of a cigarette. A man was leaning against the doorway, watching the landscape in front of the granary.

Jack watched the guy smoke his cigarette, throw the butt into the rainy darkness, turn and piss on the stored grain, then twist back to the opening. The watcher was alone.

Jack skied down the grain slope; rain drumming on the metal roof drowned out the noise of his skidding approach.

Rose behind the man, held the big knife in the palm of his hand, swung and slammed the lookout in the back of the head. The stunned man gasped, fell to his knees, looked up at Jack. He opened his mouth to cry out. Jack grabbed a handful of grain, threw it into the man's mouth. Hesitated, thought about his dad, wounded, maybe dying in the house. Stabbed the choking man in the center of his chest, just below his ribs.

The man's eyes bulged, he sighed, fell on his face. With reflexive instincts, the young man wrapped his arms around Jack's legs, held on like a small child grabbing a parent's legs. Noticed the man had dark hair: not one of the *Fist* guys.

"Fuck you, punk!" The words exploded out of his innermost core. He kicked the man's arms away, glanced outside. Saw it was completely dark. He pulled the body to the piled grain, kicked grain over the body until it disappeared.

Stepped into the rain, circled around to the backside of the one hundred twenty-foot-long, two-story barn. Moved along a pipe corral; a cluster of horses at the far end, heads bowed to the rain, didn't see him. He hoped the outside dogs were curled up under a building, hiding from the storm. Slipped in through an access door on the side of the barn near the south end. No animals in the barn, it was mainly used for storage of equipment. The second floor hayloft held hay used to sustain cattle during heavy winters when the prairie was inundated with snow. His grandfather had built the huge barn for a dairy but had given up the enterprise after a few years of low butterfat prices.

A 1929 Pierce Arrow limo on blocks—his dad's restoration project of his great-granddad's laid-aside vehicle. He paused behind it and watched: no movement, but he heard a whining animal. He tracked to the sound—a dog lying in a stall, just past the tack room. He petted the dog—it flinched, ran his fingers over its body. Shot in the midsection, the dog licked his face when he leaned close. Wet dog smell overlain with blood and feces odor. Wished he could do something, patted the dog, leaned closer and hugged the moaning dog's head to his chest. Rose and left the stall, almost fell over his favorite dog, Bullet.

The big animal whined, jumped up and licked his face.

Jack hugged the Bernese Mountain-Rottweiler-mix brute, whispered, "I know, pal. Your lady's hurt. I'll get her fixed up as soon as I can. Bad men here, be quiet."

The huge black dog whined again, settled to the floor, looked up at his master.

Finding no one on the first level, he quietly climbed the ladder to the hayloft. Bullet started to follow, but he pushed him back. Rain still pounded, drowned out his own accelerated heart rate. He crept along the side of the second floor hayloft, a gigantic expanse with a high roof arching into darkness, its atmosphere filled with the scent of straw.

A man at the end of the barn where hay was loaded into the structure: smoking, staring into the dark yard. Beside him, a long-barreled rifle on a bipod. A strong smell of stale smoke from the earlier fire Talking Dog had mentioned.

No easy approach. He considered shooting the man, wondered whether the sound would carry to the house, wished he was carrying the Heckler with its screw-on silencer as a back-up weapon. The sound of crackling thunder answered his question.

Crept closer. The man sat down, well back from the opening, which was fifteen feet wide and twenty-five feet tall, to avoid the rain. Jack stopped ten paces from the man, whose outline was barely visible when lightning flashed. Guy had blond hair that glowed white in the lightning. For the first time, he did not feel terrible about killing a man. The guy had brought himself to the ranch from the other side of the world. Sealed his fate. *Bastard probably shot the dog, left her for dead.*

Jack squeezed the pistol grip, fingered the trigger, waited: lightening flashed, thunder immediately rumbled, then crashed; he shot the man twice in the torso, walked over, didn't bother feeling the guy's pulse after looking at the wounds. Pulled the body into the hay, covered it with loose straw, dug shells out of his pocket, ejected the mag and refilled it. Checked out the machine gun: it didn't look like a military fifty caliber. It resembled an oversized M-4 with short banana clip and an oversized flash suppressor. A box of loaded clips rested next to the bipod that supported the heavy barrel. When lightning flashed, he looked closer: he quickly realized it was a Barrett XM-109, a 25mm high-power rifle. He wondered where the terrorists had gotten their hands on the gun that was capable of reaching out to 2500 meters, and could penetrate 40 millimeters of armour plating.

He crawled back down the ladder. Bullet was waiting, nuzzled him. "Stay," he ordered. Moved to the back of the barn: past the wounded dog's stall, past the old car, outside. Circled around to a small grove of spruce pines; moved through the trees to the lilac bush hedge that grew on three sides of the house. Caught a hint of lilac blooms when he ducked under a bough. Saw two men sitting under an old wagon, huddled against the downpour.

The two-story log and rock house had a covered porch that stretched across the entire front of the structure, which was one hundred feet long. Lights gleamed through all the ten windows across the front, from the kitchen, and from two double-hung windows upstairs. The security room on the second floor also showed faint lights.

Saw four men sitting on chairs, a swing, and the deck. Like the dead guards, he noticed these men were smoking ever-present cigarettes.

Ghosted through the lilacs, around to the side of the house. Heard two more men talking nearby, their voices almost drowned out by the rain. Shivered as he crawled across the water-soaked lawn—it was flooded by the downpour—icy water was about an inch deep. Worked through a prickly rose bush, rose to a windowsill, looked into a dark room. Heard a shout from the direction of the barn. Man kept yelling in an eerie singsong voice. The dog barked— a shot rang out. More frenzied barking. He thought of the white Caspian tiger he had befriended in Asia, wished Tigger was with him; sent his dog, Bullet, a prayer.

Pounding feet left the porch. He sent the dog another good luck wish, raised the window, lifted himself into the pantry, lowered the window. Listened to silence, interrupted by water dripping, splashing on the wood floor. He waited until the drips ended. Now only his heart pounding, his breath rasping.

Crossed to the door, peered into the kitchen—empty. People had left a mess. Cups and leftover sandwich clutter on the granite counter. Garbage thrown on the floor. Thought for a moment of the trash he had crawled through in the long-ago road ambush on the KKH in Pakistan.

He crossed, peeked into the huge living room; four young Arablooking guys sitting on the stairs, weapons in their laps, resting against walls, oak balusters. Two more men at the top of stairs, not alert. Also wearing American-style clothing. No ragheads or robes but the guys looked Middle Eastern. Weird to see strangers lolling around inside the house.

No way past without a major conflict. Wished he could see Dad, Penel. Longed to somehow get upstairs. Ducked back in the kitchen, found paper and pen in a drawer, wrote down a limerick that had echoed repeatedly in his mind on his approach:

Hey Mara, sweet Mara
You're just a louse,
Who's invaded my house.
Remember, Black Orchids
Don't grow in Montana.
Jack

He smiled at his childish ploy, looked around, left the note on the counter. Moved back to the pantry. Went out the window, looked up at the second floor windows that were illuminated. The log wall was climbable, even in the wet rain. He crept to the back of the house, clambered up the interlocking log ends on the corner, waited for a crack of thunder, tensed and jumped to the wood rail of a balcony, gripped the wet wood with all the strength in his climber's fingers. Stepped through a French door into an empty bedroom. He carefully opened the door, looked into the hallway.

Two guards standing in the hall, their heads together, whispering—no way to sneak up on them. Jack retreated to the balcony, stepped outside, stood on the rain-slicked rail and climbed onto the wood shake roof.

The roof shingles were large, hand-hewn slabs of cedar. He blessed the men who had built the solid roof a century earlier as he crawled across to a spot over the security room's balcony. He gripped the eave, did a slowmotion somersault, hung inches above the deck. Silently dropped.

Peered into the small window in the door, saw Dad lying on a bench, the senator and Penel sitting in chairs next to him. No one else in the room, a heavy beam barring the door. It would take axes, a chainsaw, or a fire, to get through the substantial door to the security room, an architectural design feature common to Montana houses built in the Nineteenth Century.

Opened the balcony door, stepped inside. Penel saw him first, gasped with fear. The senator swung around, also did not recognize Jack, probably because his cammo paint, streaked and blotchy—and partially washed away by the rain—made him look like a Black Lagoon monster.

As the senator moved forward in a protective maneuver, he said, "It's me, Jack."

Penel rose, hurried across the room and hugged him. "Thank you!" she exclaimed in a low voice. "Oh, Dragon God! Thank you, Jack." Her arms squeezed tight.

"Welcome to America. You didn't tell me you had travel plans."

She looked into his eyes. "I'm pregnant, Jack. You said you wanted a baby born in America. I came."

Jack didn't know what to say. He hugged her, asked, "How'd you get out of Shangri-La?"

"We decided to save the tunnel to Tajikistan. I came out that way, then overland to the Karakoram Highway."

"Amazing!" Jack crossed to the bed. "Hey, Senator—I've got a team, more coming. We're gonna get you guys outta here."

Senator Jensen clasped his hand, whispered, "We pulled Bill here when attackers got in the house, can't move him again. He needs a medevac."

"Buncha Arab-looking types, Senator. Probly snuck in from Mexico. Next time you vote on border security, remember." He turned to his father. "Hey, Dad. Can't you keep out of trouble?" Jack felt a surge of love and concern as he looked at his father's unusually pale face, tried to hide it.

Bill looked up at his son, a mirror image of himself twenty five years earlier. He smiled weakly. "Hey, thanks for coming… careful."

"Don't worry, Dad. I'll take care of these assholes. Billy an' I'll finish the job."

Bill was obviously unfit for travel. A makeshift bandage below his right ribcage, stained with blood.

Leaned forward, sniffed the wound: a faint odor of feces. "Your stomach-lining or intestine is breached—not bad but you need to get to a hospital immediately. Infection could…"

"He'll be fine," the senator hopefully reassured. "Listen, Jack. Amidst this mess, I have great news."

Jack looked at the senator. The man was unshaven, his hair in disarray, but he had the level gaze of a man who could lead in a crisis. He was tall— over six feet—had a runner's thin body, a slightly stooped carriage.

"The general that was holding up any consideration of your pardons has left the Army, dishonored. The Commandant has said—" "Later, Senator," Jack interrupted.

"Chinese government," the senator continued, "came and picked up the emeralds."

Jack stared at the man, turned to his dad. The man's words didn't mean much at the moment. Survival was a much more important issue. Shrugged off his small backpack, retrieved the first

406

aid kit. Pulled out a clear-plastic, half-liter container shaped like a liquid soap bottle. He ripped off the plastic wrapper, jabbed the catheter in his dad's arm, undid a screw clamp, handed the bottle to the senator. He pulled out a second bottle and placed it on the floor. "Doesn't look like he needs a painkiller. If he does, there's something in the pack. Give him the second bottle as soon as the first is finished. I'll be back with help."

"Jack, the tarn water is in the icebox in the kitchen," Penel said. "I had no time to fetch it and bring it to this room of safety. You must retrieve the water to save your father. If you give him the waters, he will be restored. Remember, the waters have healing powers. For now and forever."

"Sounds good," Jack placated her. "Put it on my to-do list. That and a medevac helicopter and we'll get him fixed up."

"Call the Sheriff," the senator instructed. "The phone lines're done, my cell's not working."

Jack looked at Penel, debated taking her, decided it was too risky getting her down to the ground, through the attackers. "I've got a team nearby, and soldiers on the way. I just wanted to check the place out. We'll be back in short order." He pulled a cammo stick out of his pocket, reapplied greasy paint.

Hugged Penel, whispered, "It's almost 0100 hours. I'll be back with help. Stay here. They want me, so you guys'll be safe as long as you're serving as bait. But Dad needs medical attention. Real soon."

"The tarn water," Penel grabbed his arm and urged. "It'll save your father."

"Yeah, right," Jack said, his mind on his escape route.

He stepped into the rain, climbed over the rail, hung by his fingers, dropped to the ground nine feet below. It was a soft landing, heavy thunder drowned out the splash. He retreated to the lilac hedge, deeply inhaled the fresh scent of the flowers to flush the odor of blood in his nostrils.

Bullet emerged from the bushes, frightened Jack when he rammed his head into Jack's midsection.

"Hey, big guy," Jack whispered. "Let's go."

407

The man and dog darted from grove to grove, reached the forest and ran. Jack prayed over and over, "Help Dad hang in there. Please, God." A lightning flash, thought he saw a huge figure duck behind a rock, a hundred meters away, disappear. He stared for an endless minute, saw no movement.

Knew the terrain: every tree, every bush, every obstacle—endlessly crawled over, played over, scampered over as a youth. He had never dreamed events would come to this in his own backyard.

Ran through the rain-filled darkness, his path illuminated by lightning strikes. A shout behind him—a shot rang out! Someone had noticed his movement during a lightning flash. He dodged around a big pine, ran harder, the dog bounding alongside, until he reached his rifle's hiding place.

Ten minutes later, he checked out the shed, saw no movement. Approached from the rear, pistol in one hand, rifle in the other. Edged around the side, turned his maglite on to its lowest setting, saw Talking Dog.

"Jesus Christ!" the old man exclaimed. "You're like a ghost."

Jack sank to the dirt floor, realized he was exhausted. He fumbled in a pocket, pulled out a candy bar, ate: it was a Baby Ruth—the chocolate and nuts tasted great. Bullet sat next to him, looked up at Talking Dog, whined. Billy barged into the shed doorway, put down the equipment and weapons duffle bag. When he saw the chief, he strode forward and fiercely hugged the old man. "Grandfather! It is good to see you."

The Chief smiled hugely. "Howling Dog, I have heard many good things about you as a warrior."

Abashed, Billy leaned over and patted Bullet. The dog accepted the affection as his due.

Just then, Tucson and Zhang crowded behind him. Billy turned to his brother. "What's the deal? What's goin' on?"

"Dad's hurt. There's about five thousand fucking Mujs at the house. Well, maybe a little less than ten. I took out two. We need to take the rest out, get Dad to a hospital. Dad, Penel an' the Senator're holed up in the security room upstairs."

Tucson, who was stroking the big dog, said, "Let's call the police and the Bureau."

Suddenly infuriated, Jack looked at her. "Tucson, you're nothing but a dumb ass FBI broad! You think we want a bunch of weekend warrior swat teams charging the house? That's our dad in there. Just shut up while we figure out what to do."

Tucson drew in breath, heard and understood the fear in Jack's voice, decided not to argue. Zhang sat on the floor, patted Bullet, waited in silence. The dog crowded against her, nervously whined at the tension in the air.

Jack took a deep breath, calmed his voice. "Talking Dog says there are a bunch of ragheads, less the two I took out on my recon. So there's a few less—luckily, they're a cluster fuck waiting to happen." "Sounds doable, if that's the case," Billy agreed.

"But I think *SD* is here," Jack said.

"Oh, no!" Zhang involuntarily exclaimed. "How would they know— we got rid of the electronic trace."

Jack looked at her—he couldn't see her face—too dark. "Somebody tipped them off. You?"

"I couldn't have, even if I wanted to—I haven't been alone. But why would I? They want to kill me."

"She's right, Flashy," Billy pointed at Tucson. "Has to be you."

Tucson stepped back. "Me! I don't know anything about the Second Department. Or how to get a hold of them. Nor do I have a reason." She added, "What makes you think Chinese agents are here?"

"There's only a couple of other potential suspects," Jack said.

"Talking Dog saw a big man—a very big man, and so did I."

"Let's forget about it 'til later." He paused, listened to the rain pound on the metal roof. "Mick won't be able to get in here by air, but this storm also gives us good cover. The bad guys probably discovered my recon, but I don't give a shit about that."

"If you killed two men under their noses," Talking Dog declared, "You've already put fear in their hearts."

Jack thought about what his dream grandfather had advised: *Instill fear and trembling. Then strike with overwhelming force. Shock your enemy.* Glanced at his watch: almost 0200 hours.

"We need to finish this now. First light should be around 0400. We need darkness to be successful. We only have two hours." "So what's the plan?" Billy asked.

"There's a 25 millimeter gun in the barn hayloft. It covers the whole yard, flanks of the house. I took out the gunner but they prob'ly will replace him."

"Why didn't you destroy the gun?" Tucson asked.

"Two reasons. We now know where it is. So all we have to do is take out whoever's with it. Prob'ly two guys. We need the gun for when we attack the house."

"So how do we take the shooters out?" Billy asked. "They've probably blocked off the access ladder to the hayloft."

"Remember when we were kids?" Jack asked. "When we were still pals? We used to go up the barn roof, into the ridge cupola, and capture baby pigeons for pets? One of us'd creep along the hay-loading trac system that runs along the inside of the roof ridge beam, go from nest to nest, looking for the best pigeons? That's how you'll do it."

"Holy shit, man! I was a stupid kid!"

"Cross the roof in this rain? What's a cupola?" Tucson asked.

Jack ignored her question. "Don't worry, Billy. Piece of cake: but it's too dark to shoot them from a distance, so you'll have to creep along the trac until you're right over the gun position. Then lower yourself on the hay-loading rope, take out whoever's there."

Billy grimaced. "And how do I get to the cupola in the middle of a huge rainstorm without falling off the roof?"

"Don't worry, bro—remember? There's a ladder on the west side, of the barn. Built against the wall. For roof access."

"Crawling on the roof," Billy moaned. "Easy for you to say— you know I hate heights!"

"This from a guy who's climbed mountains over 20,000 feet high in the Hindu Kush. Quit whining."

"And I haven't operated a twenty-five since Infantry Training Regiment at Camp Pendleton."

"Don't sweat it. You're a natural-born gunner. You'll figure it out." He glanced at Talking Dog. "Chief, will you help us?"

"Of course," the old man responded doubtfully. "But what'll you have me do? I'm not much of a climber."

"I want you to hit the power cut-off at the meter box on the west side of the house. The box is near the back of the house. There were men on the porch earlier, so you'll have to make a very careful approach. Do you know where it is?"

"I think so," the old man said, "But it's very dark."

"We have three NVGs—night vision goggles. I'll give you one. When Billy fires the first round, you hit the power. The 25 mike mike is loud— you can't miss it. Can you do these things, Chief?"

"Yes," the old man's voice was steady. "I am proud that you have confidence in me."

"You were a great warrior, Grandfather," Billy said. "We know how brave you are."

"Chief," Jack cautioned. "Remember, my call sign'll be Red Ryder. And we're not counting coup. Just shoot to kill like they were vermin, cockroaches. There's no honor fighting these cowards. They have no value. They'd shoot us in the back, torture an' kill us if they could. Treat em' like scum. Don't hesitate or give them any opening or any quarter. D'you understand? Promise?"

The old man nodded his head, added, "Yes, Jack. I'll do as you wish."

Jack glanced at Tucson and Zhang. "Luckily, we have two tough women, if you two're willing to help."

"This sounds very dangerous," Tucson complained. But she lifted her M-16, checked the load.

"Not as bad as it sounds," Jack responded. "Billy, post guard while I tell Zhang and Tucson what to do."

Billy stepped outside, Jack shut the shed door, aimed his maglite at the dirt floor, quickly sketched a layout of the ranch buildings. The rain on the shed roof was even louder with the door closed. Jack mentally blessed the Draco storm.

Jack pointed at the granary image. "Ladies, your station is here. I'll go with you, make sure there's no one in there. After Billy takes out the guy in the hayloft, and opens fire on the house, you'll aim to the front of the house, shoot out the first floor windows and any targets of opportunity with the M16s. Your go signal will be when Billy puts a round through the front door." He pulled a rifle out of the weapons bag, handed it to Zhang. "Check it out, make sure it's loaded. Make sure you know where the safety is. Where the selector is, but don't use autofire. We need accuracy and a constant level of suppressive fire."

He looked up at his brother. "Of course, once Billy has the twenty-five under control, he'll work the front door and windows, as well. The big gun might even go through the log walls." "What'll you do?" Zhang asked.

"I'm going up the sidewall, into the second floor security room, then attack down the hall, down the stairs. I still have a couple of flash-bangs from Arrowhead. I wish this time they were real grenades. When you see the flash-bangs go off, come to the house."

Jack looked up at the three, each in turn. "Timing on this is everything. Billy's the key."

"What if he fails?" Zhang asked.

"We can't suppress the big gun. If Billy doesn't take it out, we fail. Maybe one of you should go with him as a back-up."

"I'm not crawling on a roof in the rain," Tucson protested.

"Nor am I," Zhang echoed. "In fact, I'm not doing any of it."

Jack looked at her defiant face. Wondered if she was a threat to their plans. "Okay, Zhang, you've been through a lot. Good and bad. You're one tough lady. You hang here. We'll come get you when Mara and her gang are put for."

Billy stepped inside. "Don't worry," he said.

"No way I'm screwin' up. And I'm dry on the H."

Jack looked at Tucson, thought of the Arrowhead fracas, Omar lying near-dead in a sleazy motel room. "Tucson, we wouldn't be here if it wasn't for your help. You've been a great friend, and you're a true warrior. But you don't have to do this. It's Billy's and my responsibility."

She took his hand. "Don't worry, Jack. I'm in to the end."

He smiled, grasped her forearm, kissed her cheek. "We're not failing this time. No matter what. It'll all work. If we hit our marks, they won't know what clobbered them. It'll be Sayonara, *Saladin's Fist*, no mas, no mas."

He glanced at his watch: 0215. "Not much time, let's head out. Remember, Billy signals the attack with the 25 mike mike. We have to be in place by then."

They left the shed, stepped into the continuing downpour, moved out in single file, the dog in the lead. Jack looked back a minute later, lightning flashed, he saw Zhang watch, then hurry to catch up. He wondered what she was up to as she followed in trace. Prayed she wasn't set on betraying them.

At the edge of the ranch house meadow, Talking Dog left the others and moved along the tree line, headed for the house.

The others found the old fenceline and moved through the complete darkness to the granary, which suddenly loomed before them. Bullet moved to the shed door, whined. Jack crept around to the doorway, waited, crawled in and secured the empty shed. He went back around the corner, whispered to Zhang, "What's the deal?"

"I remembered how much I hate Mara Bhutto," Zhang whispered. "What she did to me in Kabul last year. I want to see her finished. She's evil. I want to finish her. I'm with you all the way."

Billy was already gone. Jack sent a prayer after his brother, then said good luck to the two women, headed for the house, Bullet at his side. He hoped Zhang was playing straight, wished he had warned Tucson to watch her back.

He passed the corrals; the horses were not visible until lightning flashed—they were still huddled in a downwind corner. He crawled the last fifty yards, hit the lilac bushes on the west side of the house, whispered to the big dog, "Stay, Bullet." The big dog nuzzled him, nervous about intruders on his territory, begging for a reassuring pat.

Jack inched across the cold, rain-splattered lawn on his hands and knees, turned left at the edge of the house, followed waist-high rose bushes. At the rear of the house, he tightened the slings on the two 12-gauge Benelli Tacticals and the laser gun, checked his M-9, the Casull, and the Khyber knife, climbed the interlocking log ends to the eave. He carefully grabbed the two by twelve fascia board, hung from it, fought the extra weight of all the weapons, pulled himself up and onto the roof.

Crept across the rain-slickened cedar shingles, thought of Billy, sent him a prayer. Hoped he really was off the Oxycontin. Thought of Penel below him, wondered what he was going to do with her. *Tucson in the granary. Beautiful as Penel, but FBI—a career fibbie, no doubt. A law-babe for a wife? Never happen. Too crazy a lifestyle.*

A baby. What a change! But a child could be the most normalizing thing in the world. Marriage to Penel? She's semi-crazed. Too powerful, too headstrong—not a suburban soccer mom, marrying-type.

Above the security room, he paused, looked at the landscape, felt a surge of confidence: the plan was good—it should work.

Lightning flashes revealed big trees whipping in the wind; low-lying clouds scudded past, making the sheds and the barn appear and disappear like flickering ghosts. He peered at the barn roof, but could see little across the one hundred yard expanse. Hoped he wasn't visible from the hayloft during lightning flashes.

Adjusted the weapon slings, grabbed the fascia, slowly lowered himself to the balcony, opened the door.

Penel was asleep, senator the same. Dad raised his head, gazed at his son. Jack crossed the wood floor, grabbed his dad's hand.

"I love you, son," Dad mouthed the words, too weak to talk. He looked bad, his face was ashen. Jack couldn't remember his dad ever being ill. He had always been, strong, always healthy.

"Me too, Dad. Now we're gonna get you out of here. Please, hang in there." He took the two shotguns off his shoulders, looked to make sure rounds were in the chambers. Checked the safeties.

Penel woke, started at the sight of him, rose and hugged him.

"Will thou kill the cowardly scum? Can I help send them to their 72 whores of Heaven?"

"Thanks, Penelope. Just stay here and guard this door." Jack looked at his father, who was faintly smiling. He felt a surge of love. "Hang in, Dad. My kid needs a grandpa."

He crossed to the door, sat on the floor and waited. Gave Penel the Casull.

Penel held the big revolver in two hands, looked up at Jack.

"Face your target squarely," he instructed. "Just hold it straight out with both hands, Penel. Pull the trigger. Wherever you look, you'll hit."

He checked his watch. Figured the time was almost at hand, lifted the security bar—a four by six inch oak piece. Silently rested it against the wall, removed the Benelli magazines, nervously checked again to make sure they were fully loaded. Pushed the safeties to the off position, told Penel to be ready to fling the door open.

She stood at the ready. Jack and his dad locked eyes. Dad looked drained of color, all-white hair messed up, faint smile did not waver. He slowly raised a fist and gestured with a thumb up. Jack felt another surge of love for his father. Wished for a moment they were riding to a high camp, eager to catch and fry fresh cutthroat trout over the coals of a mountain cedar campfire.

The crash of a large bullet echoed through the house! Glass shattered when the shell hit it. *Billy did it!*

Shouts from downstairs, cries in a foreign language. Thuds of feet running. Another smashing shot, then numerous windows blew in as the women targeted the house. A man screamed—a lucky shot.

Stepped into the hallway. Lights still on. At the end of the hall, two men crouching, leaning over the rail, looking below. Muscle memory took over—no pause for a cause—he leveled the shotguns, fired two doubleought shots. Clouds of buckshot hit the men in their backs, shoved them through the rails like windswept feathers. Crashed to the floor twelve feet below amid falling balusters and debris. Screams, shouts rang through the house.

Moved along the wall, a man rushed up to the top of the stairs. Knocked the guy over with a double Benelli blast. Ducked into a door alcove.

A sofa on the landing at the top of the stairs. Jack moved forward, put a shoulder against it and pushed until it slid past the blown away railing. It toppled through the air, crashed to the first floor, flattening two men helping the moaning shotgun victims. *Come on, Talking Dog, douse the lights.*

Ran down the steps on the west end of the huge living/dining room— fifty feet end to end—emptied the shotguns from the hip, fired as fast as he could in all directions, saw no targets. Hit the first floor. Another round through the entry door, into the back wall. Shots from the granary knocked out more window panes.

Dropped the empty shotguns, pulled the M-9 and the long knife. Fired the pistol into two men who stumbled around the corner. Both dropped or hid. Tang of gunsmoke, ears ringing.

A tall, chisel-faced blond man appeared in the doorway from the kitchen wildly firing an automatic weapon.

The lights went out.

Chapter 85

In a first floor bedroom: Bronze-skinned Mara Bhutto, commanding the ragged remainder of *Saladin's Fist* supplemented by the young men she had collected in Orange County from a list supplied by a Muslim cleric. She had been shocked to learn there were 200,000 Muslims living in the county— woke depressed at the thought of another day sitting in Montana, isolated, without support. She wished for the hundredth time that she could give up, get rid of the stupid, demented *Fist*, go home to Pakistan.

Mara was leaning over to pick underwear out of the clean clothes from the wash she had done the night before. She grabbed the garment on top, pulled it over her long legs. She wondered when Jack Flashhardt was going to strike. She thought of the limerick he had left for her: *Mara, sweet Mara, you're just a louse.*

He was right—he felt like a louse. He had always been good to her. He had only repaid her when she had tried to injure or kill him. On a sudden impulse, she decided to fire the house and decamp. The fate of the people in the locked room was not her concern. Then she remembered this was the third time she had decided to burn the house, but the constant downpour had dissuaded her each time. Storms and rain had dogged her and thwarted her at every step in America. *Will it ever stop raining?*

She finished dressing; her ponderous thoughts were interrupted: gunfire pounded through the front door and smashed through the windows! The crashing fire smashed the quiet of the early morning. She dove under her bed. Rolled onto her back, pulled her boots on, crawled out of the room.

A crunching noise in the living room, screams sounded. More loud concussions paralyzed her with fear. Forced herself to act: ran along a back hall to the kitchen.

The lights went out.

In the hayloft: Billy Howling Dog peered through his NVGs, aimed the Barrett rifle, growled out loud, "Wish I had a TOW missile." Squeezed the trigger, punched another round into the front door opening that had been left ajar by the second man he had shot.

Smiled at the thought of shooting at the Flashhardt home, thought to himself, *Dad 'ud whack me. Mom, the white man hater, 'ud probly cheer.* He shifted his aim, shot through each of the broken front windows. Wondered again what his mother would think if she could see him firing on her long-ago white lover's house.

Little Willow had been a hard woman, shrill and angry. Had gotten fat over the years, never cut her straight black hair. But she had loved and protected Billy, especially from scornful white society.

Rolled on his back, reached for the baggy containing the 40mg Oxycontins. Remembered his promise to his brother, stayed his hand, ached for the soothing relief.

At the granary: "Let's go," Tucson yelled to Zhang Poon t'ang. "Let's go help Jack."

"He didn't say attack the house. He said shoot out the windows. Maintain suppressing fire."

"He may need help," Tucson yelled. "Stay if you want. I'm going." She ran into the darkness, stumbled, fell sprawling in the rain-soaked mud. Kept her barrel high, the stock bounced on the ground, muck splashed in her face.

Zhang swore in Chinese and followed at a slower, more careful pace.

In the living room: Jack jumped to the side, retreated, pushed his NVGs over his eyes. Everything became visible with a green tint. The man in the doorway was gone. Jack knelt, pulled a loaded magazine out of his cargo pocket, slid it into the M-9, quietly chambered a round in the Beretta.

Heard a shot outside the rear of the house, the crack of a carbine. Wished Talking Dog good fortune. A scrape behind the fallen sofa, he pulled the Khyber knife, inched over the legs of a silenced man, then another, still wheezing for breath. From both a horrendous smell radiated. A sound behind him, someone stumbled over his legs. He whirled, slashed the man across the shins.

Guy howled, fell forward. Jack jabbed upward, pierced the man's crotch, yanked the knife out. The guy screamed, fell away.

Rolled, writhed across the floor. Jack looked in all directions: no movement.

Silence stretched: only his breath, his heart pounding in his ears. Felt tendrils of fatigue, mentally shoved then aside. His NVGs blinked twice, faded away. Dead batteries. He muttered a curse, pulled the goggles off his head, threw them across the room.

A clatter. A whispered exclamation. Two shots—the flares of gunfire blinding.

At a front window: a tinkle of glass, thuds on the floor, scratching claws—Bullet. A man fired at the dog. Bullet smelled Jack, silently joined him.

Jack sighted, waited. When the man shot blindly, he aimed the M-9 into the flash, fired, rolled away. Guy yelled, two shots lanced through Jack's last position.

He hugged Bullet, saw a flickering light from the hallway that led to the kitchen. The big dog suddenly scrabbled across the wood plank floor, jumped over the leather sofa, crashed into a man hiding behind the furniture. Snarls, frenzied barking, roars, screams of pain.

Jack crawled around an armchair, bumped into a man crawling the opposite direction. The two struggled, Jack shot and missed the guy with the last round in the Beretta, then cut him in the arm with the long knife. Guy scrambled away, tried to crawl on hands and knees. Jack stabbed, pinned the guy's lower leg to the floor. Guy arched up and a 25mm bullet hit him in the chest, jerked him away like a rag doll on a string. Jack barely hung onto the knife.

The flickering light coming from the kitchen hallway was brighter now —someone had obviously started a fire in the kitchen.

Another shot at the rear of the house. Sounded like the .30-30 carbine again. Talking Dog still doing his thing.

"American!" A guy—foreign accent. Left of the kitchen hallway.

Dim light glinting on the wood floors from the fire. Jack scrambled behind the fallen sofa, peered around the end. A man emerged from the hazy kitchen door, leveled his rifle. "American, let us end this. Why don't you give up?"

Jack threw the empty M-9 towards the questioner. Felt around for a weapon with his free hand, found nothing. Fear mounted, he gripped the knife tighter, backed behind the sofa he had sat in so many nights with his father, reading, listening to family stories. Wished he was a kid again, safe in his dad's arms. Heard footsteps approaching in the dark. Despair rose when he realized the sofa would offer no protection. He stiffened, waited for bullets to rip through him, started to scoot backwards.

A booming pistol shot from upstairs! The stalking terrorist crashed to the floor. Jack glanced up: Penel, the big Casull held in both hands. "Jack! There is fire. Smoke is coming into the safety room. And you must save the tarn waters. For your father."

"Penelope, thanks. You're… magnificent! There's a fan in the security room. Switch is by the door. That should keep the—" he suddenly remembered a fan wouldn't work without electricity. "Go to the balcony," he instructed. "Call outside for Talking Dog. Tell him Red Ryder says to hit the power."

A crash of broken glass, someone tumbled into the room from the front porch, fired two suppression shots in the air.

"Jack," Tucson called. "It's me."

"Tucson, maybe a bad guy by the fire. Mara somewhere—who knows? Only friendlies upstairs. Careful of Billy."

Someone slammed the kitchen door, the room darkened.

"Let us end this, American," a different foreign voice. "The Bhutto bitch got us into this. You've killed my brother, my friends. Sickened. Want stop. Want go home. I have two children, wife. Please, don't kill me."

"Throw your weapons across the room. Stand up, raise your hands above your head, walk outside," Jack ordered.

A clatter of a weapon. A man stood, stumbled across the littered room, stepped into the front doorway. A boom from Billy's big gun, the man screamed, flew back.

"Opps! Shit!" Jack exclaimed.

"American!" Another guy. "You liar—" sounded like he was in the library opening.

"Dude, that was an accident. I forgot about my guy in the hayloft. Just throw your weapon. You won't be hurt. Stay where you are until the lights come back on." He dug out his cell, switched it to its walky-talky mode, called Billy. No answer. Jack said anyway, "Billy, throw the Barrett out of the hayloft, come to the house before it gets light. Be careful, in case any stray SOBs are wandering around. It's over."

He glanced at the windows: the eastern sky carried the faintest gray signs of the upcoming dawn—the rain was still pounding, wind was still blowing, lightning still flashing. Looked at his watch: 0330 hours. Felt exhaustion sweeping through his body as adrenalin faded. Suddenly thought, *Where's Mara Bhutto?* Said aloud, "Hey, Mara's around, be careful. I'm going for the kitchen."

"Jack," Tucson answered, "don't expose yourself yet. The perp didn't throw out his piece."

"Got to—fire's growing. Dad an' the others're upstairs." He jumped up and ran, leaped and rolled into the hallway. Came up on his feet, threw himself forward and rolled again, smashed the kitchen door open with his shoulder. Scanned the room: empty. An intense fire on the floor, against a wall. Looked like grease had been used as a starter. It was burning hot but the log walls were barely smoldering. He dashed past the growing grease flames—now as high as his head—towards the pantry. Pulled out a fire extinguisher, sprayed and put out the flames, looked around.

Where the hell's Mara? A three-foot by four-foot double sash window over the sink was open. Yellow gingham curtains, illuminated by frenzied flashes of lightning, were blowing inward.

He opened the refrigerator, took out a *Ball* jar of water, thought, *I can't believe I'm buyin' into this crap.* He opened the bottle, drank about eight ounces, recapped it. A wonderful sensation swept through his body that made him feel rested, fresh. *Some minerals in the water, that's all.*

The lights came on. "Way to go, Talking Dog. About time," he mumbled to himself. Checked the hall, no one in sight, crept to the living room. Zhang and Tucson both inside, weapons trained on a muscular blond guy—guy resembled Bruno the Russian spy: but this was one of the *Fist*. His hands above his head.

Tucson maintained a surveillance of the library. "Come forward," she ordered. "You'll be safe."

"Where's Mara?" Jack asked.

"All dead," the *Fist* guy mumbled bitterly. "You killed all."

"Hey, I didn't invite you to this soiree," Jack shouted.

"You pricks invaded my home!" He hurried across the huge living room, noted a man lying across a bearskin, blood had matted part of the black fur.

"I can't bear this carnage," he added.

"I gotta see how Dad's doin'. Be right back."

He ran up the stairs, down the hall, knocked on the safety room door. "It's me, Jack," he called.

Penel threw the door open. Her eyes lit up when she saw Jack carrying the *Ball* jar.

"Tarn water!" She hugged him, took the water, hurried to Bill's side, held up his head and trickled water into his mouth.

Jack watched her confident movements, hoped, wished the tarn waters really were all she claimed. He certainly felt restored from his earlier state of exhaustion. Thought, *Some kind of powerful electrolytes in the mineral content of the water. Makes Gatorade taste and act like dishwater.*

Penel let Bill's head down on the jacket she had made into a pillow. Jack crossed to his dad and the senator, looked down at his father. Bill gave him a slow, feeble smile that did grow broader as Jack watched.

The senator clapped him on the back. "Amazing, son! You and your men were awesome."

"And women. But I gotta go wrap things up," Jack responded, swallowing a surge of pride. "Everything's cool—settled downstairs. Just about. Stay here. The balcony—call to Talking Dog. Tell him Jack… uh, Red Ryder says to come to the front room."

Slowly descended the stairs. Looked at the two women, mentally selected the fibbie. "Zhang, watch the guy. Tucson, let's go check on Billy.

Be careful—anything looks weird, we'll back out, reassess."

The two left by the front door, which was splintered by numerous 25mm shots. One shot had hit the upper hinge; the door was hanging cockeyed. Two dead bodies were sprawled, one across the doorway, the other on the porch.

"You did it again, Jack," Tucson whispered as they walked about ten feet apart. "Do you ever lose?"

"I dunno. Ask gutshot Omar and my dead pal, Bulldog Mahoney." He tried to see across the big yard's expanse. Wind was blowing fragments of mist and rain, cottonwoods on his flanks were still bowing and weaving in the wind, lightning was lancing earthward on all points of the compass. Like a Wagnerian opera scene. He wondered if Billy had adjusted his windage across the hundred-yard separation between the house and the barn.

"Now, that this's all over," Tucson said with a regretful tone, "I'm going to have to turn you in. I hate it."

"Don't sweat it, Tucson," Jack responded. He thought about mentioning the pardon, but worry for his brother was growing in his mind, pushing aside all else. *Where the hell is Billy?* Mo Poo? Remembered the big Casull revolver, wished he had retrieved it from Penel. Took the laser gun off his shoulder, turned it on.

Heard a yell, thought he saw a slight movement in the hayloft opening. Someone hanging upside down on the hay-loading rig? Billy? Fear started to crush his chest. He couldn't breathe.

Halfway between the barn and the house, a huge flash. An explosion. A shocking, a slamming: darkness.

Chapter 86

In the helicopter: Major Mick Nakamura, turned right at the junction that the GPS screen showed was the entrance road to the Flying Eagle Ranch. He was flying the AH-1F: the current standard Cobra. Also referred to as the Modernized Cobra, with two General Electric T700-GE-401 Turboshaft engines, each engine delivering 1,690 horsepower.

He held the powerful helicopter at fifty feet AGL because the plains below were grass-covered—no trees to be seen. In the co-pilot's seat, in the front of the tandem-seated cockpit, Sergeant Robby Tanoe—the short, wide Polynesian was asleep.

The Cobra hit an air pocket, slewed sideways. Tanoe woke, glanced around. Mick grinned, automatically adjusted the controls. He was enjoying the bucking, twisting ride through the storm-twisted air.

"Hey, Tanoe, wake up!" Mick yelled into his helmet radio. "We'll be at the ranch any minute."

The Polynesian yawned and stretched. "I'm awake, Cap'n. I'm good to go, but I still don't know what difference we're gonna make, just bein' two of us."

"My buddy needs me," Mick responded. He reversed the controls to adjust for another air pocket. "I'm just lucky I could get you, what with the rest of the team gone. Call Jack again. Just hit redial."

Tanoe, his wide-open eyes sleepy, removed his helmet and complied. After a moment he said, "No answer."

"I wonder what the hell that means," Mick mumbled. "I hope we're not too late." He noticed the sky growing brighter to the east. The sun was threatening to rise, but the violent storm cell to the front showed no sign of letting up. Lightning continued to slash and flicker across the sky.

Chapter 87

In the yard: Jack woke lying on his side, stunned, confused. Tingling flesh, twitching muscles. Zhang cradling his head, rubbing his forehead with a wet hand. Tucson lying about ten feet away, unmoving.

"I saw the lightning hit Tucson," Zhang said. "You're lucky to be alive."

He forced vibrating muscles into action. Crawled through the mud, put a finger on Tucson's neck, felt a fibrillating, racing pulse, rapidly fading. *I thought it was artillery, must've been lightning.* "Help me!" he yelled at Zhang.

He and the Chinese girl picked Tucson up by the legs, slammed her down on the ground. He felt her pulse again—still fibrillating, barely discernible. It stopped.

Zhang jerked her around, crawled on top of her, balled her fists, smashed Tucson's breastbone. A crack. Zhang began massaging her heart by compressing her chest. The unconscious woman's hair was scorched, forehead showed burn marks. Jack glanced at the barn. Zhang bent over, checked the unconscious woman's mouth, blew air into her lungs twice, returned to the heart massage.

"What about the guy you were watching?" he asked.

Zhang stared, her eyes flashing. "Couldn't leave him unguarded. You needed help."

"You shot him?"

"Of course."

He looked down at Zhang, working on the unconscious woman. Again amazed at her cold nature underneath a beautiful exterior. A minute later, Tucson, still unconscious but breathing, her heart stabilized, beating regularly.

Jack stood, staggered towards the barn, felt muscles twitching, cramping, uncramping. Zhang put his arm over her shoulders, helped him walk a straight line. The eastern sky was now an angry, storm-tossed red. *The rosy-fingered dawn,* Jack thought. *Certain sign of battle in Homer's Troy. Same here.*

Zhang shielded her eyes from the dawn, peered at the second floor hayloft. "Billy!" she exclaimed. "Up there!"

Through the hay-loading doorway, he could see his brother was hanging, motionless, ten feet above the floor, upside-down and suspended from the hay-loading trac system by the loading rope. The bipod-supported gun that had thrust out of the opening was gone.

They half-ran to the person entry next to the big double doors, Jack kicked it open; the two tumbled into the barn, dodged to the right, ran into the first stall. A boom of the big Barrett rifle crashed through the barn, a 25mm shell blew through the outer wall of the barn, just inches from the barn doors.

Jack peered around the stall divider wall, saw a huge man standing in the middle of the barn, defiantly equidistant from the stalls on each flank.

Jack instantly recognized Mo Poo's colossal form, his horribly disfigured face, even in the faint dawn's light. The giant was holding a XM 109 like it was a kid's BB gun.

Shouted, "Flashhardt, I kill you. For my lovely Chin Bit. For many other vicious acts. Step out, meet your fat, you little white rat."

Jack remembered the flashbang grenade in his pocket, mumbled, "Meet my fat? Give me a *break*—that's fate, dumbass! And call me a rat? Take this, rat's ass!" He pulled the pin, threw it at the giant Chinaman. It exploded, Mo Poo flinched, but after the dust and smoke dissipated, he raised the big gun, shot. The deafening explosion echoed throughout the barn.

Mo Poo fired the big gun again: the shell blew through the divider wall like paper, hit Jack in the chest. The force of the blow knocked him across the stall, he bounced off the next plank divider.

Alive! He remembered his words to Billy: *"—the ceramic titanium molecules harden when a bullet hits the shirt armor. Can take even a .50 caliber round..."*

He felt like a wild mustang had kicked him. Had dropped the M-199 on his short vicious flight across the stall. Zhang helped him rise to his knees. He crawled to the laser gun, picked it up. Bitterly wished for the Casull.

Glanced around the corner, aimed and hit Mo Poo. The laser burned into the giant. Mo Poo flinched, then ignored it, leveled the Barrett, fired again.

The half-inch round hit Jack's shirt-protected arm with a glancing blow—spun him like a top. Hit the concrete, smelled a faint odor of horse manure, did not move.

"Jack, are you okay?" Zhang yelled.

He gasped under his breath, "This really sucks! Big time." Another shot: a flash of searing pain; his left arm spun away from his body. He looked without moving his eyes, expected to see a stump. A gouge in his forearm, below the armor cuff, blood welling out. He pushed it under his body, pressed down. No pain yet, just a tingling numbness.

Another shot: a flare of light, a slamming blow and burst of pain in his left eye; vision gone in the eye.

Heavy steps, a rumbling basso voice so deep it made Jack's battered body resonate like a tuning fork. Harsh, barking words in Chinese from above. He didn't move, pretended death. Zhang yelled something in Chinese. The giant grunted.

Jack's cell phone vibrated against the concrete floor, making a buzzing sound. It was in his breast pocket. The giant leaned over, listened. Jack held his breath. His ribcage and his eye were on fire; he had to force himself not to tremble from the shock of his arm wound.

His left hand was under his body. M-199 thrown somewhere, wrong weapon anyway. Another buzz. *Shut up, damn it!* He stretched, eased a finger to the cell, felt for the mute button, pressed.

The big man tossed the empty Barrett aside, picked up Jack, lifted him completely off the concrete floor, threw him. Jack bit his lip, crashed, silently tumbled. Zhang yelled a stream of Chinese again, Mo Poo stalked away. Jack opened his one good eye, picked himself up, charged.

He tackled the big man at the knees. Mo Poo sprawled backwards, felt like a horse falling on Jack, knocked the wind out of him.

Helpless, he felt his body being lifted high. Thrown, he skidded, slammed into a concrete manure gutter. *Well, that went well.*

Mo Poo advanced, kicked him in the midsection—he felt his body lift, fly like a soccer ball. Zhang ran, threw herself over Jack. The giant Chinaman turned, walked to the hayloft ladder.

Jack slid his forearm under his abdomen, pressed his stomach out to put pressure on the gunshot wound in his arm. The cell, knocked out of mute mode, rang. Mo Poo stopped, looked back, then moved on.

Zhang reached under him, put the cell towards his mouth. He whispered, "Jack."

"Sir!" a tiny voice. He nudged the cell to his ear.

"Who's this?"

"Sir, it's Tanoe. Sergeant Tanoe. The Major and I are comin' in the Cobra. We're a quarter-mile west of the big barn. Major Nakamura wants to know what's goin' on."

Jack glanced towards Mo Poo. The giant had disappeared into the hayloft. He rose on one elbow, took a deep breath. "I'm in the barn with one friendly. Billy's in deep shit. Up in the barn hayloft. On the second floor. Come to the area between the house and the barn. That's the front. There's a second story opening to the hayloft. An' watch out for Tucson, the female Fibbie agent. She got hit by lightning, might still be unconscious on the ground."

"Rog, sir." Tanoe answered. "Stay on the line."

Seconds later, Jack heard a helicopter approach. He pushed himself to his feet, grabbed the dropped Khyber knife, stuck it in the scabbard at his belt, staggered towards the hayloft ladder, the cell to his ear.

"Sir, big dude starting a fire in the hay under your brother! And Billy don't look good. Not moving—just hangin' upside down by a rope! Major's gonna take the giant out."

Chapter 88

Mick Nakamura held the Cobra steady, oriented directly at the open hayloft, about twenty feet above the ground. He sighted, readied the helicopter's M197 three-barrel 20 mm gun, smiled, his eyes disappearing, a deadly grin appearing. He shot a burst at the huge Chinaman. Hit by a single round, the big man staggered, shook his fists at Mick. Opened his mouth, emitted a cry of rage that the beating rotors drowned. Mick missed with a second burst when the Chinaman dove backward. Mick aimed higher, poured fire from the 750 round ammo container until he severed the rope that held Billy in the air.

Emerging from the ladder opening, Jack saw Billy fall into the smoldering flames. He threw himself into the hayloft with a burst of energy that he didn't know he possessed. Zhang was at his heels.

"Billy!" she screamed. "Save him."

Jack ran towards Billy: hay smoked, flames were started to flicker. Billy had fallen into the middle of the burning hay.

Jack held his breath, ran through the engulfing flames, grabbed his unconscious brother by the arms, pulled the inert form, threw himself and Billy out the hayloft opening.

The wounded Chinaman dashed forward, grabbed Jack's foot, hung on. Billy slipped out of Jack's arms, fell to the ground amidst flames and ashes. He landed twenty feet below, without a sound— just a thud when he hit the wet ground. Jack dangled over the edge of the hayloft. Looked up, saw Mo Poo's ghastly face peering down. He was jerked up, into the hayloft, thrown back on the pile of burning hay.

He rolled away, Mo Poo grabbed his foot again, twisted him back to the smoldering fire. Was trying to roast him like a hot dog in a campfire's coals.

The wind and rain had dampened the hay near the entrance and the fire was barely aflame. Mo Poo backed up, pulled Jack out, then kicked dry hay onto the flickering fire. Zhang tried to tackle Mo Poo. Without looking, he grabbed her by the hair and threw her away. She bounced twice on a bare spot on the hayloft floor, did not move.

The helicopter circled around, opened fire again, but the shots went high, no damage to the monstrous Chinaman.

Jack pounded the growing flames with his hands and arms, kept his eyes on the hideously-disfigured face looming over him. Pain shot through his hands.

Mo Poo grinned, exposing his teeth where his mouth had been permanently slashed open by the tiger's attack. His eyes danced as he looked down at his daughter's killer.

Twisted around, pain shot along the side of Jack's head as flames singed his short hair and his ear. He jerked, tried to free himself: nothing. He kicked Mo Poo's leg with his free foot—like kicking the side of a tree stump.

Despair welled up, resignation, acceptance clawed at the corners of his mind. A burst from the helicopter's guns, Mo Poo staggered, ducked under another hail of bullets. Jack bent at the waist, shoved himself up, grasped a handful of hair with one hand, Mo Poo's lacerated cheek with his other. He jerked up, wrapped his arms around Mo Poo's neck, bit, then tore Poo's nose off with a savage jerk of his head. He punched the giant in the midsection— another tree trunk.

Mo Poo screamed, spun around, threw Jack to the side like a rag doll, grabbed his shredded nose, howled like a raging blizzard's winds.

The giant, bleeding from his shoulder, his face, snarled and advanced. Stomped on Jack as he scrambled to dodge the slow, smashing kicks. Zhang rose. Threw herself at the giant's legs, hung on to one leg.

Mo Poo connected with Jack's chest—ribs popped like cracking twigs. He tried to breath, couldn't.

The giant man stood back, snarled with delight, raised a foot. Jack grabbed and drew the Khyber knife, impaled the looming limb. With a wailing howl, Mo Poo unbalanced, fell across Jack, jerking the knife out of his hand.

Zhang crawled forward, grabbed the knife, stabbed desperately, sank it into Mo Poo's middle, ripped sideways. Intestines cascaded over Jack, into his mouth, across his nose and eyes. He couldn't breathe—his mouth was full of slimy gut. He involuntarily inhaled, gut slid down his throat, gunk clogged his nose. Consciousness ripped away at the edges of his mind.

With a tremendous, groaning effort, Mo Poo, unaware of Jack's desperate condition, picked him up, rose and heaved him out of the hayloft, into the brightening daylight. Air surged into Jack's throat as the guts ripped away.

Sailing backwards, Jack saw the giant rise to his feet, his innards draping to his knees like a bloody rope apron, his nose-less face and chest covered with blood. He grabbed Zhang by the hair with both hands, threw her like an inbound soccer ball. The helicopter's guns released another hail of bullets. Mo Poo staggered backwards, steadied himself, raised both arms, shook his fists at the helicopter. Another hail of bullets connected and he flew backwards into the dancing, expanding flames.

Jack hit the ground next to Billy.

Light-headed, he reeled, steadied himself, fought off blackness. Clamped his right hand on his left arm. He checked, Billy was unconscious but breathing—Jack's ribs were on fire, but he managed to drag his brother away from the building. The blaze in the hayloft was quickly expanding.

Bullet bounded up, wagged his tail, shivered, licked Jack's hand. The dog's action reminded Jack of the other dog's predicament. He stumbled into the barn, picked up the wounded dog with his able hand, huddled her to his pain-wracked ribs, staggered outside and put the injured dog down. Bullet whined, licked his face, licked the female dog's face.

The helicopter landed.

Mick jumped out, bent over Tucson. Another helicopter—a fat white Sheriff's Search and Rescue aircraft, settled beside the ultra-slender, deadly-looking Cobra. Beyond, coming from the house in the brightening, rain-free daylight, the wounded Bosnian, the senator, and Penel, were carrying Bill Flashhardt towards the helicopters on a makeshift stretcher. Talking Dog was walking next to his friend, Bill Flashhardt, comforting him. Penel fiercely hugged him.

Jack, his ribs, his eye, his forearm, his hands, all burning, started to stagger towards the stretcher. Squat Tanoe spotted him, pulled out a compress, wrapped it around his bleeding forearm, helped him to the others by placing an arm around his waist.

Tucson was still unconscious as they loaded her in the Sheriff's aircraft; the paramedics carefully laid her next to Jack's dad. Tanoe and Zhang picked up Billy, helped him to the rescue helicopter.

In scant minutes, Mick and a paramedic had the evacuees strapped down. Tanoe pushed the trussed-up Bosnian onto the ground, the senator boarded, turned and gave Jack a thumb's up. "Your dad's steadily improving," he said.

"It's a miracle. Must have been the two bags of saline solution you brought." Jack glanced at Penel. She returned his stare with a knowing smile.

"Goin' to the hospital?" Mick asked.

Jack took Penel's hand, looked into the beautiful woman's shining eyes. "I'm okay 'til the next evict arrives," Jack responded. "Just scratches and bruises. Nothing can be done for my ribs. One eye's bad but I'll be okay." Jack clasped his friend's hand. "Mick, you saved my life and Billy's.
What can I say? Thanks."

Mick grinned, his eyes disappearing and his wolfish teeth appearing. "Hey, Pilgrim. Hanging with you brings its own rewards. And they're all goo-od! I blasted the gutless big dude into shortdom. Sweet!" He put his helmet on, turned back. "I called the Sheriff's Department earlier. Told them a senator had been kidnapped. General Harmbruster called before— he's on his way—Goddam convention. I'll be back, the general wants full debrief." Mick looked at Jack, added, "You did it again, big guy! Got me a load of shithot action! I love Marines!"

"Mick," Jack fought off dizziness, replied, "You saved my ass! I love the Army!" He put his free arm around Zhang. "And

Zhang did even more! I guess I love the People's Army almost as much."

Jack, Penel, Zhang, the dog Bullet, and Talking Dog, watched the rescue helicopter lift and fly westward, towards Red Lodge. They turned and observed the fire in the barn grow and totally engulf it until they had to back farther away to escape the heat. The rain was gone, the western sky showed patches of blue: Draco had moved eastward.

In the distance, they heard another helicopter approaching: it was an MV-22.

The tiltrotar aircraft, with its twin Allison T406-AD-400 engines, at the opposite ends of stubby wings, sporting huge, thirty-eight foot long, three-bladed propellers, settled to the earth closer to the house than the burning barn.

General Harmbruster stepped out, a vast grin on his face. He was wearing camos under a black flak jacket. His aide, Major Zack Broyer, short and trim, dressed similarly, stepped out behind him, carrying an M-4 rifle at the ready. Another man, wearing a dark blue jacket with the letters FBI in bright yellow on it, climbed out and walked to the huddled Bosnian, who was still being watched by Tanoe.

"Captain Flashhardt," the general said in a voice loud enough to be heard over the Osprey's engines, "congratulations on your victory over the cowardly Moo-slim terrorist scum." He stepped to Jack and shook his hand, nodded to the others, stared at Zhang, turned and gazed at the barn. "How's your dad? Major Nakamura gave me a sketchy report on what happened over the radio. The senator and the girl?"

"Dad's gonna be okay, General. I hope. But… Captain? Does that mean the senator was right when he—"

"That's an affirm!" General Harmbruster flashed his famous grin again. "You've been pardoned and reinstated by the President of the U-nited States of America. At the Commandant's direction."

"That's wonderful, General! And Billy?"

"Same time. Pardoned. And I'm making him a E-5 immediately, as I promised. Hell! I'll make his an E-6 'fore he knows it. You boys did a fabulous job stopping *Saladin's Fist*. Your country would be grateful, if they only knew. Naturally—"

"Naturally, no one will ever know," Jack said with an ironic tone of voice. "But you gotta write up Major Nakamura and Sergeant Tanoe. Their heroic actions… saved our asses. And Zhang Poon t'ang, she—"

"I'm awarding you and your brother, Silver Stars," General Harmbruster declared. "You're eligible as you've already been reinstated. But the written awards will be sealed. You won't be able to tell any bar stories at the O Club. But I'll know, your comrades-in-arms, the President, and the Commandant will know what you've done for your country, Captain. Same deal for the Army boys."

Jack nodded in Tanoe's direction, emphasized, "Sergeant Tanoe and Major Nakamura saved the day, General. Don't forget them."

"Flashhardt, we'll take the prisoner aboard," Major Broyer yelled as he approached the group. In the background, Sergeant Tanoe shoved the plastic-handcuffed Bosnian, Mikhail al Slovenly, into the Osprey.

"We'll send him to Gitmo," the general affirmed. "He'll be detained indefinitely and debriefed. He glanced at Jack's bandaged arm, his swollenshut bloody eye. "Let's get you to the hospital in Red Lodge. We'll hold a full debrief there." The general looked around the yard, at the big ranch house. "Any idea where the leader is? Mara Bhutto?"

"She escaped in the dark, General," Zhang responded.

"Before we took the house," Jack added. He looked at the hills around the house. "She can't make it far on foot. I suggest we send in the Sheriff's Department. And the local Search and Rescue posse. They should be able to track her down."

"But they'd better be careful—she's dangerous, probably armed," Zhang offered.

Major Broyer said, "At the general's direction, you and Sergeant er— Howling Dog, are hereby granted thirty days leave after your medical treatments. Orders will follow."

"Just as soon drive into town tomorrow, General," Jack requested. "I want to rest, talk to Penel."

The general nodded agreement, shook Zhang's hand, touched Jack on the back and climbed aboard the MV-22, which immediately lifted off, spraying mist and splats of mud as it ascended.

The group watched the screaming Osprey fly away, then make its magical transformation to an airplane, climb and disappear in the cloudfilled southern skies.

"So, Jack," Zhang Poon t'ang lightly hugged him. "We won every battle. *Saladin's Fist*'s no more. Mo Poo is gone. Only Mara Bhutto escaped. What'll you do now?"

Jack Flashhardt hugged Penelope, standing on his other side, winced as she pressed a fabulous breast into his battered ribs. Smiled into her beautiful face, her wonderful wide-set eyes. "I have to check with Penelope —I'm sure she has strong ideas about our future. But I know I've got a date to put Caylynn Jones' ashes on a first summit. Then, I'm going to hang here at the ranch until the Marines need me. And climb the biggest, toughest summit of all: fatherhood."

The End

Postscript:

General Harmbruster picked up his second star and became the Far East Co-coordinator for Homeland Security.

Retired General Farley entered the service of Homeland Security, responsible for the Western and southern U.S. borders.

Zhang Poon t'ang went to Hollywood, changed her name to Xu, produced a successful rock CD.

Billy Howling Dog left the Marines to live with Xu in the San Fernando Valley, where he became a cocaine-addicted Valley Guy.

After the birth of William Andrew Jackson Flashhardt, Penelope Kong and her son, upon word that her brother had been killed in renewed clashes with Islamic inhabitants of Shangri-La, returned to Kafiristan, where she resumed her duties as queen of Shangri-La.

Captain Jack Flashhardt went AWOL and was last seen in Karachi, Pakistan.

Mara Bhutto escaped from the clutches of Red Lodge County Sheriff's Search and Rescue Force, made it back to KEGCILT in Pahrump, Nevada, to plan her next attack on The Great Enemy: America.

Omar Johnson recovered from his wound and restarted the fire-fighting school in Kingsville.

Tucson Luvabrest recovered, took a six-month leave of absence from the FBI, sails a 21-foot Ranger that has no engine in the waters off Port Ludlow, Washington.

Chopstick Mick Nakamura, at Major General Andrew Jackson Harmbruster's direction, went OPCON to the CIA to plan and implement a rescue of Jack Flashhardt from Kashgar Federal Prison in the Xinjiang region of China's far northwest.